NORTH AMERICA
Country Inns
and Back Roads

"Why should not the New Englander be in search of new adventures?"

THOREAU: *Walden*

NORTH AMERICA

Country Inns and Back Roads

25th Year—Revised Annually
1990–1991

New England, West Coast,
Canada, Middle Atlantic, South, Midwest,
Rocky Mountains

Norman T. Simpson
with Jerry Levitin

The Berkshire Traveller

PERENNIAL LIBRARY

Harper & Row, Publishers, New York
Grand Rapids, Philadelphia, St. Louis, San Francisco
London, Singapore, Sydney, Tokyo, Toronto

TRAVEL BOOKS BY NORMAN T. SIMPSON WITH JERRY LEVITIN

Country Inns and Back Roads, North America
Country Inns and Back Roads, Britain and Ireland
Country Inns and Back Roads, Continental Europe
Bed and Breakfast, American Style

COVER PAINTING: Representative painting of a New England country scene as interpreted by Janice Lindstrom, viewing a crossroads at the center of town in Monterey, Massachusetts. DRAWINGS: Janice Lindstrom

ISSN: 70-615664
ISBN: 0-06-096493-6

90   91   92   93   94   RRD   10   9   8   7   6   5   4   3   2   1

Contents

CANADA

Preface

In the early days of *Country Inns and Back Roads,* in the 1960s, country inns were virtually unknown. It was necessary to define the term. The book introduced those small, personal inns tucked away in country villages that were at that time mostly in New England. Just as there were few people who knew about the book, so were there few country inns to write about. It took a lot of hunting to find them.

By the middle '70s this situation was quite turned around. The indications were clear: they were an idea whose time had come. Within a very few years interest in country inns seemed literally to explode. Not only were people clamoring to visit them, but innkeeping as a career beckoned to many.

Buildings of all kinds were pressed into service. Existing inns, foundering or falling into disrepair, were snapped up by eager prospective innkeepers, while former gristmills, farmhouses, log cabins, stagecoach taverns, Colonial and Victorian mansions, garages, grocery stores, and the like were renovated, restored, remodeled, and generally whipped into shape as country inns or their more recent counterparts, bed and breakfasts.

Along with the proliferation of country inns and B&Bs came a host of subsidiary innkeeping enterprises: B&B registration services, regional and national guide books, magazines, newsletters, regional organizations, innkeeping seminars and how-to books. There is no question that small inns have become a permanent and important part of the hospitality business.

Such heightened attention has had some interesting results. Many beautiful and historic buildings have been rescued from demolition and brought back to useful life. In some cases, the craze for things Victorian may have perpetuated the life of more horsehair sofas and gingerbread ornamentation than seems altogether reasonable.

As I travel the countryside, I have become aware of the many configurations that list themselves as inns. The West tends to have inns that spread out with cottages or single-story lodges. More traditional inns, with the restaurant on the ground floor and the rooms above, are found in the East.

I am looking for a place that caters to the overnight guest first, rather than the dining guest. This preference eliminates some very fine restaurants with guest rooms above. My ideal is the inn that only serves houseguests. However, financial considerations often require the innkeeper to open the dining room to the general public, and occasionally I have included an inn that is an exception to this rule.

Likewise with some of my other rules. Yet I do believe the following are essential to all inns: personal involvement by the owner, or staff, with the guests; a common room where guests can meet each other, and that is distinct from the lounge or lobby; the inn's restaurant is on the premises (unless the inn operates in an urban area where fine restaurants are within walking distance); no more than two guest rooms per shared bath; cleanliness; fair and honest business practices; and an inviting atmosphere.

There is no fee for inclusion in this book. Every one of the listings has been visited and contacted. Although they are the late Norman Simpson's and my personal selections, the public, through their comments, have great influence on our final decisions. If the reader is displeased with one of the selections, or if a wonderful inn has inadvertently been overlooked, please let me hear from you.

The fundamentals of good innkeeping have not changed over the years, although most of today's innkeepers are families who have sought out innkeeping as a second career. In many cases they moved their own family heirlooms and personal furniture into the inn and are sharing them with their guests. Each inn is a highly individual enterprise reflecting the philosophies, tastes, and enthusiasms of the innkeepers and their families. That's one of the great reasons why inns continue to grow in popularity each year.

In much the same way that staying at inns is a different experience from staying at commercial, impersonal hotels or motels, so is the attitude of the inn guest different from that of the motel traveler. The ideal inn guest is someone who values the qualities offered by a country inn and who contributes to that ambience with his or her own consideration and friendliness. When visiting an inn, think of yourself as a guest in the home of a good friend—in the smaller, more intimate inns becoming friends with the innkeepers and their family is a distinct possibility. And there is always the opportunity to make friends with other inn guests.

So that the reader can see just how long each inn has been a part of *Country Inns and Back Roads,* after the heading of each write-up I have inserted the date the inn was first included in the book. As you will see, quite a few inns go back to the early years.

As I crisscrossed the United States this past year, I used many airline companies. I found the no-frills Southwest Airlines to be extremely satisfactory with respect to rate and punctuality.

As some of you may already know, I also have *Country Inns and Back Roads, Britain and Ireland* and *Country Inns and Back Roads, Continental Europe.* These are revised every other year. A fourth book, *Bed & Breakfast, American Style,* contains at least 400 recommendations for B&B establishments in North America. This is revised yearly.

I include a listing of rates in the Index. Space limitations preclude a more than general range of rates for each inn, and these should not be considered firm quotations. Please check with the inns for their various rates and special packages. It should be noted that many small inns do not have night staffs, and innkeepers will appreciate it if calls are made before 8:00 p.m.

Here are some basic guidelines for reservations and cancellations at most of the inns listed in this book:

A deposit is required for a confirmed reservation. Guests are requested to please note arrival and departure dates carefully. The deposit will be forfeited if the guest arrives after date specified or departs before final date of reservation. Refund will be made only if cancelled from 7 to 14 days (depending upon the policy of the individual inn) in advance of arrival date and a service charge will be deducted from the deposit.

It must be understood that a deposit ensures that your accommodations will be available as confirmed and also assures the inn that the accommodations are sold as confirmed. Therefore, when situations arise necessitating your cancellation in fewer than the allowed number of days in advance, your deposit will not be refunded.

To our readers in Great Britain and other countries in Europe:

Welcome to North America! Many of you are making your first visit and we're delighted that you'll be experiencing some of the *real* United States and Canada by visiting these country inns. Incidentally, all of them will be very happy to help you make arrangements and reservations at other inns in the book.

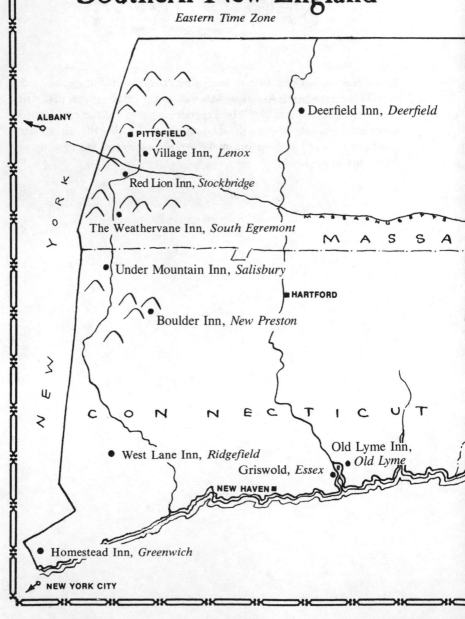

Southern New England

Eastern Time Zone

ALBANY

● Deerfield Inn, *Deerfield*

■ PITTSFIELD

● Village Inn, *Lenox*

● Red Lion Inn, *Stockbridge*

The Weathervane Inn, *South Egremont*

MASSA

● Under Mountain Inn, *Salisbury*

■ HARTFORD

● Boulder Inn, *New Preston*

NEW YORK

CONNECTICUT

● West Lane Inn, *Ridgefield*

Old Lyme Inn,
● *Old Lyme*

Griswold, *Essex*

NEW HAVEN ■

● Homestead Inn, *Greenwich*

NEW YORK CITY

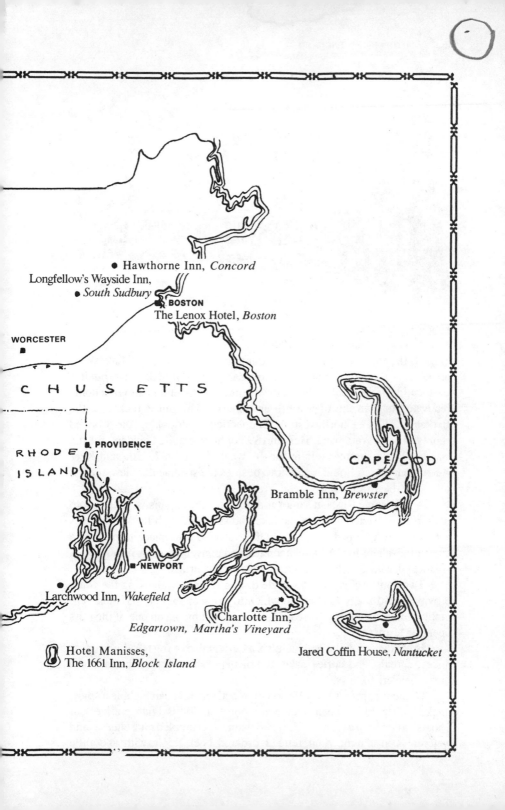

• Hawthorne Inn, *Concord*
Longfellow's Wayside Inn,
  • *South Sudbury*
  BOSTON
The Lenox Hotel, *Boston*

WORCESTER

C H U S E T T S

RHODE
ISLAND

PROVIDENCE

CAPE COD

Bramble Inn, *Brewster*

NEWPORT

Larchwood Inn, *Wakefield*

Charlotte Inn,
Edgartown, Martha's Vineyard

Hotel Manisses,
The 1661 Inn, *Block Island*

Jared Coffin House, *Nantucket*

BOULDER INN
New Preston, Connecticut (1990)

At the foot of the Pinnacle Mountains, on the shore of Lake Waramaug . . . Does this sound like an old camp song? It really isn't, but it is the location of the Boulder Inn, a lovely nineteenth-century summer home renovated into an inn of warmth and charm. The inn is tucked in the Berkshire Hills of northwestern Connecticut overlooking the wooded shores of Lake Waramaug. Built in 1895 of huge granite boulders, the inn was used as a summer retreat for the wealthy. In 1987, Ulla and Kees Adema purchased Boulder and now, besides the spectacular view, the inn offers the best in cuisine.

A handsome Russian samovar dominates the expansive living room with its unrestricted views of the lake and surrounding hills. Wing chairs and sofas are grouped with small tables around a fireplace to provide a cozy atmosphere for late-afternoon tea and conversation. A library nook is stocked with a rich selection of reading materials.

Two comfortable country-style dining rooms overlooking the water provide a restful environment in which to enjoy an exceptional meal. Or, in the summer, you may be seated under a giant maple on one of the inn's open-air terraces.

Breakfast is hearty, and includes a buffet table of fresh fruits, yogurt, juices, cereals, and coffee cake. A hot item, such as French toast or a fluffy omelet, follows.

Dinner begins with a selection of appetizers that can include a spicy, thick, Cuban black bean soup with bourbon, or Belgian endive leaf "boats" filled with a blend of chopped walnuts, crumbled blue cheese, and watercress in a light vinaigrette. I ordered beef creole with andouille sausage from the numerous choices on the menu. The flavorful Cajun sausage was garlicky, and was a perfect complement to the tender beef chunks, onions, green pepper, and fresh tomatoes that were artistically served on a bed of wild and white rice. Just as I took my last bite of the brandy-rich orange nut cake I had for dessert, the great orb of a sun sank into the lake.

The five upstairs guest rooms are furnished in antiques and have sitting areas that overlook the lake. The rooms' brass beds are covered with century-old quilts that enhance the Victorian antique walnut armoires and Ulla's handmade, painted lampshades. Eight additional rooms are located in cottages behind the inn and feature fireplaces and lake views from private porches. All seventeen rooms have private baths with tubs and showers.

If you're a ping-pong fanatic like I am, the game room in the basement will satisfy your paddle itch. There are darts and other assorted games for your enjoyment also. If you prefer outdoor sports, it's only a short hike to the private beach with its sailboats, canoes, windsurfer, paddleboats and rowboats. For those who would rather relax and watch, the beach house has a hanging wicker swing where a lazy afternoon can be spent with Fred, the inn's friendly cat.

Nearby 18th-century villages such as Litchfield and Washington offer antique shops and local crafts, and summer theaters and concerts are active from the first of July to the last of August. The hiking and biking paths of Litchfield's White Memorial Foundation also afford trails for cross-country skiing in the winter.

Ulla and Kees are gracious hosts, but when I tried to talk them into helping me compose a new camp song for Boulder Inn, my idea fell flat. I guess I'll just have to work on one over the next year, drag out my old guitar, and come for another visit with the song already written.

BOULDER INN, Route 45, New Preston, CT; 203-868-0541. A 17-guestroom (private baths) 19th-century granite inn, located at the foot of the Pinnacle Mountains on Lake Waramaug. Open all year except the two weeks after Thanksgiving. All-size beds. Modified American plan. Close to lake sports, antique shops, theater, concerts, hiking, and biking. No pets. Ulla and Kees Adema, Owners-hosts.

Directions: From Rte. 684 north, take Rte. 84 east to Exit 7, then to Rte. 7, then to New Milford Rte. 202 (formerly Rte. 25), then to New Preston. Turn left on Rte. 45 to Lake Waramaug and Boulder Inn.

GRISWOLD INN
Essex, Connecticut (1974)

Among all the things that are special about the town of Essex, perhaps foremost is its community feeling, with parades and special events on holidays, such as Memorial Day and Halloween, and its wonderful Christmas festivities. The Griswold Inn, affectionately known as "the Gris," plays a very active role in these events, which invariably occur in and around the square in front of the inn.

The Memorial Day parade was especially affecting, with the whole town participating, as it has done for a hundred years. There were paraders in uniforms from bygone wars and campaigns, a fife-and-drum corps, the school band, Boy and Girl Scouts, the fire fighters on their red fire engines, the ambulance corps, and many others. A wreath is thrown into the water to commemorate all those who died at sea, and then the parade continues to the cemeteries in the three villages of Essex township.

Bill Winterer had wheeled out the antique popcorn machine, as he has done for years, dispensing popcorn to delighted children (and some adults). The Gris wore a festive air, with windowboxes planted with geraniums and petunias. There's always something happening at the Griswold Inn, which has been owned by a total of five families since 1776. Bill and his wife, Vicky, organize all sorts of special celebrations for the holidays—they even had a splendid sendoff on Groundhog Day, for

which Bill served as grand marshal, complete with a great feast, song and dance, a magician, and costumes. Their Game Festival has become a December tradition, with pheasant, goose, wild turkey, venison, hare, and dishes made from Colonial recipes. In summer, Essex is a port of call for sailors the world over, who dock at the end of the street and troupe into town in their faded jeans and sneakers for lunch at the Griswold.

Stepping inside the inn brings back a couple of centuries of history. The Tap Room, built originally in 1738 as the first schoolhouse in Essex, was later rolled on logs drawn by a team of oxen to its present location. The pot-bellied stove and all of the marine paintings, ships' artifacts, and steamboat memorabilia are nostalgic reminders of early life in this busy little seaport town on the Connecticut River. However, there is nothing historic about the swirl of laughter and conviviality among the guests enjoying the inn's hospitality.

Within its several dining rooms and parlors, the inn has many remarkable marine paintings, including some by Antonio Jacobsen. There is an extensive collection of ship models, firearms, binnacles, ships' clocks, and humorous posters and prints. Vicky has been working over the past several years to organize it all. "Our plan is to publish a book that can be made available to our guests," Bill said, "This will list each piece in the collection, along with the history of the artist. Oliver Jensen, founder and publisher of *American Heritage,* has agreed to write the foreword."

Fresh flowers, warm woods, open fires, and candles abound, and for guests' edification, there are different kinds of entertainment almost every evening.

All of the guest rooms, furnished in "early Essex," have private baths and telephones. There are two additional buildings providing suites with living rooms and fireplaces.

GRISWOLD INN, Main St., Essex, CT 06426; 203-767-1812. A 23-guestroom (private baths) inn in a waterside town, steps away from the Connecticut River. European plan. Complimentary continental breakfast served daily to inn guests. Lunch and dinner served daily to travelers. Hunt breakfast served Sun. Closed Christmas Eve and Christmas Day. Near the Eugene O'Neill Theatre, Goodspeed Opera House, Ivoryton Playhouse, Gillette Castle, Mystic Village, Valley Railroad, and Hammonasset State Beach. Day sailing on inn's 44-foot ketch by appointment. Bicycles, tennis, and boating nearby. Victoria and William G. Winterer, Owners-hosts. (See Index for rates.)

Directions: From I-95 take Exit 69 and travel north on Rte. 9 to Exit 3, Essex. Turn right at stoplight and follow West Ave. to center of town. Turn right onto Main St. and proceed down to water and inn.

THE HOMESTEAD INN
Greenwich, Connecticut (1969)

As frequently as I have visited the Homestead over the years, I'm always delightfully re-surprised at the truly residential nature of its location, although it is only moments away from I-95. There has been an inn here for a very long time, with a long succession of different innkeepers and many different types of accommodations; now, however, I believe the Homestead has reached the pinnacle of its success.

Today, the inn reflects the sensitivities and tastes of Lessie Davison and Nancy Smith, two attractive and talented women who literally saved this 185-year-old farmhouse from the wrecker's ball. They are very proud of the historic plaque that was awarded to the inn in 1988 by the Historical Society of Greenwich.

The inn began its life as a farmhouse, built in 1799. In 1859 it was sold to innkeepers who completely remodeled it in the distinctive Carpenter Gothic architecture of the Victorian era.

The inn is set back from the road in a lovely old orchard and gardens, and the sloping lawn is highlighted by handsome hydrangea bushes. There are now twenty-three guest rooms, all with different decorative themes. They are handsomely furnished, including many antiques and such comforts as clock radios, electric blankets, two pillows for every head, lots of books and magazines, and very modern bathrooms. In many ways, the guest rooms resemble those at Rothay Manor in the Lake Country of England.

Although many of the guest rooms are in the main house, some very careful attention has been given recently to the remodeling of other buildings on the property, and guests may now enjoy a variety of rooms, some with queen-sized beds and balconies or porches, as well as a queen-bedded suite, with a lovely, large, cathedral-ceilinged bedroom and a front porch overlooking the neighbor's apple orchard.

The Homestead is the perfect alternative to the busy, noisy New York hotels, and provides a very pleasant country-type atmosphere for city dwellers who want to leave the canyons of steel for the peaceful lanes of Greenwich.

One of the main reasons for the continuing success of the Homestead is La Grange Restaurant. The chef is Jacques Thiebeult from Paris, who trained in France, Switzerland, England, and at Le Cirque and Le Cygne restaurants in New York. He has recently joined Lessie and Nancy as a partner and has the title of vice-president.

The *New York Times* restaurant reviewer awarded three stars to La Grange, pointing out that the restaurant "pays attention to every detail: salads, warm, crusty rolls, even a choice of loose tea, all are part of the seamlessly smooth dining performance."

The menu offerings include French country pâté, many marvelous soups, especially the mussel bisque, called Billi-Bi, tender sweetbreads of veal, lobster done several ways and duck with cassis sauce. Desserts made by the inn's pastry chef often include fresh fruit tarts, triple chocolate layer cake, or Linzer torte.

Incidentally, I learned recently that William Inge wrote *Picnic* here during the 1950s. This, of course, was long before Lessie and Nancy arrived on the scene, bringing with them impeccable taste and a gratifying attention for detail. I'm sure, were he to revisit now, Mr. Inge would find the atmosphere and cuisine even more inspiring.

THE HOMESTEAD INN, 420 Field Point Rd., Greenwich, CT 06830; 203-869-7500. A 23-guestroom (private baths) inn located in the residential area of a suburb, 45 min. north of New York City. Queen and twin size beds available. Lunch served Mon. thru Fri.; dinner served daily except Labor Day, Christmas, New Year's. Wheelchair facilities for restaurant. Located a short distance from Conn. countryside and shore scenes. Accessible by train from New York City. No amusements for children under 12. No pets. Lessie Davison, Nancy Smith, Owners-hostesses. (See Index for rates.)

Directions: The inn is 3 min. from Rte. I-95. Take Exit 3 in Greenwich; from NYC, turn left; from New Haven, turn right off ramp. Turn left onto Horseneck Ln. at light, just before railroad overpass. Go to next traffic light; turn left onto Field Point Rd., and continue approx. ¼ mi. to inn on the right.

OLD LYME INN
Old Lyme, Connecticut (1990)

"We haven't replaced Sassafras," innkeeper Fran McNulty said, "but we named the library after her." Confirmed cat lovers like myself appreciate such gestures, even if those long assigned to pluck Sassafras' multicolored fur souvenirs from the dark blue cushions and carpets of the Lyme Inn are less respectful.

Appropriate tribute to the memory of Sassafras is only one of the reasons I like the Old Lyme. Another is the way the guestrooms are given as much attention as the food. In other words, this place is not just another recommendable restaurant with a few rooms to rent upstairs, but a full-service inn where overnight guests are an intrinsic part of the scene.

Furthermore, it is located on a quiet, if main, street in a historic village on Long Island Sound where it is said every house belonged to a sea captain at one time or another.

The Old Lyme is an exception here too: It was built as a farm house for the Champlain family about 1850, later becoming a riding school (Jacqueline Bouvier Kennedy Onassis was one of the pupils), then a boarding house called the Barbizon Oaks, and famed for having the first iron bathtub in town. Still later, the ledger says it became a restaurant "of questionable reputation." Nary a sea captain on board, but a registered historic landmark nonetheless.

When owner Diana Field Atwood found the property, the house was charred from a fire and seemed ready only for the requiem of a wrecker. Fortunately, Diana was blessed with foresight, patience, and a treasure-seeker's eye for the possible. Marble mantels and 19th-century chestnut paneling taken from razed homes were installed; a marvelous mirror was obtained for $5 at auction; tag-sale scouring produced watercolors of the village done by unknown artists of the past.

Thirteen guest rooms—each different and including two honeymoon mini-suites—are furnished with antiques and period pieces. They have amenities like "genuine witch hazel from Essex up the road" as well as goodnight chocolates. The rooms have clock radios, but the only television set is in the Sassafras library.

Breakfast is served only to guests and is included in the room tariff. It is an expanded continental with juice, fresh fruit, just-baked breads, and homemade granola.

"Wait til you see the bar in the grill room," Fran said. "It's from one of the oldest taverns in Pittsburgh, and it fits perfectly. I don't know how Diane was so lucky." She waved her hand dramatically. "Look," she said, "original dart holes!" Sure enough. Fran hastened to add that present-day entertainment is a guitarist on Friday nights, while any evening, light suppers are served here (in winter, by the fire).

Any time of year you can expect a rose on your table in the main dining room along with a menu that changes with the season. In spring it included native lobster bolognaise as well as cream of pheasant soup and roast breast of duckling with Portobello mushrooms and a sauce of carmelized honey and thyme among other treats.

"There's so much to do around here," Fran said, producing a map marked with the "Innkeeper's Favorite Drive" and pointing out the local antique strip. "See," she said "The Connecticut River Museum is at Steamboat Dock in Essex, and our famous Goodspeed Opera House is in East Haddam. Gilette Castle is in Hadlyme. There are salt- and freshwater beaches, and we are only 5 to 25 minutes from any southern Connecticut tourist attraction."

Since the new Old Lyme Inn opened in 1976, it has garnered a stack of rave reviews from magazines and newspapers. It even won the "ultimate dessert" award at the 1989 Chocolate Expo.

Diana, who quietly admits to being a chocolate fan, maintains a low profile around the inn. Recently, however, she has found her original "Diana's Café" (a raspberry-chocolate liqueur coffee) pridefully served outside the Old Lyme. It is available at other inns who offer it by name — apparently without knowing who the "Diana" is.

OLD LYME INN, Lyme Street (P.O. Box 787B), Old Lyme, CT 06731; 203-434-2500. A 13-guestroom (private baths) full-service inn located in a historic village in southeastern Connecticut. Queen and twin beds; 2 rooms with sofa beds suitable for 3. Open all year except the first 2 weeks in January. Notable restaurant (closed Mondays) serves lunch, dinner, and light suppers. Pets accepted conditionally. Fran McNulty, Manager.

Directions: Going south on I-95, take Exit 70 and turn right off the ramp; the inn is on your right. Going north on I-95, take Exit 70; turn left off the ramp, and right at the first light. Go to the next light and you will see the inn on your left.

UNDER MOUNTAIN INN
Salisbury, Connecticut (1990)

I have always been charmed by everything English, and as a young man read as much of Charles Dickens' work as I could lug home from the library every month. So it was with "great expectations" (pun intended) that I drove to the great white farmhouse called Under Mountain Inn. I had recently read an article in the food section of a major national newspaper praising this inn's English Christmas dinner, and even though it was the middle of summer, I decided to visit for a weekend.

Salisbury is nestled in a rural valley beneath the Appalachian Trail, an area that offers unlimited walking opportunities, and is close to lakes, streams, skiing, and cultural festivals. The Under Mountain Inn sits on 3 acres that are bordered by a 7,500-acre state park and a 50-acre horse farm. The lovely old two-story home has black shutters and is surrounded by huge shade trees. The area must be just as beautiful during the winter.

Innkeepers Peter and Marged Higginson have operated the inn since 1985. The early 18th-century home has wide plank flooring, and almost every common room has a cozy fireplace. The large attractive living room is the center of activity. Many comfortable sofas and chairs are grouped for conversation. A piano is available for after-dinner sing-alongs, the library is well stocked with English literature, and game tables await a round of whist. The parlor is a bit more intimate.

The guest rooms are large and done in a color scheme of Wedgwood blue, rose, and cream. To create an 18th-century ambience, Williamsburg reproduction wallpapers and a mixture of American antiques and reproduction pieces have been used. Each room has its own bath, some of them wonderfully large.

Peter is English, and the chef, so it's no wonder that the inn's cuisine features a number of English specialties. Although I wasn't going to have the gourmet pleasure of the Christmas feast, he did invite me into the kitchen to keep him company. "We usually begin with an appetizer of imported Scotch salmon, then follow that with roast goose. I like to use a traditional prune stuffing," he explained. "Then, we serve mince pie and petit fours for dessert!" For a bit of fun, an English Christmas cracker—a tissue-wrapped "firecracker" with a pop-out trinket and hat—is placed next to each plate.

Both dinner and breakfast are included with your room. Breakfast is a full-English affair, including the special treats of sautéed mushrooms and tomatoes, and fried bread. Thursdays and Sundays, through the summer, authentic fish and chips are served for dinner. A full menu of five or six choices of appetizers, entrees, and desserts is served the other evenings. For those guests attending the Tanglewood music festival, Marged will make up a scrumptious picnic supper. The inn has a full liquor license.

Sugar and Cocoa, the inn's resident pups, escorted me to the top of the stairs when I went to bed. I took some time to choose a book from the extensive second-floor library in the hall, and after skipping over title upon title, was pleased to find what I was looking for—*Great Expectations*. As I climbed into bed to get reacquainted with some old literary friends, I decided I had to come back for some of that Christmas goose next year.

UNDER MOUNTAIN INN, Under Mountain Rd., (Rte. 41), Salisbury, CT 06068; 203-435-0242. A 7-guestroom (private baths), English-style, 18th-century farmhouse. All-size beds. Closed 2 weeks in Dec., and mid-March to mid-April. Modified American plan, with traditional English fare. Skiing, boating, hiking. Thirty min. to Tanglewood and Berkshire Theater Festival. No children or pets. Smoking restricted. Marged and Peter Higginson, Owners-hosts.

Directions: Travel to Egremont, Mass. From New York City or N.J., go north on Rte. 41 for 4 mi. to Salisbury. From Albany or Boston, go south on Rte. 41 for 8 mi. to Salisbury. The inn is 4 mi. north of the Salisbury village center on Rte. 41 (Undermountain Rd.).

The date in parenthesis in the heading represents the first year the inn appeared in the pages of Country Inns and Back Roads.

WEST LANE INN
Ridgefield, Connecticut (1980)

"Basically, I think that we have three different types of guests that find their way to our little inn." Maureen Mayer and I were seated on the broad front porch of the West Lane Inn enjoying a generous continental breakfast. "By the way," she added, "if you'd like a bigger breakfast, we have an à la carte breakfast menu that offers, among other things, grapefruit, sliced bananas, berries, yogurt, corn flakes, and poached eggs."

I might add that this breakfast was served at a table with real linen tablecloths and napkins, and there is a fine gourmet restaurant next door.

One of the things that sets West Lane Inn apart is the many additional amenities this attractive innkeeper provides for her guests. For example, there is a clock in every guest room, as well as a computerized phone system, a radio-TV, individual heating and air conditioning controls, and one-day laundry and dry-cleaning service, and a basket of fruit, cheese, and crackers is presented to newly arrived guests.

"Among our guests are families being relocated to the Ridgefield-Fairfield-Danbury area who need a comfortable, roomy place in which to stay while they look for a new home. Many come and stay for a week or two. I decided that they would be much more comfortable if we had accommodations that reflected the feeling of the area, so we have rooms with decks overlooking our lawn and the forest in the rear. Some of these have fireplaces and kitchen facilities. You see, guests can literally establish a little home for a short time. One of our bathrooms is designed for the handicapped, similar to the one at the West Mountain Inn in Vermont."

I observed that Ridgefield itself would be an ideal suburban place in which to live. Within commuting distance of New York and driving distance of the many corporations which are relocating in Fairfield County, Ridgefield is a most pleasant town with large graceful trees and excellent small shops. "There's also a very active community here," Maureen remarked. "We have a historical society, a library, the Ridgefield Symphony, the League of Women Voters, and various men's service clubs, sports groups, and business groups."

West Lane Inn is set back from the village street with a broad lawn enhanced by azaleas, tulips, roses, and maple and oak trees. It was originally built as a mansion in the early 1800s and the guest rooms are unusually commodious.

The other types of guests are commercial travelers, both men and women, and vacationers who enjoy country-inn hospitality. "I think we understand commercial travelers very well and we've done everything possible to have them feel that this is really a 'home away from home.'

"As far as the country-inn travelers are concerned, we're at sort of a crossroads for north-south, east-west travel, and many couples on their way to or from New England come back and stay every year."

The West Lane could well be a model for other bed-and-breakfast inns everywhere. Every lodging room is spotless and the furnishings and decorating are all part of a harmonious color scheme. Overnight guests are coddled even further with heated towel racks and wonderful, new, large, fluffy bath sheets.

One of the things that also appeals to me is the 100%-cotton sheets on every bed in the inn. When was the last time you slept in a bed that had 100%-cotton sheets? Outstanding!

WEST LANE INN, 22 West Lane, Ridgefield, CT 06877; 203-438-7323. A 20-guestroom (private baths; several suites with kitchens) inn approx 1 hr. from N.Y.C., in a quiet residential village in southwest Connecticut. Open every day in the year. Breakfast and light snacks available until 10:30 p.m. Restaurant within walking distance. Wheelchair access. Convenient to many museums and antique shops. Golf, tennis, swimming, and xc skiing and other outdoor recreation available nearby. No pets. Maureen Mayer, Owner-host. (See Index for rates.)

Directions: From New York City: Westside Hwy. to Sawmill River Pkwy. Take Exit 6, going right on Rte. 35, 12 mi. to Ridgefield. Inn is on left. From Hartford: Exit I-84 on Rte. 7 south and follow Rte. 35 to Ridgefield.

HOTEL MANISSES
Block Island, Rhode Island (1982)

Joan Abrams was waxing poetic about the Hotel Manisses. This in itself was nothing unusual, because she has been waxing poetic about the Manisses ever since the day, several years ago, when I first walked through the old building with her and she told me what the Abrams family had in mind in restoring this old Block Island hotel. Built in 1870, the Manisses was then known as one of the best summer vacation hotels in the East. In those days families and groups of friends arrived at Block Island by private yacht and stayed for weeks.

"We all loved the task of restoring the Manisses, and almost every week there was some decorative or furnishing highlight that was very exciting," Joan said. "For example, the twenty-three-foot-long bar, dating back to 1870, was in a Boston saloon. The century-old stained-glass inserts come from the same historic era, and the lighting fixtures are holophane glass invented by Thomas A. Edison.

"From the renowned 19th-century Plimpton House estate in Norwood, Massachusetts, we acquired many impressive Victorian items, such as the hand-grooved arches, including the one in the library lounge. We were able to purchase some handsome hooped doors from a judge's chamber in Boston.

"In keeping with the natural beauty of Block Island, natural products have been integrated with the decor. Most of it is the brick, wood, and stone of the original building. That includes the antique wood washtub divider in the dining room, now decoratively filled with green plants and fresh flowers.

"Many of our guests ask about the weathervane, mounted on the tower, which stands six feet high and is hand-forged wrought iron, about 250 years old, from a castle in Cardiff, Wales. The figure is a griffin, a mythical creature feared and admired in past centuries."

Each bedroom and bathroom at the hotel is decorated with a different wallpaper. Almost all of the furniture is of the late 19th century, and the beds are copies of that era but in king and queen sizes. Some of the smaller rooms have the original beds; all have private baths. Flowers, hanging plants, and large plants adorn every room.

The dining room is on the ground floor and includes a delightful deck area with colorful umbrellas. The luncheon menu is lively, imaginative, and satisfying. The dinner menu offers a wide choice of appetizers and entrées appealing to both the trencherman and gourmet alike. Courses include many different beef items, as well as swordfish, flounder, scallops, lobster, and bouillabaisse. The vegetables come from a 1½-acre garden just a few paces away.

The hotel is on the National Register of Historic Places. It is an

eloquent testimony to American hospitality and a tribute to what dedication, hard work, good taste, and much investment capital can accomplish.

HOTEL MANISSES, Spring St., Block Island, RI 02807; 401-466-2421. A 17-guestroom (private baths) strikingly restored and preserved hotel on Block Island Sound, off the coast of R.I. and Conn. King, queen and double beds available. Some rooms have Jacuzzis, ocean views, and private decks. Breakfast available at 1661 Inn. Open from 1st week of Apr. to Oct. 20; dining room open weekends only thru Memorial Day. Tennis, bicycling, ocean swimming, sailing, snorkling, scuba diving, salt- and fresh-water fishing nearby. Located on the Atlantic flyway. No facilities for children under 10. No pets. The Abrams Family, Owners-hosts. (See Index for rates.)

Directions: By ferry from Providence, Pt. Judith, and Newport, R.I. and New London, Conn. Car reservations must be made in advance for ferry. By air New England Airline from Westerly, R.I. Contact inn for schedules.

"European plan" means that rates for rooms and meals are separate. "American plan" means that meals are included in the cost of the room. "Modified American plan" means that breakfast and dinner are included in the cost of the room. The rates at some inns include a continental breakfast with the lodging.

LARCHWOOD INN
Wakefield, Rhode Island (1969)

Frank Browning and I were talking about lobsters, a subject that is near and dear to the hearts of those of us who are fortunate enough to live near New England's coastal waters. The Larchwood Inn certainly qualifies in this respect, since it's just a few minutes from the great beaches of southern Rhode Island.

"We buy from one source, and we know we're getting the best," he told me. "On Monday, we have special dinners of either twin lobsters or prime rib, and it is one of our most popular nights in the week. We always have a full-sized lobster every night and twin lobsters on Monday. I hope your readers will reserve ahead for lobsters because there's always a great demand. By the way, on Mondays in the summertime we have a cabaret performer and a piano player. It really livens things up."

I wandered into one of the dining rooms, where there is a mural depicting the southern Rhode Island beaches. The tables were very attractively set for the next meal with green tablecloths. I noticed the living room had been redecorated since my last visit. It was very pleasant, with comfortable chairs and a fireplace with a very impressive ship's model on the mantel. There was also an exotic bird in a cage.

At this point, Frank returned, and I asked him about the ship's model. "That is a three-masted schooner, called *L'Astrolabe,* and everything was built to scale by a friend of mine. See the little boys on the deck—he thought of everything."

The Larchwood is a large mansion, dating back to 1831, in the village of Wakefield, set in the middle of a large parklike milieu with copper, beech, ginkgo, pin oak, spruce, mountain ash, maple, Japanese

cherry trees, evergreens, dogwoods, and a very old mulberry tree. In all, there are three acres of trees and lawn.

The interior has many Scottish touches, including quotations from Robert Burns and Sir Walter Scott, and photographs and prints of Scottish historical and literary figures.

The conversation naturally turned once again to menu items, since Frank was the chef here for many years and is now carefully supervising the kitchen and dining room.

"We're in the process right now of working with the South County Hospital. They are coming out with low-cholesterol items, and they came to us to ask if we could cooperate with them. We're working on seven or eight items in our restaurant for their program. There will be lighter things, including different ways to serve chicken and fish."

I asked him about breakfasts, and I'm very glad I did. "We make the french toast with our own bread and offer it with either sour cream or whipped cream and warm strawberries. The strawberries make it absolutely fantastic. It's something that our guests really appreciate, along with our selection of different omelets."

Besides guest rooms in the main inn, there are additional attractively furnished guest rooms in the Holly House, a 150-year-old building across the street from the inn. Guests at the Holly House can enjoy breakfast, lunch, and dinner at the Larchwood Inn dining room.

My eye caught a card on the table that had a Catholic, Jewish, and Protestant grace, and also one from Robert Burns, which I am going to share with everyone.

> Some ha'e meat and canna eat
> And some ha'e nane that want it,
> But we ha'e meat and we can eat,
> So let the Lord be thankit.

LARCHWOOD INN, 176 Main St., Wakefield, RI 02879; 401-783-5454. A 19-guestroom (10 private baths) village inn just 3 mi. from the famous southern R.I. beaches. European plan. Breakfast, lunch, dinner served every day of the year. Swimming, boating, surfing, fishing, xc skiing, and bicycles nearby. Francis Browning, Owner-hostess. (See Index for rates.)

Directions: From Rte. 1, take Pond St. exit and proceed ½ mi. directly to inn.

THE 1661 INN
Block Island, Rhode Island (1976)

There are many delights to be experienced at the 1661 Inn on this historic island—the bracing salt air, the infinite expanse of ocean and sky, the masses of flowers, the easy, casual life of the inn—but my favorite delight is the animal farm. Justin and Joan Abrams have owned the inn since 1969, and it was a while before Justin began to expand his menagerie from a few goats and chickens to include horses, ponies, donkeys, sheep, and, at last report, Sarah, a little lost fawn, and a South American llama, called Humphrey.

The Abramses have been into expansion ever since I've known them. Their two married sons are pursuing careers away from the inn, but their daughter, Rita, and her husband, Steve Draper, are actively involved at the inn. And the list of grandchildren continues to expand; at last count there were five.

Over the years, other expansions have included the Guest House, next door to the inn, which Steve completely remodeled, and the Hotel Manisses across the street, which I describe in more detail on another page. Guest rooms have been enlarged and private decks have been added, which afford glorious views of the ocean. Joan tells me they have added canopies over the decks so that guests can now sit outside and enjoy the pure Block Island air in almost any season. Each room has been decorated in Colonial-period furniture, wallpaper, and draperies. There are Winslow Homer prints and quite a few original watercolors and drawings of Block Island houses.

When they first bought the inn they decided to name it in honor of the year that Block Island was settled by colonists from New England.

"At that time, we gave each of the bedrooms the name of one of the original brave settlers," Joan explained. "Our family spent many hours consulting books for authentic New England decor and redoing all the rooms. We decorated with many of our own antiques and early American paintings."

The "all you can eat" buffet breakfast is an extravaganza of baked blue fish, fresh fruit, corned beef hash, scrambled eggs, homemade muffins, bread, scones, and jams. Breakfast may be enjoyed in the sun-filled dining room overlooking the sea or on the outdoor deck. On Saturday nights, the lobster boil includes New England clam chowder, corn-on-the-cob, and gingerbread for dessert. There is also sirloin steak and chicken marinated with two mustards.

Joan tells me their Wine & Nibble Hour is always popular with their guests, who enjoy the conviviality in the cozy parlor or on the outdoor canopied deck, overlooking a panorama of countryside and the Atlantic Ocean.

May I take a moment to point out that Block Island is a very singular experience during the off-season, which is after the middle of October. There are wonderful beaches to walk and bikes to ride, and the island, with a population of only 600 during the winter, becomes a very private experience. Rita and Steve and their three boys are always on hand in the Guest House to help the island's winter visitors make it a really beautiful experience.

THE 1661 INN, Box 367, Block Island, RI 02807; 401-466-2421 or 2063. A 23-guestroom (14 private baths) Colonial inn off the coast of R.I. and Conn. in Block Island Sound. Buffet breakfast and afternoon refreshments. All bed sizes available. Open May 15 to Nov. 1. (Guest House open year-round; continental breakfast included in off-season rates; dinner upon request.) Wheelchair access. Lawn games on grounds. Tennis, bicycling, ocean swimming, sailing, snorkeling, diving, salt and fresh water fishing nearby. Block Island is known as one of the best bird observation areas on the Atlantic flyway. The Abrams Family, Owners-hosts. (See Index for rates.)

Directions: By ferry from Providence, Pt. Judith, and Newport, R.I., and New London, Conn. Car reservations must be made in advance for ferry. Cars are a convenience, but not needed on the island. By air from Newport, Westerly, and Providence, R.I., New London and Waterford, Conn. or by chartered plane. Contact inn for schedules.

THE BRAMBLE INN
Brewster, Cape Cod, Massachusetts (1977)

Although Cape Cod is not very large, there is a decided difference between the south shore, traversed by Route 27, and the opposite side, which has Route 6A. The Mid-Cape Highway runs more or less down the middle and is the fastest way to get to most places on either shore.

The Bramble Inn is on Route 6A, which is reached by turning off the Mid-Cape Highway on Route 124. This road leads through some very attractive country scenery, with bike trails off the road that provide another diversion for travelers and natives alike. It's a good example of back roads that are somewhat quiet during many months of the year and are well worth seeking out.

Route 124 joins 6A, which continues on out to exits at Chatham and Orleans with many lovely villages and pleasant views. The Bramble can be seen in the distance on the left side almost as soon as you join 124.

The inn is owned by Ruth and Cliff Manchester, who, in addition to some very practical experience in the hospitality business, also brought with them three very active and attractive daughters. Elise, now twenty-one and finishing her senior year at Amherst College, is waitressing and assisting Cliff with various duties. Suzy, twenty, graduated from the Culinary Institute in Hyde Park.

Andrea, nineteen, does the baking and she's become so adept that *Gourmet* magazine has asked for one of her desert recipes.

I can see that, as in the case of many other inns, the progress of the three Manchester sisters is going to make interesting reading in future editions of *CIBR*. Be sure to ask for them when you visit the inn.

Since taking over the inn a few years ago, the Manchesters have worked hard redoing all of the bedrooms and have put another bathroom in the 1849 House, adjacent to the inn building. The Capt. Bangs Pepper House is their latest addition. It's a Federal-style Colonial built in 1793.

Guest rooms have flowered wallpapers, antiques, and country furniture, and there's a hint of a tilt to the floors and doors, all of which adds to the fun of staying in a building that is indeed an antique itself.

Ruth has been doing some great things with breakfast (in addition to Cliff's "best ever" muffins), such as an English kedgeree; tarts made with Roquefort, chevre, and sun-dried tomatoes; frittata of ham, mushrooms, and onion; and baked apple pancakes.

The evening menu is quite different. It's a four-course fixed-price dinner that usually changes nightly. There's a choice of five items from each course; this gives Ruth, who's a gourmet cook in the true sense of the word, an opportunity to offer some dinners that are quite different. Among the more popular main dishes are tenderloin of beef with Roquefort and a white wine sauce, and rack of lamb with a cracked pepper-

corn and mustard backing. The most sought-out recipes, also requested by both *Bon Appetit* and *Gourmet,* are the lettuce and scallion bisque and the white chocolate Coeur à la Crème. Their dining room is becoming known as one of the Cape's top restaurants.

Dinner is served Monday through Saturday in season and Thursday through Saturday off-season. The restaurant is closed on Sunday.

Cliff has been very busy outside. He painted the main inn last spring and the 1849 House the year before. The shutters are a darker forest green, which adds a crisp note against the white clapboards. The gardens are coming along beautifully—Cliff added window boxes to the front of the inn with geraniums and alpine strawberries. Ruth is quite often seen picking berries to be used for garnish on the desserts.

The Bramble Inn's central location makes it ideal for enjoying all of Cape Cod's recreation and entertainment.

THE BRAMBLE INN, Route 6A, Main St., Brewster, Cape Cod, MA 02631; 508-896-7644. A 12-guestroom (private baths) village inn in the heart of one of Cape Cod's north-shore villages. Queen, double, and twin beds available. Lodgings include continental breakfast. Dinner served Mon. thru Sat. in season; Thurs. thru Sat. in fall and winter. Open mid-March to mid-Jan. Swimming, sailing, water sports, golf, recreational and natural attractions within a short drive. Adjacent to tennis club. This is a small, intimate inn and does not meet the needs of most children. No pets. Cliff and Ruth Manchester, Innkeepers. (See Index for rates.)

Directions: Take Exit 10 from Rte. 6. Turn left (north) and follow Rte. 124 to the intersection of Rte. 6A (4 mi.). Turn right, ¹/₁₀ mi. to inn.

CHARLOTTE INN
Edgartown, Martha's Vineyard, Massachusetts (1979)

It's true. Yes, in last year's edition I said that there was always something new happening at the Charlotte Inn, and my most recent visit confirmed this.

Gery and Paula Conover were taking me on an extensive tour of the fifth dwelling that makes up the complex called the Charlotte Inn. This was the Coach House, about which I had written while it was still being built and decorated.

First, perhaps I will provide a little background about the inn itself. It is located on South Summer Street in Edgartown on Martha's Vineyard Island, off the southern coast of Cape Cod. The main house, like many other Edgartown houses, is a classic three-story white clapboard with a widow's walk on the top. It is the former home of a Martha's Vineyard sea captain. Guest rooms are individually furnished, have private baths, and are very quiet and impeccably clean. Several rooms have working fireplaces, and many have four-poster beds. There are lots of fresh flowers, books, magazines, good reading lamps, and perhaps, most important of all, a very romantic atmosphere.

Besides the main house, there is the Carriage House, with a cathedral ceiling and unusual adornments, about which I wrote several years ago, as well as the Garden House, across the street from the main inn. This has been decorated with a French country look, and as is the case with the other guest rooms throughout the inn and annex, the furnishings and decorations have been done with great care and taste. This house also provides houseguests with a private lounge of their own, where they may enjoy the fireplace, play games, watch TV, and get acquainted.

Now, back to the Coach House. Entering through a downstairs tack room, I immediately felt as if I were in a British stable. Upstairs is a sumptuous two-room suite with a Palladian window and central air conditioning. It is luxuriously decorated with English antiques.

The guest rooms in the Coach House are highly individual. There are pineapple bedposts, brass beds, carved antique headboards, beautiful chests, handsome silver, and positively scrumptious bathrooms. One has a tub from 1912 that weighs about a thousand pounds and had to be lifted through the window by a crane.

Complimentary breakfast is served in the open-air terrace or in the bow-windowed conservatory. By night this room becomes the candlelit dining area.

Among the entrées on the prix-fixe dinner are roast supremes of baby pheasant, sauté of lobster and mussels in a puff pastry box, rack of lamb, and grilled swordfish steak with champagne and shrimp sauce.

October is an ideal time to be at Martha's Vineyard. The weather is usually pleasantly chilly in the morning and warms up as the hours go by. The island and the ferries are not crowded, and it's possible to enjoy the Vineyard as a place with its own personality.

CHARLOTTE INN, So. Summer St., Edgartown, Martha's Vineyard Island, MA 02539; 508-627-4751. A 25-guestroom (23 private baths) combination inn–art gallery and restaurant on a side street, a few steps from the harbor. Queen, double, and twin beds available. European plan. Continental breakfast served to inn guests except Sun. Open year-round. L'étoile restaurant open for dinner from mid-March thru New Year's Day, also winter weekends. Boating, swimming, beaches, fishing, tennis, riding, golf, sailing, and biking nearby. No pets. Not suitable for children under 15. Gery and Paula Conover, Owners-hosts. (See Index for rates.)

Directions: The Woods Hole/Vineyard Haven Ferry runs year-round and automobiles may be left in the parking lot at Woods Hole. Taxis may be obtained from Vineyard Haven to Edgartown (8 mi.). Check with inn for ferry schedules for all seasons of the year. Accessible by air from Boston and New York.

"European plan" means that rates for rooms and meals are separate. "American plan" means that meals are included in the cost of the room. "Modified American plan" means that breakfast and dinner are included in the cost of the room. The rates at some inns include a continental breakfast with the lodging.

DEERFIELD INN
Deerfield, Massachusetts (1990)

Karl and Jane Sabo became enchanted with the wonderful life-style that innkeeping offers those who don't mind living where life is slower and time together has quality in quantity. As newlyweds they toured New England, a tour that resulted in their company called Innsitters, a service that allowed innkeepers to take a needed vacation, and inns in transition to be managed. The experience changed their lives and resulted in their move to the Deerfield Inn in 1987.

The Sabos both had successful careers in New York. Karl is a graduate of the Culinary Institute of New York, and has been a chef on an ocean liner, and manager at the prestigious New York "21" Club. Jane is English, and has been an editor with publishing houses in London and New York. "We wanted a smaller, more personal, outdoor environment and we wanted a less crowded, hectic pace," Jane told me as we enjoyed afternoon tea and cookies. "We also wanted to start a family." Since taking over the two-story, white clapboard, Federal-style inn, baby John has joined them.

The Deerfield Inn is located in historic Deerfield, scene of attacks by the French and Indians during the 17th and 18th centuries. The town maintains twelve museum houses that line the mile-long Street, of which the Deerfield Inn is one. The homes are mirrors of the cultural history, art, and craftsmanship of the Pioneer Valley. The twenty-three-room Deerfield Inn was built in 1884 and modernized in 1977. All guest rooms have been named for people connected with the village's history, and some guests claim that they have seen the amiable spirit of at least one of these characters walking the halls.

All guest rooms are decorated individually. Greeff fabrics, charming print wallpapers, and period reproduction furniture are accented by old prints of the Deerfield area. Queen, double, and twin beds are available, and all rooms have private baths with combination shower and tub. A basket brimming with soaps, shampoo, and other luxury items is in each bathroom. The Sabos have also thoughtfully provided a hair dryer, ironing board, sewing kit, and extra toothbrush/paste, should you need them.

Two airy porches with rockers, a garden terrace, and a lovely herb garden are wonderful spots to spend time during the summer evenings. The common rooms are elegant, yet relaxing. Two living rooms and a large fireplace in the main inn and one living room in the south wing are furnished with cozy sofas, well-stocked bookcases, card tables, and desks.

Morning begins with a country breakfast of French toast, eggs Benedict, pancakes, bacon and sausage, home-baked sweet breads, yogurt, and fresh fruit and juices. Weekend guests are served buffet style.

Evening brings a candlelight dinner in the inn's main dining room where you will enjoy regional specialties and local wines. I particularly enjoyed my entree of cold poached salmon on a bed of sesame-sautéed spinach and sauce verte. Chef Louis Wynne uses the freshest local ingredients available, and often prepares recipes garnered from the old cookbooks in the village's archive library.

The area around Deerfield is fun to explore. History lives and breathes in almost any direction you look. In fact, farmers still unearth bones and ax heads from the Indian massacre of 1704. Inn guests are allowed a free visit on the museum house tour and a discount at the museum store. There are also country walks, nearby boating and fishing, golfing, skiing, buggy rides, and antiquing to occupy your time.

I made it a point to thank Chester Harding for the use of his four-poster bed as I crawled in that evening. I thought it wise, just in case he decided to walk the corridor.

DEERFIELD INN, The Street, Deerfield, MA 01342; 413-774-5581. A 23-guestroom (private baths) historic 18th-century village inn. Open year-round. Modified American plan, including afternoon tea; breakfast and tea, on B&B plan. Pets allowed with prior notice. Historical places of interest and outdoor sports nearby. Karl and Jane Sabo, hosts.

Directions: From New York City, take I-91 north, then Exit 24. The inn is on The Street, just off Rtes. 5 and 10. Take Exit 26 if going south on I-91.

HAWTHORNE INN
Concord, Massachusetts (1980)

First, there was Gregory Burch. No, I'm wrong there. First, there were men like Emerson, Alcott, Nathaniel Hawthorne, and others who sought out the quietude of Concord and established their homes here. Gregory Burch came along about 1976, looking for a place somewhere in New England that needed work and would provide studio space along with some sort of income. In the year of the Bicentennial, he and the Hawthorne Inn were joined.

I think it's only fair to mention that I appeared just briefly on the scene when Gregory was working day and night to whip the inn into the kind of hospitable residence that he would be proud of. In 1980 I included the Hawthorne Inn in *Country Inns and Back Roads*.

However, there are a few more persons to be accounted for in this informal history of the Hawthorne Inn. Next is Marilyn Mudry: "Having met and fallen madly in love, I, too, came to call the Hawthorne Inn my home. We are now a family of five, with Ariel Zoe, Ezra Avery, and Jasper Gardener having arrived on blessed wings from the heavens. Their angelic presence has filled our days with joy and our nights with peace."

The Hawthorne Inn is located in the historic zone of Concord just a short walk from the Alcott House on the road out of Concord toward Lexington. It is the very same road that was neatly named "Battle Road," after the events of April 1775, when the Minutemen routed the British and sent them in retreat toward Boston.

The inn is situated on land that once belonged to Ralph Waldo Emerson, the Alcotts, and Hawthorne. Bronson Alcott planted his fruit trees and made pathways to the mill brook, and the Alcott family tended their crops of vegetables and herbs here. Two of the original trees, which Hawthorne planted, are still standing and can be seen on the west side of the inn.

The guest rooms—in fact all of the rooms in the inn—have antique furnishings, handmade quilts, and oriental and rag rugs. There are original artworks both ancient and modern, antique Japanese Ukiyo-ye prints, and sculpture by Gregory. There are floor-to-ceiling bookshelves in the Common Room, which is warmed by a cozy fire in the chilly season.

Breakfast, the only meal served, is taken in the dining room and features homemade baked breads, fruit juice, a selection of teas, or a special blend of freshly ground coffee. In season, there are fruits from the gardens and vines of the inn and honey from the inn's own beehives.

Let me share just a few sentences of Marilyn's most recent letter. "We have an area of land and sky and water where a person can come and think about their life and truly feel who they are and try to learn what they need to do for themselves, their family, and this world of ours. I feel that too often we go from one day to the next, month to month, and year to year and forget to stop. Not only to stop for an early morning walk in the woods or look at a sky emblazoned with stars, but to stop and look at the love and the light and joy which can be if we take responsibility for our lives and our actions."

Henry David Thoreau, another resident of Concord, built a small cabin on the shores of Walden Pond during the 19th century and tried to find out what life was all about. Maybe he would have found a visit with Gregory and Marilyn at the Hawthorne Inn interesting and enlightening, because they would have been happy to share some of the truths that they have discovered.

THE HAWTHORNE INN, 462 Lexington Rd., Concord, MA 01742; 508-369-5610. A 7-guestroom (private baths) bed-and-breakfast village inn approx. 19 mi. from Boston. Breakfast to houseguests is the only meal served. Open all year. Within walking distance of all of the historic and literary points of interest in Concord. Limited facilities for young children but ideal for young people who have an appreciation for history and literature. No pets. Two dogs and two cats in residence. No credit cards. Gregory Burch and Marilyn Mudry, Owners-hosts. (See Index for rates.)

Directions: The Hawthorne Inn is in the historic zone of Concord, ³/₄ mi. east of the town center. From Rte. 128-95 take Exit 30B west for 3½ mi. Bear right at the single blinking light. The inn is 1 mi. farther on the left (south side), directly across from Wayside (home of Hawthorne and Alcott).

JARED COFFIN HOUSE
Nantucket Island, Massachusetts (1969)

For over 125 years, the Jared Coffin House has been dispensing hospitality on Nantucket Island, although for about 100 of those years (1857–1960) it was known as the Ocean House. Actually, Phil Read says it wouldn't be out of line to claim 150 years, since Jared Coffin built his splendid brick mansion in 1845 on the site of an old tavern.

Just a year later, when the Great Fire of 1846 burned out most of the center of the town, the English brick walls and the Welsh slate roof of the Jared Coffin House resisted the flames and helped stop the spread of the fire.

The Jared Coffin certainly offers a step back in time, with its beautiful and authentic furnishings and decorations. There are wide-board pine floors, oriental carpets, some fine examples of Chippendale and Sheraton pieces, and many objets d'art reflecting the worldwide voyages of the Nantucket whalers.

Over the many years that Phil and Peggy Read have owned the inn, they have acquired several of the surrounding historic houses, and today the Jared Coffin actually comprises six buildings, all beautifully furnished, many with queen-sized canopied beds.

On my last visit I was with friends and, being ahead of the great influx of visitors and summer people, we were in a happy May mood as we set sail from Woods Hole. It seemed almost no time at all before the *Nebska* was docking in Nantucket. Although we could have taken a taxi or the inn station wagon, we decided to walk the three blocks to the Jared

Coffin so we could admire all the well-preserved 18th- and 19th-century houses.

Phil and Peggy were their usual warm and welcoming selves, and we all enjoyed tea in the informal Tap Room with its hand-hewn beams, pine walls, and scrubbed-oak tables and captain's chairs. Phil mentioned that this is a popular gathering place for lunch and light dining.

That night we dined on quahog chowder and bay scallops, among other things, in the beautiful dining room. The table was elegantly set with Spode Lowestoft china and pistol-handled silverware. Phil describes their extensive menu as classical American, and they have received wide recognition for their fine cuisine.

The island of Nantucket, thirty miles at sea, offers many kinds of diversions, and it's a very lively place in the height of summer. It can be reached by ferry or plane. Reservations for the Jared Coffin should be made well in advance. I suggest a trip in middle to late fall or early spring. The cobblestone streets and the shops will not be crowded, and you can enjoy the beauty and intriguing history of both the inn and the island.

Christmas also is a magical time highlighted by the boar's-head buffet, Christmas Eve by candlelight, and a New England Christmas dinner.

JARED COFFIN HOUSE, Nantucket Island, MA 02554; 508-228-2400; reservations: 508-228-2405 (M–F, 10–6). A 60-guestroom (private baths) village inn, 30 mi. at sea. Queen, double, and twin beds available. European plan. Breakfast, lunch, and dinner served daily. Wheelchair access. Please verify accommodations before planning a trip to Nantucket in any season. Swimming, fishing, boating, golf, tennis, riding, and bicycles nearby. Philip and Margaret Read, Owners-hosts. (See Index for rates.)

Directions: Accessible by air from Boston, New York, and Hyannis or by year-round ferry from Hyannis, MA. Auto reservations usually needed in advance (508-540-2022). However, cars are not recommended for short stays. Inn is a 5-min. walk from ferry dock.

"European plan" means that rates for rooms and meals are separate. "American plan" means that meals are included in the cost of the room. "Modified American plan" means that breakfast and dinner are included in the cost of the room. The rates at some inns include a continental breakfast with the lodging.

THE LENOX HOTEL
Boston, Massachusetts (1985)

I like Boston. It is really a civilized city. To me the Lenox Hotel and Boston go hand-in-glove.

The time was 7:00 a.m. and the streaks of a mid-October dawn over the city were giving way to a full-fledged day. I was seated in the window of my corner room on the eighth floor of the Lenox, looking east. One by one, the street lamps were flickering out and the tail lights of the early morning traffic were becoming more obscure. There, indeed, was a potpourri of Boston architecture in front of me, with restrained 19th-century business buildings cheek-by-jowl with the single bell tower and spire of a church. The trees on Boylston Street still had a generous tinge of the fall colors. A seagull swooped by my window and perched on the very top of a modern Boston building on the opposite corner. Through the other window I could look down the street toward the Charles River and Cambridge on the other side. The runners and joggers were already out. By the way, the Lenox provides a jogger's guide to Boston.

Now the sun poked its way up over the harbor and I glanced around this most "unhotel" of all hotel rooms. A good substantial Hitchcock-style side chair was augmented by two excellent regular chairs and, of course, a Boston rocker. The furniture, draperies, and wallpaper were all in a most pleasing New England style. There wasn't a single piece of furniture that wouldn't have been in place at one of the *CIBR* country inns found throughout New England.

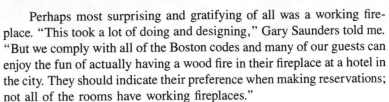

Perhaps most surprising and gratifying of all was a working fireplace. "This took a lot of doing and designing," Gary Saunders told me. "But we comply with all of the Boston codes and many of our guests can enjoy the fun of actually having a wood fire in their fireplace at a hotel in the city. They should indicate their preference when making reservations; not all of the rooms have working fireplaces."

The Lenox Hotel, a small, turn-of-the-century establishment conveniently located in the Back Bay area of Boston (next door to Copley Square), is something of a rarity in these days of corporate ownership—a family-run hotel, whose owners are very visible. Gary Saunders and his father, Roger, along with other members of the family, have owned the hotel for the past twenty-five years.

Hearty New England fare is served in the Olde London Pub and Grille, for which the main paneling, posts, and tables were shipped over from England.

Diamond Jim's Piano Bar, which has become an institution in its over twenty years of popularity, is another reason people feel so at home at the Lenox. Everybody joins in and sings; anybody can get up and perform a solo, and several professionals and young hopefuls have been "discovered" there. The annual amateur singing competition is a big event. The feeling of camaraderie and friendliness makes going to Diamond Jim's a lot of fun.

There is one particular convenience that guests at the Lenox enjoy, which pleases me very much, and that's the airport and limousine service, available at a reasonable charge for guests arriving and departing. This is particularly handy for those of us who have to fly out of Logan Airport in Boston. Incidentally, I must admit that I also enjoyed the valet parking service that eliminates the hassle of finding a garage that isn't full.

THE LENOX HOTEL, 710 Boylston St., Boston, MA 02116; 1-800-225-7676 (Mass.: 617-536-5300). A 220-guestroom (private baths) conservative hotel in Boston's Back Bay area. Breakfast, lunch, and dinner served every day. Open all year. All contemporary hotel conveniences provided. Drive-in garage with valet parking service. Convenient to business, theaters, sightseeing, and shopping. The Saunders Family, Owners-hosts; Michael Schweiger, General Manager. (See Index for rates.)

Directions: If arriving by automobile, take Exit 22 from the Mass. Tpke., the Copley Square ramp, and turn left on Dartmouth St. for 2 blocks to Newbury St. Take a left on Newbury St. for 1 block to Exeter St., take a left on Exeter for 1 block and the hotel is ahead at the corner of Exeter and Boylston Sts. An airport limo service between Logan Airport and the Lenox is available for a nominal fee.

LONGFELLOW'S WAYSIDE INN
South Sudbury, Massachusetts (1967)

It was my pleasure a few years ago to teach American history to a group of eighth-grade students, and in my endeavor to stay at least one chapter ahead of the class, I found myself once again exploring the fascinating events that preceded the American Revolution. Of course the ideal procedure to follow was to visit the scene of these remarkable events, and this trip took me to Boston, Cambridge, Concord, and other eastern Massachusetts communities that were the sites of so many of the events of 1775 and 1776.

In pursuit of these earlier times, I left the well-traveled roads to search for old buildings, mildewed markers, and ancient trees that might indeed have been witnesses to these events of history. In this way I eventually arrived at Longfellow's Wayside Inn in South Sudbury.

In my wildest hopes I couldn't have expected to find a more ideal setting. Built of red clapboard with white trim, the inn sits off a winding country road, once the stagecoach route between Boston and Albany.

The inn was built around 1702 and originally was called Howe's Tavern. In 1775, the Sudbury farmers, led by innkeeper Ezekiel Howe, were among the men who fought at nearby Concord. Revolutionary War soldiers found sustenance at the inn's tables. Today all musters of the Sudbury Minutemen take place at the inn as preparations are made for their annual reenactment of the march from Sudbury to Concord on April 19th. The 200th anniversary of the Battle of Lexington and Concord was celebrated in 1975.

Henry Wadsworth Longfellow immortalized the inn in 1863 with his *Tales of a Wayside Inn,* and thereafter it was known by its new name.

Thanks to a grant from the Ford Foundation, the buildings and priceless antiques have been preserved as a historical and literary shrine. The inn is filled with preserved and restored antiques. It combines being a museum with the more practical function of providing lodging and food.

Just up the road, a reproduction of an 18th-century gristmill is in operation grinding flour. Also just a stone's throw away is the famous Martha-Mary Chapel, a reproduction of a classic New England church and the setting for many a marriage these days.

The dining room specializes in good New England fare such as baked Cape Cod scallops, indian pudding served with ice cream, muffins made from meal stone-ground at the gristmill, and Massachusetts duckling in orange sauce.

I must echo the advice of innkeeper Frank Koppeis that anyone who is expecting to visit Longfellow's Wayside Inn either for a meal or lodgings should be sure to make a reservation in advance.

Here is an excerpt from a letter I received recently: "The Wayside Inn was as good as ever. It's got to be the classic in country inns. Probably its only fault is that it is too popular—especially on Sunday afternoon. Our first evening there we tried something new, a swordfish dinner. It was pretty darn good. When we had retired to our room for the evening we heard bagpipes and got up to see what was going on. Unbelievably, a parade of pipers dressed in Colonial uniform was marching through the inn. Quite a treat."

LONGFELLOW'S WAYSIDE INN, Wayside Inn Rd., off Rte. 20, South Sudbury, MA 01776; 508-443-8846. A 10-guestroom (private baths) historic landmark inn, midway between Boston and Worcester. European plan. Lunch and dinner served daily except Christmas. Breakfast served to overnight guests. Within a short distance of Concord, Lexington, and other famous Revolutionary War landmarks. Francis Koppeis, Manager. (See Index for rates.)

Directions: From the west, take Exit 11A from Mass. Tpke. and proceed north on Rte. 495 to Rte. 20. Follow Rte. 20 east 7 mi. to inn. From the east, take Exit 49 from Rte. 128. Follow Rte. 20 west 11 mi. to inn.

"European plan" means that rates for rooms and meals are separate. "American plan" means that meals are included in the cost of the room. "Modified American plan" means that breakfast and dinner are included in the cost of the room. The rates at some inns include a continental breakfast with the lodging.

THE RED LION INN
Stockbridge, Massachusetts (1967)

An old friend of mine, Stew Brown, who has traveled all over the world and is now living in London, once confessed that for years he had harbored the fond wish to sit in a rocking chair on the porch of the Red Lion Inn and watch the passing parade. And that's exactly what we did on his last visit, even though it was raining buckets. Although I've spent countless hours over the years rocking on that capacious porch, waving and calling out to Stockbridge friends and neighbors, it's always been a special pastime for me.

I can think of many special moments connected with the Red Lion Inn. To begin with, everyone in Stockbridge was so relieved in 1967 when Jane and Jack Fitzpatrick decided to rescue it from being torn down and replaced by a gas station. The old inn had been standing since 1793, not without experiencing any number of modifications and disasters. It had. been a stagecoach stop on the Springfield–Albany run, and in the years when Stockbridge became a summertime mecca for artists, musicians, and writers — before Tanglewood was started by Serge Koussevitsky, and Ted Shawn made Jacob's Pillow famous — in the era of the splendid Berkshire "summer cottages," Red Lion buggies would collect their guests at the Stanford White–designed railroad station.

But, back to the present. The Fitzpatricks (they are also owners of Country Curtains) set about restoring and refurbishing the Red Lion Inn and turning it into the centerpiece of the village of Stockbridge.

As often as I have walked through the lobby and parlors, I am always impressed by the beautiful collection of antiques, which includes tables, cabinets, highboys, clocks, paintings, and prints that seem to be very much at home in the low-ceilinged setting. The collection of teapots was actually started in the middle of the 19th century by a Mrs. Plumb, who owned the inn. All of the rooms and hallways show Jane's attention to detail, and the love and interest she and Jack have devoted to the inn over the years.

I mentioned special moments at the Red Lion, and there are so many — so many lunches and dinners with friends in the gracious dining room or out in the flower-filled courtyard or tucked away in Widow Bingham's Tavern . . . the times I've listened to a great jazz combo or a delightful folk singer in the Lion's Den downstairs. They have entertainment every night during the summer.

Many people equate Stockbridge with Norman Rockwell, and of course, the Corner House Museum has his original paintings. There are many Norman Rockwell prints hanging throughout the Red Lion.

In the summer, the Boston Symphony plays at Tanglewood, and there are wonderful dance companies at Jacob's Pillow and dramas at the

Berkshire Theatre Festival, along with any number of lesser-known attractions and entertainments.

The glorious autumn colors bring visitors flocking, and winter sees the skiers taking advantage of the winter package plans. Christmas at the Red Lion is a particularly joyful time, with the huge tree in the lobby, shimmering with hundreds of handmade ornaments, all the laurel roping, Christmas greens, and daughter Ann Fitzpatrick's candy sculptures. There are always several lighted Christmas trees across the porch roof and at various points around the inn. There is harp music, a concert by bell ringers, carolers on the front porch, and Santa Claus, of course.

THE RED LION INN, Stockbridge, MA 01262; 413-298-5545. A 104-guestroom (75 private baths) historic village inn, dating back to 1773, in the Berkshire hills. Queen, double, and twin beds available. European plan. Breakfast, lunch, and dinner. Open year-round. Wheelchair access. Adjacent to Tanglewood, Norman Rockwell's Old Corner House Museum, the Berkshire Playhouse, Jacob's Pillow, Chesterwood Gallery, Mission House, and major ski areas. Outdoor pool. Tennis, golf, boating, fishing, hiking, mountain climbing, and xc skiing nearby. Jack and Jane Fitzpatrick, Owners; Betsy Holtzinger, Owner-host. (See Index for rates.)

Directions: From the Taconic State Pkwy., take Exit 23 (N.Y. Rte. 23) to Mass. Rte. 7. Proceed north to Stockbridge. From the Mass. Tpke., Exit 2 at Lee, and follow Rte. 102 to Stockbridge.

The date in parenthesis in the heading represents the first year the inn appeared in the pages of Country Inns and Back Roads.

THE VILLAGE INN
Lenox, Massachusetts (1977)

"We're actually beginning our eighth year as innkeepers; it hardly seems possible that so much time has passed." I was having dinner in the Harvest Restaurant at the Village Inn with innkeepers Cliff Rudisill and Ray Wilson. We were reminiscing about their early days here, when they took over the inn in January of 1982, weathered the winter, and worked on learning the ropes and becoming acclimated.

"After Easter that year," Ray said, "we spent two weeks in England and visited seven country house hotels, sampling marvelous cuisine and learning our way around English teas. As a matter of fact, because of meeting Bronwen Nixon at Rothay Manor, we came back and established an English Afternoon Tea, as well as an authentic High Tea, which we hold, along with a chamber music concert, one Sunday afternoon a month, January through June. Rothay Manor is our 'Twin Inn' in England."

These two men, both from Texas, have established their own unique style at the Village Inn, a two-and-a-half-story yellow clapboard building with a basic Federal design. Built in 1771, and ultimately adapted to meet various needs over many years, it became an inn in 1775, and has been one ever since. Two rear wings, which were once well-constructed barns, form an L-shaped sheltered terrace with a lawn on which there are a number of beautiful maples. Plantings of irises, daffodils, petunias, roses, and tulips brighten the picture during the warmer weather, and the interior of the inn is enhanced by flowers throughout all months of the year.

On the floors above, authentic New England rooms and suites are available for overnight guests or for those with longer stays in mind. All but two of them have their own bathrooms, many have four-poster beds, and some have working fireplaces.

Ray and Cliff had invited me over for dinner to celebrate the finish of their seven-year redecorating program with the twenty-ninth and last guest room. Maybe Cliff should have been an architect. He really did an amazing job of moving walls, enlarging rooms, and creating bathrooms and closets. All of the rooms have new Colonial wallpaper and new curtains and carpets. They are air conditioned in the summer.

The Tavern in the old cellar is now completely remodeled and features professional entertainment on the weekends.

Dinner that evening was delightful and delicious, with a Shaker pie appetizer that had ham and a lovely sauce. The entrée was a perfectly poached salmon steak served with blackberries and a blackberry sauce and a side dish of fresh asparagus. Dessert was a delectable pear and macadamia nut tart. Ray pointed out that they have the area's largest breakfast menu, which includes johnny cakes—a great old New England tradition.

But let's return to the style that Cliff and Ray have brought to the inn in the past few years. Some special-interest weekends deal with California wines, computers, art and artists, literature, and Shakers, and include workshops and field trips. Write for a brochure describing these interesting weekends.

Cliff points out that "Tanglewood is just a mile down the road, and we continue the tradition of good music all year long. We always have good classical music playing in the background, and our grand piano in the large common room is frequently played by guests who share their talent with us." The inn has also been acquiring some very handsome paintings, including those of William and James Hart and other Hudson River School painters.

The Village Inn in Lenox—an inn of graceful style.

THE VILLAGE INN, Church St., Lenox, MA 01240; 413-637-0020. A 29-guestroom inn (all but 2 with private baths) in a historic Berkshire town, 4 mi. from Stockbridge, 8 mi. from Pittsfield, and 1 mi. from Tanglewood. All sizes of beds available. Breakfast and afternoon tea served daily to travelers. Dinner served Wed. thru Sun. Open every day of the year. Lenox is located in the heart of the Berkshires with many historical, cultural, and recreational features. Swimming in pleasant nearby lakes. All seasonal sports, including xc and downhill skiing, available nearby. Children over 6 welcome. No pets. Personal checks accepted. Cliff Rudisill and Ray Wilson, Owners-hosts. (See Index for rates.)

Directions: After approaching Lenox on Rte. 7, one of the principal north-south routes in New England, exit onto Rte. 7A to reach the village center and Church St. When approaching from the Mass. Tpke. (Exit 2), use Rte. 20W about 4 mi. and turn left onto Rte. 183 to center of town.

THE WEATHERVANE INN
South Egremont, Massachusetts (1984)

"Good evening, folks, how are you? I'm the innkeeper, Vince Murphy." While I was having a welcome cup of tea in front of the very cozy fireplace at the Weathervane Inn on a midwinter afternoon, Vincent Murphy excused himself at least four times to welcome new guests. Vince is a man who has the knack for making people feel welcome immediately.

Among the things that I look for in an inn are qualities of memorability. Besides innkeeper Murphy, who is, as he says, "a private investigator from the streets of New York," there are many other memorable features.

For example, there's Anne Murphy with the laughing eyes and a most pleasant manner with all of the guests. Then there's Patricia (or Trish), Anne and Vince's daughter, who had just returned from a Florida vacation at the time of my visit and must have knocked them dead on the beaches, because she had a super suntan to go with her Irish good looks.

The Weathervane Inn, listed in the National Register of Historic Places, is a small cluster of buildings set off the highway, with sections dating back to 1785. It is located in the lovely little village of South Egremont in the Berkshires, where there are many pre-1800 houses and a graceful church. Replete with wide-board floors, beautiful moldings, and an original fireplace that served as a heating and cooking unit with a beehive oven, the inn has a comfortable, warm atmosphere.

There are eleven very attractively furnished country inn guest rooms, with private baths, enhanced by Anne's eye for design and her needlework. Antique maple high double beds and some king-sized beds, all with coordinated linens, along with Anne's handmade pierced lampshades, all combine to make each room distinctive. There are many dried flower arrangements, ball fringe curtains, books and magazines, and good reading lamps.

I talked to Anne about the menu at the Weathervane. "Well," she said, "the kitchen is my domain and I'm very proud of the response that our guests have had to our entrées. Our specialties have been Cornish hens with kiwi sauce, veal Dijonnaise, pork tenderloin Normandy, duckling with black cherries seafood Mornay, and soups like split pea, New England chowders, and a hearty borscht. We've had to print our recipe for celery seed dressing because so many of our diners requested it."

Vince came cruising by and decided to make his contribution: "Let me tell you about our desserts—Trish is the pastry chef par excellence! The best homemade pies with the best crust. All kinds of fresh fruit combinations—blueberry-peach,   strawberry-blueberry,   peach-nectarine, and pear blueberry. And her cheesecake and chocolate chip walnut pie get nothing but raves!"

There are two dining areas, including a new dining room overlooking

the garden and the swimming pool, with a glimpse of the antique shop in a barn that has a feeling somewhat akin to the Sturbridge Village buildings. The shop specializes in early quilts and folk furniture. and inn guests often wander back there to browse.

Eventually, we all sat down in front of the fireplace, next to a sort of little pub corner, and for an hour and a half I was beguiled by the various members of the Murphy family. Vince really is a private investigator, but he takes all of the Mike Hammer jokes with exceptionally good grace and even adds a few of his own. "I did that for many years in the city," he said, "and I still go in about one day a week, but all of us have taken up this new life here in the country. As a matter of fact, I'm even a member of the South Egremont Volunteer Fire Department!"

THE WEATHERVANE INN, Rte. 23, South Egremont, MA 01258; 413-528-9580. A 10-guestroom (private baths) village inn in the Berkshire foothills. King, queen, and double beds available. Modified American plan in summer; in winter, modified American plan, Thurs. through Sun. Breakfast served to houseguests. Dinner served to travelers Fri. and Sat. Closed Thanksgiving to Dec. 26. Limited wheelchair access. Swimming pool on grounds. Golf, tennis, bicycling, backroading, hiking, horseback riding, fishing. downhill and xc skiing nearby. Tanglewood, Jacob's Pillow, Berkshire Playhouse, Norman Rockwell Museum, and great antique shops all nearby. No children under 7. No pets. One dog and cat in residence. Vincent, Anne, and Patricia Murphy, Innkeepers. (See Index for rates.)

Directions; From New York City follow Sawmill River Pkwy. to Taconic Pkwy. to Rte. 23 east. South Egremont and the inn are about 2 mi. past the Catamount ski area on Rt. 23.

MONTREAL

BURLINGTON

Philbrook Farm, *Shelburne*
Spalding Inn,
ST JOHNSBURY   • *Whitefield*
Rabbit Hill Inn, *Lower Waterford* Sugar Hill Inn, Christmas Farm Inn
V E R M O N T   *Sugar Hill* Inn at Thorn Hill,
                                                    • *Jackson*
Notchland Inn, *Hart's Location*
Darby Field Inn, *Conway* • NORTH CONWAY

• Middlebury Inn,
Middlebury   Snowvillage Inn, *Snowvillage*
Shire Inn,
Chelsea

Blueberry Hill Farm,
Goshen   • Lyme Inn, *Lyme*
Vermont Marble   • Tulip Tree Inn,   Moose Mountain Lodge, *Etna*
Inn, *Fair Haven* • Mountain Top Inn, *Chittenden*   N E W
• RUTLAND ■ October Country Inn, ■ HANOVER
Middletown Springs • Inn, *Bridgewater*
Middletown Springs   *Corners* • Kedron Valley Inn, *S. Woodstock*

The Governor's Inn, *Ludlow* • Rowell's Inn, Dexter's Inn,
                                    Simonsville   *Sunapee*
Barrows House, *Dorset*   • New London Inn, *New London*
1811 House, •   Inn at Long Last,   • Follansbee Inn, *North Sutton*
Birch Hill Inn, *Manchester*   *Chester*   ■ CONCORD
West Mountain Inn, • Three Mountain Inn, *Jamaica* • Mountain Lake Inn, *Bradford*
Arlington   • Meeting House Inn and
              Windham Hill,   Restaurant, *Henniker*
              West Townshend H A M P S H I R E
Four Columns Inn, *Newfane* •   • Inn at Crotched Mt., *Francestown*
Inn at Sawmill Farm, •   John Hancock Inn, *Hancock*
West Dover   Chesterfield Inn, *West Chesterfield*
Inn at South Newfane,
South Newfane   Birchwood Inn, *Temple* •

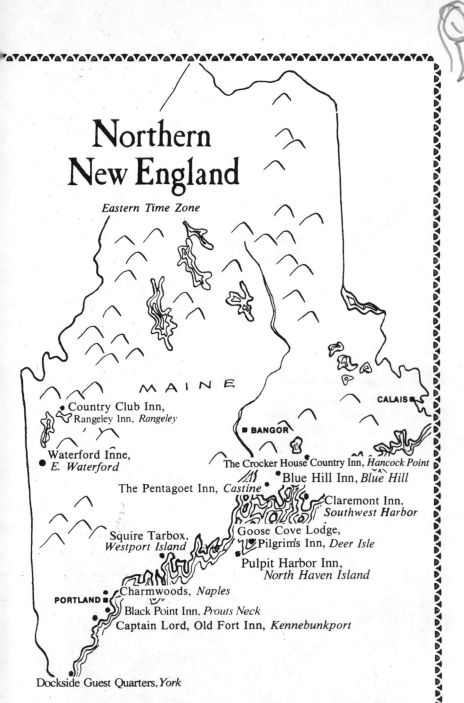

Northern
New England

Eastern Time Zone

M A I N E

CALAIS

● Country Club Inn,
Rangeley Inn, *Rangeley*

■ BANGOR

● Waterford Inne,
● *E. Waterford*

The Crocker House Country Inn, *Hancock Point*
● Blue Hill Inn, *Blue Hill*

The Pentagoet Inn, *Castine* ●

Claremont Inn,
Southwest Harbor

Squire Tarbox,
Westport Island

Goose Cove Lodge,
Pilgrim's Inn, *Deer Isle*

Pulpit Harbor Inn,
North Haven Island

Charmwoods, *Naples*

PORTLAND ■

Black Point Inn, *Prouts Neck*

Captain Lord, Old Fort Inn, *Kennebunkport*

Dockside Guest Quarters, *York*

BLACK POINT INN
Prouts Neck, Maine

The Black Point Inn was recently described as one of the "last bastions of clean air, pure water, peace — and finger bowls." It is one of the few remaining American-plan resort hotels so numerous along the New England coast at the turn of the century. The atmosphere is genteel, friendly, and understated, with gentlemen in coats and ladies in summer dresses for dinner and later dancing to a small orchestra, which also plays during luncheon at poolside.

It's always exhilarating to stand on the flagstone terrace, looking out across the gaily colored umbrellas around the pool to the vast blue sweep of ocean. There are fine sandy beaches, tennis courts, and an 18-hole golf course a few steps away. Normand Dugas joined me, and we stood for a moment watching the American and Canadian flags snapping in the breeze and the white sails of a boat on the horizon.

"Our new 28-foot fishing boat, called *The Blue Lady,* departs with a surprising number of guests at 5 a.m., in order to catch the rascals before they wake up!" Norm said. "Our guests are able to do some fishing and still get back in time for breakfast by 9 a.m. We have mackerel, bluefish, stripers, a few small sharks, and an occasional sea bass."

Norm and I walked into the indoor swimming pool room, which he tells me has been extremely well received by all of the inn guests. Those staying slightly off season have particularly appreciated this pool, since the ocean is too cold before mid-June and after mid-September. The walls of the room are lined in beautiful California red cedar, and the pool overlooks the rose garden and the putting green.

Another interesting addition to the Black Point is the "Atlantic House Library." The Atlantic House Hotel, also on Prouts Neck, is now closed after 146 years of continuous operation, and the BPI acquired most

of its library books and some other memorabilia. A lovely two-tier outside deck just off the library has been constructed for nice sunny-day reading.

The Prouts Neck path, or Cliff Walk, starts from a point next to the sea just a few steps from the main entrance of the inn and continues along the cliffs and rocks, cutting back through nooks and crannies between stately summer homes. At one point it passes in front of the studio of Winslow Homer, many of whose finest oil paintings were inspired by this coastline. Thirteen-year-old Peter Dugas is adding to the possible diversions, conducting nature walks in the adjacent Prouts Neck Bird Sanctuary, describing various trees, birds, and plant life there.

Two of Normand's other children, Marc and Michelle, are now taking active roles at the inn, working as rooms manager and dining room captain, respectively. "This gives old man Dugas a bit more time to play happy innkeeper, chat with the guests, and dream up new projects for future years," Normand said with a wink.

The evening menu emphasizes freshly caught Maine fish, and there is always lobster in some form; if you're lucky, you might even find lobster salad at the poolside luncheon buffet. Meals are essentially New England fare.

The dining room is cheerful, with windows looking out on the colorful rose garden, and the lounges are gracious and comfortable. Rooms are more readily available during the months of May, June, September, and October, when the modified American plan is optional. During recent years the weather in early June has been exceptional, and it is sometimes possible to call and make a reservation a day ahead; however, August is always a full month.

Prouts Neck became popular as a summer resort at the end of the 19th century, and time has brought few changes to this lovely neck of land stretching out into the Atlantic. The sea, birds, water, sky, and trees, all of which go to make such desirable tranquility, are still here today.

BLACK POINT INN, Prouts Neck, ME 04070; 207-883-4126. An 80-guestroom (private baths) luxury resort-inn on Rte. 207, 10 mi. south of Portland. Queen, double, and twin beds available. Open May to late Oct. American plan during July and Aug. Optional MAP May, June, Sept., Oct. During high season, 3-night minimum stay. Indoor pool, Jacuzzi, and sauna, fresh-water whirlpool, heated salt-water pool, bicycles, sailing, dancing, golf, tennis, and ocean bathing all within a few steps. No children under 8 during July and Aug. No pets. Normand H. Dugas, Manager. (See Index for rates.)

Directions: From Maine Tpke., take Exit 7. Turn right at sign marked Scarborough and Old Orchard Beach. At second set of lights turn left on Rte. 207. Follow 4.3 mi. to Prouts Neck.

THE BLUE HILL INN
Blue Hill, Maine (1990)

Sheltered by tall, graceful American elms, The Blue Hill Inn peacefully rests at the head of shimmering Blue Hill Bay and at the foot of Blue Hill Mountain. The dignified brick and clapboard building was built in 1830, and converted to a village inn ten years later. I was standing on the front lawn, admiring the lovely Federal-style architecture, and counting the many chimneys, when innkeeper Donald Hartley came around the corner with a load of wood. "Good afternoon!" he said. "I see you're here for our sailing excursion." I was excited about the day sails arranged for guests aboard the 50-foot New England pinky schooner *Summertime,* but didn't realize my new white deck shoes would be such a giveaway.

Donald told me more about the inn's history as we entered the front hallway. "We're celebrating its sesquicentennial, as a matter of fact. The inn has been in continuous operation now for 150 years." I also learned that the inn's wonderful granite foundation had been quarried locally, and that the inn is listed on the National Register of Historic Places.

Mary and Donald Hartley are very gracious hosts. Prior to their careers as innkeepers, they were both active in the management of community-based programs for the developmentally and mentally disabled. "The inn offers us the opportunity to meet and enjoy people, and to broaden our span of skills," Mary explained, as she readied the tray of scrumptious-looking hors d'oeuvres for the nightly innkeepers' reception. The reception is held in the two cozy parlors, where cocktails, wine, and soft drinks are available.

The inn's common rooms, dining room, and eleven guest rooms are decorated with 19th-century furnishings. The parlors offer comfortable easy chairs and couches grouped around attractive, working fireplaces. Oriental carpets accent polished wood floors, and colorful print wall-papers contrast with crisp, white trims. Most of the guest rooms have fireplaces, and all have private baths, some with old-fashioned tubs.

As I left for my sail, I hoped I wouldn't succumb to the bane of all landlubbers—sea sickness—because the smells from the kitchen told me that dinner would be fabulous. When Mary and Don took over the inn, they made it a priority to provide the most wonderful food possible and hired a new chef de cuisine who specializes in contemporary foods prepared with classical French techniques.

When I returned, feeling like an old salt with an enormous appetite, the aromas were even more tantalizing. Dinner is served by candlelight and includes six courses, beginning with homemade soup. I was served a subtle chicken and lentil finished with chive broth. My entree of sea scallops and spinach and mushrooms with tomato-basil coulis was melt-in-the-mouth tender. A sorbet was offered to clear the palate before a crisp, colorful salad of watercress and tomatoes dressed with walnut vinaigrette was served. A slice of rich flourless chocolate torte with a dollop of coffee cream made me wish I had room for seconds, but I knew morning would bring a full breakfast.

The Blue Hill Inn is in the center of the village, so galleries, antique shops, and fine stores are within walking distance. A weekly concert series takes place all summer at Kneisel Hall, and the famous Haystack School of Crafts is only a short drive away. Of course, all types of activities take place on the water: whale watching, canoeing, sailing, fishing. In the winter, Blue Hill Mountain has cross-country skiing and snowshoeing. But I think I'll stick to the water, and keep my deck shoes handy. Maybe I'll even add a captain's hat next year!

THE BLUE HILL INN, P.O. Box 403, Blue Hill, ME 04614; 207-374-2844. An 11-guestroom (private baths) historic inn located in the center of the village of Blue Hill. All-size beds. Open year-round. Modified American plan, and B&B rates. Wonderful food. Water sports, music festivals, and Acadia National Park nearby. No pets. Smoking limited. Children over 13 welcome. Mary and Donald Hartley, Owners-hosts.

Directions: From Augusta, take Exit 95. Take Rte. 3 south to Belfast, through Bucksport; 2 mi. east of Bucksport, take Rte. 15 south to Blue Hill. From Bangor, take Rte. 5 south. From Ellsworth, take Rte. 172 west.

THE CAPTAIN LORD MANSION
Kennebunkport, Maine (1975)

I remember it very well: in fact, it was only last summer. It was a Wednesday morning in mid-July and I joined the Captain Lord breakfast group at nine-thirty. (There had been an earlier breakfast group at eight-thirty.) Many of the guests were seated in a large but somewhat formal dining room enjoying coffee and planning the day's activities. A large jigsaw puzzle was on the dining room table and a couple of guests were playing Chinese checkers in one corner. The Chippendale chairs, beautiful cabinets, and crystal chandelier were indications that this was indeed an important room during the many years of the mansion's existence.

Meanwhile, the morning breakfast chimes were rung, and almost as one, the waiting guests rose, crossed the hallway, and walked into the ample Captain Lord kitchen, where breakfast is served.

I took advantage of the moment to walk around and admire the handsome woodwork and lovely period wallpapers of this mansion, built during the War of 1812.

I walked to the front of the house where a beautiful curving banister led up a rather formal staircase to the third floor. Throughout the mansion, Rick and Bev have collected antiques, oriental rugs, and other tasteful objets d'art. One parlor has been set aside as a gift shop offering attractive mementos of the area, as well as smaller items such as cups, saucers, plates and the like.

Ample use has been made of the generous sized hallways, both on the second and third floors, with handsome cabinets, antique children's sleighs, duck decoys, quilts, prints of sailing ships, a spinning wheel, and even a basket of washed wool.

I peeked into a few of the spotless guest rooms whose doors were open, and once again fluffy comforters, handmade quilts or 100% wool blankets, and Posturepedic mattresses reigned supreme. There are additional rooms in Phoebe's Fantasy, a beautiful Federal house next door, named for Captain Lord's wife. Furnished in much the same manner, it has king- and queen-sized four-posters and canopied beds, antiques, and working fireplaces.

I returned to the kitchen where the guests were all seated around the lovely harvest table, which provided just the right amount of intimacy. There were lots of laughter and appreciative comments about the breakfast of orange juice, fresh homemade breads, muffins, toast, and coffee, and, if desired, a soft-boiled egg.

It was at this point that Rick came in and started to tell us about the Captain's Hideaway. "It's a beautiful New England Cape Cod cottage with two wonderful guest rooms and working fireplaces," he said. "Although all of our bathrooms are very special and modern, the ones at the

Hideaway are even more so, with whirlpool baths and massage power heads in the showers. One bathroom has a fireplace and a view of the water. The upstairs bedroom has a sitting area and a canopied bed, and the downstairs bedroom has a private entrance and patio. They both have working fireplaces.

"Breakfast at the Hideaway is an epicurean delight, with homemade granola, yogurt, fresh fruit, and an egg dish. We make the same fresh muffins you have here but they're mini size." Breakfast is served in the formal dining room at the Hideaway on English china with crystal and silver. "The rates are higher," Bev told me, "but the guests who have stayed there rave about it."

THE CAPTAIN LORD MANSION, Box 800, Kennebunkport, ME 04046; 207-967-3141. A 24-guestroom (private baths) mansion-inn in a seacoast village. King, queen, and double beds available. Lodgings include breakfast. No other meals served. Open year-round. Near the Rachel Carson Wildlife Refuge, the Seashore Trolley Museum, the Brick Store Museum, and lobster boat tours. Bicycles, hiking, xc skiing, deep-sea fishing, golf, indoor swimming, and tennis nearby. No children under 12. No pets. Bev Davis and Rick Litchfield, Owners-hosts. (See Index for rates.)

Directions: Take Exit 3 (Kennebunk) from the Maine Tpke. Take left on Rte. 35 and follow signs through Kennebunk to Kennebunkport. Take left at traffic light at Sunoco station. Go over drawbridge and take first right onto Ocean Ave., then take fifth left off Ocean Ave. (³/₁₀ mi.). The mansion is in the second block on left. Park behind building and take brick walk to office.

CHARMWOODS
On Long Lake, Naples, Maine (1981)

Charmwoods is a unique type of inn. Set in an area of great natural beauty and maintained by conscientious hosts, the inn provides a perfect setting for an escape to the countryside.

Once a private lakefront estate, Charmwoods radiates all the flavor and ambience of the Maine woods but is a mere 2½-hour drive from downtown Boston.

As hosts, Marilyn and Bill Lewis make for a perfect combination. Marilyn is attractive and vivacious and delights in giving her guests personal attention to ensure the most pleasurable of vacations for them.

Bill, a former editor at the *Boston Globe* and *Boston Herald,* has unusual interests that Charmwoods guests find to be a pleasant diversion. For example, he often entertains with his 1890 Thomas A. Edison phonograph, drawing from a collection of about 500 cylindrical recordings. The newest acquisition is an antique player-piano, complete with rolls of the old favorites. Evenings, it is the center of attraction for guests addicted to sing-alongs with a keen nostalgia for this lusty entertainment of yesteryear.

Marilyn's penchant for decorating is particularly evident in all the spacious bedrooms with their selection of handsome, coordinated sheets, blankets, towels, and other accessories in distinctive colors.

The focus of activity at Charmwoods is frequently the commodious and gracious living room with its massive fieldstone fireplace and panoramic view of lake and mountains. Everything about this room encourages friendly discussions with a free exchange of information and ideas. The striking undersea photographs are provided by the Lewises' son, Jonathan.

Within fifteen minutes of my arrival, Bill and Marilyn had introduced me to their guests and we were immediately on a first-name basis — chatting like old friends. Several guests were regulars at Charmwoods, having returned year after year.

Adjoining the living room and sharing center stage during much of the year is a broad deck with an unobstructed view of Long Lake. It is equally ideal for sunny breakfasts or for chatting under the stars.

A path leads down a few steps to the shoreline of this delightfully clear lake where a rowboat and canoe are docked in the boathouse. Swimming from the white sandy beach or private sundeck is ideal, and a trim cabana provides numerous amenities, including telephone service.

The village of Naples, a short stroll down the road, offers guests some interesting upcountry diversions, not the least of which is a seaplane flight providing an excellent overview of the entire resort area. The *Songo River Queen,* an old-fashioned paddleboat, and the U.S. mailboats run

excursion trips across the ten-mile-wide lake. Plenty of backroading and quite a few antique shops can be enjoyed in the immediate area.

During my visit at Charmwoods nearly all the guests clutched tennis rackets, and the all-weather court saw plenty of play. There's a lakeside golf course and riding stables just a few minutes away.

Visiting Charmwoods is like being a guest at a houseparty for friends.

CHARMWOODS, P.O. Box 217, Naples, ME 04055; 207-693-6798. A 4-guestroom (private baths) lakefront bed-and-breakfast inn, plus a guest cottage, on the west shore of Long Lake, approx. 2½ hrs. from Boston and ½ hr. from Maine Tpke. King and twin beds available. Open June into Oct. Breakfast is the only meal served (to houseguests only). Tennis, swimming, boating, canoeing, fishing, shuffleboard, and horseshoes on grounds; horseback riding, golf, para-sailing, and windsurfing nearby. Summer playhouse just down the road. Not suitable for children under 12. No pets. No credit cards. Marilyn and Bill Lewis, Owners-hosts. (See Index for rates.)

Directions: From Boston, follow Rte. 1 north to I-95 and take Exit 8 (Portland-Westbrook). Turn right and follow Riverside St. 1 mi. to Rte. 302. Turn left (west) to Naples, which is about 30 mi. ahead. Charmwoods is just beyond the village on the right with an unobtrusive sign. From North Conway, N.H., follow Rte. 302 through Bridgton. Charmwoods sign and driveway off Rte. 302 just before Naples village.

THE CLAREMONT HOTEL AND COTTAGES
Southwest Harbor, Maine (1974)

The year was 1884. Grover Cleveland (Democrat) defeated James G. Blaine (Republican) for president. London opened the first underground railroad. Auguste Rodin created his famous sculpture *Burghers of Calais.* Harry Truman was born. The Ringling Brothers circus was organized in Baraboo, Wisconsin. The Statue of Liberty was completed and presented to the United States. Women first competed in Wimbledon tennis, and the Washington Monument was completed.

It was also the year that the Claremont Hotel was opened. Its creator was Captain Jesse Pease, a native of Rockland and a well-known sea captain. During that first year, 146 names were entered on the register. Many of these came from New York and Boston and enjoyed a simple, modest vacation at the Claremont. There were oil lamps and pitchers and basins in each room. Hot baths were ordered in advance for twenty-five cents.

Considerable contribution to the progress of this over-century-old establishment came during the long tenure of the Phillips family, who owned it for sixty years. During that time, more bedrooms and a new dining room were added, and such improvements as an elevator and a sprinkler protection system were installed.

In 1968, the Claremont was sold to Mr. and Mrs. Allen McCue of Yarmouth, Maine, who have continued in all of the traditions, as well as adding new cottages and making many improvements, including a wing with a spectacular view of Somes Sound.

In fact, the cottages have become so popular they decided just in the past year to add two more, with built-in fireplaces and hardwood floors. Adjacent to the dining room, the rooms overlook Greenings Island and Somes Sound.

The Claremont is situated on the waters of Somes Sound in a most interesting community with an identity of its very own. It always intrigues me that there are two different aspects to Southwest Harbor. On one side of the small peninsula is a working harbor with lots of fishing boats and the hustle and bustle of people who make their living with the cooperation of the sea. On the other side is a more tranquil scene, with sailboats and launches. This view over the water to Northeast Harbor is the one which is enjoyed by Claremont guests as they sit in the boathouse or on the front porch of the inn itself.

On each visit I have been struck by the wide variety of entertainment and recreation available for people vacationing on Mount Desert Island. All of the natural attractions of the area are within a very convenient distance; however, in recent years the Claremont has become well known for an important tournament of 9-wicket croquet—a game which has been played on the lawn of the inn since its earliest days. Players and spectators alike enjoy the Claremont Croquet Classic, a unique event for Claremont visitors. Many guests and staff return year after year to enjoy the serene atmosphere and the beautiful views.

Now the Claremont, on the National Register of Historic Places, is well into its second hundred years!

THE CLAREMONT HOTEL AND COTTAGES, Southwest Harbor, ME 04679; 207-244-5036. A 24-guestroom (23 private baths) rambling summer hotel with rooms also in two adjacent guest houses; on Somes Sound, Mt. Desert Island, 24 mi. south of Ellsworth. Double and twin beds available. Hotel and dining room open mid-June thru mid-Sept. Breakfast and dinner served to guest and the public. Lunch served in the boathouse during July and Aug. Guest-house rooms and 11 housekeeping cottages available May thru Oct. Hotel and Phillips House rooms available only on Modified American plan during the season. Off-season, all rooms available either EP or MAP while hotel is open. Tennis, rowboats, croquet, badminton, golf, bicycles, riding, boating, and sailing rental nearby. No credit cards. Personal checks accepted. The McCue Family, Owners-hosts; John Madeira, Jr., Manager. (See Index for rates.)

Directions: From Maine Tpke., exit at Augusta and proceed east on Rte. 3 to U.S. 1. At Ellsworth, pick up Rte. 3 again and follow Rte. 102 on Mt. Desert Island to Southwest Harbor. Follow inn signs approaching and in Southwest Harbor.

The date in parenthesis in the heading represents the first year the inn appeared in the pages of Country Inns and Back Roads.

THE COUNTRY CLUB INN
Rangeley, Maine (1981)

Rangeley, Maine, is one of those places in the world that has a special kind of charisma. There are few locations that offer such beauty and grandeur in all seasons. The combination of wide skies, vast stretches of mountain woodland, and the placid aspect of Rangeley Lake have been drawing people to this part of western Maine since long before the roads were as passable and numerous as they are today.

Innkeeper Sue Crory of the Country Club Inn says, "The dramatic lake and mountain scenery surrounding us will tranquilize even the most jangled nerves." At an elevation of nearly 2,000 feet, the Country Club Inn offers a magnificent view. Each of the guest rooms has a picture window, and the dining room and lounge both offer a scenic view of the lake, which reminds me of similar stretches of lake and mountains in certain sections of Scotland—Loch Ness being one. The cathedral-ceilinged living room has heavy beams, wood paneling, and many, many different comfortable sofas, armchairs, and rocking chairs. There are jigsaw puzzles in various states of completion, huge shelves of books, and a great moosehead over one of the fieldstone fireplaces.

We were all gathered at one of the focal points at the Country Club Inn—the deck, with its sweeping panorama of sky, lake, and mountains. Sue shares innkeeping duties with her son, Bob, Jr., and daughter, Margie, and husband Steve Jamison. And now there's Margie and Steve's "Little Kate," born in August. Sue mentioned how pleasant it is to have all the family working together. "Our staff is small enough so that everyone becomes part of the family and we find our guests love this kind of atmosphere.

"Of course, we all change hats, so to speak, and move from one job to another, so the guests really receive lots of personal attention.

"We have all known for a long time that what we wanted was to have our own small country inn. We've found just that in the Country Club Inn."

Sue elaborated on how they are enjoying being a year-round operation and mentioned the many activities during the summer season—excellent fishing (landlocked salmon and square-tailed trout), hiking the many trails (including the Appalachian Trail, which goes through this area), boating, canoe trips, a swimming pool, and a variety of lawn games. For those who love golf there's a challenging 18-hole public golf course adjacent to the inn. Tennis courts are nearby.

The inn is located in the heart of the northwestern mountains of Maine's ski country, surrounded by Saddleback and Sugarloaf mountains, which offer downhill and cross-country skiing. Margie, Steve, and Bob, Jr., commented on how beautiful Rangeley is during their winter season. "Many of our guests cross-country ski right from our doorstep. Snowmobilers enjoy over 100 miles of well-groomed trails and, at the end of the day, drive right up to their rooms in time to freshen up for a sumptuous dinner."

Sweeping an arm towards the view, Sue said, "September is a golden month. The fall foliage color starts a little earlier in this section of Maine than in other parts of New England. It is a good opportunity to enjoy nature's great show and still experience the wonderful peace and solitude."

THE COUNTRY CLUB INN, P.O. Box 680C, Rangeley, ME 04970; 207-864-3831. A 19-guestroom resort-inn (private baths) overlooking Rangeley Lake in western Maine, 45 mi. from Farmington. King, queen, and double beds available. Modified American plan. Breakfast and dinner served to travelers by reservation. Open mid-May to mid-Oct. and late Dec. to late March. Near many cultural, historic, scenic, and recreational attractions. Swimming pool, horseshoes, bocci, volleyball, and croquet. A public 18-hole golf course adjacent to the inn. Tennis and lake swimming nearby. Fishing, hiking, and canoeing. Snowmobiling and xc skiing at doorstep. Downhill and xc skiing at Saddleback and Sugarloaf Mts. The Crory and Jamison families, Owners-hosts. (See Index for rates.)

Directions: From Maine Tpke., take Auburn Exit 12 and follow Rte. 4 to Rangeley. From Vt. and N.H., take I-91 to St. Johnsbury; east on Rte. 2 to Gorham and Rte. 16 north to Rangeley. From Bar Harbor, Rte. 1A to Rte. 2 to Rte. 4. From Montreal, Rte. 10 to Rte. 112 to Rte. 147 to Rte. 114; then Rte. 26 to Rte 16 to Rte. 4.

THE CROCKER HOUSE COUNTRY INN
Hancock Point, Maine (1987)

Finding a beguiling, secluded place for an overnight stay on a trip to Canada via U.S. 1 would delight many a weary traveler. And it could be the perfect solution for those who enjoy the activity and excitement of Bar Harbor, Acadia National Park, and Blue Hill, but also want a quiet hideaway nearby. On Hancock Point, three minutes from the ocean, the Crocker House Country Inn is all of the above.

The entrance leads into a living room that is eclectic, to say the least, with good comfortable old wicker furniture, a big window seat, some rather striking modern primitive paintings, a very handsome rug of Indian design, a backgammon set, and lots of growing plants. At the very moment I walked in I was greeted with a flute concerto by Jean Pierre Rampal wafting from the stereo. It all seemed quite casual and quite natural.

The guest rooms are bright and cheerful. Almost all of them have been redecorated and some have stenciling on the upper walls. They are large enough to accommodate two people very comfortably.

Innkeeper Richard Malaby told me a little bit about the past history of this part of Maine. "A lot of people think that the most northern part of Maine is Ellsworth and Bar Harbor," he remarked. "Hancock was once a thriving shipbuilding community and also the terminus of the Washington, D.C., to Bar Harbor express train. It was the port from which the famed Sullivan Quarry shipped its cobblestones to pave the streets of Boston, New York, and Philadelphia. I'm afraid that the Crocker House is a lone survivor of those days of the past."

He continued, his eyes alight with enthusiasm, "Up here we're rather out of the way, but we have quite a few of our own activities. For instance, the Monteux Symphony Orchestra performs biweekly in Hancock during June and July and the Somesville Acadia Repertory Theater provides professional theater during the summer. Hancock is the site of one of the two reversing tidal falls in North America.

"We have clay tennis courts available for our guests a short stroll away, and the ocean is just a three-minute walk from our front door. Many guests come to enjoy Acadia National Park and then stay on here an extra day to recover from all of that activity."

One might expect the dinner menu to consist of good hearty upcountry Maine food; therefore, I was quite surprised to find some international dishes such as poached salmon Florentine, gray sole meunièrc, and veal Monterey, which I ordered. It is very thinly sliced veal, sautéed in Madeira with avocado and tomato and topped with Monterey jack cheese. The menu also has filet au poivre, scallops in sorrel and cream, broiled swordfish, broiled halibut Dijon, and other treasures from the sea.

If you happen to be there on Sunday, the brunch is very spiffy indeed, with brandied french toast, eggs Benedict, steak and eggs, and something interesting called the "Cromlet," featuring three eggs, scallions, bacon, and Cotswold cheese.

In the morning, after a very pleasant breakfast, I walked around this little neck of land, enjoying the birch trees and the grass beside the water. It's great for bicycling and running, and I came upon a little harbor with lots of sailboats and mountains in the distance and lobster traps bobbing in the tide. Would you believe that not a single automoblie passed in either direction during my morning walk?

Taken all in all, I found the experience at the Crocker House Country Inn most refreshing. I particularly enjoyed my conversation with innkeeper Malaby, who, because of the relatively small size of the inn, can take the time to meet his guests and to share some of his enthusiasm for this quiet, sequestered corner of the Maine coast.

THE CROCKER HOUSE COUNTRY INN, Hancock Point, ME 04640; 207-422-6806. A 10-guestroom (private baths) secluded country inn about 8 mi. north of Ellsworth, Me. Breakfast and dinner served daily. Open from May 1 to Thanksgiving. Bicycles and dock moorings available for guests. Tennis, swimming, and walking nearby. Just 30 min. from Mount Desert Island, Acadia National Park, and Bar Harbor. Blue Hill and the east Penobscot peninsula easily accessible. Richard Malaby, Owner-host. (See Index for rates.)

Directions: Follow Rte. 1 approx. 8 mi. north from Ellsworth. Turn right at sign for Hancock Point and continue approx. 5 mi.

DOCKSIDE GUEST QUARTERS
York, Maine (1975)

"There must be something special that happens here on the Fourth of July; don't I remember that you have a special little celebration?"

Harriette Lusty and I were having a light luncheon on the porch of the dining room at Dockside Guest Quarters. It was a day such as I have experienced here many times in the past, watching the wonderful harbor traffic as all kinds of craft make their way through the harbor to the ocean. Even though it had been a very hot day out on I-95, here on this lovely porch there was a wonderful breeze that made even sitting in the sun a joy.

"Oh, we do some very wonderful things here on the Fourth of July," Harriette exclaimed. "We have a thirty-five-foot-long flag with only thirty-seven stars that is brought out, unfolded, and placed on the lawn, because it is much too large for any flagpole. At noontime we set off our cannon, and all of our staff and their families and friends, as well as our neighbors, come over and stand by. It's really quite a ceremony and we leave one of our postcards at each door, inviting all the guests to come up to the shoot. It takes place right over there by the flagpole. We use that little brass one-pounder cannon originally kept in the hallway near the front door. Everybody gets into a wonderful Independence Day mood."

The Dockside Guest Quarters is composed of the original New England homestead of the 1880s, called the Maine House, and four other multi-unit cottage buildings of a contemporary design, with guest rooms that have their own porches and water views. The three-level restaurant is also separate and overlooks the harbor and marina docks.

The innkeepers are David and Harriette Lusty. David is a real "State of Maine" man, complete with a wonderful Down East accent. They have raised four sons at Dockside, and now their second son, Eric, has returned to take a hand in the running of the inn.

Harriette continued, "The days in early June can be spent in many different ways. We have a number of sandy beaches, and it's great fun to wander around the stretches of beach and have them almost entirely to one's self. It's one of our favorite off-season pastimes. Golf and tennis are available at the golf club, and the marina has rental outboards, great for picnics on the York River. We're doing something very interesting during the month of June; we have arranged a special three-day bargain package that includes a sightseeing cruise with a luncheon stop at Portsmouth Harbor. It also includes a lobster dinner, all at very attractive pre-season rates."

There's always a great deal of history to share in the York area, and this time I learned about the famous statue that is the figure of a Confederate soldier, instead of a "Boy in Blue." David tells me that they have now located the town somewhere in South Carolina where the statue of the

Union soldier has been resting for almost a hundred years. Everybody has decided that they're going to leave the statues the way they are.

So the combination of Dockside life, generous dollops of history, the pleasant vista from Dockside of the harbor craft. and the opportunity to enjoy a good dinner at the Dockside dining room, managed by Steve and Sue Roeder, makes staying at this little seaside inn an enjoyable experience in any season of the year—perhaps just a tad more satisfying in June.

DOCKSIDE GUEST QUARTERS, P.O. Box 205, Harris Island Rd. York, ME 03909; 207-363-2868. A 21-guestroom 19 private baths (some studio suites with kitchenettes) waterside country inn 10 mi. from Portsmouth, N.H. American plan available. Queen and twin beds available. Continental-plus breakfast served to houseguests only. Dockside Dining Room serves lunch and dinner to travelers daily except Mon. Open Fri. and Sat. only during May; daily from Memorial Day weekend thru third week in Oct. York Village is a National Historic District. Wheelchair access. Lawn games, shuffleboard, badminton, fishing, and whale-watching from premises. Golf, tennis, and ocean swimming nearby; safe and picturesque paths and roadways for walks, bicycling, and jogging. Credit cards are not welcome for amounts over $75. Personal checks accepted for payment of food and lodgings incurred by registered guests. Eric, Carol, David, and Harriette Lusty, Owners-hosts. (See Index for rates.)

Directions: From I-95, take the last exit before the northbound toll gate at York to U.S. 1, then to Rte. 1A. Follow 1A thru center of Old York Village, take Rte. 103 (a side street off Rte. 1A leading to the harbor), and watch for signs to the inn immediately after crossing bridge.

GOOSE COVE LODGE
Deer Isle, Maine (1981)

George Pavloff says when someone asks how he would describe Goose Cove Lodge, he answers, "Think of *On Golden Pond*—loons included." Basically, it's a rustic lodge on the ocean, surrounded by woodlands with fascinating nature trails where flora and fauna abound.

It's the kind of a place where guests can really unwind and be themselves. Some people bring their paints, others bring their binoculars for some serious bird-watching, others like to paddle a canoe, sail a boat, take walks along Waldron or Wolffe trails, where spruces tower overhead, lovely mosses and lichens line the paths, and they are likely to come upon a magical patch of pink and white ladyslipper orchids. Or some guests just like to sit on one of the huge granite boulders, debris from a glacier that passed this way millennia ago, and gaze, mesmerized, at the ever-changing sea. There are many other choices for diversion: boat trips to the outer islands, a drive to Bar Harbor, shopping in crafts and antiques shops, sailing lessons, or even a deep-muscle massage.

Rustic cottages sit on the great granite rocks and are scattered among the trees for complete privacy and seclusion. Each has its own special view; all but two have native stone fireplaces, and all have bathroom facilities. There are also guest rooms in the main lodge. There is a one-week minimum-stay policy during July and August. Typically, guests arrive about 5:30 on Saturday, which is the beginning of the Goose Cove week.

The atmosphere is relaxed and friendly, and on arrival guests are presented with a copy of George's newsletter, "Mother Goose Says," which gives the names of the current guests and their home towns, lists the dinner entrées (three seafood entrées each week), and describes the after-dinner entertainment—local musicians, perhaps a slide show of a trip to Antarctica, or a guest nuclear physicist talking about "The Origin and Possible Destinies of the Universe."

Over hors d'oeuvres in the lodge, George and Elli Pavloff introduce guests to each other. By dinnertime first-timers are beginning to realize that many of the other guests have been coming to Goose Cove for quite a few years.

Young parents are ecstatic when they find out the arrangements in July and August for children under twelve. The baby-sitting crew takes over from 5:30 to 8 o'clock, giving the children their dinner and then entertaining them during the adults' social hour and dinner.

By Friday night, the lobster cookout on the beach is like the last night of summer camp. Physical and mental tensions are erased, faces are relaxed, and fellowship is high. Guests are exchanging addresses at breakfast the next morning, and George and Elli and their staff are all saying goodbye. The result is obvious and in marked contrast to those guests who are trying to do New England in a week by touching down briefly in a different place each night.

Elli says she particularly loves the wide span of ages of their guests, ". . . middle-aged folks like ourselves, honeymooners, parents with newborns to teenagers, octogenarians who seem to have a beatific secret. . . . Goose Cove Lodge is a special place of peace and beauty for them all, and for me, too."

And for me, too, Elli.

GOOSE COVE LODGE, Sunset, Deer Isle, ME 04683; 207-348-2508. A 22-guestroom (60 people) (private baths) resort-inn on beautiful Penobscot Bay approx. 1 hr. from Rte. 1 at Bucksport. All-size beds available. Open mid-June to mid-Oct. Modified American plan mid-June to mid-Sept.; 7-day minimum stay (Sat.-Sat.) in July and Aug.; 2-day minimum stay other times. Meals served to houseguests only. Wheelchair access. Swimming, boating, canoeing, hiking, and bird watching all available at the inn. Other outdoor sports, including backroading, golf, tennis, etc., nearby. Especially adaptable for children of all ages. Elli and George Pavloff, Owners-hosts. (See Index for rates.)

Directions: From Bucksport, it is approx. 1 hr. to inn. Drive 4 mi. north on Rte. 1 and turn right on Rte. 15 down the Blue Hill Peninsula to Deer Isle Village. Turn right in village at sign to Sunset, Maine. Proceed 3 mi., turn right at Goose Cove Lodge sign. Follow dirt road 1½ mi. to inn.

OLD FORT INN
Kennebunkport, Maine (1976)

"Beaches are fun and I enjoy salt water, but to me there's something very special about having the privacy and quietness of a swimming pool."

A group of us were seated around the pool at the Old Fort Inn when this particular observation was made by a Canadian guest. Someone else had said, "I like to play tennis and I like to know that not only is there a good tennis court here, but there are frequently people who play a good game."

The Old Fort Inn is a very special kind of country inn that provides a complete change of pace from the hustle and bustle of Kennebunkport. A few years ago, the main building of the hotel that originally had been on the property was torn down, and the handsome stone carriage house was converted into a most attractive inn, with a large common room filled with English pine pieces and fourteen large guest rooms with four-poster or canopied beds and Laura Ashley wall papers. The rooms are large enough so that guests can stay for longer periods without feeling cramped. Some of them have Jacuzzis and small efficiency units.

Guests gather for breakfast at the main lodge in a converted barn, built around 1880. It has a big fireplace that serves as a focal point on spring and fall evenings, and its open deck next to the swimming pool makes it a very comfortable place where guests may gather in the warmer weather.

The innkeepers are David and Sheila Aldrich, two very attractive people originally from California, who came here several years ago and have made the Old Fort Inn and Kennebunkport their new home. They are considerably assisted by their perky daughter, Shana, who must be at least twelve years old by this time.

I think it might be fun if I shared a description of my bedroom at the Old Fort Inn. For one thing, it's large enough to be comfortable for two people, with plenty of room for a third person on the little sofa bed. There is a big double cannonball bed with blue sheets and a harmonizing blue comforter, blue carpeting, and a blue cover on the daybed. There are good reading lights on both sides of the bed. A wood table and chairs for two, a Victorian table with an attractive lamp, a wicker armchair, and a beautifully refinished chest of drawers complete the picture. A painting of a duck is part of the great collection of duck decoys and paintings found throughout the inn. They also have a wonderful collection of Victorian clothing and prints.

David is on hand at the breakfast buffet, which features freshly baked croissants and fruit breads and all kinds of fresh fruits, as well as sticky buns on Sunday.

The village of Kennebunkport still retains much of the ambience it

had when clipper ships sailed from its shores. The lovely old sea captains' houses remain, and the beautiful streets and winding river make it a very pleasant vacation experience.

During my most recent visit I found that guests spend quite a bit of time in the antiques shop that's mainly Sheila's project. "David and I feel that it has added considerably to the attractiveness of the inn," she said. "I'm glad that we put in that lovely English garden. The flowers change with the seasons, and it is the first thing the guest sees upon arrival."

Spring is an excellent time to visit this part of the Maine coast, and between mid-April and mid-June, and November and mid-December, David and Sheila have arranged for a very special midweek "Escape Plan" that I'm sure many of our readers would find most attractive.

OLD FORT INN, Old Fort Ave., P.O. Box M, Kennebunkport, ME 04046; 207-967-5353. A 16-guestroom (private baths) resort-inn within walking distance of the ocean in a historic Maine town. All-size beds available. Includes an ample buffet continental breakfast. Fireplace lodge. Open from mid-Apr. to mid-Dec. Efficiencies, heated pool, tennis court, shuffleboard and bicycles on grounds. Golf, salt-water swimming, and boating nearby. Not comfortable for children under 12. No pets. Sheila and David Aldrich, Owners-hosts. (See Index for rates.)

Directions: Take Exit 3 (Kennebunk) from Maine Tpke. (I-95). Take left on Rte. 35 and follow signs through Kennebunk to Kennebunkport. Take left at traffic light at Sunoco station. Go over drawbridge and take first right on Ocean Ave. Take Ocean Ave. to the Colony Hotel; turn left in front of the Colony, go to the Y in the road, go right ¼ mi. Inn is on left.

THE PENTAGOET INN
Castine, Maine (1988)

For many years I regarded Castine as one of the best-kept secrets in the world. I also discovered that when I ran into other people who knew about Castine, we felt as if we belonged to an exclusive club — something akin to people who have climbed Mount Everest.

I'm sure that many people do stumble on Castine, but it's not on the road to anywhere. Its principal claim to fame is the fact that originally it was settled by British Loyalists, who, after the American Revolution, decided they preferred to remain under King George and so moved, many of them, from Boston up to this lovely out-of-the-way location. There are many markers in the town reminding us that such an exodus did take place.

The Pentagoet Inn has made people sit up and take notice of Castine. I first discovered it quite a few years ago, when it was run by Natalie Saunders. Today, I think it's safe to say the Pentagoet far exceeds her finest dreams under innkeepers Lindsey and Virginia Miller.

One of the first things that Lindsey, Virginia, and I have in common are porches. I've always loved them and I've spent many a happy hour rocking on porches of country inns all over North America. "That's just the way we feel," said Virginia. "As a matter of fact, that's why we have extended the porch all the way to the back of the main building. You'll notice that we've put window boxes and standing flowerpots in as many places as possible, and our new green awning has been a real blessing."

Well, the talk went on from porches to breakfast. "I must step in here," Lindsey declared. "This morning, besides a cup of fresh tropical fruit, we had a creamy, fresh herb omelet. Our french toast is thick homemade slices filled with cream cheese and fresh orange, topped with blueberry sauce. In addition to that there are sausage links or grilled rib eye steak and we continue with the famous Pentagoet muffins that you wrote about when Natalie owned the inn."

In the ensuing conversation we talked about many other interesting changes the Millers had made. "When we first arrived in the fall of 1985 we became aware that the inn needed more dining space and more common areas for the guests. We spent the first winter correcting this by creating a very inviting library with an upright Bosendorfer piano and most of our personal collection of books." I agreed that it provides a good place for guests to relax with a book, play the piano, or listen to some classical music.

"The addition of the back dining room was an inspiration," Virginia said, "and I'm happy to say we are well known for our dinners. Part of this is because we have an excellent chef and we offer a variety of main dishes including Maine lobsters, lobster pie, grilled fresh salmon steak with dilled hollandaise, a peppered rib eye steak, and a roast leg of lamb. It's part of a five-course meal which includes soup and dessert."

Things have happened above the first floor of the Pentagoet which I found very important and exciting. For example, by redesigning the second- and third-floor guest rooms, the Pentagoet now has twelve guest rooms with private baths and two with half-baths. In addition the annex next door, 10 Perkins Street, also has very attractive guest rooms.

"Virginia has a knack for details," Lindsey said, "and guests like such touches as the baskets with a large supply of fresh towels, vases with fresh flowers in each room, and nightly room freshening with beds turned down."

So the Pentagoet is attracting more country inn enthusiasts than ever.

THE PENTAGOET INN, Main St., P.O. Box 4, Castine, ME 04221; 207-326-8616. A 17-guestroom (private baths) inn in a seacoast village on the Penobscot Peninsula, 36 mi. from Bangor. Modified American plan includes breakfast and dinner. Dinner available to outside guests by reservation. Open Apr. 1 to Dec. 1. Tennis, swimming, backroading, village strolling, craft shops, chamber music concerts, Maine Maritime Academy, Acadia National Park, and Blue Hill nearby. Children over 12 welcome. No pets. Smoking on porches only. Lindsey and Virginia Miller, Owners-hosts. (See Index for rates.)

Directions: From the south, follow I-95 to Brunswick and use Rte. 1 exit. Follow Rte. 1 to a point 3 mi. past Bucksport. Turn right on Rte. 175 to Rte. 166 to Castine. Look for Maine Maritime Academy sign; turn left onto Main St.

THE PILGRIM'S INN
Deer Isle, Maine (1980)

Travelers really have to be looking for Deer Isle and the Pilgrim's Inn. It's a good hour's drive from U.S. 1, east of Bucksport, to the Blue Hill Peninsula. Deer Isle sits just off the southern flank of the mainland, and no matter how you arrive, it's necessary to cross over the suspension bridge at Eggemoggin Reach.

This is really "down home" Maine and even the 1939 bridge has failed to disturb the naturalness of both the islanders and the area.

A four-story, gambrel-roofed red house, this building has overlooked the long harbor on the front and the millpond in the rear since 1793. Jean and Dud Hendrick moved here a few years ago after acquiring the Pilgrim's Inn. Much of the original building has remained almost completely unchanged, with the original Colonial feature of two large rooms and a kitchen on the ground floor still intact. One of these rooms is the Common Room of the present-day inn.

Most of the guest rooms are quite large with richly hued pine floorboards, wood stoves, country furniture, and a selection of books and magazines. They are enhanced by coordinated Laura Ashley fabrics, used for curtains, lampshades, quilts, and cushions.

Although I visited there last summer as part of a hilarious dinner party with some friends from nearby Blue Hill, where everybody vowed that it was "the best time ever," I'd like to share a portion of a yearly letter that Dud and Jean write me.

"Jean has enjoyed sharing the cooking with a bona fide chef, Terry Foster, and the two of them have been 'knocking them dead.' It is a very rare night that we couldn't fill the dining room twice over. Dinner at the Pilgrim's Inn is the hottest ticket in the area.

"Number 15 is our enchanting house in the village. 'Enchanting' understates it. Number 15 sits over the harbor, affording the occupants unparalleled sunset views from its back deck. It is completely furnished and equipped so that guests may choose to prepare their own meals if they are so foolish as to pass up Jean's fabulous cuisine. It is the quintessential honeymoon cottage or retreat for four friends (it has a hide-a-bed in front of the fireplace in the living room in addition to the upstairs bedroom).

"We discovered that guests really didn't have a room in which they could quietly read, free of socializing fellow travelers, and turning one of the first-floor parlors of the main inn into a warm reading room and library has worked very well."

The Pilgrim's Inn provides far more than can really be done in a single- or two-night stay. Guests can bike, hike, sail, canoe, and even learn to kayak in whitewater or the sea with a certified instructor. Guests also play tennis and golf, and do many of the less energetic things. The mail boat run to Isle au Haute is a most romantic day trip, and the sailing here is terrific. There are many, many art galleries and crafts shops a short distance away, and Acadia National Park is just close enough for a day trip.

Pilgrim's Inn, as I said before, is a special place, so tell only your very special friends about it.

THE PILGRIM'S INN, Deer Isle, ME 04627; 207-348-6615. A 13-guestroom (8 private baths) inn in a remote island village on the Blue Hill Peninsula on the Maine coast. Queen, double, and twin beds available. Modified American plan, May 15 to Nov. 1, includes a hearty breakfast and a creative dinner. In season, outside dinner reservations are accepted. A 4-day minimum reservation is requested in Aug. Bicycles, badminton, table tennis, regulation horseshoes, croquet, and a rowboat for the millpond on the grounds. All types of cultural and recreational advantages, including golf, fishing, sailing, hiking, and browsing nearby. No pets. Dud and Jean Hendrick, Owners-hosts. (See Index for rates.)

Directions: From Boston, take I-95 to Brunswick exit. Take coastal Rte. 1 north past Bucksport. Turn right on Rte. 15, which travels to Deer Isle down the Blue Hill Peninsula. At the village, turn right on Main St. (Sunset Rd.) and proceed one block to the inn on the left side of the street, opposite the harbor.

PULPIT HARBOR INN
North Haven Island, Maine (1990)

At Pulpit Harbor Inn, pint milk bottles holding colorful bunches of fresh flowers are reminders of the dairy it used to be, supplying North Haven Island families with milk. The cows and barn are gone, but innkeepers Christie and Barney Hallowell have maintained the wonderful country feeling of the original 120-year-old farm house.

North Haven Island is one of Maine's least commercial islands, and one of its most lovely. Surrounded by tall spruces and pastoral views of the Hallowells' sheep pasture and the Camden Hills beyond, Pulpit Harbor Inn sits just across from the town's old grange hall. The village of North Haven is small, and virtually traffic-free, a real treat to those who enjoy evening walks and early-morning bike rides.

Christie and Barney were teachers in North Haven for some time before deciding to open their inn. "We were looking for a business to help support the failing economy," Barney told me, as we sat in the cheerful glassed-in sunroom, "and this farmhouse came up for sale five years ago. It seemed perfect. We've got a view to the ocean and the Camden Hills, and guests seem to really enjoy the farm atmosphere." Barney is still active in the community as a full-time teacher and assistant principal at the high school.

The Hallowells' commitment to their community can also be seen in their collection of wonderful local artwork that hangs throughout the inn. Christie is particularly pleased with the new custom-made mantlepiece in the living room. "It inspired us so much that we had to repaint the whole room!" she said. Both the living room and library are casual and comfortable. Two large couches and a wood-burning fireplace invite quiet conversation or evening reading.

In the simply furnished bedrooms, tiny calico prints are a unifying theme in bureau scarves, quilts, pillows, and pillow shams. Somehow, sleeping in an old farmhouse always brings me such wonderful dreams.

Christie is quite a cook and baker. Breakfast and dinner are both served in one of the inn's three dining areas: the dining room, sun porch, or outside on the brick terrace. A continental breakfast that may include two lemon poppy seed or Maine blueberry muffins, juice, coffee, tea, or cocoa is included in your room fee. An omelet or eggs and bacon are available at extra cost. Sandwiches with a creamy garlic herb spread and brown-sugar coconut bars can be made into a picnic lunch to take to the beach. Dinner has four courses and includes two entrees. Ripe garden produce is an integral part of summer dinners, and Christie makes use of the fresh fish in season.

The inn's island location offers wonderful solitude and peace, or you can take part in outdoor activities. Biking, sailing, golfing on the nine-hole course, tennis, beachcombing, fishing, or perhaps a trip on a lobster boat can be enjoyed during the summer months. Winter brings cross-country skiing and ice skating. And even though the farm's old barn has been torn down, be sure to visit the inhabitants of the creamery: four sheep, a rooster and hens, two ducks, and the rabbits, Mr. and Mrs. Claus.

Christie and Barney have created a comfortable, clean, and nonpretentious environment. In Christie's words, "North Haven remains an escape." And so is the Pulpit Harbor Inn.

PULPIT HARBOR INN, Crabtree Point Rd., North Haven, ME 04853; 207-867-2219. A 6-guestroom (3 private baths) century-old farmhouse on the lovely island of North Haven, in the middle of Penobscot Bay. Open all year. Double and twin beds. Continental breakfast included with tariff; a picnic lunch and dinner available. Quiet and solitude. Hiking on Ames Knob, golf, tennis, beachcombing. Winter xc skiing and ice skating. Pets by advance arrangement, plus a $5 cleaning fee. Christie and Barney Hallowell, Owners-hosts.

Directions: From Boston, take Rte. 95 north. In Brunswick, take Rte. 1 to Rockland. In Rockland, board the ferry to North Haven Island.

"European plan" means that rates for rooms and meals are separate. "American plan" means that meals are included in the cost of the room. "Modified American plan" means that breakfast and dinner are included in the cost of the room. The rates at some inns include a continental breakfast with the lodging.

RANGELEY INN
Rangeley, Maine (1989)

I was talking to Rick Litchfield of the Captain Lord Mansion about Rangeley Inn. "One of the great things is that when you come in after skiing, there's a roaring fire and people are sitting around, telling stories about their last run down the mountains," he said. "And then there's always plenty of hot water to soak in and big, thick towels."

I could certainly see what Rick meant about the homey, country feeling. Coming into the town of Rangeley, perched on scenic Rangeley Lake, I thought the big blue clapboard building with the long veranda across the front had the look of one of those grand old summer hotels.

Meeting Fay and Ed Carpenter in the roomy lobby with its country-print wallpaper and comfortable wing chairs and sofas, I had an immediate feeling of warmth and friendliness. I was not surprised to discover they had earned an Innkeeper of the Year award. "We've found innkeeping to be a very rewarding career," Ed told me. "We really enjoy getting to know our guests with all their varied backgrounds and interests."

Looking through some of the comments and letters from their guests, I realized that their cuisine played an important part in the overall picture. "Our daughter Sue is responsible for making our kitchen one of the finest in Maine," Fay said. "She's self-taught, and there just isn't anything she can't do." "That's absolutely true," Ed broke in, "I never cease to be amazed by how creative she is with her seasonings, garnishes, textures, and taste."

I had the opportunity to sample Sue's cooking, and it was indeed a pleasure. I tried the sole Victoria, which was stuffed with crabmeat, shrimp, cream cheese, finely chopped vegetables, and wrapped in phyllo dough. Some other interesting entrées were blueberry chicken, sautéed in fresh blueberries, blueberry schnapps, and spices, and lemon grass shrimp, prepared with garlic, ginger, sliced carrots, scallions, snow peas, peppers, water chestnuts, and lemon grass.

I found the total dining experience most enjoyable. The dining room, with its high ceiling and many windows, has an elegant but informal atmosphere. The dining tables were carefully laid with china and stemware on double rose tablecloths. The fresh flowers and candlelight added a note of romance.

"That's a beautiful antique ceiling," I exclaimed, looking up at the peach-colored, ornate pressed tin admiringly.

"I'll tell you a secret, I put that ceiling up myself," Ed replied, with refreshing candor.

I think refreshing candor may be the keynote of this inn. Ed and Fay and their two daughters, Sue, who is the chef, and Janet, who served me breakfast with a most infectious smile, have a straightforward, friendly manner that puts everyone at ease.

The guest rooms are simply furnished with country-print wallpapers and various-sized beds. Fay told me that some of the rooms still have the old clawfooted, cast-iron "soakers." "We've started to add the old-fashioned shower heads and duck curtains." There are additional motel-style rooms in a separate building, which looked very clean and comfortable.

Ed showed me around the several acres of lawn and garden bordering on Haley Pond, a bird sanctuary. Not only are there ducks, Canada geese, and herons, but at the moment, Ed tells me, they have two pairs of loons.

This is a pristine area, and with spectacular Rangeley Lake and the Longfellow Mountains, including Saddleback Mountain, there are marvelous opportunities for glimpsing wild animals, such as moose, deer, beaver, red fox, or possibly a black bear. As a resort area for nearly a hundred years, Rangeley offers endless recreational pursuits. We are happy to welcome the Rangeley Inn to our pages for the first time.

RANGELEY INN, P.O. Box 398, Main St., Rangeley, ME 04970; 207-864-3341 or 5641. A 51-guestroom village inn and motor lodge (private baths) on the eastern shore of Rangeley Lake in western Maine. Breakfast and dinner served daily; limited dining in early Dec. and late spring. Wheelchair access. Summer events such as Blueberry Festival and Fiddlers' Contest and evening entertainment, also pool table and board games on premises. Guided canoe trips, dogsled races, and all the summer and winter activities of lake and mountain areas. No pets. One cat in residence. Limited smoking. Fay and Ed Carpenter, Owners-hosts.

Directions: From Me. Tpke. take Auburn Exit 12 and follow Rte. 4 to Rangeley. From N.H. Rte. 2, take Rte. 16 north to Rangeley. Inn is at southern end of village on Rte. 4 (Main St.).

THE SQUIRE TARBOX INN
Westport Island, Maine (1974)

Karen Mitman and I were walking through the woods behind the Squire Tarbox Inn toward Squam Creek. We were two people being escorted by seven lively, handsome Nubian goats in various shades of brown and beige. It being June, we passed through patches of buttercups and lupine, and our group occasionally paused while one of the goats decided to nibble.

"Come on, Garbo," Karen called. "We call her Garbo because she thinks she's kind of dramatic. We arrived at the serene saltwater inlet that has a little dock and a screened-in shed for just sitting and looking through the binoculars provided. A rowboat waits patiently for the energetic guest.

"Most of our guests are from the city, and it's just nice for them to come here and sit. The combination of the water, the sky, the clouds, the little marshy island, and the trees offers a special quiet privacy."

The Squire Tarbox is in a section of Maine that is sufficiently off the beaten track to be unspoiled and natural. The main house has both the wainscoting of the early 1800s and the rustic wide-board construction of the 1700s. It is quite small—eleven guest rooms have a cozy "up country" feeling with Colonial prints and colors and some working fireplaces. A large hearth with the original bake oven, pumpkin pine floors, and hand-hewn beams set the tone for this rambling Colonial farmhouse.

There are several choices for sitting around in front of fireplaces to enjoy reading or conversation, especially in a captivating three-story barn with large doors that open out on a screened-in sundeck. There is a player piano, an antique music box, Colonial wooden toys, and English wooden puzzles for further amusement.

Karen and her husband, Bill, are very friendly, conversational people, who make innkeeping seem almost deceptively simple. Their background at the Copley Plaza in Boston must have much to do with this.

Karen and I sat in the little shed and continued our conversation while the goats cavorted on the pine needles. "I know you remember when we brought in our first goats," she said. "We were a little hesitant, but they have been a most rewarding experience for our guests. Now we have a new cheesemaking room and have packaged some goat cheese for sale to our guests. The cheese is served every night before dinner as well."

Our conversation turned naturally to food, and she mentioned that the Squire Tarbox serves breakfast and dinner to their guests. "Dinner is at seven o'clock in an intimate Colonial dining room and usually begins with a soup that could be made with fresh fruit or vegetables. The second course is a salad, and the main course is usually local fish or chicken or an occasional roast, always served with three vegetables that reflect some

creative thinking, such as mint-glazed carrots, cranberries with red cabbage, or spinach with cheese and pasta. One of the most popular desserts is a chocolate concoction known as the Squire's 'Sin Pie.' "

Karen had to return to the inn and suggested that I might find it interesting just to sit here and enjoy the sounds of silence. So she took all of the goats and set back up the hill. I mused that this simple little path through the woods down to the saltwater pond provides guests with the unique opportunity to have the feeling of really being in the country, and yet it's within easy driving distance of the many diversions of the Maine coast.

THE SQUIRE TARBOX INN, Westport Island, R.D. 2, Box 620, Wiscasset, ME 04578; 207-882-7693. An 11-guestroom (private baths) restored Colonial farm midway between Boston and Bar Harbor on Rte. 144 in Westport, 10 mi. from Wiscasset. King, queen, and double beds available. Modified American plan—includes continental breakfast and full leisurely dinner. Open late May to late Oct. Within a 30-min. drive of L. L. Bean, beaches, harbors, shops, and museums of midcoast Maine. No amusements for children under 14. Bill and Karen Mitman, Owners-hosts. (See Index for rates.)

Directions: From Maine Tpke., take Exit 9 and follow Rte. 95 to Exit 22 (Brunswick, Me.). Take Rte. 1 to Rte. 144, 7 mi. north of Bath. Follow Rte. 144 for 8½ mi to inn.

The date in parenthesis in the heading represents the first year the inn appeared in the pages of Country Inns and Back Roads.

THE WATERFORD INNE
East Waterford, Maine (1980)

"Last July was our tenth anniversary," Barbara Vanderzanden exclaimed, "and we are still maintaining our strict adherence to quality and immaculate housekeeping." Rosalie, who is Barbara's mother, added, "We frequently have guests comment on how clean everything is." We were sitting on the porch enjoying the view.

The Waterford Inne certainly reflects their loving care and hard work. They seem to take on a new project every year. "One year we added this screened porch, which is so pleasant for dining on warm evenings. Our tenth and final guest room is on the drawing board. It will be very special, with its own deck."

My eye happened to travel to what was one of the most sumptuous-looking vegetable gardens I have ever seen, and it prompted a question: "What are some of the things that you grow in your own garden for your kitchen?"

"Well, we grow practically all our own herbs," explained Rosalie, who is the cook. "We like fresh herbs in the salad dressing. We also have tomatoes, brussels sprouts, broccoli, peppers, squash, and pumpkins."

Their food has received a four-star rating by the food reviewer of the *Maine Sunday Telegram,* who gave them a rave review.

"We serve tenderloin of beef with béarnaise, shrimp Pernod, and various veal and pork dishes as entrées. Dinner is fixed-price every evening for both houseguests and visitors. We do all our own baking, and our guests seem to enjoy it very much."

At the Waterford Inne, located in the little-known Oxford Hills area of western Maine, "small and tidy" is beautiful. It can be truthfully said that the Waterford Inne is an intimate inn. The inn is small enough to

MAINE   89

provide a really cozy country inn experience. The original house was built in 1825 and has five upstairs bedrooms that step out of the 19th century. These are augmented by four additional rooms created in a wing leading to a very large barn.

All of the bedrooms have been carefully decorated, usually with some theme in mind. For example, the Chesapeake Room has a fireplace stove and a private porch. The decorations are in the Eastern Shore theme, with duck decoys and waterfowl. Even the sheets and towels have colorful waterfowls on them. All of the rooms have either antiques or attractive country furniture. My bed was a four-poster with a lace canopy.

Guests gather in the main living room, where there are many different books and magazines, including several from England, because Barbara and Rosalie are Anglophiles and in fact followed *Country Inns and Back Roads, Britain and Ireland* in a trip they made to England.

Our chat was over, and as Rosalie went to the kitchen, Barbara and I strolled around to take a closer look at the big barn. "The Oxford Hills section of Maine abounds in much beautiful scenery," she remarked. "It's hard to drive more than four or five miles without coming to a lake. It's quite a popular area for summer camps, so we are rather well booked in advance for the camp visitation weekends. Many camp parents stay at the inn and then stay on extra days, because it's such a lovely, tranquil experience."

THE WATERFORD INNE, Box 49, East Waterford, ME 04233; 207-583-4037. A 10-guestroom (7 private bath) farmhouse-inn in the Oxford Hills section of southwest Maine, 8 mi. from Norway and South Paris. Double and twin beds available. Closed March, April, and Thanksgiving week. Breakfast and dinner served to travelers by reservation. European plan. Within a short distance of many recreational, scenic, and cultural attractions in Maine and the White Mountains of New Hampshire. Cross-country skiing and badminton on grounds. Lake swimming, golf, rock hunting, downhill skiing, hiking, canoeing nearby. Alcoholic beverages not served. Well-behaved pets welcome; however, advance notification is required and a fee is charged. No credit cards. Rosalie and Barbara Vanderzanden, Owners-hosts. (See Index for rates.)

Directions: From Maine Tpke.: use Exit 11, follow Rte. 26 north approx. 28 mi. into Norway, then on Rte. 118 west for 8 mi. to Rte. 37 south (left turn). Go ½ mi., turn right at Springer's General Store, up the hill ½ mi. From Conway, New Hampshire: Rte. 16 to Rte. 302 east to Fryeburg, Me. Take Rte. 5 out of Fryeburg to Rte. 35 south, thence to Rte. 118, which is a left fork (with Rte. 35 going right). Continue on Rte. 118 east, past Papoose Pond camping area, then watch for right turn onto Rte. 37. Go ½ mi. to Springer's General Store. Take immediate right turn, ½ mi. up hill.

THE BIRCHWOOD INN
Temple, New Hampshire (1986)

Judy and Bill Wolfe and I were enjoying a quiet moment in the back parlor of the Birchwood Inn, and I could see by the light in his eye that Bill was most enthusiastic about being an innkeeper. They are both very proud of the fact that they were chosen as one of New Hampshire's best country inns in a poll taken by the *Manchester Union Leader*. The paper described the inn as having a "New England homespun hospitality, conviviality, and a casual, relaxed atmosphere in a scenic New Hampshire village."

The Birchwood Inn, sitting on one corner of the village green, is listed on the National Register of Historic Places and is believed to have been in operation since 1775. The present Federal-style brick building, along with the adjacent barn, was probably built about 1800, and the records document a history of changing uses that mirror the evolution of the small town tavern in New England.

"We as a young nation of Americans are really just developing a true nostalgia of our own." Bill remarked. "Just since the Bicentennial has this craving grown tremendously, and an old country inn allows guests to turn back the clock and immerse themselves almost totally in an atmosphere of the roadside travel of the 18th and 19th centuries in America."

The small, tucked-away village of Temple has no telegraph wires in the center of the town, and it's pretty much the same as it's been for two hundred years, with the Grange Hall, Congregational Church, village store, Revolutionary cemetery, and old blacksmith shop.

In 1965, probably the most interesting and prized feature of the inn was discovered when some early wall murals were uncovered under layers of old wallpaper. The paintings proved to be the work of the well-known muralist Rufus Porter, painted between 1825 and 1833. Fortunately, they were restored and are now being carefully preserved by Bill and Judy.

Today, the inn is characterized by comfortable furniture, a Steinway square grand piano, wide floorboards, checked tablecloths of yellow, red, brown, and blue, music in the background, and many tiny little areas where guests can enjoy a tête-à-tête. On the other hand, there is much opportunity for sociability. Judy said, "We have developed countless friendships with lovely people from all over the world without ever leaving the comforts of our little inn. The opportunity to reach out to people of all interests is a rare privilege afforded to both innkeepers and their children alike." The Wolfes find that their three children enjoy being involved with inn activities.

The guest rooms are decorated according to different themes — there is the Music Room, the Seashore Room, and the Train Room, among others. Homemade quilts add a real country touch. Five rooms have private baths, while two rooms share two hall baths.

The kitchen is handled in an interesting way because Bill does the cooking. Judy bakes breads and desserts, including blueberry-lemon bread, blueberry cobbler, chocolate cake, and various pies and tortes. The evening menu is on a slate blackboard, and on the night of my visit included crab soup, baked stuffed lobster, and chicken piccata. They have a new cookbook, titled *The Birchwood Sampler*, with 255 of their most requested recipes.

Bill remarked, "Serving meals as innkeepers is like hosting a dinner party each evening, except it's a lot easier since you don't have to sit down with the guests. By the time they're finished, you're nearly finished as well."

THE BIRCHWOOD INN, Rte. 45, Temple, NH 03084; 603-878-3285. A 7-guestroom (5 private baths) village inn in southern New Hampshire. Double and twin beds available. Open year-round. Breakfast included in room rate. Dinner not served on Sun. or Mon. Wheelchair access. Hiking, horseshoes, xc skiing, hayrides, summer theater, ice skating, superb backroading, and numerous historic houses nearby; also the Cathedral in the Pines. No credit cards. Judy and Bill Wolfe, Owners-hosts. (See Index for rates.)

Directions: Take Rte. 3 north to Nashua. At Exit 7W follow Rte. 101 west through Milford to Rte. 45. Turn left 1½ mi. to Temple. From I-91 at Brattleboro take Rte. 9 east to Keene to Rte. 101 through Peterborough, over Temple Mtn. to Rte. 45. Turn right, 1½ mi. to Temple.

CHESTERFIELD INN
West Chesterfield, New Hampshire (1990)

I've always had a soft spot in my heart for country inns that have histories as farmhouses. The Chesterfield Inn is one of these. The traditional New England center-hall Colonial, with its two attached barns, is more than 200 years old. Built in the 1780s, the building first functioned as a tavern and then as a private farmhouse. The clapboard structure was renovated in 1984. Sitting on a hill above the Connecticut River, the panoramic views are to the lovely Vermont Green Mountains to the west.

After looking at more than eighty country inns, Phil and Judy Hueber hiked the Chesterfield Inn's 10 acres and knew it was "the one." Phil had been a marketing director for Dun & Bradstreet, and Judy was a manager for Mutual of New York, prior to the move to their "dream inn," and a much less stressful way of life.

One of the most attractive aspects of the inn comes from its unusual construction. In order to reach the three intimate dining rooms, one must walk through the kitchen. Here, head chef Carl Warner enjoys his "stage," as guests stop by to listen while he explains the nightly specials and trades recipes. It isn't often that I get to discuss the merits of raspberry vinegar with a chef trained at Cambridge's Creative Cuisine Culinary School!

The dinner menu is changed every couple of months and takes advantage of fresh seasonal offerings, including fish. The candlelit dining room tables are set with crisp white linens, Dudson floral china, and crystal water glasses. The rooms are softened by Oriental carpets.

Dinner is leisurely. My first course was a colorful salad of roasted red peppers with fresh basil. An exotic main course of Brazilian fish and shrimp, stewed in a sauce of coconut, tomatoes, peanuts, and ginger, was exceptional. A crisp garden salad, using tender bibb lettuce from the inn's garden, was tossed with a tangy, homemade house dressing. Along with my after-dinner espresso, I ordered pumpkin cheesecake, one of Carl's specialties. I made a mental note to ask him how he makes it so creamy.

Cathedral ceilings, weathered barn boards, and exposed beams highlight the nine spacious guest rooms. Many of the walls are hand-stenciled, and period antiques and handmade quilts—a hobby of Judy's—decorate the comfortable rooms. As an avid reader, I particularly appreciated the rooms' cozy sitting areas and three-way reading lamps. All rooms have full baths, two with Jacuzzis, and thick, large towels. Some have fireplaces and two have balconies. My room had a lovely view onto the inn's pond.

The Huebers have stocked the rooms' small refrigerators with chardonnay, champagne, mineral water, and imported beers. Air-conditioning is quiet, and telephones and television are available.

A beehive fireplace dominates the sitting room. Colonial furnishings, a brass chandelier, a 20-foot-high ceiling, and lots of windows make this room a wonderful place for relaxing.

Judy whips up a super breakfast that might include fruit-filled crepes or summer vegetable custard, which is served on the cheery remodeled sun porch, or outside on the terrace.

The inn is located in an area appropriately termed "the elegant gateway to New Hampshire and Vermont," near Brattleboro, with its fascinating museum, annual Bach Festival, River Playhouse, and diverse shopping. Skiing, mountain climbing, boating, fishing, and swimming are all close by. Or, in the winter, skate under the stars on the inn's lighted pond.

The latest news from the dedicated Huebers is that they're planning six additional guest rooms. One thing is certain: I'd like to return for their traditional New Year's Eve sleigh ride.

CHESTERFIELD INN, Rte. 9, Chesterfield, NH 03466; 603-256-3211. A 9-guestroom (private baths) country inn on a hill above the Connecticut River Valley. Open all year. King and double beds. Breakfast included. Gourmet dinners Wed. to Sun. Close to outdoor activities and cultural offerings. Children over 10. Judy and Phil Hueber, Owners-hosts.

Directions: Traveling north on Rte. 9, take Exit 3 and follow to lights. Go straight, across river, 2 mi. Inn is on the left. From Keene, N.H., travel west on Rte. 9 for 20 min. Inn is on the right.

CHRISTMAS FARM INN
Jackson, New Hampshire (1989)

Sydna Zeliff was welcoming some golfers who were returning for their fifth year. There was a lot of laughter, with jokes and references to past seasons—some of which they surely wanted to forget. But it was all in fun, and I enjoyed watching the camaraderie between Sydna and her guests. Both she and Bill are most genial and warm hosts, and their guests obviously feel comfortable and very much at home here.

Christmas Farm was given its name many years ago, and Sydna and Bill found it inspirational. Using subtle variations of red and green in the decor, naming their guest rooms after Santa's reindeer and elves, sending out semiannual newsletters from the North Pole, and having a big Christmas celebration in the middle of July, they keep the feeling and spirit of Christmas alive all year.

As I drove up the country road my first view of the inn, with its white clapboards and green shutters, was very inviting. The main house, built in the 1770s, is set back on a little knoll, across a green lawn with huge maple trees and masses of flowers. The green rocking chairs on the long front porch with its overhanging roof, hanging plants, and flowers seemed to beckon me to "come and set a spell." The screen door is the kind I expected to slam when it closed.

Bill obligingly took me on a tour up the little road that wound around the hill and through the woods. There are several cottages with names like

the Sugar House, the Smoke House, and the Livery Stable, in a lovely, woodsy setting, with little yards and porches where you can sit out and enjoy the birds and the flowers. They are all different, with attractive and comfortable furnishings. Some have fireplaces, and all have beautiful mountain views. The 1777 Saltbox and the Barn are closer to the main house and have several guest rooms and suites. The ground floor of the huge Barn is also a leisure center with table tennis, a piano, and a TV.

Guest rooms in the main house are decorated in Laura Ashley fabrics and antique reproductions. Two rooms have Jacuzzis. Cheerful plaids cover the settees and chairs in the two cozy sitting rooms; one room has a corner fireplace with a raised hearth, and the other has a TV and VCR. There's an old-fashioned phone booth in the entry.

My dinner in the pleasant dining room with its many windows overlooking the flower gardens was delightful. The chef is from the Four Seasons in Boston, and the extensive menu shows his sophisticated touch. Everything was excellent, from my appetizer of ravioli of crab with saffron and chives, to the entrée of grilled tuna with spinach, garlic, herbs, and diced tomatoes, to the ambrosial finale of an amaretto-soaked sponge cake served in a raspberry sauce and topped with chocolate. All of the breads and rolls are freshly baked. I gently awakened the next morning to that wonderful aroma wafting in my bedroom window.

The fresh, pure mountain air drew me outdoors to the promise of a brilliant day of clear blue skies and hot sun. I didn't want to miss the once-a-week garden trail tour that the gardeners conduct in the summer, after which I planned a dip in the pool and possibly lunch poolside at the Cabana. There are so many things to do here in the summer and, of course, in winter Jackson is a mecca for skiers. I can just imagine Christmas Farm is like a Christmas card in the winter.

CHRISTMAS FARM INN, Jackson Village, NH 03846; 603-383-4313. A 37-guestroom (36 private baths) comfortable farmhouse inn with cottages and suites on 14 acres on a country road in the rolling farmlands and forests of the White Mountains. Modified American plan. Breakfast and dinner served to travelers by reservation. Open year-round; various packages available. Swimming pool, sauna, putting green, horseshoes, shuffleboard, volleyball, table tennis on grounds. Golf, tennis, fishing, hiking, all summer/winter sports, and cultural and sports events nearby. No pets. No smoking in dining room. Sydna and Bill Zeliff, Owners-hosts. (See Index for rates.)

Directions: From Rte. 16, go through village. Follow Rte. 6B up the hill ½ mi. to the inn.

THE DARBY FIELD INN
Conway, New Hampshire (1981)

There's a real sense of adventure involved in just making the last stage of the journey to reach Darby Field Inn. I turned off Route 16 and followed the Darby Field sign, plunging into the forest on a wonderful dirt road that seemed to climb ever upward. Following this road through the forest, again I had the great feeling of expectation that something would emerge at the top of the mountain that was going to be grand, and grand it is.

The Darby Field Inn has a most impressive panoramic view from its terrace dining room and many of the bedrooms. On this particular day Marc and Marily Donaldson, the innkeepers, took turns making sure that I saw all of the redecorating that had been accomplished in the inn, and we also had a chance to talk about the great view of the mountains.

"Over there is South Moat Mountain," Marc explained, "and that's Mount Washington just to the right. We can also see Adams and Madison and White Horse Ledge in the center."

The Darby Field Inn sits on the edge of the White Mountain National Forest, where guests can cross-country ski, snowshoe, and hike to nearby rivers, waterfalls, lakes, and open peaks. Fortunately, there's a very pleasant swimming pool on the terrace, providing guests with not only a cooling dip in the hot days of summer, but still another view of the mountains.

Marily and I did a short tour of the rooms. "Each room has its own country personality," she observed. "Some have four-poster beds, patchwork quilts, and braided rugs. Most of them have private baths and, as I'm sure you've noticed, many face our special view of the valley."

There is a cozy little pub, where both guests and Marc and Marily's friends can come together. This is adjacent to the living room, which has as impressive a massive stone fireplace as I have ever seen.

I was curious about the origins of Darby Field Inn. "Samuel and Polly Chase Littlefield first came up here in 1826, when it was hard work farming through all those generations of hard winters and long distances," she recounted. "Later on, the home took in summer guests, and it was then that the innkeeping tradition began. In the 1940s, a man from Boston and his family came here, and the original farmhouse became the living room section of what was to be known as the Bald Hill Lodge. The barn and blacksmith shop came down and in its place the dining room and kitchen section was built. The swimming pool was added and even a small ski lift for guests."

As one might expect, the menu is a bit on the hearty side with lamb chops, filet mignon, veal piccata, and roast duckling satisfying outdoor-oriented appetites.

Marc and Marily met in Venezuela, Marily's homeland, and came to Darby Field in 1979. They saw it as a country home for their children and an opportunity to meet guests from all parts of the world.

Many guests at Darby Field really enjoy going through the three volumes of scrapbooks containing brochures from inns all over New England. They provide a very pleasant few hours of relaxation in the living room in front of the big fireplace, and invariably lead to making new acquaintances among other guests.

As Marc and Marily walked me out to the car, she said, "We can't let you go without pointing out our garden where we get so many of the good things we serve at the inn, including snow peas, peppers, cabbage, corn, lettuce, and brussels sprouts."

THE DARBY FIELD INN, Bald Hill, Conway, NH 03818; 800-426-4147 (NH: 603-447-2181). A 16-guestroom (14 private baths) White Mountain country inn, 3 mi. from Conway. Queen, double, and twin beds available. Modified American plan. Closed Apr. and early Nov. Bed and breakfast offered at various times, so I would suggest checking with the inn in advance. Within convenient driving distance of all of the Mt. Washington Valley cultural, natural, and historic attractions, as well as several internationally known ski areas. Swimming pool and carefully groomed xc skiing trails on grounds. Tennis and other sports nearby. Marc and Marily Donaldson, Owners-hosts. (See Index for rates.)

Directions: From Rte. 16: Traveling north turn left at sign for the inn (½ mi. before the town of Conway) onto Bald Hill Rd., and proceed up the hill 1 mi. to the next sign for the inn and turn right. The inn is 1 mi. down the dirt road on the left.

DEXTER'S INN AND TENNIS CLUB
Sunapee, New Hampshire (1978)

What a day! The sky was the bluest of skies, the sun was the sunniest of suns, and New Hampshire during the last week in June was really showing off for the rest of the world. I crested the hill and found Dexter's Inn basking in all of this glory, its bright yellow paint and black shutters blending well with the black-eyed Susans, Queen Anne's lace, and other summertime flowers and the green trees in the background.

After parking my car, I strolled up the granite steps, and stepped into the entrance, over which was the date 1804. Here again was the comfortable library-living room with some appropriate paintings of New Hampshire mountains and countryside. The furniture had been brightly slipcovered, and the room was wonderfully cool after the midday heat. I took a moment and stepped out to a screened-in porch with white wicker furniture and a ceiling painted to look like a canopy. It looked like a wonderful place to spend an evening.

Now I opened the door to the side terrace with its round tables and bright yellow umbrellas, remembering that I first sat here perhaps ten years earlier. There were tennis courts on both sides of the broad lawn and some tennis players were having a lively game. I could hear guests splashing in the swimming pool.

Suddenly, innkeeper Frank Simpson appeared, and true to his promise, recorded in the last edition of the book, he had a pitcher of lemonade. We sat and had a long conversation about innkeeping, including a word or two about Norman Arluck, who at eighty-three was spending his fourteenth consecutive year at Dexter's.

"Shirley and I have turned over the reins to our daughter, Holly, and her husband, Michael, who are now the official innkeepers. I am going to be known as 'Innkeeper Emeritus,' and I will be doing what I love best—grounds keeping—and Shirley is very busy decorating our new house."

Now I heard the reassuring sounds of lawnmowers—lawnmowers always sound wonderful unless you're pushing them yourself, and it's a sound that perhaps a great many city folk don't hear very often. Frank continued about Holly. "She's added some very nice main dishes to our menu, including fresh poached salmon, fillet of sole Capri, and chicken with red peppers and scallions. In addition to some exceptional cheesecakes and lemon meringue pies, for dessert there's walnut torte and Wellesley chocolate cake."

Frank was called to the phone and I took a look at the bulletin board. It's small wonder that this part of New Hampshire is so popular with country-inn guests because there is always something to do, including a regular series of band concerts in nearby Sunapee, and drama and music at the Dartmouth Hopkins Center and the Barn Theater in nearby New London.

Frank returned, and we went to see some of the guest rooms in the main house, which are reached by funny little hallways that zigzag around various wings, and also the guest rooms in the barn across the street. Everything looked tiptop.

So, there is a changing of the guard at Dexter's. To me it looks as if nothing is really different, it's all as great as ever.

DEXTER'S INN AND TENNIS CLUB, Box R, Stagecoach Rd., Sunapee, NH 03782; 603-763-5571. Also, 800-232-5571. A 19-guestroom (private baths) resort-inn in the western New Hampshire mountain and lake district. All-size beds. Modified American plan; European plan available in late June and Sept. Breakfast, lunch, and dinner served to travelers by advance reservation; closed for lunch and dinner on Tues. during July and Aug. Lunches served only July, Aug. Open from early May to mid-Nov. Three tennis courts and teaching pro, pool, croquet, and shuffleboard on grounds. Lakes, hiking, backroading, and championship golf courses nearby. Pets allowed in Annex only. Michael and Holly Simpson-Durfor, Owners-hosts. (See Index for rates.)

Directions: From north and east: use Exit 12 or 12A, I-89. Continue west on Rte. 11, 6 mi.—just ½ mi. past Sunapee to a sign at Winn Hill Rd. Turn left up hill and after 1 mi., bear right on Stagecoach Rd. From west: use Exit 8, I-91, follow Rte. 103 east into NH—through Newport ½ mi. past junction with Rte. 11. Look for sign at Young Hill Rd. and go 1½ mi. to Stagecoach Rd.

FOLLANSBEE INN
North Sutton, New Hampshire (1990)

Dick and Sandy Reilein are innkeepers who know the true meaning of the word *hospitality.* They're not only cordial and generous but lots of fun. When they purchased Follansbee Inn in 1985, they were already in love with the area surrounding the small country village of North Sutton. Dick left a career in computer sales and Sandy gave up her position as a hospice worker to realize their dream of having an inn. "We wanted an inn since staying in many in England on our honeymoon," Sandy told me. "And since we've had one, we have no regrets!"

The Follansbee Inn is nestled near lovely, peaceful Kezar Lake, four miles from, as Sandy says, "the nifty New England town of New London." The Follansbee family built the rambling, distinctive farmhouse in 1840, and it was expanded in the 1920s. Crisp and clean, the white clapboard and green-trimmed house has a traditional old fashioned front porch for evening "dawdling."

"We don't have any television here," Dick told me as he ushered me into the cozy sitting room, "just great conversation." I was pleased to practice this rather rare art as we sat in overstuffed chairs next to the wood-burning stove. The room is paneled with weathered barn wood, which lends an air of timelessness. Another meeting room has comfortable sofas, a fireplace, and a small service bar.

In the winter months, hot kir and cider are served around the fire: a welcome treat after an afternoon of cross-country skiing. Summers bring

Follansbee slush, served as guests relax on the front porch. The inn also has a nice selection of wines and beer. Several local brews are offered. By the way, Follansbee is a nonsmoking inn. "We want our guests to enjoy this clean New Hampshire air, inside and outside," Dick said.

The twenty-three guest rooms are each decorated differently. Carpeting, new mattresses, and lovely antiques create a comfortable atmosphere. Shared baths are large, with claw tubs and showers, and private baths have either tub showers or shower stalls. The bayberry soap waiting in my soap dish was an aromatic surprise.

One of the most wonderful things about Follansbee Inn is Kezar Lake. First of all, the view to the lake is spectacular. There's something about the sight of a peaceful lake the first thing in the morning that just starts the day off on the right note. Dick and Sandy invited me to the inn's private lakefront and pier to show me their new handmade wooden rowboat one afternoon. "Isn't she great!" Sandy proudly said. "We have quite an armada now: a sail board, rowboat, canoe, and paddleboat." For an afternoon of lazing, take one of the boats to the small island in the middle of the lake and enjoy one of Sandy's picnic lunches as you soak up some sun.

Breakfast begins in the dining room, with homemade granola, juices, coffee, and tea. Guests are then invited into the cozy kitchen to feast on lots of fresh fruit, muffins, and either an egg casserole, pancakes, or French toast. Evening dining is leisurely. Dick can suggest just the perfect wine to accompany your meal.

I left Follansbee feeling completely rested and rejuvenated. I wish I could have captured the sense of tranquility I felt as I sat on the comfortable front porch and gazed across the lake. But, since I can't, I'll just have to return for another visit!

FOLLANSBEE INN, P.O. Box 92, North Sutton, NH 03260; 603-927-4221. A 23-guestroom (11 private baths), authentic New England country inn on Lake Kezar. King, double, and twin beds. Closed portions of Nov. and April. Hearty breakfast included; picnic lunch and dinner available. Boating, fishing, hiking, biking, picnicking, golf, tennis, xc skiing from doorstep, summer playhouse, and musical concerts. Children over 10 welcome. No pets. Nonsmoking inn. Dick and Sandy Reilein, Owners-hosts.

Directions: Take I-89 to Exit 10. Follow signs to North Sutton, about 2 miles. The inn is behind the big white church.

THE INN AT CROTCHED MOUNTAIN
Francestown, New Hampshire (1981)

Once again I turned off Route 202 at Bennington, New Hampshire, and followed Route 47 toward Francestown. I noticed that an unusual number of beaver dams had been built by our industrious friends. Admiring the farms on both sides of the road, I wound my way ever upward through the grove of trees, coming once again to the Crotched Mountain Inn, just a few paces from the base of a ski area.

The brilliant sunshine of the day glittered in the waters of the swimming pool and intensified the radiant hues of the uncountable irises. I stopped for a moment to admire the view. One of the intriguing things about this view is that it gets better with each visit.

Rose Perry came around the corner of the inn, and after warm hellos we wandered across the broad back lawn. The subject of how many years the inn had been included in *CIBR* came up. The first entry was in the 1981 edition. Interestingly, some of the things I mentioned then are still true today. I had visited Crotched Mountain early in June, when the late New England spring is most delicious with apple blossoms and lilacs, and I was smitten by the wonderful panorama stretching out for miles.

I made a second visit that year when the fall colors were as magnificent as only they can be in the Monadnock region, where occasionally the full range of color is reached before October 1.

It was during this second visit that I enjoyed a leisurely dinner and the opportunity to see John and Rose Perry and the inn in a different light. There was a glowing fire in the low-ceilinged parlor of the little pub, where after-dinner guests and other couples dropped in during the evening.

The inn was originally built as a farmhouse in 1822. The first owner constructed a secret tunnel from his cellar to the Boston Post Road, incorporating his home as a way station to shelter runaway slaves on the Underground Railroad. During the late 1920s, it was to become one of the most spectacular farms in New England, boasting an internationally recognized breed of sheep, champion horses, and Angora goats.

Unfortunately, the house was destroyed by fire in the mid-30s, rebuilt, and John and Rose came on the scene in 1976.

Rose is an attractive Indonesian woman. She is in complete charge of the kitchen, doing a great deal of the cooking. The menu includes roast duck with plum sauce, sautéed bay scallops, and Indonesian-style scallops with sautéed tomatoes, onions, pepper, and ginger.

Although several years have intervened, both Rose and John looked like the same fresh-faced young innkeepers they were at our very first meeting. I asked John what he thought was the most important thing about innkeeping, and he unhesitatingly replied, "People." He went on to

explain that it is really the returning guests who make innkeeping such a joy. "We have had people who have been back every year since we first took over," he said.

As I was leaving, Rose walked out to the car and said, "Do tell your readers that we love children to come here, and we have many things for them to do and see, and they always seem to have a good time."

THE INN AT CROTCHED MOUNTAIN, Mountain Rd., Francestown, NH 03043; 603-588-6840. A 13-guestroom (8 baths) mountain inn in southern New Hampshire, 15 mi. from Peterborough. Double and twin beds available. European plan. Open from mid-May to the end of Oct., and from Thanksgiving thru the ski season. During winter, dinner is served on Fri. and Sat., and during holiday periods. Dinner is served from Tues. thru Sat. during the remainder of the year. Within a short distance of the Sharon Arts Center, American Stage Festival, Peterborough Players, Crotched Mt. ski areas. Swimming pool, tennis courts, xc skiing, volleyball on grounds. Golf, skiing, hill walking, and backroading in the gorgeous Monadnock region nearby. No credit cards. Rose and John Perry, Owners-hosts. (See Index for rates.)

Directions: From Boston, follow Rte. 3 north to 101A to Milford. Then Rte. 13 to New Boston and Rte. 136 to Francestown. Follow Rte. 47 for 2½ mi. and turn left on Mountain Road. Inn is 1 mi. on right. From New York/ Hartford, take I-91 north to Rte. 10 at Northfield to Keene, N.H. Follow 101 east to Peterborough, Rte. 202 north to Bennington, Rte. 47 to Mountain Rd. (approx. 4½ mi.); turn right on Mountain Rd. Inn is 1 mi. on right.

INN AT THORN HILL
Jackson, New Hampshire

What a transformation! When I last saw Mount Washington from my guest room, it had been at sundown the previous day. The mountain's eminence had caught and reflected the last rays of the sun, until it finally disappeared in the ever-deepening hues of blue that marked a mid-September evening in northern New Hampshire.

This morning the top of the mountain was completely white. A 6-inch snowfall had powdered several peaks of the Presidential Range, and Jack Frost had brushed some streaks of red, orange, yellow, and russet through the greenery. When I went down for breakfast there was an electricity in the air that comes with the arrival of a change in season.

Innkeepers Peter and Linda LaRose moved to Jackson Village in 1987. Coming from Washington, D.C., they had been accustomed to a much more cosmopolitan environment than the village of Jackson (population 650) provided. But the LaRoses had no trouble adapting, and quickly left any attachment to their previous careers in communications and accounting behind.

The Thorn Hill Inn was designed by noted architect Stanford White, who also designed the Washington Square Arch in New York City. A bit of gossip, unproven of course, hints that White was shot to death by a jealous husband. Built originally as a private mansion for Katherine Prescott Wormeley, a distinguished translator of the works of Balzac, the property with its gambrel-roofed main house on 7.5 quiet country acres became her winter abode. The quintessential grand country residence was completed in 1891.

Three different types of accommodations are available at the inn: the main inn, the carriage house, and the cottages. Each room has a private

bath and is individually decorated with Victorian antiques, lovingly chosen by Linda and Peter. The inn is by no means rustic, catering to a clientele who appreciate a genteel atmosphere.

The first floor, with its forty-two-seat dining room, has a Victorian flavor. The parlor offers the inn's only television, and the spacious drawing room with its soapstone wood stove, lace curtains, and antique furnishings provides a comfortable ambience that is hospitable and welcoming. The inn's long living room has been divided into three separate areas where guests can gather for conversation or for games at the gaming tables.

Views to the surrounding mountains, and unique Victorian accents, highlight the guest rooms. The Carriage House next door offers a 20- by 40-foot great room with a fireplace and seven comfortable guest rooms. The decor is country-inspired and the environment perfect for group get-togethers. The other three cottages offer the ultimate in privacy with the option to participate in the group environment. All rooms and cottages have modern baths with either showers or shower/tub combos.

The inn's dining room is reserved exclusively for guests. In addition to individual tables for those who desire romantic privacy, there is a common table that seats eight, for the adventurous who love to swap travel stories and good conversation. Besides the scrumptious, full breakfast, a varied dinner menu is prepared to order, offering appetizers like a country pâté of veal, pork, and chicken livers flavored with brandy, and entrees of lobster pie and paella valenciana with the traditional Spanish saffron rice. All entrees are served with fresh vegetables and a baked, stuffed potato.

The inn's built-in pool and winter sports, including the Jackson Ski Touring cross-country trail network, provide enjoyable exercise for any season. Plays, dance troupes, and concerts take place at various times during the year.

Be sure to spend some time looking at Linda's antique Victorian light fixtures. She has spent many hours pursuing this unusual, noteworthy collection.

INN AT THORN HILL, Thorn Hill Rd., Box A, Jackson, NH 03846; 603-383-4242. A 20-guestroom (private baths) inn within sight of Mount Washington. Various packages available, including European, Modified American, and B&B plans. Breakfast and dinner served daily. All-size beds. Closed April. Many cultural and recreational activities nearby. Smoking in pub only. Children over 12. Kennel nearby. Linda and Peter LaRose, Owners-hosts.

Directions: Take I-95 to the Spaulding Turnpike and follow Rte. 16 north to Jackson. Once in Jackson Village, take Rte. 16A through the covered bridge to Thorn Hill Rd. and turn right; go up the hill.

THE JOHN HANCOCK INN
Hancock, New Hampshire (1971)

"One of the things I'm most proud of," Pat told me, "is our listing on the National Register of Historic Places. Our Hancock Historical Society did all the necessary research and received a listing for our entire Historic District. Glynn and I are so grateful and pleased. We've always wanted to be listed but never had the time to do the research."

It's true that they are always busy with some new project—building new dining rooms, redecorating, expanding the grounds, and making additions and improvements to the menu. Because, as Pat says, "You just cannot stand still; you have to move with the times and the circumstances."

When people interested in knowing more about country innkeeping come to visit me, I often suggest that they visit the John Hancock as an example of a certain type of village inn. It is the center for community activity and small enough so that villagers and visitors have the opportunity to get acquainted. It is New Hampshire's oldest continuously operating inn, with appropriately furnished guest rooms, many with double and twin canopied beds.

I had arrived in Hancock on a rainy day, and the trees arching over the village streets provided a very welcome shelter for many of the umbrella-carrying villagers and visitors. There was a special gleam from many of the white narrow-clapboard Federalist homes. For instance, directly across from the John Hancock Inn there is a pleasant white clapboard house with a Victorian porch and next to that is a typical New Hampshire double-galleried, peak-roofed, three-story white clapboard house with pillars on the front.

Pat had met me at the door with exciting news of the inn's past history. "We'll be telling guests of the colorful past, of the Rufus Porter murals and the Moses Eaton stenciling. We discovered the Porter murals while we were doing some redecorating. Both men were itinerant 19th-century artists. And we know stories about the times of Squire Patton and the other twelve innkeepers, along with some humorous anecdotes. Our neighbors are already searching old trunks in their attics for memorabilia."

I was ready for lunch, and with a choice of four different dining rooms, I decided on the one with the dried-flower arrangements hanging from the exposed beams and overlooking the back lawn. Pat mentioned that their creative culinary staff has developed some lighter dishes on their extensive menu, and the Chef's Choice at each meal is a great way to showcase their talent.

After looking over the display board with the luncheon specials and the luncheon menu, which included fried haddock, chicken shortcake, and other unusual sandwiches, I decided on roast beef hash with a poached egg. Pat explained that the Sunday brunches are not buffet style. "We prefer to offer our guests table service," she said. "In many cases, our Hancock neighbors join with the out-of-town guests—it's becoming a regular stop-off after church or after the morning trip out for the paper."

As I drove away from the John Hancock Inn and my dear friends Pat and Glynn, I remembered the thought expressed by them a few years ago.

"I think that the whole business of innkeeping has been an act of faith for us. God has been good these years. We believe that with His strength and guidance we have made the inn a haven for others, a source of pride for the town, and a deep and rich experience for our family."

THE JOHN HANCOCK INN, Hancock, NH 03449; 603-525-3318. A 10-guestroom (private baths) village inn 9 mi. north of Peterborough, on Rtes. 123 and 137, in the middle of the Monadnock region of southern N.H. King, double, and twin beds available. European plan. Breakfast, lunch, and dinner served daily to travelers. Sun. brunch. Closed Christmas Day and 1 wk. in spring and fall. Wheelchair access. Bicycles available on the grounds. Antiquing, swimming, hiking, alpine and xc skiing nearby. Glynn and Pat Wells, Innkeepers. (See Index for rates.)

Directions: From Keene, take either Rte. 101 east to Dublin and Rte. 137 north to Hancock or Rte. 9 north to Rte. 123 and east to Hancock. From Nashua, take 101A and 101 to Peterborough. Proceed north on Rtes 202 and 123 to Hancock.

THE LYME INN
Lyme, New Hampshire (1971)

On my most recent visit, Judy Siemons showed me the lovely new Lyme Inn notepaper, with a very delicate watercolor of the inn by a local artist, showing all four of the red brick chimneys and the four-plus stories of the inn itself. The second- and third-story open porches in the front of the building are plainly visible. Everything is set off by a trim white fence. It might be that in some future edition of *Country Inns and Back Roads* we would use this for our cover.

I was also pleased to discover the expanding crafts area on the second floor, with many delightful handcrafted gifts by mostly local artisans.

Judy was overflowing with news about the "Garrison stove in our third dining room. What a difference it makes, both in direct heat and warming up the atmosphere. We found a wonderful source of braided rag rugs, and have replaced many of our older rugs and covered previously bare floors with some of the nicest braided rugs I've ever seen. We've also added quite a few Hitchcock chairs and tables to our dining rooms."

The Lyme Inn is an antique-laden gem that sits at the end of a long New England common. The twelve guest rooms with private baths and two rooms with shared baths have poster beds, hooked rugs, hand-stitched quilts, wide pine floorboards, stenciled wallpaper, and winged chairs. I feel certain that children would not be comfortable, because there is no entertainment particularly designed for them.

This inn is a treasure-trove of nostalgic memorabilia; one room displays old farm tools, and reminds us that this is good snowshoeing country. The house boasts a number of antique maps and salt-glazed pottery, and one of its bedrooms is outfitted in a rare suite of 19th-century painted "cottage" furniture, reminiscent of Eastlake.

My attention was drawn to the unusual collection of framed samplers on the wall of the dining room. "Oh, I am definitely into samplers," exclaimed Judy. "I am always anxious to know more about them and sometimes our guests are able to be of assistance.

"Samplers are a form of American folk art," she continued, "and I find that the real old ones are fast disappearing. A friend of mine who lives nearby does most of our framing and we are doing everything we can to preserve them, including using acid-free paper."

Judy told me they are now on the modified American plan, which includes breakfast and dinner. Breakfast features juice, fresh fruit in season, fried or scrambled eggs, french toast with local maple syrup, and blueberry muffins. It is served from 8:00 to 8:45 a.m.

Chef Hans Wickert, trained in Germany and Switzerland, has introduced several Continental specialties, including hasenpfeffer. He offers a different menu for summer and winter, but always a veal dish and a shrimp dish, and always makes his own soups from scratch.

Guests are intrigued with the four sheep, two black and two white ewes. Judy says they are kept as added "lawn mowers." They're sheared every spring and she talked about possibly trading their wool for blankets at one of the crafts shops in the area. I'm sorry to report that Duffy, their well-loved, fourteen-year-old sheep dog is no longer there. I know many guests will miss his friendly presence.

Although the village feels quite remote, it is nonetheless just ten miles from Hanover, New Hampshire, the home of Dartmouth College, and inn guests have the opportunity to enjoy some of the sporting and theatrical events taking place there. It is just a few minutes from the Dartmouth Skiway, and there's plenty of cross-country skiing nearby.

THE LYME INN, on the Common, Lyme, NH 03768; 603-795-2222. A 14-guestroom (12 with private baths) village inn 10 mi. north of Hanover on N.H. Rte. 10. Double and twin beds available. Modified American plan includes breakfast and dinner; reservations necessary. Dinner served to travelers by reservation. Dining room closed on Tues. Closed from Sun. following Thanksgiving to Dec. 26, and 3 wks. in late spring. Convenient to all Dartmouth College activities, including Hopkins Center, with music, dance, drama, painting, and sculpture. Alpine and xc skiing, fishing, hiking, canoeing, tennis, and golf nearby. No children under 8. No pets. Fred and Judy Siemons, Owners-hosts. (See Index for rates.)

Directions: From I-91, take Exit 14 and follow Rte. 113A east to Vermont Rte. 5. Proceed south 50 yards to a left turn, then travel 2 mi. to inn.

THE MEETING HOUSE INN AND RESTAURANT
Henniker, New Hampshire (1990)

Located in the beautiful Contoocook Valley, nestled at the base of Pat's Peak Ski Area, The Meeting House waits for those who love and appreciate a small rural environment. Henniker is home to New England College and takes its name from the original meeting house, built more than 200 years ago, at the base of Craney Hill.

Located on a quiet, secondary country road, the refurbished farmstead is bordered by two meandering mountain-fed streams. Its 5 acres of wooded land provide wonderfully peaceful hiking trails. As innkeeper Cheryl Bakke stated, "The inn is a quiet jewel awaiting your discovery."

And a jewel it is. Bill and June Davis, and Cheryl Davis Bakke and her husband, Peter, have owned and operated The Meeting House Inn and Restaurant for seven years. They were charmed by the quaint town of Henniker, and chose it as an ideal location to begin "hands-on" innkeeping. For them, the "hands-on" part started immediately. They purchased the buildings, which previously had not been used as an inn, and began renovating. "We literally started from scratch," Bill, the former owner of an executive search firm, told me. "We wanted the inn to have our own signature."

That unique family signature is apparent throughout The Meeting House. The style is eclectic, with personal family antiques and treasures in all the rooms. Even the intricate needlepoint pieces have been stitched by family members.

Each guest room has its own personality. "Rooms are *chosen* by our guests rather than *assigned*," Cheryl told me as she showed me to my romantic suite. "We want people to relax in the comforts of their own personalities and thoughts."

Wide pine floors, canopy brass beds, comfortable furnishings, designer sheets, and fluffy extra pillows are just part of what encourage total relaxation. All rooms have private baths. I really luxuriated as I soaked in a deep, hot bath, made fragrant by a few drops of complimentary home-made Henniker wild rosewater cologne.

The common room has a phone, television, VCR, and some interesting mystery puzzles that can be taken back to your room for an evening of *who-dunit*. A solar recreation area, comprised of a hot tub and sauna, is also available for guest use. Tiny twinkling Christmas tree lights peep from the plants surrounding the tub, creating a magical atmosphere.

Breakfast is always a surprise. Delivered in a charming country basket, each morning's unwrapping brings a delightful selection, including a home-baked goody. The menu is changed seasonally. Accompanied by Grensil, the inn's affectionate Maine coon cat, I took my treasure basket to breakfast on the sunny deck where I could appreciate the rock gardens and flowers that surround the inn.

In the evening, hearty New England cookery can be enjoyed in The Meeting House restaurant, housed in the inn's authentic, carefully preserved barn. Open to the public, dinner is available Wednesday through Sunday. The recently added solar greenhouse bar is just the spot to have one of Bill's famous fourteen-ingredient Bloody Marys. The bar is full-service, and includes nonalcoholic selections. An extensive wine list is also available.

A unique display of small plastic bags, filled with sand from around the world, hang from the restaurant walls: "The Sands of Time." What began as one guest's way of sharing a vacation experience has grown into a nostalgic collection that former guests send from such exotic locations as Mt. Everest and the floor of the Atlantic Ocean. Such "sharing" is an indication of just how much warmth and friendliness is found, and remembered, at the Meeting House. As the inn's brochure states, it is "A place in time to return to again and again."

THE MEETING HOUSE, 35 Flanders Rd., Henniker, NH 03242; 603-428-3228. A 6-guestroom (private baths) country inn located in the Conoocook Valley. All-size beds. Open all year. Breakfast included, dinners available Wed. through Sun., Sunday brunch. Gift and antique shops, downhill and xc skiing, water sports, theaters nearby. No smoking or pets. June and Bill Davis, and Cheryl and Peter Bakke, Owners-hosts.

Directions: From Henniker, take Rte. 114 south about 2 mi. to Pat's Peak Sign. Turn right (Flanders Rd.); the inn is about ½ mi. on the right.

The date in parenthesis in the heading represents the first year the inn appeared in the pages of Country Inns and Back Roads.

MOOSE MOUNTAIN LODGE
Etna, New Hampshire (1984)

Checking my own directions, I stopped at the Etna General Store and met a very attractive young woman who told me that I should take the second road on the right and follow the road up the mountain and the signs for the lodge. I set off for Moose Mountain Lodge with my heart high, reflecting that on my earlier visits it had been wintertime and sometimes necessary for Peter Shumway, the innkeeper, to come down to the bottom of the last steep incline to pick people up in his four-wheel drive. Up I went to the lodge and its fabulous view.

Moose Mountain Lodge is a rustic building high on the western side of Moose Mountain, built in the late 1930s, mostly of logs and stones gathered from the surrounding forests and fields. The broad porch extends across the entire rear of the lodge, and has foreground views of the rolling New Hampshire countryside and, in the distance, of famed Vermont peaks as far away as Rutland.

I passed through the new entryway and walked into the kitchen, as almost everyone does, joining Peter and Kay Shumway around the big table for a wonderful breakfast visit.

The kitchen is one of the centers of activity at Moose Mountain Lodge. "We run an open kitchen here," Kay said. "I like it when guests wander in and ask 'what's for lunch?' Incidentally, most of the time it's soup and salad." This is Kay's domain and it reveals her many interests besides cuisine, including flowers and plants. In the middle of the big butcher-block table was a copy of *Webster's New Collegiate Dictionary*. How can you go wrong in a kitchen that is also a haven for the intellectually curious!

There are twelve lodge-type, rustic bedrooms with colorful quilts, lots of books and magazines, bunk beds and conventional single and double beds, and a rustic air that I seldom find these days.

"Many things are different here in the summer, including the menus," Kay remarked. "Summer meals have lots of fish and some meats with light sauces; all of the vegetables from the garden and all the fresh fruits that I can pick; sometimes cold soups. We have salads and home-made breads and generally fruit desserts.

"However, in the wintertime we serve stuffed squash, lots of potatoes and big roasts, and always a huge salad and all kinds of desserts. Everything is put out on the buffet table so guests can have whatever they want and they can sit wherever they wish."

In winter there are extensive cross-country ski trails everywhere, and the winter scenery is spectacular. It's great to come in after skiing and grab a cookie from the seemingly bottomless cookie jar.

A recent letter from Kay said, "Peter is enjoying working with a

forester to formulate a plan for the best use of our recently acquired over 300 acres of land, including extending our trail system for hiking and cross-country skiing. The Appalachian Trail, about a mile away, intersects our new land. In the summer, our spring-fed pond with its sandy beach is a real boon.

"It's a beautiful fall morning here on the mountain, and the fog is covering the floor of the valley below us, looking like a lake, with the hills like islands and the mountains like the far shore. Down in Hanover they don't know what a beautiful day it is going to be yet. The fall colors increase every day, and two days ago we had an early morning blizzard with two inches of snow on the ground for a while. I love this time of year and we feel so fortunate to be able to live here and share our mountain home with people who love it as we do."

MOOSE MOUNTAIN LODGE, Etna, NH 03750; 603-643-3529. A 12-guestroom (5 shared baths) rustic lodge a few miles from Hanover, New Hampshire. Queen, double, and twin beds available. Closed April and May, and from Nov. 15 thru Dec. 26. Breakfast, lunch, and dinner served to houseguests only. Xc skiing for all abilities on grounds or nearby. Ski equipment available. Hiking, biking, walking, canoeing, backroading, and many recreational and cultural attractions nearby, including Dartmouth College. No pets. Peter and Kay Shumway, Owners-hosts. (See Index for rates.)

Directions: If arriving for the first time, stop in Etna at Landers Restaurant or the Etna Store and telephone the lodge for directions. The last mile up the mountain is steep, and when the road is icy, guests are met at the bottom parking lot with a 4-wheel-drive vehicle. Etna is on the map, a few miles east of Hanover.

MOUNTAIN LAKE INN
Bradford, New Hampshire

I took one look at the wide expanse of manicured lawn that stretched from the screened-in front porch of the Mountain Lake Inn and my hands began to itch for a croquet mallet. Located in the foothills of the White Mountains on 167 acres of woods and streams, the inn has served guests since it was built in 1760. White with black shutters, the immaculately maintained inn overlooks a spectacular view to its own private sandy beach just across the highway on Lake Massasecum.

Carol and Phil Fullerton spent almost six years searching for just the right inn when they decided to leave the Boston area where Bill was a stock and commodity broker and Carol ran a successful catering business. Neither have regrets about the change of careers. "We find this life-style rejuvenating," Carol said. Their search was over when they stayed one night at the Mountain Lake Inn. "We fell in love with it driving up the driveway," she continued. Well, you've heard of love at first sight; the next day the inn became theirs.

The Fullertons are hard-working partners. They immediately used their skills of refinishing and restoring "just about everything in our various urban and suburban houses during the last thirty years," to upgrade the inn's nine homey guest rooms and private baths. American and English antiques combine fluidly with contemporary furnishings. Soft earth tones, quilts, crisp eyelet curtains, stenciling and wallpapers, along with unique touches like Phil's Scottish grandfather's 1820s clock, create a relaxed atmosphere. Handmade New England crafts are tucked here and there.

Currier and Ives prints decorate the charming front parlor with its large fireplace. Another pine-paneled sitting room, where you will enjoy your country breakfast of fresh fruit, homemade muffins, cereals, and either a hot egg dish or French toast, has a cozy wood stove and a beautiful view of the front lawn.

Carol gives full vent to her creativity preparing dinner. After years of catering for a variety of epicures, she has developed a repertoire of recipes to please even the most discriminating. My mouth still waters at the thought of the tender beef burgundy, with a hint of sweet paprika and thick with mushrooms, that was served the first evening. I also sampled the beef fondue, accompanied by Carol's three diverse sauces for dipping: zippy horseradish, sweet-hot mustard, and a rich wine sauce.

Dinner is served in the antique-decorated dining room where unique mismatched chairs surround polished wood tables spread with woven mats. An eighty-five-year-old pool table dominates one corner. The dining room is open to guests only, so dinner is usually an intimate affair.

Carol and Phil enjoy the company of their guests. After raising five sons, their in-house family is now limited to a pair of cats, Pepper and Sam, and Parker, their "extremely friendly" English springer spaniel. Having been parents, they understand the need for time away from the kids, so are happy to arrange for babysitting.

Besides swimming and sunbathing, fishing, canoeing, skiing, and snowshoeing are available. A horseshoe pit and badminton net also lie in wait. Oh, by the way, I did satisfy my itch. Phil set up the croquet wickets and I knocked away to my heart's content.

MOUNTAIN LAKE INN, Rte. 114, P.O. Box 443, Bradford, NH 03221; 603-938-2136. A 9-guestroom (private baths) charming country inn in the foothills of the White Mountains. Near 3 major ski areas. Closed 2 weeks in November. King, queen, and twin beds. Modified American plan. Restaurant for guests only. Private sandy beach on lake. No pets. Children welcome. Smoking restricted. Carol and Phil Fullerton, Owners-hosts.

Directions: From Boston, take I-93 north to Exit 5, then west to Rte. 114. Go north 5 mi. From New York, take I-84 to I-91, north to Exit 3 in Vt. Go east on Rte. 9 to Henniker, then 5 mi. north to Rte. 114.

"European plan" means that rates for rooms and meals are separate. "American plan" means that meals are included in the cost of the room. "Modified American plan" means that breakfast and dinner are included in the cost of the room. The rates at some inns include a continental breakfast with the lodging.

NEW LONDON INN
New London, New Hampshire (1990)

On three lovely landscaped acres, the New London Inn overlooks the town green of the village of New London. Located on the main street of what will soon be a designated historic area, the three-story white clapboard, green-shuttered, Federal-style building has been operated as an inn for more than 150 years. Innkeepers Maureen and John Follansbee informed me that they would soon be applying for inclusion in the National Historic Register.

Extensive renovation of the inn began three years ago. The thirty guest rooms, decorated in subtle shades of green, yellow, lavender, blue, and pink, are furnished with antiques and wicker. The result is a fresh, airy atmosphere. Telephones were recently installed in each room. The private baths were modernized, but some still offer the old-fashioned charm of claw-foot tubs.

After busy careers in New York, Maureen and John made the decision to pool their talents and open an inn. Maureen had spent seventeen years in human resources, and John had worked for twenty-five years in international insurance, prior to their search for an inn. When they finally found what they wanted, the cart rather came before the horse. "First, we fell in love with the town and the area," Maureen told me. "Then we decided we really wanted the challenge of restoring this beautiful inn."

Maureen is an avid gardener, and eager to give you a guided tour of her prize-winning horticultural masterpieces. John can direct you to the nearby cross-country ski areas. A golf course and the Mount Sunapee lake region are less than two miles away. And, for those who love the thrill of uncovering that long-sought-after, one-of-a-kind hat pin, antique shops are in the immediate area.

A cozy mixture of antique and contemporary furnishings assure comfort in the common rooms. Television is available in the living room and bar. The inn has a full liquor license, and serves beer, wine, and spirits.

Breakfast is included with the room tariff and is served in the lovely dining room. Surrounded by Federal-period wallpaper, raised paneling, and new Windsor chairs, you will be treated to fresh fruit, juice, and a choice of entree and side dish. On chilly mornings, the 200-year-old fireplace warms the room.

Dinners offer wonderful appetizers, such as pepper pasta with Italian bacon and fresh vegetables. Soup usually follows, and could be something like chilled tomato lime and scallop. I had an entree of spiced beef medallions with lime-cilantro butter and avocado sauce. What a combination of flavors!

I took my morning coffee to the long, downstairs veranda and began reading the Sunday morning paper, when an impromptu game of touch football began on the village green between some Colby-Sawyer College students. I tipped back in my chair, closed my eyes, and began reminiscing about my college years; I promptly fell asleep. What bliss.

NEW LONDON INN, Main St., P.O. Box 8, New London, NH 03257; 603-526-2791. A 30-guestroom (private baths) Federal-style inn on 3 acres overlooking the New London village green. Open all year. All-size beds. Breakfast included, dinner available. Skiing, golf, public beaches, antique shops, and theater nearby. No pets. Maureen and John Follansbee, Owners-hosts.

Directions: From I-89, inn is approximately 3 mi. off Exit 11 from the south, or Exit 12, from the north. Follow signs to New London.

"European plan" means that rates for rooms and meals are separate. "American plan" means that meals are included in the cost of the room. "Modified American plan" means that breakfast and dinner are included in the cost of the room. The rates at some inns include a continental breakfast with the lodging.

THE NOTCHLAND INN
Hart's Location, New Hampshire (1990)

New Hampshire has the highest mountains in the Northeast, including the majestic Mount Washington. The air is almost crystalline, and the granite, evergreen forests, and icy snow-fed streams offer an invigorating atmosphere for body and soul.

Only 10 miles from Mount Washington, at the entrance to Crawford Notch, The Notchland Inn sits on a picturesque knoll with a commanding view of the Saco River valley. The 400 acres spread to touch the bases of four different mountains.

Off a major highway, the inn has served travelers for more than a century, and played an active role in the history of New Hampshire's White Mountains. Dr. Samuel Bemis, a successful dentist and inventor, completed the English-style manor house in 1862. Using native granite and timber, the handsome mansion was constructed by methods Dr. Bemis had studied in Europe. To achieve the clean cuts so obvious in the stone even today, the granite was drilled by hand at intervals. The holes were plugged with wooden dowels, which, when wet, split the granite with amazing precision.

John and Pat Bernardin purchased Notchland in 1983. The inn had been abandoned for some time, so the Bernardins began the work-intensive process of restoring the inn to its former Victorian grandeur. The huge brick chimneys, embossed metal ceilings, tiled fireplaces, and hardwood interior have been carefully and lovingly refurbished. Modern updating, like private tiled baths, has been done to complement the Victorian design. The atmosphere is delightfully casual and comfortable.

All eleven guest rooms have their own fireplaces and private baths. The rooms are bright and airy. The placement of beds and chairs takes advantage of the incredible views to the mountains beyond.

Pat and John are a couple with varied interests, and an unending flow of energy! Believing in the tradition of the country inn, where the family runs the business, they have no staff, choosing rather to do everything themselves. And they do *everything*. When I asked John, a former nuclear engineer, what he did for fun, he laughed and said, "I like bicycling, skiing, and fixing up the place, and fixing up the place, and . . ."

One of the Bernardins' hobbies is their sanctuary for endangered species of domestic animals. I had never heard of endangered domestics, but Pat immediately educated me. "They're rare, almost extinct, breeds of goats and sheep." You can visit their collection of llamas, ducks, and their famous golden retriever, Ruggs, who has rescued many a misdirected hiker. Wild critters also wander in now and then: deer, moose, and that masked bandit, the raccoon. Recently a large barn complex was completed to house the animals.

It's difficult to imagine Pat having much time to spend whipping up gourmet breakfasts and dinners, but she does. A former chief chef, she focuses her culinary expertise on preparation of fabulous five-course dinners that include hearty homemade soups, crisp salads, a choice of three of four entrees, like beef Wellington, and luscious desserts. Complimentary drinks and appetizers are served before dinner, and wine is available with dinner. Breakfast is equally wonderful. Both meals are served in the inn's intimate dining room by the fire.

Notchland has a wealth of outdoor sports. John just recently cleared 5 miles of cross-country ski trails to add to the 12 already in use. After a nippy day in the snow, you can return for a soak in the hot tub by the pond, and then relax in the library with a video. Or read in one of the other three sitting rooms where you'll find comfortable chairs and warming fires.

The Bernardins are a generous, resourceful family who have kept the tradition of Notchland Inn alive and well.

THE NOTCHLAND INN, Hart's Location, NH 03812; 603-374-6131. An 11-guestroom (private baths) Victorian manor house nestled in the mountains near Crawford Notch. All-size beds. Modified American plan. Open all year. Excellent winter sports, hiking, and boating. Antique shops, outlet centers, and theaters nearby. No pets. Pat and John Bernardin, Owners-hosts.

Directions: From North Conway, follow Rte. 302 north for 20 min. into the White Mt. National Forest. The inn is very noticeable on a knoll above the highway.

PHILBROOK FARM INN
Shelburne, New Hampshire (1978)

I can't think of another inn in North America that has been under the ownership of the same family for 125 years. In 1986, that is exactly what Philbrook Farm Inn was celebrating—although they were so busy with their innkeeping that nobody remembered it until mid-1986. Then they had a party and invited about sixty guests who had been coming to the inn over many years. In some cases, their guests were members of families who have been coming there over generations.

Nancy Philbrook and her sister, Connie Leger, and Connie's son, Larry, have been joined by Larry's sister, Ann, and her friend, Madonna, which has swelled the family members of the staff considerably.

The main house of Philbrook Farm was built in 1834, and the first addition with the blue porch and old-fashioned door was put on in 1861. The east end was built in 1905, and the dining room, along with the "new kitchens" was added when the big barns burned in 1934.

The Philbrook Farm *is* New Hampshire. There are New Hampshire prints, paintings, and photographs, some of them really irreplaceable. There are some tints of old prints, hooked rugs, and many, many books about New Hampshire. A whole library of books is just on the White Mountains, some of them written by former guests of the farm.

In the kitchen there is a *ten-burner* wood-burning range built by the McGee Furnace Company of Boston during the 1890s. "Yes," said Nancy, "we do almost all of our cooking and baking on this range. We only use the electric stove in case of emergencies or to keep things warm." Imagine a country inn where almost all of the cooking is done on a wood-burning range!

Meals are New England–style home cooking. "It's all homemade with no mixes," said Connie. "There is one main dish each night, and the dinner usually consists of a homemade soup, some type of roast, such as

pot, pork, or lamb. The vegetables are as fresh as possible, and we try to stay away from fried foods. Most of the guests enjoy roasts, because these days they are not served as much at home. All of the desserts are homemade. There's pie, ice cream, and pudding.

"For lunches, we serve salads, chowder, hot rolls, hash, macaroni and cheese, and things like that. On Saturday night we have a New England baked bean supper, and we almost always have a roast chicken dinner on Sunday night. We always serve a full breakfast, and on Sunday morning we have New England fish balls and cornbread."

The latest news is that the old barn next door has been put into operation as a stable, and horseback riding, trail rides, instruction, and boarding for horses are now available.

The swimming pool adds one more option to the summertime activities, which include hikes, picnicking, and nature walks on Mount Washington and the Appalachian Trail. In winter, there are cross-country trails on the 900-acre property and downhill skiing nearby.

Guests, friends, and family have been busily making cross-stitch door plaques with the names of many of the long-time returning guests, and another popular pastime is putting together one of the fantastic collection of ninety-eight jigsaw puzzles, all cut by Larry and Ann's great-grandfather and kept in a special cupboard.

If you're looking for a fine rustic inn, you won't go wrong at Philbrook.

PHILBROOK FARM INN, North Rd., Shelburne, NH 03581; 603-466-3831. A 19-guestroom (10 private baths) country inn in the White Mountains of northeastern N.H., 6 mi. from Gorham and just west of the Maine/N.H. line. King, double, and twin beds available. American, Modified American, and European plans available. Open May 1 to Oct. 31; Dec. 26 to Apr. 1. Closed Thanksgiving, Christmas. Wheelchair access. Swimming pool, shuffleboard, horseshoes, badminton, table tennis, croquet, billiards, hiking trails, xc skiing, snowshoeing trails, horseback riding on grounds. Swimming, golf, hiking, backroading, birdwatching nearby. Pets allowed only during summer season in cottages. No credit cards. The Philbrook and Leger Families, Owners-hosts. (See Index for rates.)

Directions: The inn is just off U.S. Rte. 2 in Shelburne. Look for inn direction sign and turn at Meadow Rd., cross R.R. tracks and river, and turn right at North Rd. The inn is at the end of the road.

SNOWVILLAGE INN
Snowville, New Hampshire (1990)

Frank, Trudy, and Peter Cutrone are a family after my heart, and Snowvillage Inn is one of my favorite inns. Not only is it unusual to have a father-mother-son team pool their diverse skills to operate an inn, but Trudy also shares my interest in writing. The trio purchased the 1900s inn in May 1986. "When we do 'business', I call my parents partners," Peter informed me, smiling. "When we talk 'family', it's Mom and Dad."

Originally a retreat for historical writer, Frank Simonds, the country inn is located 1,000 feet up Foss Mountain in the New Hampshire rural village of Snowville. Mr. Simonds valued the peace and solitude, the absolutely spectacular view of the White Mountains, and the property's 10 acres of forest and lawns that keep neighbors and traffic at bay. The Cutrones did too. They chose Snowvillage Inn after first deciding to adopt a new life-style, then agreed on their approach to innkeeping: "country casual." Snowvillage was to be a place where guests could relax and put up their feet. And it is.

Coming up the graceful, flower-edged drive, three attractive buildings meet your gaze: the many-gabled main house with attached chalet, the converted 150-year-old red barn, and the quaint chimney house. Though separated by a lush center lawn and old stone walls, the three buildings are closely connected by driveways. The New England architecture is enhanced with colorful window boxes of flowers.

The living room and lounge are elegant, adorned with Oriental rugs, a huge brick fireplace, and well-stacked bookcases. Games like chess and

Tak-a-Radi are available in a beautiful, hand-carved Swiss cupboard. Peter's expertise as a wood craftsman is apparent in his handsome oak grandmother clock in the comfortable living room. Paintings of Trudy's Austrian ancestors smile down from the walls, and sprays of fresh flowers appear everywhere.

In keeping with the inn's literary heritage, each of the nineteen guest rooms is dedicated to a writer and displays a selection of the author's work. The rooms are romantic and cozy with a blend of New England and Alpine Provincial furnishings ranging from period antiques to quality reproductions. Colors of dusty rose, blue, mint, and fiery poppy red accent country cottons and natural muslin linens. I found the welcome basket in my room a particularly friendly gesture, especially when I uncovered the buttery chocolate chip cookies.

I told Trudy that I wanted to meet Boris, the inn's handsome Samoyed and unofficial greeter. (He must surely have been attending to more important business when I arrived.) Boris is quite a character, and has made an enduring impression on most guests. "Our guests end up sending postcards and pictures to *him!*" Trudy said. "He even has his own photo album." The Cutrones also have cats: Skunk, Elvira, and Virginia, touted as the world's loudest *purrer.*

Dining at Snowvillage Inn is exquisite. My dinner began with a warm loaf of walnut beer bread, accompanied by a salad course of greens topped with an unusual bourbon dressing. This was followed by creamy tomato soup and an entree of Viennese beef tenderloin in a delicious sauce, rice pilaf, and a colorful sauté of squash with yellow and red peppers. Trudy's luscious French silk pie, slathered in whipped cream and shaved chocolate curls, completed the meal. Breakfast is also included with the room fee.

I was treated to an exceptional final evening at Snowvillage Inn when I attended Trudy's Americanized version of her native Austria's traditional Solstice Festival, a celebration of the return of light to the land. Tiki torches represented more traditional ones, but the spirit brought on by song, wine, and good food created an evening truly worthy of this ancient ritual.

SNOWVILLAGE INN, Snowville, NH 03849; 603-447-2818. A 19-guestroom (private baths) mountain inn retreat. Closed April. All-size beds available. Modified American plan; breakfast with B&B rates. Clay tennis courts, sauna, fitness course in woods, volleyball, horseshoes, and a wide, restful screened porch on premises. No pets. Frank, Trudy, and Peter Cutrone, Owners-hosts.

Directions: Follow directions to Crystal Lake. On the far side of Crystal Lake, turn right at the town beach onto Snowville Rd. Follow 1 mi., then turn right at Snowvillage Inn sign and come up the mountain ³/₄ mi.

SPALDING INN & CLUB
Whitefield, New Hampshire (1976)

Many years ago the White Mountains in New Hampshire had numerous summer resorts where mother and children might come up early in the season and father joined them for the last four weeks or so. These resorts were wonderful, gay places where everything that was needed for a long, complete vacation was either on the grounds or nearby. The lure of the mountains drew people in great numbers from Boston and New York.

Now, with few exceptions, all of these family-run resorts have disappeared, but not the Spalding Inn & Club, which is thriving under the ownership of William A. Ingram and his partner, Lore Moran. Many of the amenities of earlier times are still preserved; for example, gentlemen wouldn't think of going to dinner without a jacket and tie. The inn is a focal point for the sports of lawn bowling and tennis, with several tournaments scheduled from mid-June to mid-September, including the U. S. National Singles and Doubles Lawn Bowling Championships.

The Spalding Inn & Club is an excellent example of entertainment and hospitality that can be provided for a family with many different preferences. For example, on the inn grounds there are four clay tennis courts, a swimming pool, a nine-hole par-3 golf course, two championship lawn bowling greens, and shuffleboard. Five golf courses are within fifteen minutes of the inn, and plenty of trout fishing and boating and enticing back roads are nearby. The Appalachian Trail system for mountain climbing is a short walk from the inn.

In addition to opportunities for a well-blended balance of vigorous outdoor activity, there are also facilities for quiet times, including an extensive library, a card room, and a challenging collection of jigsaw puzzles. Groves of maples, birches, and oak trees native to northern New Hampshire are on the inn grounds, and there are over 400 acres of lawns, gardens, and orchards.

There are real country-inn touches everywhere. The broad porch is ideal for rocking, and the main living room has a fireplace with a low ceiling, lots of books and magazines, baskets of apples, a barometer for tomorrow's weather, a jar of sour balls, and abundant arrangements of flowers.

Those country-inn touches also include the traditional hearty menu items so satisfying after a day of outdoor activities in the White Mountains. Among other offerings in the air-conditioned dining room are delicious clam chowder, oyster stew, broiled scrod, poached salmon, pork chops, roast duckling, roast tenderloin, and sweetbreads. Children love the indian pudding. All of the pies, including hot mince, and the breads and rolls are made in the bakery of the inn.

Bill Ingram and Lore Moran have instilled a really fresh new spirit at

this lovely inn. As Bill says, "We are confident that guests of all ages will enjoy our resort. We now have live piano music in the tea room and lounge and a variety of special events is available upon request. With seventy guest rooms we are larger than the average inn in your book, but we are still able to retain a personal touch."

I agree.

SPALDING INN & CLUB, Mountain View Road, Whitefield, NH 03598; 603-837-2572. A 70-guestroom (private baths) resort inn in the center of New Hampshire's White Mountains. King and twin beds available. Full American plan includes lunch. Modified American plan available on request. Open early June to mid-Oct. Breakfast, lunch and dinner are served daily to travelers. Heated pool, tennis courts, 9-hole par-3 golf course, 18-hole putting green, 2 championship lawn bowling greens, and shuffleboard on grounds. Also Sunday night movies. Guest privileges at 5 nearby golf clubs. Trout fishing, boating, summer theater, and backroading nearby. William A. Ingram and Lore Moran, Owners-hosts. (See Index for rates.)

Directions: From New York take Merritt Pkwy. to I-91; I-91 to Wells River, Vt./Woodsville, N.H. exit; then Rte. 302 to Littleton, then Rte. 116 thru Whitefield to Mtn. View Rd. intersection—3 mi. north of village. From Boston take I-93 north thru Franconia Notch to Littleton exit; then Rte. 116 thru Whitefield to Mtn. View Rd. intersection—3 mi. north of village. From Montreal take Autoroute 10 to Magog; then Autoroute 55 and I-91 to St. Johnsbury, Vt.; then Rte. 18 to Littleton, N.H. and Rte. 116 as above. The inn is situated 1 mi. west on Mtn. View Rd.

SUGAR HILL INN
Sugar Hill, New Hampshire (1990)

Stepping onto the wide veranda of Sugar Hill Inn, with its flowers and white wicker furnishings, I was reminded of the gracious old homes I've visited in the South. The 17th-century farmhome is set on a natural rock foundation, and is stretched along a spacious lawn dominated by an old horse-drawn surrey. A powerful telescope on the veranda invites night-time star searching.

Sugar Hill Inn was built as a home for one of the hardy early-American families who came to the White Mountain area in search of a better way of life. The home was built in the traditional way, using post and beam construction, and relied on handsome rock fireplaces in the principal rooms for heat. Wide pumpkin pine boards were used for woodwork and flooring. Over the years, three cottages were added in a cluster to the west of the original inn. In 1972, improvements were made to the total facility and the inn was renamed Sugar Hill Inn.

Jim and Barbara Quinn, Rhode Island residents who had been in the grocery business, purchased the inn in 1986 and made substantial efforts to infuse the inn with their own personal warmth and, in Jim's words, "their desire to develop first-time guests into longtime friends."

The two charming common rooms have original fireplaces, mantels, and stone hearths. Decorated in a Colonial style, with beautiful sugar-maple flooring accented by Oriental rugs, the rooms are quite lovely and comfortable. The living room has an antique 1906 player piano with a large assortment of piano rolls. I had particular fun with the rousing rendition of "Alexander's Ragtime Band" that we played during an after-dinner sing-along. A television is available, and board games and a variety of reading materials and puzzles are set out for entertainment.

I stayed in one of the country cottages adjacent to the main inn and found it spacious and homey. Each cottage has its own covered front porch for enjoying the evening twilight. All the guest rooms are individually decorated with handmade quilts on antique beds and hand-braided rugs on the floors. Barb has used her artistic flair to design and paint wall stencils modeled after original patterns found during renovation. As an inveterate late-night reader, I was happy to find good lighting for reading in bed. All rooms have immaculate private baths with mostly tub/shower combinations.

The inn's light, airy dining room is a perfect spot for enjoying a breakfast of such specialties as walnut pancakes, along with fresh fruits and home-baked muffins served on country crockery. In the evening, the ambience is changed with candlelight for a dinner that features two entrees and the finest of fresh and locally grown fruits, vegetables, poultry, and meats. Jim prepares all of the meals and has some wonderful specialties like his chicken Washington, a tender chicken breast stuffed with rich crabmeat and sauce. I recommend the excellent pecan bourbon pie for dessert. The inn has a fine selection of wines, beer, and full spirits to accompany your dinner.

Both summer and winter sports abound in the area, and the inn is ideally located for antique and outlet shopping, and visits to the Sugar Hill, Robert Frost, and Ski museums. In the summer, the repertory theater and chamber concerts provide entertainment.

After dinner on my final evening at the inn, I sat on the front veranda and peered through Jim's telescope. I was granted an especially clear sky: Orion's belt was never more beautiful.

SUGAR HILL INN, Rte. 117 (Sugar Hill), Franconia, NH 03580; 603-823-5621. A 16-guestroom (private baths) traditional New England inn and cottages. Open May thru mid-Nov., and Dec. 26 thru March. All-size beds. Full breakfast included; dinner available on premises. All seasonal sports. Antique and outlet shopping, museums, theater, and chamber concerts nearby. No pets. No smoking. Jim and Barbara Quinn, Owners-hosts.

Directions: From Boston, take Exit 38 from I-93. Turn right on Rte. 18 through Franconia. Turn left on Rte. 117. The inn is ½ mile up the hill on the right. From New York, take Exit 17 from I-91. Go east on Rte. 302 and turn right onto Rte. 117. The inn is on the left ½ mile before Rte. 18.

BARROWS HOUSE
Dorset, Vermont

I received a wonderful postcard of a reproduction print depicting the Barrows House by primitivist painter, Natalee Everett Goodman, and turned it over to find an invitation from innkeepers Sally and Tim Brown. "When you come up next summer, plan on enjoying a scrumptious brown-bag lunch under our new awning over the patio by the tavern!"

The Browns have been operating the 18th-century inn since 1986, and love the small Vermont town of Dorset. "We thought that the Barrows House was really a unique property," Sally said. "Its got such a lovely parklike setting, and the multiple buildings (eight in all) offer privacy for guests." The main house was built around 1784, two of the other seven were built in the 19th century, and the remaining five buildings were finished in the mid-20th century. To provide continuity, the Browns have painted all the buildings in the Colonial style: a crisp white with black shutters.

Only a two-minute walk from town, the inn is spread over 11 acres that include a tennis court and swimming pool. Neighboring homes are nearby, creating a pleasant rural village atmosphere.

The Barrows House is ideal for family visits. The Browns are only the fourth family to have owned the inn since 1900, and their children often help out during the summer months. Their son, Thatcher, enjoyed cooking in the inn's kitchen so much during the past summer that he enrolled at the Cornell School of Hotel Administration. The only "kid" left at home now is their keeshond, Katrina, who, according to Sally, "has become a special hostess in the tavern and on our new cocktail terrace."

Four of the eight buildings have been completely renovated, and all have new rugs, fabrics, curtains, and paint. The common areas are comfortably furnished and, in keeping with the inn's Colonial origins, are decorated with stenciling and many antique period pieces.

The bedrooms are individually furnished in a variety of country styles using combinations of floral and print fabrics interspersed with period and antique furnishings. Television, air-conditioning, and refrigerators are in all the suites, and some of the other rooms. All rooms but two have private baths.

Enhancing the inn's dining reputation was one of the interesting challenges that drew the Browns away from careers in finance. The Barrows House is a full-service inn, where a country breakfast and dinner are served daily. Dinner is a four-course gourmet treat, with six to ten choices of appetizers, a main course, and dessert. A crisp green salad with three dressings comes paired with fresh hot bread.

Breakfast begins with juice, fruit, and cold cereals followed by a pancake special and an egg dish, served with bacon, sausage and great home fries.

Although lunch is not available regularly, a brown-bag picnic can be arranged. I took the Browns up on their postcard invitation and enjoyed a chicken salad sandwich on the patio by the tavern, with Katrina to keep me company. The inn has a complete liquor license and offers an interesting selection of imported and domestic wines and a wide variety of beer.

The Barrows House is only 6 miles from historic Manchester for sightseeing and shopping, and a close 15 minutes to Merck State Forest for hiking and cross-country skiing. You can also borrow one of the inn's bikes for a relaxing ride down one of the peaceful country roads.

THE BARROWS HOUSE, Rte. 30, Dorset, VT 05251; 802-867-4455. A 30-guestroom (28 private baths) 200-year-old colonial country inn on 12 acres in the heart of the picturesque Vermont village. All-size beds. Open year-round. Modified American plan. Close to historic Manchester and shopping. Swimming pool and tennis courts on premises. Close to shopping, hiking, and skiing. Well-behaved pets permitted in two of the cottages. Sally and Tim Brown, Owners-hosts.

Directions: On Rte. 30 north, 6 mi. northwest of Manchester, Vt. Coming from Manchester, the inn is on the right-hand side of the road before the town of Dorset's Green.

The date in parenthesis in the heading represents the first year the inn appeared in the pages of Country Inns and Back Roads.

BIRCH HILL INN
Manchester, Vermont (1982)

There was a pleasant hum of conversation and occasional bursts of laughter in the spacious, low-ceilinged, many-windowed living room, as Jim Lee moved around among the guests, carrying a tray of hors d'oeuvres. Everyone was back from a day on the ski slopes or one of the many cross-country woodland trails that start right from the door of the inn, and we were more than ready for one of Pat Lee's great dinners.

Four generations of Pat's family have lived in this lovely old farmhouse, the main part of which is over 190 years old. As I have mentioned in other editions, I often admired it on my trips through the valley over the years. Pat and Jim decided to turn it into an inn, and have been welcoming guests here since 1981.

Pat sat down beside me on the deep, comfortable sofa in front of the big fireplace where a fire danced and crackled. We watched Jim talking animatedly with a couple on the other side of the room. "He's a terrific innkeeper," Pat said. "He's enthusiastic, friendly, and always has time to answer questions and listen to guests."

"But do you both take time for yourselves?" I asked. "Oh, yes," she replied, "usually one of us will ski or play tennis while the other one holds the fort. But we work very hard, partly because we love what we're doing and partly because we feel very strongly that everything should look terrific, taste fantastic, and feel real good."

The living room is a warm, comfortable place with a spinet piano, a never-ending jigsaw puzzle, and innumerable books and magazines. Over the fireplace is a print of George Washington's triumphal entry into New York City after the Revolutionary War. There is an obvious interest in history, art, and music here.

Pat showed me the sun room that was recently added onto the living room. It's very attractive with wicker furniture and lots of plants.

Dinner was being served, and Jim led us into the dining room, where we all sat down at the large, round mahogany table. It was a convivial group and there was much good conversation, along with the excellent dinner of tomato bisque, veal Marsala, fresh vegetables, a crisp salad, and a delectable dessert.

Many of the vegetables are fresh from their garden, and of course their flower gardens provide wonderful flowers for the house.

Dinner is offered only to houseguests every night except Wednesday and Sunday. I was most interested in what Pat Lee had to say about the Beefalo that she often serves. "Beefalo," she explained, "is a breed of cattle originally developed by the introduction of American bison (buffalo) genes into domestic cattle. Beefalo meat contains less cholesterol and fat than supermarket beef, and is completely natural without hormones or antibiotics. There are beefalo in the fields around the inn."

Accommodations are in five comfortable, large, and cheerful guest rooms in the main house, all of which have views toward the mountains, farm, and pond. They are well decorated with paintings and furniture from the family home. A nearby cottage on the grounds has been converted into an ideal family-style accommodation as well.

In summertime there's good swimming and a trout pond, where the fish are reproducing at such a rate that guests can bring them back to the inn to be cooked for breakfast. There are also all those beautiful ski trails that are great for walking or running.

I remarked to Jim that he and Pat provide a wonderful opportunity for their guests to get acquainted. "People who come here love the homey feeling—sounds a little trite," he smiled, "but guests really like being in an inn that feels like a private home."

It may be trite, Jim, but it's nevertheless true.

BIRCH HILL INN, Box 346, West Rd., Manchester, VT 05254; 802-362-2761. A 5-guestroom (all private baths) extremely comfortable country-home inn, with a family cottage, 5 min. from downtown Manchester Center. Queen and twin beds available. Modified American plan includes dinner and breakfast. B&B plan available. Dinners offered to houseguests only, every night except Wed. and Sun. Open after Christmas to mid-April, and May to late Oct.; 2-night minimum preferred (be sure to make reservations). Swimming pool, xc skiing, trout fishing, and walking trails on grounds. Alpine skiing at major areas nearby as well as tennis and golf facilities; great biking. Children over 6 welcome. No pets. No credit cards. Pat and Jim Lee, Owners-hosts. (See Index for rates.)

Directions: From Manchester Center, where Rtes. 7, 7A, and 30 meet, take Rte. 30 north 2 mi. to Manchester West Rd. Turn left on West Rd. and continue ¾ mi. to Birch Hill Inn.

BLUEBERRY HILL
Goshen, Vermont (1973)

Tony Clark was an innovator in 1972 in what now has become a very popular winter pastime. Today, most inns in New England, or in fact anywhere in the mountains, have some kind of cross-country skiing facilities on the premises or nearby.

In the meantime, Tony has continued to look for new paths to follow. Let me put it in his words:

"As you know, we are open for skiing from December through March. But, May through October, and especially summertime here in the Green Mountains is just fabulous. We're very popular with summer and fall backpackers and walkers. Many, many of our cross-country trails are used for walking and hiking, and it's possible to use the inn as a central point for such activities or to include it on an itinerary. We use our ski trails as nature and educational paths, providing all kinds of guides to help our guests learn the names of the trees and birds."

"Actually," he said, pronouncing it as only a native-born Britisher can, "we have a lot of other summertime activities here, including a kite flying weekend during the second week in September. There are all kinds of kite contests, and with this wonderful open field immediately across from the inn, it's ideal for such activity. We also have a Mozart festival and a chamber music festival in the offing.

"I think the biggest attraction in summer is the peace, quiet, and fresh air. These are some luxuries that we sometimes take for granted—the luxury of fresh air, clean water, and no noise pollution—which are pretty special to people who live in cities."

Blueberry Hill is very definitely family style. Everyone sits around the big dining room table, and there is one main dish for each meal, cooked in the farmhouse kitchen. This main dish is likely to be something quite unusual, depending upon the cook's gourmet proclivities.

Bedrooms are plain and simple with hot water bottles on the backs of doors and handsome patchwork quilts on the beds. It is truly like visiting a Vermont farm.

In late July, to continue the summer saga, there has been an annual cross-country footrace and Blueberry Festival. The course covers ten kilometers on the paved and gravel roads, leading the runner down through the cool, shaded heart of Goshen, up a series of hills, and back through the woods and pastures, with beautiful views of the Green Mountains. Following the race, the Blueberry Festival, open to competitors and spectators alike, features a chicken barbecue with salads, homemade breads, and blueberry baked goods. An old-time square dance wraps up the festivities.

In June, Blueberry Hill hosts the annual Vermont croquet competition, and all competitors are asked to wear whites.

"As far as the cross-country skiing season is concerned, there is a ski touring center right across the road from the inn, which has a waxing area, repair shop, and an expert staff. There are seventy-five kilometers of trails with both challenging and moderate terrain."

Blueberry Hill is an unforgettable experience, whether it's early-morning coffee in the greenhouse, a day-long ski tour, or a romantic evening of relaxation in front of a roaring fire. There is great fishing, hiking, biking, and tennis nearby and always a refreshing dip in the pond.

Reservations for winter accommodations should be made as early as possible, as the inn is often booked solid for weeks at a time in winter.

BLUEBERRY HILL, Goshen, VT 05733; 802-247-6735. A 12-guestroom (private baths) mountain inn passionately devoted to xc skiing, 8 mi. from Brandon. Double and twin beds available. Modified American plan for overnight guests. Open from May thru Oct and Dec. to March. Public dining by reservation only. Closed Christmas. Wheelchair access. Swimming, fishing, hiking, nature walks, and xc skiing on grounds. Much other recreation nearby. Tony Clark, Owner-host. (See Index for rates.)

Directions: At Brandon, travel east on Rte. 73 through Forest Dale. Then follow signs to Blueberry Hill.

The date in parenthesis in the heading represents the first year the inn appeared in the pages of Country Inns and Back Roads.

1811 HOUSE
Manchester Village, Vermont (1990)

Except for the brief period when Mary Lincoln Isham, President Lincoln's granddaughter, used the 1811 House as a residence, it has been used as an inn. Built in the 1770s, the home has been carefully and authentically restored to the Federal period of the 1800s. Twelve-over-twelve windows and clapboard siding are only two of the details that earned the inn its position as a registered National Landmark building. The inn sits on more than 3 acres of lawn, landscaped with flower and rose gardens, and is directly on the green in Manchester Village. Views through pristine white birches to the Green Mountains and the Equinox Golf Course are exceptional.

All rooms are filled with authentic English and American antiques. I felt as if I had walked into a living museum, yet one where I was encouraged to relax and enjoy the comforts of home. Innkeepers Jack and Mary Hirsts' splendid collection of antique furnishings, Oriental rugs, Chinese lamps, and sterling and china artifacts create an ambience that signifies superior taste and sensibilities. The art collection alone, with original oils, prints, and drawings, is of a quality usually seen only in private collectors' homes.

Roaring fires warm each of the public rooms on chilly evenings. Pull up a chair in the library–game room where a hand-carved chess set waits, or prop your legs over the arm of an easy chair in the restful living room. Whatever your choice, sooner or later you will end up at the hub of the inn, the beam-ceilinged English pub.

In the pub, the hum of conversation and thud of darts goes on long into the evening, enhanced by gleaming brass horns, authentic tavern tables, and a wonderful pewter collection. The well-stocked bar is open to guests, who partake on the honor system. Jack, a retired Wall Street stock specialist, is responsible for the near-regulation dart setup. An avid player and teacher, he has made certain that participants have the best in equipment: a set of balanced brass darts, an illuminated board, and distance markers on the floor, properly placed for anyone who tries to sneak a few feet closer.

The fourteen bedrooms, all with private bath and shower, exhibit the same tasteful consideration to period decoration as the public rooms. Each room is different. I stayed in Robert Todd Lincoln, with its lovely old four-poster canopied bed and my own fireplace. Plump pillows and cheerful designer fabrics, along with the colorful handmade quilt, made me feel as if I'd been tucked in by someone's loving hands. The modern bathrooms have been expertly designed to blend with the period surroundings.

After a wonderful, restful night, I wandered down to the elegant dining room for a sumptuous breakfast. Amidst Georgian silver and china plates, I enjoyed fresh-squeezed orange juice, a savory English omelet, and rich fresh-brewed coffee with cream. Breakfast can also be taken in the pub, just in case a dart rematch had been planned the night before.

Although the 1811 House does not offer dinner, four very fine restaurants are within walking distance from the inn: three serving French cuisine and one serving steaks and seafood. The Hirsts are happy to make reservations for you.

The inn is close to many outdoor activities, a perfect way to work off that extra glass of stout. Besides golf and tennis at the Equinox, you might try cross-country skiing or hike one of the trails at the nearby Merck Forest and Farmland Center. Stop at the center on your way back and sample some of the traditional Vermont maple sugar, and give one of the Center's hefty draft horses a pat.

1811 HOUSE, Box 39, Manchester Village, VT 05254; 802-362-1811. A 14-guestroom (private baths) classic Vermont inn with traditional English pub. King, queen, and double beds. Closed Christmas week. Breakfast included. Restaurants within walking distance. Hiking, skiing, water sports, biking, and antique shops nearby. No pets. No children under 16. Jack and Mary Hirst, and Jeremy and Pat David, Owners-hosts.

Directions: In Vermont, take Rte. 7 north to Manchester. Turn left at the blinking light and go back on 7A for 1 mile. The inn is on your left.

THE FOUR COLUMNS INN
Newfane, Vermont (1990)

Newfane is a quintessential New England rural village, and one of the most photographed spots in Vermont. And according to innkeeper Jacques Allembert, "The Four Columns Inn is one of the reasons why!"

Set back from the main roads on 150 acres of gardens, woodlands, ponds, and streams, the graceful white facade of the main house includes four Greek revival columns. Built by General Pardon Kimball of hand-hewn timbers and beams, the over 150-year-old home has lost none of its stately yet relaxed elegance.

Jacques has owned the inn for eight years. His twenty-plus years as a New York restaurateur have honed his skills as a gracious host to a fine art. "I love the hospitality industry," he told me as he took my bags in the foyer.

The decor of the inn is lovely, with polished antiques, handmade rugs warming the floors, and attractive accents, like a period spinning wheel tucked into a sunny corner. The living rooms are cozy and invite reading, television watching, or visiting with other guests.

Seventeen unique rooms and suites, all with private baths, are located in the main house, the cottage, and the renovated barn. The clean, airy rooms, some with fireplaces, are decorated with antique and wicker furnishings. Most are papered with quaint prints. The beds range from four poster to brass. One has a lace-topped canopy. "All our rooms have a living connection with a quiet and relaxing world," Jacques said as we admired the view of the village green from my window.

I accepted his invitation for a glass of wine before dinner and we met at the inn's distinctive pewter-topped bar that presides over the tavern room. I was impressed with the superb wine list. Victorian and Colonial antiques, along with wide plank flooring and Oriental rugs, provide a warm atmosphere for easy conversation. I could almost imagine General Kimball sitting across from me, tipping a glass of homemade brew to my health.

The excellent reputation of the inn's restaurant had preceded my visit. Over our wine, I asked Jacques to give me a brief overview of the menu. "Well, we offer a blend of fine European and New American cuisine. Our chef, Gregory Parks, uses the finest and freshest Vermont food products. Why don't we go in and you can see for yourself."

As we entered the barn that houses the restaurant, I was impressed by the quality renovation that had been done. Dark beams set off the cream tones of the room, while a large, brick fireplace warms one end, and antique copper cook pots, baskets, and country crafts offer interesting accents. Fresh garden flowers and soft candlelight create a romantic mood.

The menu is intriguing. Chef Gregory gives full rein to his creativity, making use of local Vermont gamebird, rabbit, milk-fed veal, and North Atlantic seafood. Unique, inventive sauces are used, such as a blend of rhubarb and radish, yes, radish. The hot-sour-sweet combination is perfect. A full array of desserts, each created in the restaurant's kitchen, can't help but tempt even the most staunch abstainer. I had the creamy chocolate mousse pie, delicately accompanied by fresh blueberries, strawberries, and *real* whipped cream.

After such a splendid dinner, I had doubts about having much more than coffee for breakfast. But the buffet table, set with fresh berries, fruit, homemade granola, and local Grafton cheddar cheese, was too inviting. Besides, what little I did have left on my plate I shared with the inn's two resident white ducks, who seemed genuinely pleased to have my company in the garden.

THE FOUR COLUMNS INN, P.O. Box 278, West St., Newfane, VT 05345; 802-365-7713. A 17-guestroom (private baths) inn located in one of Vermont's most picturesque rural villages. King, queen and twin beds. Closed for 2 weeks after Thanksgiving. Breakfast, wonderful gourmet dinner, plus all gratuities included in tariff. Hiking, bicycling, swimming, alpine and xc skiing nearby. Children over 10. Pets by arrangement. Jacques Allembert, Owner-host.

Directions: 100 mi. from Boston, and 220 mi. from New York. Take Exit 2 from I-91 at Brattleboro to Rte. 30 north. Inn is 100 yards off Rte. 30 on the left.

THE GOVERNOR'S INN
Ludlow, Vermont (1987)

"You've missed our complimentary three o'clock tea for our house-guests," Deedy scolded me, laughingly. "But that's your own fault. It is served on our beautiful Victorian silver service. We actually have second- and third-time guests who try to get here in time for tea. It's a wonderful way to begin a country visit. It gives you a chance to meet the other guests."

Although I missed tea, I was still in ample time to join the other guests in the "front room." Deedy introduced all of us and we were soon chatting away about what a wonderful time of year it was to be in upper New England. We were then individually escorted to our tables in the candlelit dining room by one of the turn-of-the-century-clad waitresses. Deedy, who is an artist-cum-chef, described the six-course dinner. As each course was served, the dish was again described, in much the same way it is done at the Old Rittenhouse Inn in upper Wisconsin.

Whether there are five courses or six, dinner always begins with cream cheese and the Governor's sauce (the only recipe, incidentally, not included in the inn's delightfully refreshing cookbook). I don't see how any guest could leave the inn without a jar of this sauce, which is available for purchase.

Here are a few brief hints on the menu: Appetizers include mushroom strudel or marinated fish l'orange or steak strips with horseradish cream. Some of the main dishes are Lamb Gourmet, bluefish flambé, and Village Inn Steak Diane. These are augmented by intriguing side dishes. Desserts include chocolate walnut pie and peach ice with raspberry melba sauce.

If all of these seem to be a bit unusual it's because both Deedy and Charlie (he does the wonderful breakfasts) are passionately devoted to cookery. They have attended cooking schools in France, and their skills are evident in the menu.

Another of their innovations is the gourmet picnic hampers, for which the Governor's Inn has now become rather well known.

I had driven to the inn on a perfectly splendid mid-September day. The roads weren't crowded, and there were sudden bursts of orange, yellow, and red amid the backdrop of greenery covering the hills and valleys.

Deedy Marble had met me at the front door of the inn, and as she showed me to my guest room on the second floor, she pointed out five generations of family photographs along the staircase. My bedroom had a beautiful brass head and footboard that had been in Deedy's family for over 100 years. The furnishings and decorations were pure Victorian, with the exception of two watercolors by artist Virginia Ann Holt, whose work is also found throughout the inn. The rooms tend to be too small.

Some of the amenities include the option of a morning tray of coffee and sparkling Mimosa delivered to your room, some special Governor's Inn chocolates, and in the hallway a "butler's basket" of necessities for guests who forgot toothbrushes, toothpaste, and the like. By the way, my bed was turned down at night and my towels had been changed.

This brief account of the Governor's Inn has not done justice to this handsomely restored and preserved Victorian mansion, built by a governor of Vermont in 1890. It is beautifully furnished with family antiques and all the appointments and decorations are done with impeccable taste. However, I did want to leave sufficient room to say that there are many qualities about the Governor's Inn that will delight both confirmed and novice inn-goers. Among these are devoted attention to detail, dedication to making certain that guests' needs are met, and, perhaps best of all, a sincere, deep-rooted desire to bring loving care to everyone. However, those sensitive to traffic should be aware the inn is located on a busy road.

THE GOVERNOR'S INN, 86 Main St., Ludlow, VT 05149; 802-228-8830. An 8-guestroom (private baths) village inn in central Vermont. Modified American plan includes dinner, breakfast, and afternoon tea. Twin and double beds available. Open all year. Downhill skiing at Okemo Mountain and cross-country skiing nearby. Conveniently located to enjoy all of the rich recreational, cultural, and historical attractions in central Vermont. No facilities for small children or pets. Charlie, Deedy and Jennifer Marble, Owners-hosts. (See Index for rates.)

Directions: Ludlow is conveniently reached from all of the north-south roads in Vermont. It is located just off the village green, where Rte. 100 crosses Rte. 103.

THE INN AT LONG LAST
Chester, Vermont (1990)

Artists are created in many forms: painters, sculptors, writers, composers. Some people, however, are artists of another fashion: artists of life. Jack Coleman is one such artist. Instead of paints or stone mallets, pens or paper, Jack has used his experiences to mold, form, and color a work of art he calls The Inn at Long Last.

Few inns are so representative of their innkeeper's personalities as this three-story Victorian located in the middle of the quiet village of Chester. Author Studs Terkel should have interviewed Jack for his book *Working,* since Jack has had more careers than most of Terkel's subjects: a college president, professor, foundation president, blue-collar worker, labor economist, author of seven books, and now an innkeeper. All to satisfy his search for "the dignity of all human beings."

"I've never done anything in which I've used every resource I've got," he told me as we sat in the airy breakfast room drinking coffee. "But every experience I've had I'm drawing on now, and I need everything to make it through the day!" If it sounds as if Jack thinks innkeeping is difficult, he does. But, he also loves what he does: "The work is harder than anybody can possibly describe to you, and the satisfactions are greater than you can ever imagine."

Jack saw the potential of the original old dilapidated inn when he came to see it in 1985. A million dollars later, the once haggard-looking building has been restored to its present grand state. From the moment you enter the lobby, you feel a sense of peace. The inn is spacious, with polished hardwood floors and Oriental rugs. The very large lounge has a

huge stone fireplace and comfortable antique furnishings. Jack has a most interesting collection of books in the library, over 3,000, where you will most certainly want to relax by the firelight and share a good-night sherry.

One of the most unique areas of the inn is the upper floors that Jack has turned into a private museum. The thirty guest rooms have been decorated and named for fond memories or passions of his life. Some are named for cities he has called home. Others are named for the experiences he has had, or jobs he has held. His favorite authors, composers, and painters are also represented. For example, one set of adjoining compartments is named for Currier and Ives. "I gave Ives the bigger room because he always comes second," he laughed as we walked to the Grand Opera Room, where programs from some of his favorite operas line the walls.

Breakfast and dinner are eclectic and the domain of chef Mark Dickerson. Jack helps, of course, and served me a tasty chicken sauté with a spicy peanut sauce. My wife had baked salmon, with dilled Harvarti and Pernod cream, that was absolute heaven. Each entree includes salad with sourdough rolls. The Shaker lemon pie is luscious.

A Quaker, Jack believes that humility is an essential lesson of life that we all need to learn. Therefore, no task at the inn is beneath him. You may find him welcoming guests at the front door, taking their bags to their rooms, then scurrying down to the kitchen to whip on his green apron and sprinkle parsley into steaming bowls of split pea soup. As you leave, he'll be back at the front door, wishing you a safe trip and waving you off.

Visit The Inn at Long Last. Visit because it's a warm, comfortable, and gracious inn. But most important, visit for the joy of meeting Jack Coleman and taking part in the art of living.

THE INN AT LONG LAST, Chester, VT 05143; 802-875-2444. A 30-guestroom (mostly private baths) renovated Victorian country inn. Closed April and mid-Nov. All-size beds. Modified American plan. Historical area, tennis courts, swimming pool, fishing, golf. No pets (except goldfish in their own bowls). No smoking. Jack Coleman, Owner-host.

Directions: Head north on Rte. 91 in Vermont to Exit 6. Then go 9 mi. on Rte. 103 into Chester. Follow Rte. 11 west one block in Chester to the village green.

"European plan" means that rates for rooms and meals are separate. "American plan" means that meals are included in the cost of the room. "Modified American plan" means that breakfast and dinner are included in the cost of the room. The rates at some inns include a continental breakfast with the lodging.

INN AT SAWMILL FARM
West Dover, Vermont (1970)

It was mid-November. The southern Vermont sky was lowering, and all around me were signs and portents of snow. I was driving north from Dalton, Massachusetts, on Route 8A to the Mount Snow area in Wilmington, Vermont. This road goes through some most interesting northern Massachusetts and southern Vermont country with many villages. I was headed toward Sawmill Farm in West Dover, Vermont, and the reports on the radio indicated that snow was, indeed, on the way. Just imagine being snowbound at Sawmill Farm! Boy, oh boy!

With Wilmington behind me, I could now see the buildings of Sawmill Farm on my left. My last turn was over the bridge, which had been reconstructed since a previous visit.

I asked Rod Williams what he would do if all the guests were snowbound. "We would try to amuse them by getting everyone out to cross-country ski," he said. "If you can walk, you can cross-country ski. It's not like downhill. We can even start off with people who have never been on skis. Then we would organize picnics on the trails. We'd keep the fire in the fireplace going bigger and better than ever, and normally we would do tea at four o'clock, but on a snowbound day we start around one."

When Rod and Ione Williams made the "big break" from the pressures of urban life, they brought their own particular talents and sensitivities to this handsome location, and it is indeed a pleasing experience. There was plenty of work to do—a dilapidated barn, a wagon shed, and other outbuildings all had to be converted into lodgings and living rooms. However, over the years, the transition has been exceptional. The textures of the barn siding, the beams, the ceilings, the floors, and the picture windows combine to create a feeling of rural elegance.

Guest rooms have been both added and redecorated, and again I was smitten with the beautiful quilted bedspreads, the bright wallpaper and white ceilings, the profusion of plants in the rooms, and all of the many books and magazines that add to their guests' enjoyment. Lodgings are also found in outbuildings, including the Cider House Studio, which has a bedroom, dressing room, bath, and living room. The king-sized bed is in an alcove facing a fireplace.

In the living room of the inn there is a superb conversation piece that perhaps symbolizes the entire inn—a handsome brass telescope mounted on a tripod, providing an intimate view of Mount Snow rising majestically to the north.

Brill Williams, Rod and Ione's son, was a teenager when the family moved to West Dover. Now, he is the chef and officially one of the owners of the inn. The menu selection and quality of the food has been praised by

many national restaurant and food reviewers. The menu changes with the seasons; for example, the fall menu includes grilled marinated duck breasts, backfin crabmeat, fillet of salmon, and a rack of lamb for two. Appetizers include clams Casino, backfin crabmeat cocktail, and cold poached salmon.

With a picture-book Vermont setting like this, accommodations like these, and an almost inexhaustible supply of ideas for sumptuous dining, the idea of being snowbound at the Inn at Sawmill Farm certainly had a great deal of appeal for me.

INN AT SAWMILL FARM, Box 8, West Dover, VT 05356; 802-464-8131. A 21-guestroom (private baths) country resort-inn on Rte. 100, 22 mi. from Bennington and Brattleboro. All-size beds. Within sight of Mt. Snow ski area. Modified American plan omits lunch. Breakfast and dinner served to travelers daily. Closed Nov. 29 to Dec. 18. Swimming, tennis, and trout fishing on grounds. Golf, bicycles, riding, snowshoeing, alpine and xc skiing nearby. No children under 8. No pets. No credit cards. Rodney, Brill, and Ione Williams, Owners-hosts. (See Index for rates.)

Directions: From I-91, take Brattleboro Exit 2 and travel on Vt. Rte. 9 west to Vt. Rte. 100. Proceed north 5 mi. to inn. Or take U.S. 7 north to Bennington, then Rte. 9 east to Vt. Rte. 100 and proceed north 5 mi. to inn.

THE INN AT SOUTH NEWFANE
South Newfane, Vermont (1990)

I purposely skipped lunch in anticipation of the gourmet dinner I was going to enjoy at The Inn at South Newfane, located in the Currier and Ives village of South Newfane, Vermont. A very good friend had spent a wonderful weekend at the inn, and was still raving about chef Lisa Borst's catfish jambalaya. As I pulled in front of the 19th-century country manor house, my stomach was growling and I hoped Lisa was already busy in the kitchen.

Lisa's parents, Connie and Herb, opened The Inn at South Newfane in 1984, and it has since received high marks for its hospitality and excellent cuisine. The Federal-style home sits next to a natural spring-fed swimming pond on over 100 private acres. Wide lawns and manicured grounds invite strolling. The views to the surrounding Green Mountains are spectacular during all four seasons.

I had some time to explore before dinner, so I wandered through the first floor, beginning with the great room entry. The room is warm and comfortable, decorated in tones of antique gold. Well-stocked bookcases frame the windows and overstuffed chairs are available for quiet reading time. The more luxurious living room is just off the entry. Here, coffee is often served before a roaring fire after dinner. Both rooms are spacious and mostly furnished in antiques.

Antiques also adorn the six comfortable guest rooms. Extra pillows, firm mattresses, fluffy comforters, and handmade quilts make the beds islands of contentment. All the rooms have modern private baths with plenty of towels.

The afternoon was so lovely that I decided to spend the last predinner hour on the inn's old-fashioned porch with a glass of wine. I must say that there is nothing quite as relaxing as gently rocking on a porch while a slight breeze softens the air and cicadas sing. I could have fallen asleep, but my stomach kept reminding me of my mission.

Herb and Connie realize that, in addition to the bliss of porch sitting, eating is one of life's most divine pleasures. The inn's dining room is well known for its superb cuisine, which is French in style, but makes full use of local seasonal produce, some of which comes from the gardens behind the inn. Lisa is an award-winning CIA-trained chef and brings great energy and creativity to her work. "We don't use shortcuts here," she told me. "Everything is made from scratch daily, including all our pastries, breads, and desserts."

All entrees are prepared to order and are served with fresh garden vegetables, a unique rice dish, or potatoes or noodles. I chose baked Vermont goat cheese, with diced plum tomatoes in basil and capers, to begin my meal. The goat cheese was a lovely texture and the tomatoes had vine-ripened sweetness. I had difficulty choosing from the wonderful entrees, but finally decided on the roast loin of pork. The pork was succulent and juicy, and the creamy apple-wine sauce that was served alongside added just the right tang. The assorted goodies on the pastry table literally begged to be sampled, so I had two.

I took my cup of decaffeinated espresso to the informal "map room" to relax. Herb had opened the French doors onto the porch, and the scent of fresh cut grass drifted into the room. I couldn't have been happier.

Just before I climbed the staircase to bed, Lisa poked her head around the corner and said, "I'm making a special treat for breakfast— sticky buns!" I sighed, knowing I'd need to add at least five more laps to my morning swim.

THE INN AT SOUTH NEWFANE, Dover Rd., South Newfane, VT 05351; 802-348-7191. A 6-guestroom (private baths) turn-of-the-century manor house in the charming village of South Newfane. Closed 3 weeks in April and all of Nov. Queen and twin beds. Modified American plan. Swimming, hiking, skiing, antique shops, Marlboro Music Festival. No pets. Connie and Herb Borst, Owners-hosts.

Directions: From Brattleboro center, go north on Rte. 30 for 9 mi. Turn left at the Inn sign, and go 2 mi. through Williamsville. Go over covered bridge, and proceed for 1¼ mi.

The date in parenthesis in the heading represents the first year the inn appeared in the pages of Country Inns and Back Roads.

KEDRON VALLEY INN
S. Woodstock, Vermont (1990)

The stately Kedron Valley Inn has welcomed travelers since the 1820s, and is one of Vermont's oldest hotels. Innkeepers Max and Merrily Comins always longed for the country life but, coming from New York, were concerned about the lack of culture and access to interesting people that sometimes go hand-in-hand with a rural environment. After a two-year search, they found Kedron Valley, an inn that more than satisfied their needs. Located only five minutes from the famed retreat and artists' colony of Woodstock, the inn is set in the middle of 15 lovely acres of rolling foothills.

The main brick and clapboard buildings are excellent examples of Federal-style architecture, with expansive front porches. Colorful flowers overflow the porch-railing planter boxes. The third, more modern rustic log-cabin-style structure, is the perfect accommodation for guests who travel the inn-to-inn horseback riding tours in the summer and fall.

Merrily's family heritage is exhibited on guestroom beds and the inn's walls in the form of gorgeous heirloom quilts. The collection of forty-two quilts, in traditional patterns like *Grandmother's Flower Garden,* is one of the largest in Vermont. The eleven quilts from Merrily's family, two of which are more than 100 years old, are displayed with photographic histories of the women who made them.

The twenty-eight guest rooms are charmingly decorated with canopy beds, fireplaces and Franklin stoves, needlepoint rugs, and antiques or collectibles. Hand-stenciled walls adorn some rooms. A marvelous heirloom linen collection has recently been restored for guests' appreciation. Other collectibles, like a turn-of-the-century cotton-batiste dress, add interest to almost every corner. Two of the rooms have private decks, and one has its own airy veranda. All have televisions and private baths.

The living room, with its unusual horseshoe-shaped oak bar, is a warm and relaxing place to enjoy a prize-winning glass of wine. On Friday and Saturday nights, a pianist is seated at the baby-grand, and Max steps forward to sing your favorite tunes while a fire crackles in the background.

Dinner and breakfast are served in the dining room, on the spacious front porch, or on the recently completed al fresco dining patio, with its breathtaking view of the inn's exuberant perennial gardens.

I thoroughly enjoyed a sumptuous Sunday brunch on the porch, beginning with fresh muffins, juice, and coffee. Crisp waffles covered with juicy strawberries, along with some spicy sausages, followed. Pancakes and a daily special omelet, or eggs any style, are also available. Dinner can offer specialties such as grilled Vermont rack of lamb and chicken with peaches.

"How about some beachcombing?" Max teased, just after I had finished brunch. Well, he wasn't teasing. Kedron Inn has a most unusual feature: a clean, white sand beach—in the mountains! A refreshing, spring-fed lake is bordered by the private beach, where an on-duty lifeguard is available during the summer months. In addition to swimming and beach lounging, guests can take advantage of championship golf courses, tennis, and cross-country and downhill skiing, all within a 20-mile radius.

I took Max's suggestion and strolled the beach until I found a peaceful spot for sunning. When I'd wriggled the warm sand into the shape of my body, I closed my eyes and listened to the mesmerizing lap-lap of the lake water. My peace was pleasantly broken by Blondie, the Cominses' "love bug" of a golden retriever, as she tactfully dropped her tennis ball beside my head. Laughing, I sat up and heaved it into the lake, happy to be a guest at this wonderful country inn.

KEDRON VALLEY INN, Rte. 106, S. Woodstock, VT 05071; 802-457-1473. A 28-guestroom (private baths) country inn filled with heirloom quilts and antiques, only 5 mi. from the famed artists' colony of Woodstock. Closed April. Double, queen, and king-size beds. Modified American plan, or deduct for breakfast only. Close to skiing, golf, tennis. Private beach and lake with lifeguard. Pets on leash welcome. Merrily and Max Comins, Owners-hosts.

Directions: From I-89, take Rte. 4 west into Woodstock. Turn south on Rte. 106 and travel for 5 mi. The inn is on the right.

THE MIDDLEBURY INN
Middlebury, Vermont (1989)

The gaily striped yellow and white awnings and bright flowerbeds of this historic 162-year-old village inn add a festive feeling to the town square and green.

The three-story red brick Middlebury Inn, with its pristine white shutters, was erected on the site of a tavern built in 1794. The inn now stands in the center of the historic district and is listed on the National Register of Historic Places.

While I sat on the West Porch, enjoying my lunch of vichyssoise and a grilled Vermont cheddar cheese sandwich, I remembered that this was the home of Middlebury College, internationally renowned for its foreign language programs. It was fun to watch the clusters of students laughing and talking as they biked and walked and ran around the town. Across the street, near the bandstand, a blue and white tent was being set up for the early July week-long Festival on the Green, which features different events every day.

It had been some years since I visited the Middlebury Inn, and I was delighted to see what a fine job of refurbishing and redecoration Frank and Jane Emanuel had accomplished. The spacious lobby, done in shades of rose and burgundy, is warm and inviting, with several comfortable sitting areas furnished with antiques, a fireplace, and a handsome grandfather clock.

Jane Emanuel greeted me and introduced me to Aunt Kitty, who really is Frank's aunt, and who devotes herself to making guests feel at home. Frank had the great idea of calling her out of her retirement from a forty-year teaching career to come and help at the inn. She says her job is to "mix, mingle, and pour," and this delightful lady plays an important part in giving this inn its personal quality.

The day I was there, Frank was in Washington. In the eleven years that the Emanuels have had the inn, Frank has become very active in the hospitality industry, serving on committees and as a board member or an officer for various organizations. As Jane was holding down the fort that day, she took me in hand to show me the inn.

The Colonial blue of the walls, the collection of Flow Blue china on display, and the high windows of the formal dining room, called the Founders Room, provide an elegant setting for dinner. "We have a nightly buffet-style candlelight dinner, called the Carverie," Jane told me. "Our chef specializes in New England cuisine, and a very popular dish is our chilled strawberry soup."

I got a kick out of riding the vintage Otis elevator to the second floor and walking along the wide hallways that, as Jane put it, "wander and dip." The guest rooms I saw in the main inn were all pleasantly furnished with antique reproductions, restoration papers, private baths, books, magazines, and various amenities. There are additional rooms in the Porter Mansion and also in a contemporary motel building.

After returning to the first floor and peeking into the pine-paneled Morgan Tavern and the Country Peddler Cafe and Gift Shop, I took off for a walk with Aunt Kitty. We had a wonderful tour across the green and through the town. We explored the Vermont State Craft Center, watched the geese on Otter Creek, and even slipped into the church and eavesdropped on the organist, who was practicing. Then we headed back to the inn, where Aunt Kitty was due to serve High Tea.

Those sensitive to traffic noise should be aware that the inn is located on a busy road.

THE MIDDLEBURY INN, P.O. Box 798, 14 Courthouse Square, Route 7, Middlebury, VT 05753; 802-388-4961 or (toll-free) 800-842-4666. A 75-guestroom (private baths) historic village inn consisting of the main building, Porter Mansion, and a contemporary motel midway between Burlington and Rutland in the Champlain Valley. European plan. MAP and other packages available. Breakfast, lunch, tea, and dinner served to the public. Open year-round. Wheelchair access. Gift shop, arrangements for tours and other recreation, and mystery weekends on premises. Historic walking tours, antiquing, fairs, Vermont State Craft Center, Middlebury College, Morgan Horse Farm, Lake Dunmore, Fort Ticonderoga, Shelburne Museum; also golf, tennis, swimming, bicycling, hiking, downhill and xc skiing nearby. Frank and Jane Emanuel, Owners-hosts. (See Index for rates.)

Directions: Middlebury is accessible by major highways from all directions. The inn is located at junction of Rtes. 7 and 125.

THE MIDDLETOWN SPRINGS INN
Middletown Springs, Vermont (1982)

The Middletown Springs Inn is located on a picturesque green in the middle of this very quiet village. The green itself has a brave Civil War laddie on top of a pedestal and an American flag on a slightly bowed flagpole. These are protected by a cannon of some indefinite years. Around the square is the church and a nice Vermont home with a porte cochère, and across the way is a Federal-period brick house. The entire town is on the National Register of Historic Places.

The inn is an 1879 Victorian mansion, built at the time when Middletown Springs was quite a thriving place, mostly because of the springs that still bubble up. At one time the town's reputation for its water rivaled that of Saratoga Springs.

After a three-year search for an inn, Steve and Jane Sax are very happy with their choice. Jane showed me into the parlor with its impressive curved wall on the left of the central hall. This leads into the library, which is a little less formal, and then on into the large center music room with its grand piano.

A handsome carved stairway to the second floor reminds me of the one at the Mainstay Inn in Cape May, New Jersey. Again, there is a center hallway with antique-furnished guest rooms on either side. Terrycloth bathrobes are provided for rooms that have shared baths.

"We brought with us our collection of antique china, glassware, pewter, clocks, and furniture," Jane told me. "Even though the inn retained many of its antiques from previous owners, there was still enough room for our own treasures, including the pictures of my great-great-great-grandparents and their grandfather clock. We added two poster beds and some antique chairs and rockers.

"We've discovered that many guests enjoy our special-interest weekends featuring antique clocks in the spring, guided country walks and bicycle touring in the summer, hiking and antique collecting in the fall, and cross-country skiing and snowshoeing in the winter.

"Our big country kitchen is the heart of the inn," Steve said, "where all our guests find their way in the morning or evening. I am the chef and I make freshly baked bread, blueberry muffins and bubbling homemade soups. We also serve beef Victorian, baked stuffed haddock, and chicken Roquefort. Jane prepares the desserts, with rum torte and English Trifle being the house specialties. A morning favorite is our country breakfast of fruit, cereal, spiced German pancakes and locally produced Vermont maple syrup. We treat all our guests like company. Actually, we have a lot of fun presenting riddles and brain teasers along with our breakfast menu. Sometimes Jane has been known to write a limerick for and about the guests.

"We're always delighted to assist in planning the day's activities, arranging bike rentals and sharing our favorite meandering routes. Actually, we're located near some of the best hiking, biking, skiing, and picture-taking in New England, and there's lots of jogging and running, and cross-country or downhill skiing."

The Christmas holidays at the Middletown Springs Inn are most unusual, with sleigh rides, treasure hunts, a Victorian mystery, and gifts. Each evening features the food of a different country, and on the final evening, guests are encouraged to join the innkeepers in wearing Victorian costume.

THE MIDDLETOWN SPRINGS INN, Middletown Springs, VT 05757; 802-235-2198. A 10-guestroom (8 private baths) Victorian mansion on the green of a lovely 18th- and 19-century village. Queen, double, and twin beds available. Modified American plan includes full breakfast and dinner. B&B plan also available. Meals served to public by prior reservation. Open year-round; however, call in advance for reservations. Within easy driving distance of all central Vermont summer and winter recreation. Mt. Killington, state parks, summer theater, trout fishing, hiking, xc and alpine skiing, bicycling, horseback riding, swimming, golf, tennis nearby. Not suitable for young children. No pets. Jane and Steve Sax, Owners-hosts. (See Index for rates.)

Directions: From Manchester Center, Vt., follow Rte. 30 to Pawlet and turn north on Rte. 133 to Middletown Springs. From Poultney, Vt., follow Rte. 140 to East Poultney and on to Middletown Springs.

MOUNTAIN TOP INN
Chittenden, Vermont (1987)

The first time I visited Mountain Top it was an exceptionally brilliant winter's day; the sky couldn't have been bluer, and the sun on the freshly fallen snow made the road up the mountain positively dazzling. As I pulled into the parking lot in front of the inn, I could hear the sound of sleigh bells, and, sure enough, along the country road came some guests in a horse-drawn sleigh, which was later to carry me to the maple sugar house, where the inn's syrup is boiled down. Particularly in evidence were the skating rink, toboggan hill, and cross-country ski facilities, where there were dozens of skiers of all ages.

On the occasion of my second visit, I went up this very same Vermont road, and the trees, which before had been delicately mantled in snow, now formed a green, arched canopy, and the farms and meadows blended into a midsummer's idyll.

Inside Mountain Top Inn, I gazed in wonderment through the two-story staircase window at the sweeping view of a beautiful lake, where inn guests were canoeing, sailing, and swimming.

"Mount Carmel is the high peak over there," innkeeper Bill Wolfe commented. "There are hiking trails, and that is a five-hole golf course you're looking at."

"We've enlarged things considerably," Bill told me. "Cross-country skiing has really come into its own, and we have 110 kilometers of trails and state-of-the-art grooming equipment, which makes them among the finest anywhere in the world. Our ski shop is in a former barn and has snowshoe furniture and wood-burning stoves. We have an excellent staff of instructors also."

Bill and I continued our tour of the inn, and I noticed how nicely the country inn atmosphere comes across in the guest rooms, which have reproductions of antiques, very pleasant quilts, quilted wall hangings, and Shaker-style rockers.

Bill told me that the horseback riding program has been very popular. "We are the only resort that I know of with riding and cross-country skiing included in our rate."

Mountain Top is a deftly orchestrated example of how a country-inn experience can also include a great deal of entertainment and enjoyment for outdoor-minded guests of all ages. With fifty guest rooms it is somewhat larger than the average New England inn included in this book; however, thanks to innkeeper Wolfe, there is a good personal rapport among the staff and the guests.

The modified American plan offers truly gargantuan menus, most of which are very hearty country fare although the kitchen is often inconsistent.

Among all the helpful literature is a booklet called "Get Lost in Vermont . . ." with maps and many suggestions for trips to nearby historic and natural attractions. Above and beyond all the possibilities for recreation and diversion, I think the chance to walk to secluded spots where beavers have built lodges in mountain ponds helps make Mountain Top a special place.

MOUNTAIN TOP INN, Mountain Top Rd., Chittenden, VT 05737; 802-483-2311 or 800-445-2100. A 33-guestroom (private baths) four-season resort-inn located in the Green Mountains, between Middlebury and Rutland. Cottages and chalets nearby. Various guestroom categories. Modified American plan. Open year-round. Wheelchair access. Sailing, canoeing, fishing, swimming, horseback riding, tennis, golf, walking, hiking, xc skiing, ice skating, toboggans, horse-drawn sleigh rides, and lawn games all available at no additional cost. Many nearby historical and cultural attractions. Special attention for children. William Wolfe, Owner-host. (See Index for rates.)

Directions: Chittenden is north of Rte. 4 and east of Rte. 7. After arriving in the village, turn left at the little bridge and stay to the right of the war monument. This is Mountain Top Rd.; follow it up the mountain and to the inn.

OCTOBER COUNTRY INN
Bridgewater Corners, Vermont (1990)

Richard Sims and Patrick Runkel came to the October Country Inn by a rather circuitous route. As a travel agency manager, Richard became intrigued with the idea of purchasing an inn. Since they both love to scuba dive, why not open an inn in the Caribbean? So, Richard took off to St. Kitts, Antigua, and St. Lucia, and Patrick began working in a restaurant and at a gourmet catering business to prepare himself for the eventual career change.

Unfortunately, what initially sounded quite simple became a bit more complicated, and the two moved their search to the United States, eventually settling in Vermont. After countless hours "pressing our noses against innumerable windows," they finally found the October Country Inn.

Located just 8 miles from the quaint village of Woodstock, the rambling, mid-19th-century New England clapboard farmhouse sits on a hillside on 5 acres. Two airy porches, complete with rocking chairs, and a large flower-framed deck tempt guests to laze away an afternoon. Although civilization is near, the area feels wonderfully rural. There's even a delightful country store only a short walk from the inn.

Indoors, the comfortable living room, with its cozy overstuffed furniture, has a fireplace at one end and a charming pot-bellied stove at the other. It's a great place to relax and peruse the inn's eclectic selection of books. I spent an engrossing evening with E. L. Doctorow, while one of the other guests giggled her way through Gary Larson's humorous view of the world. A variety of interesting games are also available. An unusual art collection, some of it local work, decorates the walls.

Richard and Patrick are gregarious hosts and encourage guests to feel at home. "We want our guests to be comfortable, satisfied, and content," Patrick told me. The whole style of the inn conveys a homey feeling. The ten guest rooms are airy and restful, decorated in off-white, pale green, and touches of blue and pink. Two of the rooms have hand stenciling. The beds are comfortable, with new mattresses, and the bathrooms, eight private and two shared, are clean and basic.

In this wonderful family farmhouse atmosphere, I ate one of the most unexpected and memorable meals I have had. The inn specializes in unusual ethnic cuisine, with Patrick conjuring up whatever country's cuisine inspires him. I was served an exotic African menu that began with a flavorful chicken peanut soup. It was followed by tajine of lamb and green beans, traditional couscous, spiced vegetables, vegetarian spiced lentils, a cooling cucumber and yogurt salad, and rich date-nut cakes with orange custard sauce. The pairing of distinctive flavors and textures was a real treat to the palate. The inn has a full liquor license, and just the right wine, beer, or ale is available to accompany the meal. Richard told me that guests often linger after these feasts, laughing and swapping stories until long after the last plate has been washed.

Breakfast starts with a buffet of homemade granola, fresh fruits, juices, and toast. A selection of muffins are then served along with a hot dish, like scrambled eggs with Vermont cheddar cheese.

I enjoyed reading some of the entries in the inn's colorfully illustrated guest book, and added my own compliments and a laughable drawing of Zoe, the resident cat. Comments like "the food is out of this world," and "we're back, and enjoying it even more," and from a seven-year old, "thank you very much for making our family feel like at home," confirmed my conclusion that this is a very special inn.

OCTOBER COUNTRY INN, Box 66, Upper Rd., Bridgewater Corners, VT 05035; 802-672-3412. A 10-guestroom (8 private baths) 19th-century farmhouse inn on 5 acres, 8 mi. from Woodstock. Closed April and part of Nov. Modified American plan. Double and twin beds. Close to all winter and summer sports. No pets. Richard Sims and Patrick Runkel, Owners-hosts.

Directions: From Woodstock, travel 8 mi. to junction with 100A. Continue for another 100 yards and take first right. At fork in the road, turn right again. Go up the hill. The inn is the second house on the left.

"European plan" means that rates for rooms and meals are separate. "American plan" means that meals are included in the cost of the room. "Modified American plan" means that breakfast and dinner are included in the cost of the room. The rates at some inns include a continental breakfast with the lodging.

RABBIT HILL INN
Lower Waterford, Vermont (1990)

Just above the Connecticut River in the hamlet of Lower Waterford, Vermont, Rabbit Hill Inn rests amid the steepled church, the 150-year-old tiny post office, honor-system library, and cluster of restored homes. The village has remained virtually unchanged for more than 150 years. Lower Waterford is one of the most picturesque, and hence photographed, villages in Vermont. The location takes advantage of the spectacular views of the White Mountains and accompanying outdoor sports, including fishing, sailing, canoeing, nature walking, mountain climbing, and downhill and cross-country skiing.

The inn boasts two wonderfully restored buildings, originally built in 1795 and 1825. Wide pine floor boards, five spacious porches, and eight fireplaces accompany antique and reproduction furnishings. As you arrive, you are welcomed into the Federal-period parlor for a full high tea, which includes freshly baked pastries such as scones slathered with fresh whipped cream and preserves.

"Our commitment to this beautiful old inn, to our guests, to our staff, and to our presentation, is tremendous," innkeeper Maureen Magee told me. "But with all this effort, we still have a creak in the fifth stair!" she laughed, showing me to my room. Each of the eighteen guest rooms has a special theme to the decor: hat boxes and bonnets, reproduction wooden toys, or antique letters. My room's particular motif was based on the life of a 1900s woman named Clara. You can choose from king, queen, and double beds, most with canopies. Twin beds are also available. All rooms have private baths.

Guests may congregate for conversation and relaxation in the Federal-period parlor, the After-Sports Lounge, or the Library Nook. A television, VCR, and small video library are available, and chamber music concerts take place almost every evening. A large selection of musical tapes has been recorded for guests to use with their in-room radio-cassette players. Lawn games inspire healthy competition, and guests may choose to venture out on snowshoes or toboggans in the winter, or canoes in the summer.

Breakfast, dinner, and high tea are all included in the room rate. Dinner is outstanding, offering five courses superbly prepared by chef Bob Reney, who was trained in the European tradition. Maureen seated me in the lovely candlelit setting, then quietly disappeared. As I enjoyed my appetizer of chicken and smoked cheddar cheese in puff pastry, salad of garden lettuce, and entree of steak Elizabeth—a filet mignon wrapped in bacon and topped with shrimp—I was pleasantly surprised to hear Maureen, in another role, that of flutist, as she unobtrusively entertained from the next room!

Breakfast offers juice, homemade granola, rice pudding, cobblers, homemade donuts, an egg dish, or pancakes and French toast. "We often concoct our special breakfast treat, a Rabbit Hill banana split. Its made with yogurt or whipped cream cheese, granola, and fresh fruit," John Magee told me as we sipped our first cup of fresh roast coffee. "You know, people who have stayed here have given us wonderful memories. One of the best was the couple who fell asleep on the second-floor porch, and remained there all night!"

During an after-breakfast stroll to the freshwater lake nearby, I was accompanied by Hershey, the Magee's collie/shepherd mix. "He's quiet and slow moving," Maureen warned me, "but he's a superb listener." That was just the sort of companion I needed. Apparently many love this place as I did. As Emerson said, "The ornament of a house is the friends who frequent it." From the guest entries in the room diaries, Rabbit Hill has been exquisitely ornamented.

RABBIT HILL INN, Rte. 18, Lower Waterford, VT; 802-748-5168. An 18-guestroom (private baths) restored country inn in one of the most photo-graphed villages in Vermont. Closed April and the first 2 weeks in Nov. Modified American plan; includes high tea. Evening chamber music concerts. Hiking, swimming, boating, summer hayrides, xc skiing. Warmly hospitable. No pets. John and Maureen Magee, Owners-hosts.

Directions: From I-91, take Exit 19, then Exit 1 onto Rte. 18 south. From I-93, take Exit 44, Rte. 18 junction; turn north (left) on Rte. 18.

ROWELL'S INN
Simonsville, Vermont (1985)

"How do you make apple pie?" It was a natural question because as soon as I walked through the front door the delicious aroma of baking apples had enticed me through the downstairs hallway and the dining room, with its alternate floorboards of cherry and maple, and into the kitchen where Beth Davis was taking three more pies from the oven.

Without missing a beat, she said, "I make it with a crumb crust, and the filling is my grandmother's recipe. Maybe we can have a piece a little later on."

What an inn kitchen! It's just the kind of a place that guests cannot resist. Fortunately, Beth enjoys their company and is still able to perform all of her varied culinary tasks. There were cookies in a cookie jar, bread cooling, a jar of cinnamon sticks, a long string of pepper pods, bunches of garlic, a little sign that says "Kiss the Cook," an old cabinet with many cookbooks, a big old refrigerator with four doors and jars on the top that said "Apple butter," "Relish," and "Jam." There was everything the accomplished cook needs, within arm's length.

Meanwhile, Lee Davis came down from the second floor where he had been finishing redoing the guest rooms, and we stepped from the kitchen into the Tavern Room, which has all kinds of wonderful things on the walls and tables. There was another old-fashioned refrigerator, not with ice in it, but jampacked with books. There were dried flowers, duck decoys, a moose head, a piano, a mounted fish, all kinds of magazines, a checker game, a big copper pot for holding firewood, and a shoeshine chair. I made a mental note to ask Lee where it came from. There was a present-day cast iron stove, which was radiating heat all over this room and adjacent rooms. The Tavern also has an old-fashioned soda fountain

and a collection of syrup dispensers. There's a big tray of peanuts for shelling. Isn't it interesting that one never forgets how to shell peanuts? I went back into the kitchen and asked Beth, "What's for dinner tonight?" She said, "We're going to start out with mushroom strudel, potato and leek soup, orange and grape salad on fresh greens with a homemade dressing, our own bread, beef tenderloin, new potatoes with dill sauce on them, broccoli and cheese—we use a Vermont cheddar. The dessert will be that apple pie with ice cream. We always have a five-course dinner."

Rowell's Inn is an authentic historic inn, built for that purpose in 1820 by Major Simons, who was the founder of the village, located at a bend in Route 11, across from Lyman Brook. This handsome red brick building, with the highly distinctive wooden porches added to the front, is on the National Register of Historic Places. The five guest rooms are furnished in the tradition of the inn's prosperous past, as are the front parlors.

Lee is very proud of the new sun room, just off the dining room and the kitchen. "Our guests are able to enjoy sitting by the fire on a cool morning and yet feel the warmth of the sun while they enjoy coffee or, in the late afternoon, have a cup of hot chocolate or another refreshing drink. They can look out the windows and see all the natural beauty."

As I was leaving, I asked Beth about Christmas at Rowell's Inn. "Well, we start pretty early, along about the 11th or 12th of December, when our inn guests come, and the men go out and cut the trees and the women stay home and pop popcorn and string cranberries. We decorate both trees, one for the sun room and one for the living room. We don't have guests on Christmas Eve, but we do leave the Christmas decorations up through Valentine's Day at the request of our guests."

Everybody was gathered on the porch saying goodbye and I tiptoed back into the kitchen, and as quiet as a mouse I opened the cookie jar and took out one delicious sugar cookie.

ROWELL'S INN, RR 1 Box 269, Simonsville, VT, 05143; 802-875-3658. A 5-guestroom (private baths) inn in the mountains of central Vermont. Modified American plan with 2-day minimum on weekends. Bed and breakfast also available midweek. Dinner is served by request to houseguests only. Closed 3 wks. in April and 1 wk. in Nov. Convenient to all the cultural, recreational, and historic attractions in the area, including, hiking, biking, trail riding, golf, tennis, fishing, theaters, downhill and xc skiing. Children over 12 welcome. No pets. No credit cards. Beth and Lee Davis, Owners-hosts. (See Index for rates.)

Directions: Rowell's Inn is between Chester and Londonderry on Rte. 11.

SHIRE INN
Chelsea, Vermont (1986)

If the word "idyllic" had not already been created, I would certainly have invented it myself just to describe this bucolic scene.

Standing on a sturdy wooden bridge immediately behind the Shire Inn, gazing down on a branch of the White River below, I caught the flash of a trout slipping through the cool, rushing waters. Some early owner of the house so appreciated this scene, he placed a bench long enough to hold eight people here on the bridge.

I had just driven through some exceptionally beautiful Vermont country, following Route 14 north from Lebanon, alongside the White River, to Chelsea. The village is listed on the National Register of Historic Places, and has two commons and several early-18th-century homes and buildings.

Built of Vermont brick in 1832 and surrounded on all sides by gardens and lawns, the Shire Inn, with its fanlight doorway and black shutters, is certainly one of the most attractive of these historic homes.

The entrance hallway is dominated by a handsome circular staircase. On one side of this hallway is a most comfortable living room with deep chairs and sofas, as well as lots and lots of books. "This is the gathering room for our guests," remarked Mary Lee Papa, who with her husband, James, is the innkeeper.

"We're open year around," James told me, "and it's a good base from which guests can explore the variety of recreational and cultural opportunities that abound up here in this area. We've got good cross-country skiing here in Chelsea—actually, right from our own backyard. There's also downhill skiing at the Sonnenberg Ski Area near Woodstock, and there's hiking and bicycling in fair weather, as well as swimming and boating in the summer, and skating in the winter on Lake Fairlee."

The six guest rooms are most attractively furnished and four of them have working fireplaces. Mary Lee referred to the one on the right side of the entranceway as "our toasty room, because the boiler is just underneath." Upstairs, there are two high-ceilinged rooms with fireplaces on the front, one with a delightful canopy bed. Each has a little sign that says, "Good night, rest well. Breakfast at 8:30." Another has a spool bed and ruffled curtains. Very pleasant country bedspreads and comforters are found in each of the guest rooms, and all the beds have triple sheets. The beautiful "pumpkin pine" floorboards have been brought back to their lovely natural finish. All the guest rooms, named after Vermont counties, have a bountiful supply of books and magazines, but each has its own distinctive quality.

Breakfasts are really almost beyond description. There are three courses, and the emphasis is on fruits of all kinds, including baked fruits,

as well as all kinds of pancakes and homemade breads. There is also a cream cheese omelet, now and then, served with mint.

Dinner could include scallops in a caraway sauce, veal in vermouth sauce, chicken in a spice or curry sauce, pork chops with caraway stuffing, or fillet of sole in wine. For dessert there might be fresh blueberry pie or an amaretto mousse, chocolate-brandy cake, a grasshopper mousse, or chocolate cheese cake.

You will, as I did, have some fun getting there and after you arrive, I hope you'll agree with me that Chelsea and the Shire Inn have just the kind of withdrawn New England atmosphere that you hoped to find.

SHIRE INN, Chelsea, VT 05038; 802-685-3031. A 6-guestroom (private baths) village inn in a beautiful central Vermont setting. Open all year with a vacation break in Nov. and Apr. Breakfast included in room rate. Evening meal available by advance reservation. Bicycles available. The Justin Morgan horse farm, the Joseph Smith memorial, xc and downhill skiing, fishing, swimming, boating, and walking nearby. No children under 8. No pets. No smoking. James and Mary Lee Papa, Owners-hosts. (See Index for rates.)

Directions: From I-89 use Exit 2, proceed west on Rte. 14, then northward on Rte. 110 to Chelsea. From 1-91, take Exit 14 and turn left on Rte. 113 proceeding northwest to Chelsea. Both of these roads are extremely picturesque.

THREE MOUNTAIN INN
Jamaica, Vermont (1982)

Here I was once again sitting on that very comfortable couch in front of that tremendously impressive huge fireplace at Charles and Elaine Murray's Three Mountain Inn, talking with Sarah, another teenage Murray beauty. I'd been smitten with her sister Claire some years earlier. Claire is now in graduate school in California in international policy studies, and Sarah is a junior at Cushing Academy. "When I'm home I help out with serving and other things," she informed me.

"What sort of other things?" I inquired, charmed by her irrepressible enthusiasm. "Well, one of the things our guests really seem to appreciate," she replied, "is all the help we give them in finding their way around. We have our own detailed map showing all the surrounding villages and back roads, where to see the best views, crafts and antiques shops, Morgan horses, old cemeteries, fishing, wonderful cross-country and hiking trails . . ." She got a copy of the map to show me. "This trail is only four blocks from here. It wanders along the West River and then climbs to a spectacular waterfall where three natural pools cascade down into each other—it's very dramatic. This is a great area for walking and running as well as for skiing."

"Do you ski a lot?" I asked. "Oh, yes I'm a ski instructor at Stratton." That reminded me that Three Mountain Inn is close to three famous ski areas: Stratton, Bromley, and Magic.

"Our guests seem to like to do all kinds of things, but they always say how relaxed they feel here—it's casual and comfortable and they do like our lovely landscaped pool." She gave me a dazzling smile and said very confidentially, "I think it's really romantic, don't you?" "In what way?" I asked, mesmerized. "Well, tucked away in this tiny village, it's so cozy. It was built in the 1780s, and it has the original Dutch oven in this fireplace and the wide-plank pine walls and floors. The bedrooms are so pretty, with four-poster beds, comforters, and flowered wallpaper. I think both our little dining rooms are romantic, with their fireplaces and the pretty table settings, don't you agree?" Yes, I did agree.

There are additional guest rooms next door in Robinson House and also in Sage Hill House, a small farmhouse across the street that has kitchen facilities and can sleep four to seven people.

Sarah and I put our heads together over the menu, and she was glowingly complimentary about her mother's cooking, which features freshly baked breads and desserts, as well as Elaine's own salad dressing. Some menu favorites are trout amandine, scallops maison, chicken paprikash, carrot vichy soup, and butter pecan ice cream pie with hot caramel pecan topping. Guests have a choice of several appetizers and entrées, as well as three or four great desserts.

"Last year my mother and father celebrated their tenth year at Three Mountain Inn," Sarah exclaimed. "That means you were a very little girl when you first came here," I answered. "Yes, I grew up at the inn," she said.

Not only have Elaine and Charles raised three lovely daughters (I hope to meet Kelley, their oldest), but they have created a warm, welcoming environment where guests feel well taken care of. What more could anyone ask?

THREE MOUNTAIN INN, Rte. 30, Jamaica, VT 05343; 802-874-4140. An 18-guestroom (14 private baths) inn (some rooms in adjacent houses) located in a pleasant village in southern Vermont. All-size beds. Modified American plan (rates include breakfast and dinner). Dinners also served to travelers nightly except Wed. Closed Apr. 15 to May 15; Labor Day to Sept. 10. Swimming pool on grounds. Tennis, golf, fishing, horseback riding, nature walks and hiking trails in Jamaica State Park, downhill and xc skiing, Marlboro Music Festival, Weston Playhouse, all within a short drive. No pets. No credit cards. Charles and Elaine Murray, Owners-hosts. (See Index for rates.)

Directions: Jamaica is located on Rte. 30, which runs across Vermont from Manchester (U.S. 7) to Brattleboro (I-91).

The date in parenthesis in the heading represents the first year the inn appeared in the pages of Country Inns and Back Roads.

TULIP TREE INN
Chittenden, Vermont (1990)

Like the town crier, innkeeper Ed McDowell announces breakfast and dinner at the Tulip Tree Inn by ringing a bell and, in a resonate baritone, descriptively recites the menu. Does this sound a bit dramatic? Well, that's only one of the dramatic roles Ed plays as owner-host. "I never get sick of being the host because that's the fun of the job. If you want to hide out, what's the sense of being an innkeeper?" He and his wife, Rosemary, left New York City, where Ed owned a taxi and limousine service, and Rosemary worked for the Carnegie Foundation, to open a country inn in Vermont.

Ed's wonderful sense of humor is infectious. With a theater background, he is no stranger to storytelling, and willingly spins yarns while guests lounge on comfortable couches around the huge stone fireplace in the spacious sitting room. Windowed on three sides, you feel as if you are sitting outdoors. A comfortable living room and a small library/pub are also available for guests. The pub has a wide selection of imported beers including stout, spirits, and wines.

Nestled in the Green Mountain National Forest, the Tulip Tree is an ideal example of what you expect from a country inn. Built as a farmhouse in 1842 and purchased by Thomas Barstow, a wealthy collaborator of Thomas Edison in the early 1900s, the serene forest-green house, with its crisp white shutters and trim and airy porch, could be a model for a picture postcard.

This inn is one of my favorites. Although its location inspires solitude, Ed and Rosemary make certain you're never bored or lonely. In fact, from the moment Ed greets you and personally shows you to your room, you will be entertained, by the McDowells, their playful shag of a sheep dog, Guinness, or the other charming guests.

The eight guest rooms vary in size, but are all warm and cozy. Tucked under the fluffy French print comforter of my oak four-poster, I fell asleep listening to the sound of the river drifting through my open bay window. The McDowells have made every effort to decorate the rooms authentically, and have purchased New England-made braided rugs and furniture. All guest rooms have private baths, some with Jacuzzis.

Two of the guests staying at the inn had hiked in along the Long Trail, a network of Vermont hiking trails linking country inns. In the afternoon I joined them for a soak in the common-use hot tub and enjoyed hearing about their trail adventures.

Breakfast and dinner are included in the price of the rooms, and are Rosemary's specialty. Both excellent gourmet meals are served in the pleasant dining room, where everyone sits communally at two or three large tables set with tasteful china and silverware, and glasses for water, wine, and an after-dinner sherry or liqueur.

Our dinner began with a lovely hot curried carrot soup, swirled with tangy plain yogurt. The color alone was heavenly. The soup was followed by a crisp green salad with juicy sections of ripe tomato, Vermont cider sorbet, strips of succulent veal in white wine and cream, tender egg noodles, steamed broccoli, and a luscious dessert of pumpkin cheesecake with warm Vermont maple syrup. Breakfast is just as appetizing.

After dinner, I took my glass of sherry and joined some of the other guests in the living room, only to be met by a reproachful-looking Andrew Carnegie staring down from his portrait on the wall. Had he seen how much I'd eaten? I didn't care. I was happy, contented, and ready for an evening of Ed's storytelling.

TULIP TREE INN, Chittenden Dam Rd., Chittenden, VT 05737; 802-483-6213. An 8-guestroom (private baths), lovely, small country inn nestled in the Green Mt. National Forest. Open Memorial Day weekend thru end of March. Queen, double, and twin beds. Modified American plan. Hiking, fishing, and xc skiing at the doorstep. Ed and Rosemary McDowell, Owners-hosts.

Directions: From Rutland, Vt., go north on Rte. 7. Just past the red brick power station on the left, watch for a red country store. Keep right of the store, and go approximately 6 mi. Just past the fire station, go straight ½ mi. The inn is on your left.

"European plan" means that rates for rooms and meals are separate. "American plan" means that meals are included in the cost of the room. "Modified American plan" means that breakfast and dinner are included in the cost of the room. The rates at some inns include a continental breakfast with the lodging.

VERMONT MARBLE INN
Fair Haven, Vermont (1990)

What do three people who had careers in the fields of insurance, cab driving, and machine tools have in common? What they have in common is a desire to provide excellent service to the public by doing whatever it takes to make the customer happy. Another thing they have in common is the Vermont Marble Inn.

Innkeepers Shirley Stein and Bea and Richard Taube used to live and work in New York City. In 1986, the three decided to open a country inn and leave the big city life behind. Why did they make this decision? "That's a very good question!" laughed Bea. "Sometimes I think we were out of our minds."

Looking for an appropriate inn proved time consuming, but ultimately worth the trouble. "We were looking for a mansion," Shirley remarked, "but we were never looking for anything this grand." Bea and Richard agreed. "There are mansions, and then there are *mansions.*"

The splendid, delicately veined, golden Vermont marble-block mansion was built in 1867 by Ira C. Allen, reportedly a member of the renowned Ethan Allen family. The main mass is almost square, with two and one-half stories and a mansard roof surmounted by an elaborate cupola. A wonderful example of Second Empire Italianate Victorian styling, the home has seven chandeliers suspended from imposingly high ceilings, elaborate plasterwork decoration, carved marble fireplaces, and an Art Deco suite that was added in the 1930s.

Immediately upon entering the heavy walnut doors, one is enfolded in luxury. Comfortable furnishings in the double parlors are grouped around the fireplaces for easy conversation. Wing-back chairs in the cozy library encourage evening reading.

The fourteen beautifully decorated guest rooms, named after the owners' favorite poets, are romantic and luxurious. Some of the rooms are complemented with high, four-poster queen-size beds, draped with antique hand-crocheted lace curtains, while others have wood-burning fireplaces. All have lush linens and private baths.

Past the towering staircase and down the long hallway are the inn's two dining rooms. One overlooks the 5 acres of tastefully landscaped grounds with its delightful herb garden, while the other, more formal room, displays an elaborate ceiling of papier-mâché and plaster, cast in a design of fruit bordered with grape leaves.

Within these two dining rooms you will be served with what chef Donald Goodman calls gourmet American, which according to Don means "that I can take different styles from Italy or France, everywhere, and apply them to regional American concepts using ingredients indigenous to New England."

Although the main dining room is small, barely ten tables, it is charming and gracious. The goblets sparkle, as does the elaborate crystal chandelier overhead, and the entire ambience reflects Victorian elegance. Small details distinguish the Vermont Marble Inn from its competitors, like chilled salad forks, and tart, homemade lemon sorbet between courses to clear the palate. You may choose to begin with an appetizer of pungent duck soup, or a rich bacon, potato, and bell pepper chowder. Each entree on the menu is handled in an innovative way. The roast tenderloin of pork with a grain mustard sauce and fresh tomato chutney served on tender snow peas was exceptional. Your complimentary breakfast is Shirley's specialty.

Shirley, Bea, and Richard will make your stay memorable. "We want to pamper a guest so they can't walk out, they have to be carried," quipped Shirley. As I left, I wondered if she saw my knees wobble while I walked down the drive.

VERMONT MARBLE INN, 12 West Park Pl., Fair Haven, VT 05743; 802-265-8383. A 14-guestroom (private baths) mansion located on the town green in Fair Haven. Open all year. Continental breakfast. Gourmet dinner available. A short drive from one of the largest ski areas in the East, golf, tennis, fishing, hiking, and horseback riding. Bea and Richard Taube, and Shirley Stein, Owners-hosts.

Directions: From N.Y., take State Thruway to Exit 24 to Northway, to Exit 20. Then take Rte. 149 east to Rte. 4; then go north to Exit 2. Follow sign to Fair Haven. From Boston, take Rte. 93 north to Rte. 89; then go north to Rte. 4 west (sign reads to Rutland), to Exit 3. Follow signs to Fair Haven.

WEST MOUNTAIN INN
Arlington, Vermont (1984)

It's not often (probably never) that a quiet, secluded country inn has helicopters hovering overhead and swarms of reporters and photographers lurking in the bushes. But that was definitely the scene on a weekend one July, all because actors Michael J. Fox and Tracy Pollan decided to hold their small, private wedding at the West Mountain Inn. "We were honored they decided to get married here," Wes Carlson said afterward. "It was crazy, but a lot of fun."

As if that weren't enough excitement for one inn, Mary Ann and Wes celebrated their tenth anniversary as innkeepers in June with 250 other people, balloons, music, and a barbecue. Before that, Wes completed their long-time dream of a two-story addition on the south side of the inn, which gives them a larger dining room and two beautiful suites.

Both Wes and Mary Ann personify the very highest spirit of innkeeping. As Mary Ann explained it to me while we were walking through the snow to see some of the animals: "I think we are all gathered together as one people living on a beautiful planet and we would like to share our part of it with other people.

"Wes likes to feel that he is involved in international peace and love, so our animals are from all over the world. There are dwarf rabbits from the Netherlands, African pigmy goats, and Peruvian llamas. Wes is getting serious about building his llama herd. Our new baby, Annadonna, is a year old, and we are planning to buy more llamas. We also have assorted artifacts from around the world, including nutcrackers from

Germany and Holland, and a collection of Norwegian trolls in our library area. A small collection of African crafts is in the Daniel Webster Room. We like to think of ourselves as including everyone and wanting everyone to be here."

As we walked back across the snow, I noted the wonderful view, looking right down to the Battenkill River, out through the valley, and over to the Green Mountains. Mary Ann told me more than twenty-five species of birds visit here throughout the year, and I enjoyed seeing the birds fluttering around the many bird feeders.

There is a wide variety of outside diversions on the 150 acres of meadows and hills, where wilderness trails abound. The cross-country ski trails have been extended considerably, especially with the novice skier in mind. The area is famous for its fishing, and there is canoeing on the Battenkill.

The guest rooms are in many sizes and shapes: some with outside porches, one with a working fireplace, one with a bedloft for children, two with high, pine-paneled cathedral ceilings, and all attractively and comfortably furnished. There is a room on the first floor equipped for disabled persons.

"We've named our guest rooms for Robert Frost, Norman Rockwell, and Rockwell Kent," Mary Ann told me. "These, and others, are people who lived in the area or had some significance here. We have rooms named after Governor Chittenden, Ethan and Ira Allen, and Dorothy Canfield Fisher, a wonderful author. We have a room with about fifty of her books. There is also a room named after Carl Ruggles, a wonderful gentleman who lived here in the 1950s. He was an avant-garde composer, and not too many people played his music because it was discordant."

There's more to a good inn than food, facilities, and atmosphere. The West Mountain Inn has all of these plus a highly commendable *esprit*.

WEST MOUNTAIN INN, Arlington, VT 05250; 802-375-6516. A 13-guestroom (private baths) comfortable hilltop country estate with a view of the Green Mountains. All-size beds. Modified American plan. Breakfast and dinner served to travelers daily. Open year-round. Wheelchair access. Swimming, canoeing, hiking, fishing, nature walks, xc skiing, and tobogganing on grounds. Special weekend programs from time to time; call for information. Children welcome. No pets. Mary Ann and Wes Carlson, Owners-hosts. (See Index for rates.)

Directions: Take Rte. 7 or Historic Rte. 7A to Arlington. Follow signs for West Mountain Inn, ½ mi. west on Rte. 313; bear left after crossing bridge.

WINDHAM HILL INN
West Townshend, Vermont (1989)

"Aren't you lucky!" I exclaimed. Linda and Ken Busteed were showing me some of the wonderful treasures they had found in the attic, trunkloads of memorabilia and all kinds of furnishings that belonged to the Lawrence family, the original 1825 homesteaders and owners of the house. "We found that quilt in the attic," Linda said, pointing to a beautiful antique quilt hanging on the wall in the Wicker Room.

"William and Matilda Lawrence had twelve children," Ken took up the story, "and Miss Kate was the last of the Lawrences. She farmed the land until she died in her mid-eighties in the late 1950s."

This rambling old farmhouse, perched on a remote hillside with spectacular views of the West River Valley and the eastern edge of the Green Mountains, was turned into an inn a few years before Ken and Linda bought it in 1982. They have since created a most delightful, truly country inn, simply but fetchingly furnished and decorated with country fabrics, many antique pieces, and all sorts of interesting touches, such as Linda's collection of antique high-button shoes (the handmade white calf wedding shoes are captivating). Three sitting rooms allows you to join guests or be alone.

While we were chatting in the cheerful, floral Wicker Room, a guest came to tell us there was a deer in the yard, and we all rushed to the parlor window to look. Sure enough, there was the big, beautiful creature grazing on the lawn and not at all concerned about the two wood sculptures of black and white Herefords standing nearby.

Ken and Linda are very relaxed with their guests. They have two dining rooms, one with an oval mahogany table for up to twelve, and the other with several smaller tables. "Sometimes," Linda observed, "guests who originally preferred a separate table, decide they want to sit at the group table. We've had some lively conversations there."

The dinner was exquisite. We had asparagus en croûte, sherry-peach soup, an endive salad with mustard-vinaigrette dressing, a homemade strawberry-rhubarb sorbet with mint, scallops provençale with herbs, onions, garlic, and swiss cheese served with snow peas, homemade poppy seed rolls, and a wedge of scrumptious frozen chocolate cheesecake.

For guests who are inclined toward activities beyond sitting on their balconies, drinking in the spectacular scenery, dreaming in the natural gardens, listening to the birds and the bees, and watching the butterflies, there are walking and hiking trails in the summer, which become cross-country ski trails in the winter. Ken told me they are right next to a preserved area of 1200 acres that will never be developed. Forget the traffic noise—there isn't any.

When we were standing on the deck of one of the guest rooms in the

barn, Linda pointed out a couple of the trails that led out through openings in the old stone walls. "The trail that goes over the third mowing is a little steeper than the others," she said.

Linda explained that they created a cross-country learning center with a private trail system for the use of inn guests only.

Standing on the balcony outside my room before climbing into bed, I felt as if I could reach out and touch the brilliant moon and the millions of stars. This is indeed one of my favorite special country experiences.

WINDHAM HILL INN, West Townshend, VT 05359; 802-874-4080. A 15-room (private baths) 1825 country farm inn on a secluded hillside in the scenic West River Valley of southern Vermont, 23 mi. northwest of Brattleboro. Modified American plan includes breakfast and dinner. Open mid-May to Nov. 1; Thanksgiving; mid-Dec. to April 1; 2-night minimum stay on weekends. Nature walks, biking, xc skiing and lessons, swimming, summer chamber music concerts, and horse-drawn carriage picnics on grounds. Backroading, Marlboro and Bach Music Festivals, state parks, and antiquing nearby. Children over 12. No pets. Smoking in sitting rooms only. Ken and Linda Busteed, Innkeepers. (See Index for rates.)

Directions: From I-91, take Exit 2, following signs to Rte. 30. Take Rte. 30 north 21½ mi. In West Townshend, turn right at red country store and drive 1½ mi. up hill to inn.

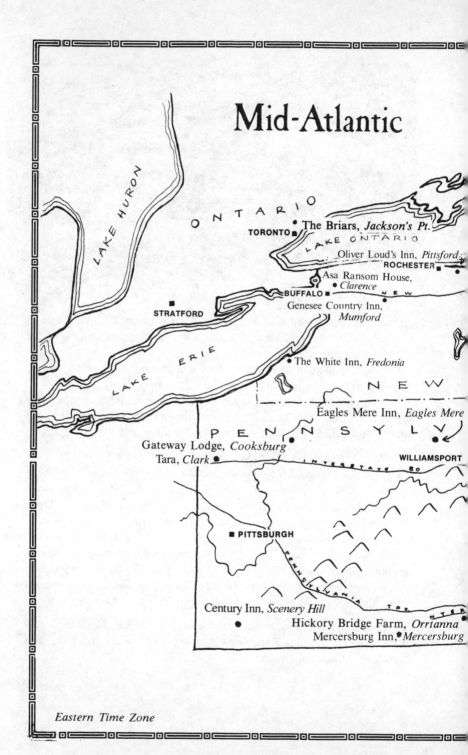

Mid-Atlantic

LAKE HURON

LAKE ERIE

ONTARIO

LAKE ONTARIO

TORONTO ● The Briars, *Jackson's Pt.*

Oliver Loud's Inn, *Pittsford*
ROCHESTER

Asa Ransom House,
● *Clarence*
BUFFALO

Genesee Country Inn,
Mumford

STRATFORD

N E W

● The White Inn, *Fredonia*

N E W

Eagles Mere Inn, *Eagles Mere*

P E N N S Y L V

Gateway Lodge, *Cooksburg*
Tara, *Clark* ●

WILLIAMSPORT

INTERSTATE 80

■ PITTSBURGH

PENNSYLVANIA TPK.

NYS

Century Inn, *Scenery Hill*
●
Hickory Bridge Farm, *Orrtanna*
Mercersburg Inn, ● *Mercersburg*

Eastern Time Zone

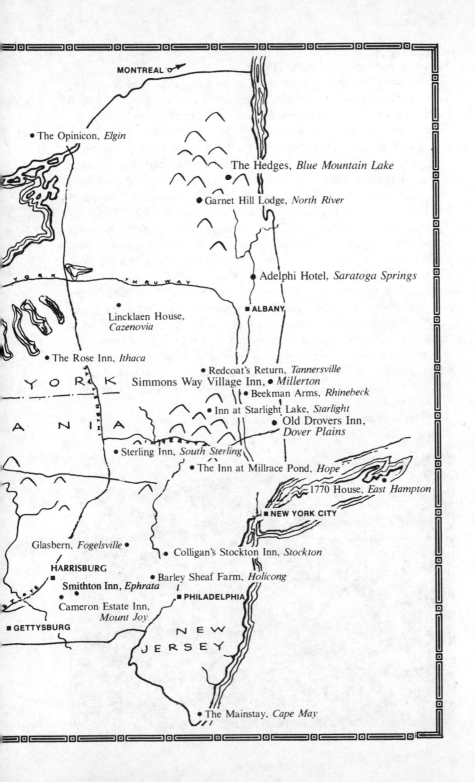

ADELPHI HOTEL
Saratoga Springs, New York (1990)

In the 1800s, Saratoga Springs was called Queen of the Spas. The very wealthy and artistic flocked to the resort for the concerts, garden parties, horse racing, and gala balls held in the elaborate hotel ballrooms. Today, Saratoga Springs has two distinct seasons: In July the New York City Ballet has its center at the Saratoga Performing Arts Center, and in August the social set returns to attend polo matches and horse racing.

Sheila Parkert and Gregg Siefker purchased Saratoga's Adelphi Hotel just as plans were being made to tear it down, as its more grandiose sisters had been. "It was in unimaginably bad shape, though," Sheila told me. "People thought we were crazy." But the enterprising couple literally dug in and began the almost unbelievable task of renovating the huge, 19th-century Victorian. Since money was short, they did almost all the work themselves, including construction and decorating.

In 1979, they opened the lobby and the bar. Then three guest rooms were completed. And now, there are only five rooms of thirty-nine left to finish. Through this whole process, they studied magazines, collected antiques, and traveled to little country inns in Europe to gain inspiration.

It takes a well-developed sense of personal style and natural talent to take elements that are both eclectic and eccentric and combine them to produce a work of art. Sheila and Gregg have done it: The Adelphi Hotel is just that.

The building is a spectacular example of high Victorian architecture.

A facade of Lombardian brick work is fronted by three-story wooden columns adorned by elaborate masses of fretwork. The opulent lobby could now be considered Gilded Age. Gilt peeks out from corners, pillar pediments, mirror frames, and ceiling panels. Dark woods and hunter-green walls set off the period chairs and sofas. The light from tiny lamps and chandeliers creates shadows as it filters through the glossy leaves of brass-potted plants. The antiques throughout the inn are all originals and attest to the dedication of the collectors. Prints and engravings of old Saratoga adorn the walls, and fresh flowers add color.

The couples' full artistic vision is evident in the spacious guest rooms. Most are done in the Victorian style, but always with unique touches that make them lively. A few rooms are worlds unto themselves, such as the Riviera Room with its wall murals of the French Riviera and the southwest-inspired Adirondack Mission Suite. All individual window treatments in the inn have been designed and sewn by Sheila, who has a great philosophy about interior design: "a building tells you what to do."

Each room has a full bath, air-conditioning, television, and special little touches, like trays with a glass decanter and glasses, and a special bottle of wine. Sheila's handmade comforters cover the beds, and antique armoires are filled with extra pillows and blankets.

A breakfast of fresh fruits, coffee cake, and a beverage is brought to your room. But finish your morning coffee from one of the wicker rockers on the inn's loggia, just off the parlor. Coffee, tea, and cakes are also available on the parlor sideboard throughout the day.

The inn's bar has a full liquor license, and in July and August lunch and a light dinner can be enjoyed in the Cafe Adelphi, or outdoors in the cafe's courtyard. Fine restaurants are also within walking distance.

Sheila and Gregg have achieved their goal of creating "a small grand-luxe hotel in the finest European tradition," and, from the enthusiastic way Sheila was talking about a new wallpaper pattern, they have no intention of stopping.

ADELPHI HOTEL, 365 Broadway, Saratoga Springs, NY 12866; 518-587-4688. A 34-guestroom (private baths) elegant Victorian in the center of historic downtown Saratoga. Operated in the European tradition. Open May through Oct. Queen, double, and twin beds. Continental breakfast included; lunch and light dinner available during the summer. Walk to restaurants. Close to Saratoga Performing Arts Center, Spa State Park, Saratoga Race Track, mineral baths, shopping. No pets. Sheila Parkert and Gregg Siefker, Owners-hosts.

Directions: From New York City, take I-87 to Saratoga Springs; take Exit 13N.

ASA RANSOM HOUSE
Clarence, New York (1976)

The letter was typical of several I have received from readers who have stayed at the Asa Ransom House: "A delightful surprise; we didn't realize that such a wonderful old place existed near Buffalo. Here we were treated as personal guests. Our bedroom was really beautiful, furnished with old pieces and decorated with exquisite taste. The bathroom was one of the prettiest and cleanest I have ever seen. The dining room was crowded, but our table was kept for us until we arrived and then we sat down to one of the finest meals I have had for years. The next morning a complimentary breakfast was served because we were remaining overnight. Everything seems to be homemade and from organically grown produce. We intend to return."

As long as I am at it, let me quote till another reader's letter: "Driving down the main street of Clarence at dusk on a December day my spirit was brightened when I saw the warm glow of the lights of the inn reflected on the snow. I could see through the windows that everyone was thoroughly enjoying themselves. Upon entering I was greeted by Judy Lenz, who showed me to my bedroom and gave me a bowl of fruit."

The inn has four totally different guest rooms. The Lavender and Green Room has a lovely view of the front lawn and boasts a king-sized bed. Room 2 is in hues of blue and peach with a lovely cherry canopied bed. A queen-sized bed presides in the Gold Room, impressive with its originally designed stenciled walls and fireplace. The larger Green Room has a view of the herb garden and has two pine cannonball double beds.

The Asa Ransom Library is the guests' living room, complete with a wonderful selection of books and periodicals, a puzzle and game table, and a roaring fire (in season, of course) in the Franklin stove.

Both dining rooms share a fireplace, and the menu reflects the

Lenzes' innovative flair. Besides an impressive assortment of main dishes, such as grilled salmon steak (or baked in a puff pastry), baked sole Florentine, country pot pies, and the Ransom mixed grill, the dinner includes steaming soup from the kettle, fresh green salad and vegetables, and the inn's famed rolls and muffins. The kitchen uses many of the fifty-two culinary herbs from the Asa Ransom garden. Everything is made from scratch here, including the tempting desserts and ice creams.

A full breakfast for houseguests consists of fresh fruit, hot muffins, and toast, as well as the special breakfast pie or a special creation of that morning. Summer guests may enjoy their morning repast on the veranda.

The two younger "innkeepers," Abigail and Jennifer, have been taking an active interest in their parents' endeavors. Abby enjoys helping guests in the gift shop, and Jennie is an assistant waitress.

The Asa Ransom House is closed on Fridays and Saturdays because of the religious beliefs of Bob and Judy, who are members of the Church of God.

ASA RANSOM HOUSE Rte. 5, Clarence, NY 14031; 716-759-2315. A 4-guestroom (private baths) village inn approx. 15 mi. from Buffalo; near the Albright Knox Art Gallery, the Studio Arena Theatre, the Art Park, and Niagara Falls. European plan. Dinner served on Mon. through Thurs., 4:00 to 8:30 p. m.; Sun., 12:00 to 8:00 p.m. Jackets required. Lunch is available on Wed. only. Closed Fri. and Sat. Wheelchair access to dining room. Tennis, golf, fishing, swimming nearby. Limited amusement for children under 12. No pets. No credit cards. Bob and Judy Lenz, Owners-hosts. (See Index for rates.)

Directions: From the New York Thruway traveling west, use Exit 48A-Pembroke. Turn right to Rte. 5 and proceed 11 mi. to Clarence. Traveling east on the N.Y. Thruway, use Exit 49; turn left on Rte. 78, go 1 mi. to Rte. 5 and continue 5¼ mi. Coming from the east via Rte. 20, just east of Lancaster, N.Y., turn on Ransom Rd., go to end and turn left.

BEEKMAN ARMS
Rhinebeck, New York (1967)

"I've heard lots of explanations for the name 'Rhinebeck' or 'Rynbeck,'" said Chuck LaForge, as we sat down for dinner in the low-ceilinged Tap Room of the Beekman Arms, "but recently I learned that on the same ship with Peter Stuyvesant was a German, William Beckman, who originally came here from the Rhine Valley. His son received a land grant here in 1703 from Queen Anne of England, and he named the property Rhinebeck. 'Beckman' could have been changed to 'Beek' through a clerical error in later years."

By 1769, the Beekman Arms, which started from rather humble beginnings, had increased in size to two full stories with a roomy attic that later became a ballroom. When trouble arose with the Indians in the area, the entire community would take refuge within the inn's walls.

During the Revolution, George Washington and his staff enjoyed the fare of the inn, and the window from which he watched for his couriers is still in place. Those were anxious days also for Lafayette, Schuyler, Arnold, and Hamilton, who spent many hours at the inn. In fact, over the years hundreds of men who have helped fashion the destiny of our nation partook of the inn's hospitality.

Tonight, the light from the flickering candles was reflected in the varnished tabletops and overhead beams. The walls were hung with ancient documents and prints and sabres and muskets, many of them dating back to the days of the American Revolution. This was the same place where pioneer families and early tradesmen enjoyed a roaring fire and perhaps took a pipe similar to the white clay pipes that also adorned the walls.

While earlier Colonial Beekman Arms menus probably included such items as roast beef, venison, bear steak, pheasant, quail, and turkey, tonight chef Dan Smith's menu had varieties of boned roast duckling (raspberry sauce or hunter's style), fresh seafood, scrumptious veal preparations, as well as a few select recipes from other inns featured in *CIBR*. Casual but elegant country dining is the fare.

During most of the more than twenty years I have visited the Beekman Arms, Chuck has been kind enough to share news of the ongoing new developments with me. These have included the creation of a greenhouse dining area in the front of the building, the Antique Barn with thirty shops, and the growth of still another adjunct to the Beekman Arms—the Delamater House, built in 1844.

Chuck suggested that we take a stroll to the Delamater House to see all of the recent developments. "This is the Delamater courtyard," he commented, as we walked into an open-ended square area. There were buildings on three sides, including one that had been there earlier and a Federal house of batten-and-board design similar to the original Delama-

ter House, which had been moved from another point in the village and is now a conference center.

The guest rooms in this section are furnished with a very pleasant restraint; each has a four-poster bed and a fireplace, and there is split wood for the fire. Each of them has its own little refrigerator. There are thirty-five rooms in this complex.

Right in the center of the bustling village of Rhinebeck, Beekman Arms offers a variety of diversions. As Chuck says, "It is a wonderful walking village with many shops of all kinds, a foreign movie house, and other interesting restaurants in addition to our own."

The Beekman Arms today is more than a historic inn, listed on the National Register of Historic Places, where thousands of guests enjoy its fascinating and authentic Colonial decor and menu; like many other village inns, it is still the community meeting place.

BEEKMAN ARMS, Rhinebeck, NY 12572; 914-876-7077. A 13-guestroom Colonial inn (with 39 rooms and 2 suites in nearby guest house) (private baths) in the center of a busy village in the Hudson River Valley. European plan. Breakfast, lunch, and dinner served to travelers daily. Open year-round. Wheelchair access at Delamater House. Amtrak station at Rhinecliff 1 mi. (2-hr. train ride from Grand Central Station). Short drive to Hyde Park with F.D.R. home and library, Rhinebeck World War I Aerodrome, and Culinary Institute of America. Golf, tennis, swimming nearby. No amusements for young children. Chuck LaForge, Owner-host. (See Index for rates.)

Directions: From N.Y. Thruway, take Exit 19, cross Rhinecliff Bridge and pick up Rte. 199 south to Rte. 9. Proceed south on Rte. 9 to middle of village. From Taconic Pkwy., exit at Rhinebeck and follow Rte. 199 west 11 mi. to Rte. 308 into village.

GARNET HILL LODGE
North River, New York (1980)

September in the Adirondacks! It's hard to imagine a more gorgeous place. I was having a morning cup of coffee on the balcony of my bedroom, one of the six recently remodeled guest rooms at Garnet Hill. All of them have an excellent view of Thirteenth Lake, below the ridge on which the lodge sits.

I thought of my last visit in late March, when I had joined George and Mary Heim and a group of *CIBR* innkeepers for a meeting and some of the last cross-country skiing of the season. Now it was early September and one of the best times to travel, when the weather is marvelous with just a slight chill in the air.

I reluctantly left my vantage point, collected my tape recorder and camera, remembering that George had told me that all of these rooms in the Log House have private baths and are finished in a nice combination of original pine paneling and wallpaper. There were also fresh flowers adding a pleasing touch.

Garnet Hill Lodge is an all-season resort-inn. The Log House was built in 1936, and it is a true rustic lodge, with a big combination living/ dining room of varnished Adirondack white pine in a post-and-beam construction—the bark has been left on in many cases. Guests gather around the big fireplace for some good conversation and fun.

Even on rainy days there are things to do in this lodge, including watching movies, television, or the VCR, or playing games. And there are books and books and books. The room is big enough to accommodate several different groups comfortably.

While we were taking a short tour of the property, George and Mary expressed great pride in the new nature trail. "All the trees have been

carefully marked," Mary told me, "and one of the trails is used for skiing in the winter."

Besides walking and hiking, there is canoeing and fishing. Among the many other outdoor activities are white-water rafting trips on the upper Hudson River through a fifteen-mile gorge, which has some of the most spectacular rapids and scenery in the Adirondacks. "Fishing is another big thing here," George commented. "We have land-locked salmon and brook trout right here on the lake, and the nearby lakes and streams have lake trout, rainbows, brownies, bass, walleyes, and pickerel.

"I'd say we have two faces up here on the mountain," George said. "Our wintertime face is cross-country skiing. The Adirondacks offer some of the best snow in the East. We get over 125 inches here, and there is downhill skiing at Gore, Whiteface, and Lake Placid. Our own cross-country skiing includes forty kilometers of scenic, groomed trails, and we have a well-equipped ski shop with an experienced staff for lessons and tours."

Winter or summer, the evening meal is a big event at Garnet Hill Lodge. The menu includes a sizeable group of appetizers—pâté, shrimp cocktail, and soups. Entrées might be fish, scallops Provençale, baked stuffed shrimp, fillet of tenderloin, chicken in many different forms, center-cut pork chops broiled and then sautéed in a savory brandied apple sauce, as well as several game dishes like pheasant or venison.

I asked George about the animals one might see on a walk in the woods. "Well, we have black bear, although they are very seldom seen; however, you can see white-tailed deer, red foxes, minks, an occasional beaver, and the other day a coyote came right up on the ski trail. You don't see them very often, but they're out there."

GARNET HILL LODGE, 13th Lake Rd., North River, NY 12856; 518-251-2821. A 21-guestroom rustic resort-inn (private baths) high in the Adirondacks, 32 mi. from Warrensburg. King, double, and twin beds available. Modified American plan. Breakfast, lunch, and dinner served to travelers. Open year-round except 2 wks. in June and Nov. Wheelchair access to dining room. Swimming, boating, hiking, fishing, and xc skiing on grounds. Downhill skiing, long-distance hikes, Hudson River white-water rafting trips, and beautiful Adirondack drives nearby. The area has many museums, arts and crafts centers, and historical points. No pets. No credit cards. Taxi service provided to bus stop 30 mi. away. George and Mary Heim, Innkeepers. (See Index for rates.)

Directions: From the Northway (I-87) take Exit 23 and follow Rte. 8 north. Take Rte. 28 for 22 mi. to North River. Take second left (13th Lake Rd.) 5 mi. to lodge. For more explicit directions, write for brochure.

THE GENESEE COUNTRY INN
Mumford, New York

What a great place for breakfast! Seated on the airy sun porch of The Genesee Country Inn, looking over a beautiful millpond surrounded by woods, I had just finished a delightful cheddar cheese egg bake with Dijon mustard and broccoli. After a final freshly baked muffin covered with quince jelly, innkeeper Glenda Barcklow invited me to join her on a walk around the grounds.

We passed the pretty gardens and the gazebo under the pines, and Glenda said good morning to the ducks as they came waddling toward us. "Sometimes I'll see a blue heron out here on the water," she said. As we walked to the brook, I saw a brown trout flash by, rippling the water. "Yes," Glenda added, "I have both rainbow and brown trout, and people do fish in the spring-fed ponds. Spring Creek and Allen Creek come together here and they flow down to a waterfall farther on in the woods. I'm going to create a picnic area overlooking the falls. There were about forty mills in this area during the 1800s, and you can see the ruins of many of them when you walk through the woods."

The Genesee Country Inn actually began its life in 1883 as a mill, and the original section had two-foot-thick walls of native limestone, with later additions completed in plaster and clapboard. The original mill was used as the residence of the company manager in the 1900s. Glenda Barcklow bought the property in 1982 and turned it into a lovely inn.

I was really taken with the very fine stenciling in several of the rooms. The stenciling was done by Glenda and two local artists, one of whom also painted a charming fire board and the inn's sign.

Glenda is very proud of her Garden Rooms with fireplaces and French doors opening onto private balconies overlooking the millponds and gardens. All of the rooms are most attractively furnished with some antiques, country prints and fabrics, and a guest diary.

"I suppose many of your guests take the twenty-minute drive over to Rochester, for all the cultural programs and historic attractions," I said. Glenda nodded in agreement, "But there are all sorts of things to do and see right here in Mumford. The Genesee Country Village is less than a mile from here. This is a restored village—a 'living museum,' very much like Williamsburg and Sturbridge—with about sixty buildings on 200 acres. It depicts a range of architectural styles, interior furnishings, as well as life-styles and occupations, covering the entire 19th century. They have many interesting events from spring into fall. Letchworth State Park is called the 'Grand Canyon of the East,' and they have an Olympic-size pool, hiking and nature trails along the river gorge, and beautiful water-falls. Of course, nearby schools and colleges always have something going on."

"And I imagine it must be beautiful here in the winter," I mused. "Oh," she exclaimed, "there's just nothing like it. It's so lovely, the grounds are spectacular, and it's so peaceful and quiet. You feel as if you're in another world."

Glenda did a good job of convincing me with her enthusiastic attitude. I know I'll be back to take advantage of some of the peace and quiet this winter.

THE GENESEE COUNTRY INN, 948 George St., Mumford, NY 14311; 716-538-2500. A 9-guestroom (private baths) restored historic 1833 mill inn on 6 acres of woods with ponds and waterfalls. Complimentary full breakfast is the only meal served. Afternoon tea. Seven good restaurants within walking distance. Open year-round. Queen and double beds. Trout fishing, nature walks, Genesee Country Museum, Letchworth State Park, Niagara Falls, historic sites, antiquing, biking, hiking, xc skiing, golf, swimming, and all attractions of Rochester nearby. No pets. Glenda Barcklow, Owner-host.

Directions: From N.Y. Thruway (I-90), take Exit 47 and Rte. 19 south to Le Roy. Go east on Rte. 5 to Caledonia, then north on Rte. 36 to Mumford. Turn left at George St.

THE HEDGES
Blue Mountain Lake, New York (1990)

The Hedges has remarkably maintained the truly rustic quality of the traditional country inn. The main house, with its lovely textured bark exterior, was built over a span of two years, beginning in 1880. The accompanying house, with its hand-cut stones and imported cypress shingles, was built some years later. Located on 12.5 acres on Blue Mountain Lake, The Hedges opened to its first guests in May 1921.

The almost primitive nature of The Hedges during those first few years, with no electricity or plumbing, attracted the first guests. Now, even though modern accommodations have been added to the rustic rooms, the attractiveness of the environment, and the surrounding mountainous vistas and quiet restfulness of Blue Mountain Lake, still attract the appreciative soul.

Decoration of the hotel enhances its rustic nature. The beauty of the lodge and stone house is stunning. Large, comfortable Adirondack furniture beckons from wide porches and shaded lawns . . . a perfect place to write those six letters that you've put off for months. You'll be surprised at the creative inspiration that the invigorating mountain air gives to your prose.

The library houses some fun old westerns, a great collection of children's books for a dip into the world of Lewis Carroll, and a piano for evening sing-alongs. Backgammon, cards, chess, ping-pong, and other games offer entertainment at the end of the day or during inclement weather. In the afternoon, horseshoes, volleyball, tennis, or an eye-opening swim in Blue Mountain Lake can stimulate stress-weary minds. Additionally, water-skiing equipment and boats are available for rental at the hotel's boat livery.

Breakfast and dinner are included in the room fee, and are served at your reserved table. Dinner includes one entree with vegetable, a salad selection, and crunchy homemade breads. Breakfast is hearty; on Saturday, a wonderful buffet is spread; and Sunday's midday dinner is ample. At a slight additional cost, a picnic lunch can also be arranged.

Guest rooms are cozy and comfortable with wooden-beamed ceilings and rockers. Before bed each evening, complimentary hot chocolate, coffee, and tea are served along with cookies or cakes.

I really think there can be nothing more peaceful than drifting off to sleep while the haunting sounds of a loon float across the lake. A stay at The Hedges can provide such a tranquil nocturnal experience.

THE HEDGES, Blue Mountain Lake, NY 12812; (518) 352-7325. A 14-guestroom, 14-cottage (private baths) rustic inn noted for its Adirondack resort quality. Open from mid-June to Columbus Day. Double and twin beds. Modified American plan. Boating, swimming, tennis, and water skiing on premises. No pets. Smoking restricted. Richard J. Van Yreren, Owner-host.

Directions: From west: N.Y. State Thruway to Utica, Exit 31, Rte. 12 to Alder Creek, Rte. 28 to Blue Mt. Lake. From south: N.Y. State Thruway to Exit 24 at Albany and I-87 to Exit 23 and Rte. 9 north. About 3 mi. north of Warrensburg take Rte. 28 to Blue Mt. Lake. From north: Rte. 3 or Rte. 30 to Tupper Lake; Rte. 30 to Blue Mt. Lake.

"European plan" means that rates for rooms and meals are separate. "American plan" means that meals are included in the cost of the room. "Modified American plan" means that breakfast and dinner are included in the cost of the room. The rates at some inns include a continental breakfast with the lodging.

LINCKLAEN HOUSE
Cazenovia, New York (1968)

Our dear friend Helen Tobin is no longer with us; it is indeed sad news; however, her son, Ed Tobin, has taken up the reins at Lincklaen House and promises his guests the same kind of warmth, hospitality, and dedication for which his mother was famous.

Ed, who grew up in Lincklaen House, has many plans of his own, naturally enough, and he has been knee-deep in a number of projects, including painting, wallpapering, and the more mundane but necessary things like plumbing and electrical repairs.

If an old-time stagecoach driver were to pull up his team in front of Lincklaen House today, he would find the hotel looking almost the same as it did in 1835, at least outwardly. The locally made brick, the fine chimneys, the broad front steps, and the columns flanking the doorway were built to last—and they have. Twenty or more stagecoaches passed through Cazenovia each day traveling over the Third Great Western Turnpike, and the snap of the drivers' whips was a familiar sound. The stages carried the mail and as many as fourteen passengers, and Lincklaen House must have been a welcome respite from hours spent in those lumbering horse-drawn conveyances.

Lincklaen House has been called one of the best examples of early-19th-century architecture in central New York State. Its Greek Revival lines are in harmony with other buildings in this college town. The inn was named after the founder of the village, and over the years, many famous guests have enjoyed its hospitality.

Cazenovia is one of the attractive towns along Route 20 in central New York State. This road, by the way, is a very interesting alternative to traveling across the state entirely on the Thruway, just a few miles to the north.

"We are getting to be a very special-event-minded community," Ed tells me. "We have the winter festival every February; the Lorenzo needlework exhibit the whole month of June; arts and crafts on our village green; plus a parade and fireworks over the 4th of July; the Lorenzo driving competition, which takes place in July; the Franklin car reunion each year in August; and our own events here at Lincklaen House at Christmastime."

Cazenovia provides a wide variety of sports and diversions. Swimming, fishing, sailing, waterskiing, and in winter ice skating and ice fishing are available on the lake, and there is also tennis, horseback riding, and skiing nearby. A small folder outlines five lovely motor tours in the vicinity of the town, and eventually all roads lead back to Lincklaen House for afternoon tea.

LINCKLAEN HOUSE, Cazenovia, NY 13035; 315-655-3461. A 21-guestroom (private baths) village inn, 20 mi. east of Syracuse. King, double, and twin beds available. European plan. Modified American plan upon request. Breakfast, lunch, and dinner served to travelers daily. Open year-round. Near several state parks, the Erie Canal Museum, and the Canal Trail. Tennis, golf, bicycles, alpine and xc skiing nearby. Ed Tobin, Owner-host. (See Index for rates.)

Directions: From west on N.Y. Thruway, take Exit 34A, follow Rte. 481 south, take Exit 3E and follow Rte. 92 east to Cazenovia. From east on N.Y. Thruway, take Exit 34 and follow Rte. 13 south to Cazenovia. From Rte. 81, take Exit 15 (Lafayette) and follow Rte. 20 east, 18 mi. to inn.

"European plan" means that rates for rooms and meals are separate. "American plan" means that meals are included in the cost of the room. "Modified American plan" means that breakfast and dinner are included in the cost of the room. The rates at some inns include a continental breakfast with the lodging.

OLD DROVERS INN
Dover Plains, New York

"You know, New England had cowboys during the 1700s," innkeeper Alice Pitcher told me, much to my surprise. "During the early days when John and Ebenezer Preston opened this inn as the Clear Water Tavern, cattle drovers used to drive their herds down this post road to New York City markets and stop in here for their hot buttered rum and mulled ale—and some pretty wild midnight gambling sessions!"

So well has the inn's old-world ambience been preserved that it's easy to imagine the dusty, rough-booted drovers as they relaxed in the stone-walled tap room by a crackling fire, swapping stories of wild-eyed heifers and their balling, spindly legged calves. In fact, a portion of the inn has even been relocated intact, to be used as a museum display.

The Old Drovers Inn is nestled in the Berkshire foothills on 12 rural acres. The charming white clapboard colonial is surrounded by majestic maples and gardens. Alice and her partner, Kemper Peacock, had been patrons of the inn for many years before purchasing it in 1988. "We've tried to keep the feeling of days gone by," Kemper explained, "but we've also made sure our guests have the comforts of modern conveniences."

Cable television and a VCR are available in the parlor, and the library has an extensive collection of books. The sitting rooms are comfortable with down-filled couches and fireplaces. Hooked rugs warm polished pine floors, and antiques furnish most of the rooms.

As Alice showed me to my room, a small gray dynamo flashed past us on the stair. "That's Jed, our Yorkie," Alice laughed, following my questioning glance. "His ears are too big for his head, but he can sure zip around." Antique double beds covered in satin comforters, and bureaus and wing-back chairs are featured in each room. Chintz cheerfully frames the windows. All rooms have private baths, two with old-fashioned claw-foot tubs.

Guests enjoy a complimentary breakfast that includes three meats, eggs, griddle cakes, French toast or grits, and homemade baked goods served on polished mahogany tables in the old tap room, now called the Federal Room. Murals depicting the area's historical landmarks decorate the walls.

Dinner is also served in this handsome dining room. The original low, smoke-darkened wood-beamed ceilings are illuminated by candles on tables set with lustrous old glassware and Georgian flatware. The room's 18th-century character has been so well preserved that as I glanced into a softly lighted corner I half expected to see General Lafayette creating a historically rumored scandal by dining with two questionable ladies.

The menu is Old English chophouse-style with curries and excellent

meats. Soups like Russian cabbage, and a rich cheddar cheese drizzled with sherry, are served along with fantastic hot popovers. I had the double-cut prime rack of lamb chops that was crusty-charred and succulent, accompanied by a spicy tomato chutney. The inn's full-service bar also has an extensive wine cellar.

The area surrounding the Old Drovers Inn has a rich selection of sites to explore. Nearby, the museums at the Roosevelt and Vanderbilt estates are certainly of interest. Golf, downhill skiing, and horseback riding are a short drive away. In summer, music lovers can enjoy the Berkshire Music Festival at Tanglewood, and gourmet cooks can visit the Culinary Institute of America in Hyde Park.

The traditional hospitality of the Old Drovers Inn has survived for more than 250 years, and the comfortable warmth that greeted those early drovers still greets you today.

OLD DROVERS INN, Old Rte. 22, Dover Plains, NY 12522; 914-832-9311. A 4-guestroom (private baths) traditional country inn at the end of a narrow country road in the Berkshire foothills. Open all year. Double beds. Complimentary full country breakfast; dinner by reservation. Croquet, badminton, bicycling, golf, skiing, horseback riding. Museums and antique shops nearby. Pets by arrangement. Alice Pitcher and Kemper Peacock, Owners-hosts.

Directions: Take Major Deegan Expwy. to the N.Y.S. Thruway; go north to Exit 7A, then north on Saw Mill River Pkwy. until it merges with Rte. 684 north. Follow Rte. 684 until it becomes Rte. 22 north; the inn is 23 mi. along Rte. 22.

OLIVER LOUD'S INN
Pittsford, New York (1989)

For nearly ten years Richardson's Canal House, the oldest surviving tavern on the Erie Canal, offered superb dining in a beautifully restored building, but there were no overnight accommodations. Then, in 1985, owner Vivienne Tellier learned that the Oliver Loud Tavern in Egypt, four miles away, was scheduled for demolition. Within twelve months, the building was moved to its present site near Richardson's, fully restored to its 1812 Federal and Greek Revival splendor, and taking overnight guests.

Oliver Loud had built his tavern in the style of the clapboard farmhouses of Massachusetts, where he was born. In 1812 the hamlet of Egypt was a busy stagecoach stop on the road to Syracuse, and Mr. Loud was something of an entrepreneur, providing bed and board to travelers, operating the first sawmill in the area, writing pamphlets, and as an amateur astronomer, watching the heavens and probably forecasting the weather.

He had introduced considerable refinements to his inn, and Vivienne wasted no effort in recreating such special features as the Federal moldings, French and English wallpapers and borders, and paint colors. Mr. Loud's "receipt for making any wood look like mahogany" was used as an inspiration for the present hand-grained "mahogany" doors.

Vivienne has filled the rooms with fine reproductions of antique furniture and Early American paintings and artifacts. A display in the common room of the "Nanking Cargo" porcelain plates over the Federal-style mantel, which boasts gold-leaf panels and marbleized insets, was part of the cargo of a Dutch ship that sank in 1752 in the South China seas. Vivienne bought them at an auction in Amsterdam.

The guest rooms have king-sized and canopied beds and beautiful 1800s documentary and handscreened borders; four of them have a view of the canal.

You will find a chilled split of champagne, Saratoga water, fresh fruit, crackers and cheese, and homemade cookies when you arrive in your room. A continental breakfast basket will be delivered with the morning paper to your door, or you may enjoy it in a rocking chair on the porch overlooking the canal.

Lunch and dinner are available at Richardson's Canal House, a few steps away. Built in 1818, it retains virtually all of the original exterior and interior architectural detail. There are two-storied porches on the front and rear, a great cooking fireplace in the old kitchen, and delicate but simple Federal trim in its public rooms, which are painted in the intense original colors.

"For the most part the cuisine gets its inspiration from French and American regional cooking," Vivienne told me as we sat under the gay umbrellas on the terrace of the inn, which is separated from the canal by a lovely grassy bank.

"For dinner we present a five-course, fixed-price meal, including appetizers, soup, a main dish, salad, and dessert. Everything is made right here. We have our own herb garden and bake all our own breads. There's always a variation of fish, fowl, a beef dish, and perhaps one or two others on the evening menu. For instance, we get very good veal from Wisconsin and duckling from Long Island. Our area has a lot of beef eaters and they seem to like our tenderloin of beef and New York strip steaks. We frequently have entertainment on Friday nights with musicians playing original instruments and tunes from the 1800s."

This is a most appealing country setting in an Erie Canal village with its century-old locust trees.

OLIVER LOUD'S INN, 1474 Marsh Rd., Pittsford, NY 14534; 716-248-5200. An 8-guestroom (private baths) historic inn on the Erie Canal, 10 mi. east of Rochester. Continental breakfast included. Lunch served Mon. thru Fri., and dinner served Mon. thru Sat. at the famous Richardson's Canal House, on the National Register of Historic Places. Open year-round. Canal towpath for walking or running, xc skiing, scenic Finger Lakes, Letchworth State Park, museums and galleries, and other sightseeing and historical landmarks nearby. Children over 12 welcome. No pets. Vivienne Tellier, Owner-hostess. (See Index for rates.)

Directions: From NY Thruway, take Exit 45 to I-490 west to Bushnell's Basin exit. Turn right off ramp, and proceed to Richardson's Canal House and Oliver Loud's Inn.

THE REDCOAT'S RETURN
Tannersville, New York (1977)

I think it's fair to say that every inn I have written about in my books is unique. Each has its own personality and its own particular brand of hospitality. However, I have noticed certain similarities among various inns. In the case of Redcoat's Return, I am reminded of some British inns. One is the Royal Oak in Yattendon, another is the Collin House in Broadway in the Cotswolds, and still another is the Pheasant in the English Lake District.

I suggest that one of the reasons I see similarities is that Tom Wright, who with his wife, Peggy, is the innkeeper at Redcoat's Return, is a true Britisher. He was brought up in England, apprenticed at the Dorchester Hotel in London, and was at one time with the Cunard Line as a chef on the Queen Mary.

The furniture and decorations at Redcoat's, as it is familiarly known, could well be at home in many English pubs. For example, the paintings in the pub room include a bravura treatment of the Battle of Waterloo and an oil painting of a young boy coming home with a mess of fish and a fishing pole over his shoulder. Another oil painting could well be of a thatched cottage in the Cotswolds. Adding to this wonderful "hands across the sea" feeling is a family room with a solarium and a group of Hogarth prints.

For regular readers and followers of Redcoat's progress there is good news and bad news. First of all, the dining room and deck have been very successful, and, as Peggy Wright points out, the air conditioning is certainly a blessing during the summer. The room faces west toward some beautiful sunsets, and the deck is very popular as a gathering place in the summer, and for an occasional wedding as well.

The bad news is that their beloved cat, Quilty, is no longer with them.

However, they now have Winston, the baby brother of Humphrey, their big Swiss mountain dog, who loves to take guests on hikes. Winston is trying to follow in Humphrey's footsteps.

There are fourteen guest rooms in the inn, most with wash basins and several with private baths. "We've tried to preserve the best of what is really appropriate for the building," Tom says, "and have made a few major changes that will provide more bathrooms." These guest rooms are rather small and cozy and definitely of the country inn variety.

The Wrights' preoccupation with things artistic also includes their sign in front of the inn, on one side of which is a red-coated soldier, looking surprisingly like Tom, and on the other side, a pretty woman in a period costume, who looks surprisingly like Peggy.

The British theme extends to the menu, where steak-and-kidney pie is one of the most popular items, along with prime ribs of beef, usually served on the weekends. Beef Stroganoff is another hearty favorite, as is the duckling.

The inn is built at an elevation of 2,000 feet, and there's plenty of both downhill and cross-country skiing nearby, particularly at Hunter Mountain. This is the kind of countryside that creates hearty appetites.

Whenever I visit Redcoat's, I like to sit down in front of the fireplace and soak up some of the atmosphere. I also positively have to go look at my favorite painting of the Indian maiden with a headband and a coy look, wearing an Indian costume that includes knee-length stockings. "That's one of our prize possessions," Peggy says. "She's a kind of Hiawathan Betty Boop."

Peggy and Tom's exciting vacation in Hawaii last year had two results: (1) they brought back some rather odd souvenirs, and (2) after a helicopter ride over an erupting volcano Tom decided to take flying lessons.

THE REDCOAT'S RETURN, Dale Lane, Elka Park, NY 12427; 518-589-6379. A 14-guestroom (private baths) English inn approx. 4 mi. from Tannersville, N. Y., in the heart of the Catskill Mts. Lodgings include breakfast. Dinner served daily except Tues. and Wed.; no lunches served. Open from Memorial Day to Easter. Closed 1 wk. in early Nov. Please call for details. Wheelchair access to restaurant. Within a short drive of several ski areas and state hiking trails. Nature walks, trout fishing, croquet, skiing, swimming, ice skating, riding, tennis nearby. No pets. Tom and Peggy Wright, Owners-hosts. (See Index for rates.)

Directions: From the New York Thruway, going north, use Exit 20; going south, use Exit 21. Find Rte. 23A on your map and follow it to Tannersville; turn left at traffic light onto County Rd. 16. Follow signs to Police Center, 4½ mi. Turn right on Dale Lane.

THE ROSE INN
Ithaca, New York (1986)

Perhaps it is because I am so attuned to the characteristics of central New York State that the flat-topped cupola of the Rose Inn attracted my eye. Many 19th-century homes have such cupolas. I was driving north from Ithaca along the shore of Cayuga Lake, and there on top of a small hill was a gorgeous mansion with the easily recognizable, graceful lines of a mid-19th-century Italianate home. Innkeeper Charles Rosemann met me as I was parking the car, and together we started on a lovely tour of the inn.

About the first thing I learned is that the Rose Inn is known locally as "the house with the circular staircase."

As Charles explained, "The house is a gem of woodcraft, built of heavy timbers with large, heavy handcut doors of chestnut. The floors are laid with quarter-sawn oak, inlaid in parquet fashion. It was built and completed in 1851, with the exception of a center staircase that would have led to the cupola. No one capable of completing it could be found. Hundreds of feet of priceless Honduras mahogany were stored for over half a century. In 1922 a master craftsman appeared, and he worked for two years building a circular staircase of that solid mahogany, which extended from the main hall through two stories to the cupola."

The inn displays the ambience of its period. High ceilings, the warm glow of woods from indigenous American trees long gone, marble fireplaces, and period antiques provide an elegant but surprisingly comfortable setting. Sherry and Charles really have been ingenious in adding new rooms—it's hard to distinguish the old from the new. The honeymoon suite has a king-sized bed, a working fireplace with an antique mantel, a sunken whirlpool bath for two, and a solarium overlooking the apple orchard and the fish pond. All of the rooms display Sherry's creative touch. One room with forest green walls has a beautiful 1850s walnut bed and a fine armoire imported from England. The new addition has its own elegant parlor with a TV set and a well-stocked refrigerator.

Dinner is something special. Sterling silver settings and candlelight set the mood for such four-course dinners as rack of lamb with an herbed sauce or scampi Mediterranean cooked in a light curry and cream sauce. There is Chateaubriand grilled over charcoals, and for those who like surprises there is the chef's *entrée du jour*. Eclectic and ethnic meals are also available, and since dinners are served only with advance reservations, the innkeepers have a chance to create something quite different.

My visit was true to form and I was delighted. At breakfast (Sherry cooks the evening meal and Charles cooks breakfast), Charles explained, "We like to give our guests a good start, and so we have full breakfasts, including hand-squeezed orange juice, our own blend of coffee, home-

made jams and jellies, along with fresh fruits, German apple pancakes, french toast, or eggs Benedict."

There are many, many more things to share about the Rose Inn, but I think the best way for such sharing is a visit to the inn itself. It may be known as the inn with the circular staircase, but I think the second most wonderful thing is that Sherry and Charles Rosemann appeared on the scene—just the right people to maintain this beautiful building and permit those of us who love inns to enjoy its hospitality.

THE ROSE INN, 813 Auburn Rd., Rte. 34—P.O. Box 6576, Ithaca, NY 14851; 607-533-7905. A 12-guestroom and 3 suite (private baths) elegant New York State mansion just a few minutes from Cornell University. Breakfast included in room rate; gourmet dinner offered by advance reservation. Open all year. Conveniently situated to enjoy the beautiful Finger Lakes scenery and attractions, including Cayuga Lake, wineries, and college campuses. No facilities for children under 10. Arrangements can be made for pets. Cat in residence. No smoking anywhere in the inn. Charles and Sherry Rosemann, Innkeepers. (See Index for rates.)

Directions: From N.Y. State Thruway take Exit 40 and Rte. 34 south about 36 mi. The inn will be on your left before arriving in Ithaca. From I-81 use Exit 11 (Cortland) to Rte. 13 to Ithaca. Take No. Triphammer Rd. right, 7.4 mi. to inn.

The date in parenthesis in the heading represents the first year the inn appeared in the pages of Country Inns and Back Roads.

1770 HOUSE
East Hampton, Long Island, New York (1980)

"Aquiring the 1770 House was part of a longtime dream for us," recounted Sid Perle. "We spent many months searching outer Long Island for just the right place for the ideal country inn." Sid and I were seated in the main living room of the inn, where some of the most recently acquired pieces are from the old Easthampton Post Office. They have been used very cleverly. There was one window labeled, "General Delivery." Another one for money orders now has a tiny television set that disappears completely, if necessary.

We were joined momentarily by Miriam Perle, who is the chef at the inn. She formerly ran a cooking school in Great Neck for twelve years and studied earlier at the Cordon Bleu in Paris.

The menu changes weekly and, with the exception of desserts and beverages, it is a complete meal. There are such appetizers as spaghettini with a robust fresh tomato sauce, fresh poached salmon served with three sauces, stuffed artichoke Siciliano, crabcake Edna Lewis—lump crabmeat cake sautéed in a butter and mustard dressing. The salads are different every week, as are the salad dressings.

I asked Miriam about the main dishes. "Well, as you know, we're here on the end of Long Island, where there is lots of fresh fish available. So, our entrées very frequently include stuffed fresh swordfish, lobster creole, and other fish dishes. Tonight, we also have stuffed filet mignon, rack of lamb, roast loin of pork with a lemon-garlic marinade, and your favorite, roast duck with a lingonberry glaze." She knows my great love of roast duckling and knew that she had, indeed, made a conquest.

Downstairs in the Tap Room there is a beautiful beehive fireplace, with many old trivets and other artifacts on the wall. The atmosphere is quite similar to an English pub, and the room is now used as an antiques shop for their guests.

The bedrooms are delightful. Several of them have canopied beds and combinations of French and American Victorian antiques, including several bedside tables with marble tops. They are all very romantic, and one in particular on the ground floor overlooking the garden struck my fancy as being an ideal honeymoon suite.

Incidentally, guests at the 1770 House can also be booked at the Philip Taylor House, a few doors away. It's an English manor house with canopied beds and fireplaces in three luxurious guest rooms.

Sid said there have been several references to my quotation from Owen Meredith, which is occasionally used on their menus:

We may live without friends, we may live without books, but civilized man cannot live without cooks.

Sid put an arm around Miriam. "I always tell them that I'm the luckiest guy in the world because my wife and daughter, Wendy Van Deusen, are two of the world's great cooks."

1770 HOUSE, 143 Main St., East Hampton, Long Island, NY 11937; 516-324-1770. An 8-guestroom (private baths) elegant village inn near the eastern end of Long Island. Queen, double, and twin beds available. Open all year. Dinner served Thursday thru Sunday during the summer months. During the off-summer months, dinner served Friday and Saturday only. During July and August weekends, 4-day minimum reservations are required; mid-week, 3-day reservations are required. Convenient to many cultural and recreational diversions, including antiquing and backroading. Not comfortable for children under 14. No pets. The Perle Family, Owners-hosts. (See Index for rates.)

Directions: From New York City, take the Long Island Expressway to Exit 70, and then turn south to Rte. 27 East, the main street of East Hampton. The inn is located diagonally across the street from Guild Hall.

"European plan" means that rates for rooms and meals are separate. "American plan" means that meals are included in the cost of the room. "Modified American plan" means that breakfast and dinner are included in the cost of the room. The rates at some inns include a continental breakfast with the lodging.

SIMMONS' WAY VILLAGE INN
Millerton, New York (1990)

For me, one of the most memorable things about the Simmons' Way Village Inn is that it is indeed a *village* inn. There is no typical village inn; each is a unique establishment. Yet, somehow I always look for that special feeling of communal social activity that characterizes innkeepers' involvement with guests, and with their community. Simmons' Way fits my criteria perfectly.

The twin of an English inn, the Manor House, Moreton-in-Marsh, the gracious 1800s Victorian mansion is located on the village square of Millerton. Although on a highway, the inn is set back on a hill, with an expansive, shaded lawn stretching to the street. Striding up the walkway to steps lined with Halloween jack-o'-lanterns, I was appreciating the spacious front porch when innkeeper Nancy Carter poked her head out the door. "You're just in time! We're serving cocktails in the drawing room. Come and join us."

Richard and Nancy were both professionals prior to their purchase and renovation of the inn in 1987. Richard spent an interesting career as a United Nations official, and Nancy worked as a vice-president in banking and financial services. They have made many friends during their years at Simmons' Way. "Our repeat clientele first stay with us as inn guests, and later purchase second homes in the area and continue their relationship with us as dining guests and friends," Richard told me. "I guess that's 'proof of the pudding.'"

Highly photographable, the majestic wooden-frame house has a porte cochere, a third floor, and several balconies. The interior has been almost completely renovated. From the broad front veranda, tall doors

open onto the center hall, which separates the comfortable lounge area from the smaller, charming parlor. Wicker furnishings, cozy couches, antiques, Oriental rugs, and wood-burning fireplaces offer a relaxing environment. The finish has been removed from the original wood in all the inn's rooms, resulting in glowing, honey-toned floors and wainscoting.

Climbing a twisty little paneled-oak staircase, illuminated by two stained-glass windows, I made my way to my room. The guest rooms are most romantic, truly within the European tradition. All rooms are light and airy, with distinctive color themes. Spool beds, four-poster beds, brass beds, and draped-canopy beds all have down pillows, lush linens, and antique furnishings to comfort the weary traveler. Some rooms have fireplaces, and most have restful sitting areas. All rooms have private shower/baths.

Afternoon at Simmons' Way brings traditional English tea, particularly popular due to the inn's private tea blends. Predinner cocktails are served "à la Hotel Algonquin style," according to Nancy.

Dinner is served in the inn's formal dining room and can begin with some wonderful appetizers, like Icelandic Gravlax. Main entrees can be anything from Cajun blackened steak to my delectable choice of the evening: creole eggplant stuffed with shrimp and crabmeat. A fine wine list is also available. The restaurant is open to the public by reservation only.

A wonderful breakfast of home-baked muffins, granola, fresh fruit, goat's cheese, and coffee cake or croissants is served in the smaller dining room, on the lovely front veranda, or most decadently in your suite.

The Carters' pets, Baden, an enormous but absolutely loving two-year-old Bernese mountain dog, and discriminating Sam, a black Siamese-mix cat, are pleased to act as surrogate pets for those travelers who might be pining for their "pup" or "kitty" left behind.

While visiting at Simmons' Way, you will be close to music festivals, theater, historic homes, and hiking and outdoor sports. Furthermore, the inn is in a perfect place for parents to make private school visits with their children, since there are at least a half-dozen schools within a short distance.

SIMMONS' WAY VILLAGE INN, 33 Main St., Millerton, NY 12546; 518-789-6235. A 9-guestroom (private baths) Victorian village inn in a rural environment only 2 hours from Manhattan. Open year-round. Modified American plan. All-size beds. Convenient to cultural and recreational activities, antiquing, and shopping. No pets. Nancy and Richard Carter, Owners-hosts.

Directions: From New York City, take Henry Hudson Pkwy. to Sawmill River Pkwy. to Rte. 684 north, and follow Rte. 22 to Millerton.

THE WHITE INN
Fredonia, New York (1989)

This is the story of the renaissance of an inn and a village, and of how two professors of philosophy became experts on historical restoration. Sounds ponderous, doesn't it? Actually, Dave Palmer and Dave Bryant are two great guys, who laugh about the way people get them mixed up—they look a lot alike.

The day I met them, Dave Palmer was wearing a tie and Dave Bryant was in work clothes, repairing the air conditioning, so I had no problem. "How did two university professors get involved in historical restoration and innkeeping?" I wanted to know.

"We became friends in 1970 when we both arrived at the State University of New York here," Dave Palmer replied, "and Dave, being a very skilled craftsman, got me interested in renovating some historic buildings in our spare time. My wife, Nancy, who is an art historian, also joined us in developing the design and decoration of the buildings."

Dave Bryant took up the story. "By 1980 when we bought the White Inn, I had given up my teaching career for the world of restoration, and although Dave still teaches philosophy at the university, he is very much involved with the inn and continuing restoration projects." As I learned later, these two men were the catalysts for what developed into a major restoration of historic buildings in Fredonia and nearby Dunkirk. Part of the town is now listed on the National Register of Historic Places.

I was impressed with the White Inn from the moment I saw the beautiful lawn, the flowers and two ancient maples beyond the wrought iron fence, and walked up to the two-story, pillared portico with a long, spacious porch extending on both sides across the front. As we walked through the inn, every room seemed more beautiful than the last. Nancy Palmer has furnished and decorated the rooms with a great sense of style. She uses designer wallpapers and fabrics, and many handsome antique pieces and special touches that make each guest room different and delightful. There are several two-room suites, and they are all quite spacious.

From 1868, when Dr. Squire White's son replaced the original 1821 house with a brick mansion, until the early 1900s, this was a private residence. As the White Inn, it has undergone many changes and additions; in the early 1930s it was included in the first edition of *Adventures in Good Eating* by Duncan Hines.

Dave Palmer pointed out that they are very community oriented, as shown by some wonderful displays of memorabilia donated by area residents. There are displays of Victorian lace, oriental silks, drawings, paintings, photographs, posters, and old newspaper clippings about the White Inn. The antique stained-glass and brass tulip chandelier hanging over the registration desk was donated by a community member.

Their three dining rooms have an enthusiastic following among townsfolk, and Chef Richard Orloff's meals have established the White Inn's reputation for fine dining. Dinner menus might feature rainbow trout stuffed with a mousseline of scallops, shrimp, and whitefish and served with a dill sauce and fresh vegetables, or medallions of pork with wild rice and a basil brandy sauce, as well as a number of other equally tantalizing dishes.

Congratulations to the two Daves for their impressive work of preservation and restoration. We welcome the White Inn to our pages.

THE WHITE INN, 52 E. Main St. (Rte. 20), Fredonia, NY 14063; 716-672-2103. A 20-guestroom (private baths) village inn, off U.S. Rte. 20 and 1 mi. from Lake Erie in Chautauqua County. All-size beds available. Continental breakfast included in rates. Full breakfast, lunch, and dinner served daily to public. Open year-round. Wheelchair access with assistance. Bicycles, basketry and gift shop on premises, sailing on Lake Erie on inn's sloop. Sightseeing in historic area, wineries, and the many events at SUNY and Chautauqua nearby. No pets. David Palmer and David Bryant, Owners-hosts.

Directions: From N.Y. Thruway, take Exit 59 and follow Rte. 60 to Rte. 20. Turn right to the inn.

BARLEY SHEAF FARM
Holicong, Pennsylvania (1982)

I sat on the terrace of Barley Sheaf Farm looking down across the lawns over the old stone fence, bordered by gorgeous spring flowers and covered with vines, into what could best be described as the next lower level of lawn, where the pond and the swimming pool are.

Ann Mills told me that I should not miss the pair of Canada geese that herd their four goslings in and out of the pond every morning. "The mother and father arrive every spring and stay long enough to produce the eggs and guide the family, and then a few weeks later they all fly away. The parents come back again every year."

Earlier that morning, lying abed in my room, which had been fashioned out of one of the original outbuildings of the farm, I became aware of the fact that Barley Sheaf was a series of foregrounds and backgrounds. For example, on the walls and window sills beside my brass bed there were several country artifacts. Then out of one of the windows, I could look over the red brick walks and farm fence in the foreground across the fields to the line of trees in the background. The other window provided a wonderful view of the old barn on the property. This handsome building, which saw service on this property for most of the 19th century, if not longer, has the recognizable earmarks of an early Pennsylvania antiquity. The stone pillars and walls support the second and third floors, constructed of long plank siding. Meanwhile, the sounds of the mourning doves and busy birds filled the Bucks County morning air with their anticipation of another busy day.

Located in the heart of Bucks County, north of Philadelphia, Barley Sheaf Farm has been designated a National Historic Site; the original part of the farm dates back to 1740. There are poled Dorsets on the property, and the raspberries and grapes are made into jam. There are also bee-hives, and the wildflower honey they yield is often taken home by the guests. Almost everything comes from the farm, and the bread is baked fresh every day.

In the 1930s and 1940s it was the country home of the eminent playwright George S. Kaufman. Apparently Moss Hart and Kaufman enjoyed many hours of collaboration here. The Marx brothers were frequent guests, and I understand that Harpo was a special friend of the Kaufmans.

The emphasis of Barley Sheaf Farm is more on knowledgeable hospitality than on farming. The living rooms and reception areas are adorned with impressive Early American oils and prints, and there's a decided interest by all the Mills family in Early American antiques.

Guest rooms indicate a continuous labor of love, as country antiques abound and personal touches, such as the international doll collection in one of the bedrooms, provide a homey feeling. Each room has its own distinct character and flavor; one has a mahogany sleigh bed with a Hitchcock dresser, and still another has an antique iron bed with a very handsome quilt. There's an antique brass bed and a fireplace in the master bedroom suite, with a lovely view of the terrace.

Plans are afoot to put aside a corner of the old barn for antiques and local artwork to be enjoyed and purchased by guests.

Now, what about my Canada geese? I hadn't seen them yet. Could they have indeed flown off on the very morning of my arrival? Ah, I could now see a long graceful neck among the grasses along the edge of the pond and, sure enough, a four-gosling flotilla was heading out across the placid waters. Whatever else might happen today, the geese would be at Barley Sheaf Farm.

BARLEY SHEAF FARM, Box 10, Holicong, PA 18928; 215-794-5104. A 10-guestroom (private baths) bed-and-breakfast inn, 8 mi. from Doylestown and New Hope, Pa. King, queen, and double beds available. A full breakfast is the only meal served. Tea is served in the afternoon. Open Valentine's Day thru weekend prior to Christmas; weekends only mid-Jan. to mid-Feb. Minimum 2-night stay on weekends; 3-night minimum on holiday weekends. Near Delaware River, Bucks County Playhouse, Washington's Crossing. Croquet, badminton, swimming pool, farm animals on grounds. Tennis, boating, canoeing, and horseback riding nearby. Near all of the natural and historical attractions of Bucks County, Pa. Recommended for children over 8. No credit cards. Don and Ann Mills, and Don Mills, Jr., Innkeepers. (See Index for rates.)

Directions: Barley Sheaf Farm is on Rte. 202 between Doylestown and Lahaska.

CAMERON ESTATE INN
Mount Joy, Pennsylvania (1982)

Betty Groff was telling me about the history of the Donegal Presbyterian Church, which adjoins the Cameron Estate Inn property. We had been wandering around the parklike grounds of the inn and quite naturally gravitated toward this historic spot.

"Founded by Irish settlers prior to 1721, this is the church with the famous Witness Tree. On a Sunday morning in September, 1777, an express rider came to the church with the news that the British Army under Lord Howe had left New York to invade Pennsylvania. Challenged to show proof of their patriotism, they joined hands around the historic tree and declared their loyalty to the new cause of liberty and to the founding of a new nation."

As we walked beside a woodland stream, she pointed out the many trout darting about in it. "We stock this stream with trout, for which our guests may fish." Standing for a moment on an old stone bridge, she continued the narrative. "As you know, Abe and I live right here in Mount Joy and we've been operating the Groff Farm Restaurant for quite a few years. But we've always wanted to own an inn and we had our envious eye on this estate for a long time."

Agreeing to meet for dinner later on, Betty and I separated at the front door of the inn, a most impressive red brick mansion, built in 1805, with attractive dormer windows on the third floor. I speculated mentally that the broad veranda running around three sides of the inn probably had been added later in the 19th century.

Stepping inside, I found the interior to be exactly what one would have expected in a mansion: large living rooms, a library, generous-sized bedrooms, some with canopy beds and a great many with fireplaces. There are many oriental rugs and period furnishings chosen by Abe and Betty to define the historical significance of the inn. These are fitting complements to the fine paneling and marble embellishments.

Dinner that evening in the main dining room was another baronial experience, with excellent service, delicate china, and fine silverware against pristine napery. The menu included roast Long Island duckling with a mandarin orange sauce; chicken sauté "Simon Cameron" served with ham and complemented by a wine-and-cheese sauce, and white asparagus; and a succulent Steak Diane. These are an interesting contrast to the family-style dinners offered at nearby Groff's Farm Restaurant, which specializes in Pennsylvania Dutch food. Inn guests also eat there.

Betty Groff is the author of three best-selling cookbooks: *Good Earth Country Cooking, Betty Groff's Country Goodness Cookbook,* and *Betty Groff's Up-Home-Down-Home Cookbook.* She's also been seen on many TV programs and featured in magazine articles.

CAMERON ESTATE INN, R.D. #1, Box 305, Donegal Springs Rd., Mount Joy, PA 17552; 717-653-1773. An 18-guestroom (16 with private baths) elegant inn in a former mansion, 4½ mi. from Mt. Joy and Elizabethtown. All-size beds available. Complimentary continental breakfast. Lunch and dinner served every day except Sun. and Christmas. Open year-round. Convenient to all of the attractions in the Pennsylvania Dutch Amish country, as well as the Hershey and Lancaster museums, art galleries, crafts shops, and theaters; halfway between Gettysburg and Valley Forge. No children under 12. No pets. Abram and Betty Groff Owners-hosts. (See Index for rates.)

Directions: The inn is situated in the heart of the triangle formed by Harrisburg, York, and Lancaster. Traveling west on Pennsylvania Tpke. take Exit 21. Follow Rte. 222 S to Rte. 30 W to Rte. 283 W. Follow Rte. 283 W to Rte. 230 (the first Mt. Joy exit). Follow Rte. 230 through Mt. Joy to the 4th traffic light. Turn left onto Angle St. At first crossroads, turn right onto Donegal Springs Rd. Go to the stop sign. Turn left onto Colebrook Rd. Go just a short distance over a small bridge. Turn right, back onto Donegal Springs Rd. Follow signs to inn—about ½ mi. on the right. Traveling east on the Pa. Tpke. take Rte. 72 at Lebanon Exit to the Square in Manheim. Turn right on W. High St. This becomes the Manheim-Mt. Joy Rd. Follow directly into Mt. Joy. At the first traffic light, turn right onto Main St. Follow Main St. to the next traffic light. At light turn left onto Angle St. Follow above directions from Angle St.

CENTURY INN
Scenery Hill, Pennsylvania (1972)

"So this is a joggling board," I observed. "Yes," responded Megin Harrington, "we've had it here for a number of years and the guests really like it."

Megin and I were sitting on this great long, suspended board that "joggles," and that's all I'm prepared to say about it. "It's been tempering for at least seventy-five years," she said. "You just sit on it and it goes up and down."

Pointing to a magnificent black locust tree, she said, "Lafayette and Andrew Jackson probably passed under the branches of that tree. The Century Inn was built before 1794, and is the oldest continuously operating tavern on the National Pike, most of which is today's U.S. 40. Consequently, the inn has played an important role in the history of southwestern Pennsylvania. Lafayette stopped here on May 23, 1825, and Jackson was a guest twice, once on the way to his inauguration as President of the United States."

The inn remains what it has been for so many years: the pride of the community and a place sought out by true lovers of country inns. They've been coming for many years to enjoy stuffed pork chops, roast turkey, seafood, whipped potatoes, sweet potatoes, absolutely scrumptious cole slaw, and homemade pies.

As many times as I have visited the inn I always delight in visiting Room 5, which will probably never be occupied because it is jampacked with dolls of all sizes and descriptions.

Guests stopping at the inn today are attracted as much by the vast array of antiques as they are by the bill of fare. All of this restoration was started by Gordon and Mary Harrington, the parents of Megin's late husband, Skip Harrington. Gordon and Mary purchased the inn in 1945, and restored and furnished it with rare and valuable antiques collected during their lifetime.

I had arrived at high noon on a beautiful warm September day. There were generous flowers in the front of the inn and large potted geraniums interspersed with rocking chairs and benches on the porch.

The room on the right, off the main hall, has the Whiskey Rebellion flag, just as it was during the time of my first visit many years ago, when I met Gordon and Mary Harrington. We talked all through dinner and far into the night of the things that inn-seekers enjoy so much: history, music, art, and the lovely countryside.

"Let's go down the street and look at our new shop," Megin said. "There are twenty-three little shops in Scenery Hill, and we are gaining a wonderful reputation among people who like to have a personal shopping experience." Well, walk we did, and when I stepped into It's Always

Christmas, Megin's shop, I realized I was in a place where Christmas never ends. It has all kinds of Christmas everythings, including a Christmas tree hung with miniature dolls, a corner cupboard with more of the same, still another tree decorated differently, toys, paintings of ducks, and dozens of things one can mix with Christmas. Each of the little rooms of the shop, which is a former house, has been decorated differently.

After a chance to see a few of the other shops, we walked back up the street, returning to the inn to enjoy lunch in the Keeping Room, with its huge fireplace and truly astonishing collection of old tools and artifacts decorating the mantel. It's a cozy dining room, and many a lovely meal have I enjoyed in this pleasant atmosphere.

All of this and a joggling board!

CENTURY INN, Scenery Hill, PA 15360; 412-945-6600 or 5180. A 9-guestroom (private baths) village inn on Rte. 40, 12 mi. east of Washington, Pa., 35 mi. south of Pittsburgh. All-size beds available. European plan. Breakfast served to houseguests only. Lunch and dinner served to travelers daily. Open Mar. 16 to Dec 23. No pets. No credit cards. Personal checks welcome. Megin Harrington, Owner-hostess. (See Index for rates.)

Directions: From the east, exit the Pa. Tpke. at New Stanton. Take I-70W to Rte. 917S (Bentleyville exit) to Rte. 40E and go 1 mi. east to inn. From the north, take Rte. 19S to Rte. 519S to Rte. 40E and go 5 mi. east to inn or take I-79S to Rte. 40E and go 9 mi. east to inn. From the west, take I-70E to I-79S to Rte. 40E and go 9 mi. east to inn.

EAGLES MERE INN
Eagles Mere, Pennsylvania (1990)

The village of Eagles Mere sits near Eagles Mere Lake, a 90-foot-deep crystalline lake that is thickly capped with ice in the winter. Rich forests of laurel and pine climb the surrounding mountains. It is a nature photographer's dream come true. From 1892 until 1923, the Eagles Mere Railroad Company transported excited children and their well-heeled parents up the 2,057 feet to the lovely little village referred to as "The Town Time Forgot . . . in the Heart of the Endless Mountains." During its height in the 1920s, the village housed these affluent folks in magnificent Victorian "cottages," or the seven grand hotels.

The area can be reached in about three and one-half hours from either New York or Philadelphia on an often breathtakingly beautiful drive through the Allegheny Mountains. All the trappings of a high-powered ski resort are most wonderfully missing here: no whining chair lifts, no growling snowmobiles, no exorbitant rates for lodgings, and most appreciably, no pretensions.

As I climbed from my car, I filled every inch of my city-polluted lungs with crisp, clean mountain air and immediately felt revived. I mentioned this to innkeeper Lou Fiocchi as he welcomed me on the inn's large front porch. "You're hooked!" he laughed. "That's exactly what happened to me when we first came up here for a visit." Lou and Joan, his wife, purchased the inn in 1983. The magnificent architecture of the 1878 structure, with its three stories, splendid front porch, and gables and fireplaces, helped the Fiocchis make their choice.

The stately home is located in a residential area of the historic village, only a two-block walk from the center of town and the lake's natural sandy beach. The Fiocchis have redecorated, but maintained the inn's unspoiled, relaxed atmosphere.

Large overstuffed chairs and sofas in the common rooms invite unhampered lounging. A fireplace, arm chairs, and tables for card playing inspire lively evening games.

The fifteen guest rooms are all comfortable; some are quite cozy. Lace curtains create an airy quality in a few rooms, while others are pleasantly color coordinated. All rooms have rockers and sturdy reading chairs. The private baths are modern and clean. The bedrooms and baths are all fully carpeted, an asset much appreciated when one steps from bed on a chilly winter morning.

A full country breakfast and a five-course dinner are served in the dining room. The food is basic and filling. Dinner might begin with a homemade soup and fresh baked bread. Usually three entrees are offered: fish, chicken or pork, and beef or veal. The mouth-watering desserts are made in the inn's kitchen. Joan oversees preparations and makes certain

that no boxed, frozen foods are used. An extensive wine list and full beverage service are also available. The downstairs pub offers drinks and darts before dinner.

Eagles Mere Inn is in a perfect location for almost every outdoor sport you could desire. Hunting, fishing, hiking, golf, and skiing are exceptional. But, for an experience you'll never forget, be sure to visit during the winter so you can take a ride on the renowned "Slide."

The Eagles Mere Toboggan Slide is quite famous: a 120-ton, 1,200-foot-long channel of ice down which you can plummet at speeds of up to 45 miles an hour! After much cajoling on the part of my fellow "sliders," and assurances of safety precautions, I closed my eyes and down I went with eight other adventuresome souls. All I can say is that the experience was one of total exhilaration. After hurtling across the thick lake ice at the bottom of the slide, my only thought was typically childlike: I wanted to do it again!

EAGLES MERE INN, P.O. Box 356, Eagles Mere, PA 17731; 717-525-3272 or 717-525-3273. A 15-guestroom (private baths) small village inn high in the Allegheny Mountains. Open Mother's Day thru Oct., then weekends only Nov. thru mid-March. Closed March 15 to April 15. Modified American plan. All outdoor sports nearby. No pets. No smoking. Joan and Lou Fiocchi, Owners-hosts.

Directions: From New York City, take I-80 west to Rte. 42 north (Exit 34). Rte. 42 is Eagles Mere Ave. Inn is one block south on the corner of Mary and Sullivan avenues.

GATEWAY LODGE
Cooksburg, Pennsylvania (1983)

In the past two editions I have begun the account of my visit to the Gateway Lodge by sharing a conversation I had with innkeepers Linda and Joe Burney about the black bears in Cook Forest. This time, as we were enjoying a candlelit dinner, we talked about the other animals in the woods. "Besides the bears," Joe said, "we also have bobcats, raccoons, porcupines, skunks, deer, turkeys, rabbits, chipmunks, gray squirrels, and an uncountable number of birds."

I must point out that since 1981 it has been the lodge's custom to allow the first caller who makes a dinner reservation to set the menu for that evening. The choices might include prime rib, veal with a spinach dressing and mushroom sauce, chicken Cordon Bleu, thick pork chops with bread stuffing, country-style barbecued spareribs, chicken and biscuits, or baked trout, among others. On that particular night the main choice, chosen by an earlier telephone caller, was braised sirloin steak.

Linda and Joe were enthusiastic about the wicker picnic baskets they are now offering. "There are wonderful places for picnics, and we include a blanket, tablecloth, and everything for a lovely lunch."

Gateway Lodge is a rustic country inn in Cook Forest, where the pine and hemlock may be seen in all their majesty, towering 200 and more feet above the pine-needle-carpeted forest. Hundreds of years of growth, untouched by human progress, has preserved for us some of the most magnificent forest scenery east of the Rocky Mountains. The pine and hemlock logs of the lodge suggest the ruggedness of our pioneer forebears.

The big living room of the main lodge has log walls and a beautiful big fireplace, with lots of deep, comfortable chairs gathered around it. The guest rooms have beds with chestnut headboards, and all have comforters and dust ruffles. Most rooms with baths down the hall also provide fluffy robes for the trip.

In addition to the rustic guest rooms in the main lodge, there are eight cabins across the road in the forest, which require a minimum three-night stay June through August, and two nights the rest of the year. These cabins have kitchen conveniences, porches, and fireplaces, and are very snug with lots of firewood; however, such items as bed linens, towels, dishes, and cooking utensils must be provided by the guests.

The Cook Forest really serves as the recreational motivation to visit this rustic hideaway. It has twenty-seven miles of hiking and over seventeen well-marked trails for good cross-country skiing. It's possible to fish for trout and warm-water fish in the Clarion River, and over ninety species of birds have been identified in the park. Canoeing and inner-tubing can also be enjoyed, as well as golf, horseback riding, swimming, superb backroading, and there's even a summer theater nearby.

After dinner I strolled down to the Mountain Greenery Gift Shop, a little rustic building just a few steps away, where there are all sorts of gifts, made mostly by local craftspeople. "It makes a very nice place for our guests to browse in both before and after dinner."

"Our winters are very active here," Joe commented, as we wandered back up to the front porch of the lodge. "We have all kinds of carefully maintained cross-country ski trails, ice skating, and miles of snowmobile trails." "Yes," Linda chimed in, "as a matter of fact, winter is one of our busiest times."

"A really popular spot is our indoor pool, which is kept at a balmy 92° in the winter," Joe added. "Our houseguests can come in after a strenuous day in the snow and completely relax in the pool."

Linda made a sign to me and put her finger to her lips. She pointed down the forest road to where three deer were crossing. "It happens all the time," she whispered, "but it always gives me a big thrill."

GATEWAY LODGE, Rte. 36, Cooksburg, PA 16217; 814-744-8017 (Pa.: 800-843-6862). An 8-guestroom (3 private baths) rustic lodge in the heart of Cook Forest in western Pa. Double and twin beds available. Cabins require 2- and 3-night minimum stay. Open year-round, except Wed., Thurs., and Fri. of Thanksgiving week and from Dec. 22 to 25. Indoor swimming pool. Beautiful backroading and many trails in forest. All types of seasonal outdoor recreation available. The Burney Family, Owners-hosts. (See Index for rates.)

Directions: Because Cooksburg is accessible from all four directions, locate Cook Forest State Park on your map of Pa., and find Rte. 36. The lodge is on Rte. 36, 15 min. north of I-80.

GLASBERN
Fogelsville, Pennsylvania (1989)

Dusk was gathering as I turned off old Route 22 and followed first one back road, and then another, deep into Pennsylvania Dutch farmland. I thought the tiny lights I glimpsed in the hills before me were the Glasbern's, but I wasn't sure. Then, down a dip and over a bridge, I turned into the driveway, bordered with split-rail fences. Up ahead loomed the outline of a huge, impressive barn.

Al and Beth Granger welcomed me into the awesome Great Room of the Barn, which they have reconstructed and converted into an inviting country inn. The incredibly high vaulted ceiling soars twenty-six feet into the far reaches, banded by many hand-hewn beams and punctuated with several skylights. The farmer's ladders still climb to where the hay mow once was. The original stonework of the massive walls provides interesting textural contrast to the smooth, clean line of the plaster fireplace and chimney.

As we sat comfortably ensconced before a cheery fire that danced on the hearth, the Grangers told me that the barn is a 19th-century post-and-beam Pennsylvania German bank barn. "I named it Glasbern, which means 'glass barn' in Middle English," Beth said, "because I felt as if all of the windows across the front give it a kind of all-glass look."

Beth and Al are a very cordial and accommodating couple, who formerly owned a bed-and-breakfast inn and come from a background of business and teaching. "When we saw this fabulous barn and the beautiful country surrounding it," Al said, "we knew it would make a great country inn."

In addition to the Barn, where there are several guest rooms, the Carriage House is a converted tractor shed with paneled barn-siding walls, and the original Farmhouse has suites with kitchen facilities. The Carriage House rooms all have skylights, fireplaces, and whirlpool baths; in fact, in two corner rooms you can relax in a double whirlpool bath and enjoy a view of the countryside. All of the guest rooms are attractively and comfortably furnished with queen- and king-sized beds, air conditioning, telephones, and cable television.

Tucked into a fold of rolling meadows and woods, there are sixteen acres with trails for nature walks in the clear, pure air and, when there's snow, cross-country skiing. A flagstone patio surrounds the swimming pool, where a cooling splash could be followed by an hour of tranquil reflection, broken only by the distant buzz of bees, the twitter of birds, the rustle of the busy little nearby stream. In autumn the color must be breathtaking because of all the wonderful trees.

Hearty breakfasts are served at the large oval mahogany table in the dining area of the Great Room, where guests can exchange plans for the

day or their adventures. Sometimes breakfast is in the Sun Room, over-looking the valley, and might include something as scrumptious as whole-wheat pecan pancakes with maple syrup and bacon. Arrangements for a fixed-price, family-style dinner can be made in advance.

"We like to think that this is a place where our guests can find sanctuary," Beth commented, "a respite from the world in a peaceful, pastoral setting."

GLASBERN, Pack House Rd., R.D. 1, Box 250, Fogelsville, PA 18051-9743; 215-285-4723. A 20-guestroom (private baths) country inn on a back road in rolling Pennsylvania Dutch farmland, 10 mi. west of Allentown. King and queen beds available. Hearty breakfast included. Dinner can be arranged in advance. Open year-round. Minimum 2-night stay on weekends. Wheelchair access. Swimming pool, nature walks, xc skiing, and hot air ballooning on grounds. Hawk Mountain Sanctuary, Blue Mountain Ski Area, festivals, antiquing, covered bridge tours, and wineries nearby. Limited accommodations for children. No pets. Beth and Al Granger, Owners-hosts.

Directions: From I-78 take Rte. 100 north, turning left at 1st light north of I-78 onto Old Rte. 22. Turn right on No. Church St., continue about ½ mi. to right turn at Pack House Rd. Continue about 1 mi. to inn.

HICKORY BRIDGE FARM
Orrtanna, Pennsylvania (1978)

The breakfast deck over the creek behind the farmhouse is a wonderful place to sit and listen to the gurgling waters as they flow under the deck. The remnants of breakfast had been cleared away, and overnight guests had gone off on their various pursuits. Nancy Jeane Hammett took advantage of a quiet moment to sit with me. "Sometimes our guests stay out here so long I have to shoo them out so that we can get the breakfast dishes done," she said. "This is a great place for birders—they come out with their spyglasses."

"Has it been a busy summer?" I inquired. "Oh, my, yes," she replied. "We just finished canning some of the best peaches we've ever had from our neighbor's orchard, and of course we always do apple butter. Although it's been a long, hot summer, the gardens and orchards have done well. Our vegetables, honeydew melons, and cantaloupes were fine. Being at the foot of the south mountain range, we have a wonderful water supply. Our guests really appreciate a good glass of water. They say that's why my coffee and tea taste so good."

She left me to answer the summons from a telephone, and I thought about my drive over here. The road from Fairfield to Orrtanna is one of my favorite back roads. There are great cornfields on one side and apple orchards on the other and, in the midst of all, a large farmstand with a wonderful collection of pumpkins out in front, and every imaginable type of the fresh farm produce that is abundant in this highly agricultural area.

I turned at the inn sign, passed over the railroad track, and was in sight of Nancy Jeane and Doctor Jim Hammett's Hickory Bridge Farm. There were the big red barn, the many flower gardens, the old farmhouse, and the ever-growing collection of old farm machinery and carts. The

newest addition was a natural swimming pond with a diving platform. All of this was set against the background of beautiful, swaying trees, which in late September were beginning to take on their autumnal colors.

When Mary Jeane returned, I asked her if that was her son-in-law, Robert, I saw out in the field. "Yes, indeed," she replied, "Robert and Mary Lynn are taking on more responsibilities here. Dr. Jim and I are gradually exchanging hats with Mary Lynn and Robert, who will be the official innkeepers in the near future. However, Dr. Jim is always busy around the farm on his days off, and I will always be on hand to serve our guests. This is truly a family operation. Even our grandchildren love to entertain the guests."

The bedrooms in the main house are Pennsylvania farm bedrooms. Many have washstands and one even has an old-fashioned radio on the shelf. There are many additional touches, such as good country-type fixtures on the walls, that make the bedrooms very pleasant, including a rocking chair for two in one room. Additional accommodations are in two cottages beside the brook in the woods.

We took a little tour around the grounds, ably assisted by one of the eight grandchildren. One of the points of interest is a country store museum, where there is penny candy, molasses, sarsaparilla, and apple butter for sale. However, it is basically a museum store, with an old post office money window, and it provides a great deal of amusement for guests.

HICKORY BRIDGE FARM, 96 Hickory Bridge Rd., Orrtanna, PA 17353; 717-642-5261. A 7-guestroom (5 private baths) country inn on a farm (with cottages) 3 mi. from Fairfield and 8 mi. west of Gettysburg. Queen and double beds available. Open year-round except Dec. 20 thru Jan. 1. Deposit required. Full breakfast included in rates. Dinner served to guests and travelers some weekdays and every weekend by reservation. Less than 2 hrs. from Wash., D.C., Baltimore, Lancaster, Amish country, and Hershey, Pa. Near Gettysburg Battlefield Natl. Park, Caledonia State Park, and Totem Pole Playhouse. Hiking, biking, fishing, and country store museum on grounds. Swimming privileges at local country club. Golfing, horseback riding and antiquing nearby. The Hammett Family, Innkeepers. (See Index for rates.)

Directions: From Gettysburg take Rte. 116 west to Fairfield and follow signs 3 mi. north to Orrtanna. From south, take U.S. 81 north to Green-castle, Pa. Then east on Rte. 16 to 116 east to Fairfield. From south, take U.S. 270 to Rte. 15 to Emmittsburg, Md., then west on 16 to Rte. 116 east through Fairfield. From west of Pa. Tpke., get off at Blue Mt. exit and go south on Rte. 977 to Rte. 30 east for 9 mi. Turn south at Cashtown, Pa., and follow the signs.

THE INN AT STARLIGHT LAKE
Starlight, Pennsylvania (1976)

The orchestra was playing "Moonglow." The peepers were peeping and the sunset afterglow was lighting the western sky. I had wandered out on the front porch of the Inn at Starlight, speaking, as everyone else did, to the mother cat and her two brand-new kittens. I wandered down the steps through the little grove of trees next to the lake and out onto the long dock, off of which were moored boats and sailboats.

I turned around to look at the lights of the inn and could hear the voices of some of my innkeeping friends from Pennsylvania and New York, who had gathered here to enjoy the opportunity to exchange experiences, tell good stories, and perhaps lend encouragement and counsel to each other. The trees along the shore created lacy silhouettes against the darkening blue sky. Then I noticed that several other innkeepers had decided to take a walk along the shore of the lake to help digest the wonderful evening meal. The small orchestra changed to a bit more up-tempo with "String of Pearls."

My evening meanderings also brought me within sight and earshot of four ducks who had taken up residence in the lake near the inn. Three of them were feathered in beautiful hues and the fourth was an ordinary white barnyard duck. They all had names and, as Judy McMahon explained, they had "just sort of all arrived and never left. They are busy morning and night rooting in the lush green grass at the edge of the lake for some succulent tidbits, and then cruising energetically to this end of the lake, occasionally diving down into the depths after some elusive fish."

This inn is on a back road, overlooking beautiful Starlight Lake. It is a rambling, old-fashioned, comfortable place with an accumulation of furniture from over the years. The combination lobby/living room has a fireplace in one corner, and there are reminders that the McMahons are originally from show business. Besides the piano and the guitar, books of plays or sheet music may be found on the tables or on the bookshelves.

Guest rooms are in the main building and also in adjacent cottages that have been redecorated and winterized. The inn is on the modified American plan, meaning that dinner and breakfast are included in the room rate. Lunch is offered every day at an additional charge.

There's a TV room, a game room in the main house, and lots of outdoor activity, from canoeing, sailing, swimming, and bicycling to ice skating on the forty-five-acre lake and cross-country skiing on eighteen miles of marked trails. Incidentally, their bicycle built for two is a real test of togetherness for their guests. There is a very pleasant lakeside play area, and many lovely walks and dirt roads for backroading in the picturesque woods. By the way, the McMahons have a fabulous collection of old films.

Their chef, Michael O'Neill, a graduate of the École Cordon Bleu in Paris, creates some wonderful dishes, like filet mignon with duxelles in brioche with Bordelaise sauce, veal medallions in a green peppercorn sauce, and lobster and shrimp marinara over his own fettucini. He makes his own pasta, as well as mayonnaise, stock, sauces, sherbets, and ice cream.

The newest feature is Starlight's occasional murder mystery weekend. I've been offered a small role in a future production—probably the victim!

Now I could hear Jack McMahon's high tenor voice wafting out from the living room, and I knew it was time to go back for a very pleasant evening at the Inn at Starlight Lake. It's always a pleasure to visit.

THE INN AT STARLIGHT LAKE, Starlight, PA 18461; 717-798-2519. A 27-guestroom (17 private baths) resort-inn, 5 mi. from Hancock, NY. All-size beds available. Modified American plan. Breakfast, lunch, and dinner served daily between May 15 and Apr. 1. Closed Apr. 1 through Apr. 15. Wheelchair access. Swimming, boating, canoeing, sailing, fishing, hunting, tennis, hiking, bicycling, xc skiing, and lawn sports on grounds. Golf nearby. No pets. Judy and Jack McMahon, Innkeepers. (See Index for rates.)

Directions: From N.Y. Rte. 17, exit at Hancock, N.Y. Take Rte. 191S over Delaware River to Rte. 370. Turn right, proceed 3½ mi.; turn right, 1 mi. to inn. From I-81, take Exit 62 at Tompkinsville. Follow Rte. 107 east 4 mi. to Rte. 247N and Forest City. Turn left on Rte. 171 (the main street), and continue 10 mi. north to Rte. 370. Turn right and go 13 mi. east to Starlight. Turn left, 1 mi. to inn.

THE MERCERSBURG INN
Mercersburg, Pennsylvania (1990)

The colonial village of Mercersburg, located in the beautiful Cumberland Valley at the foot of the Tuscarora Mountains, has maintained its historic architecture and small-town character. Once a frontier trading post, rumor has it that the property was purchased from Indians with guns and beads. As I drove down Main Street, dotted on either side with historic structures of limestone, brick, and log, most dating back to the early 1700s, I was unprepared for my first sight of the elegant Mercersburg Inn.

Constructed in 1909 of Berlin brick, the Georgian mansion's impressive main entrance is accentuated by six massive columns. Large double porches at either end overlook 5 acres of gently terraced lawns. In 1986, Fran Wolfe Guy, an artist with more than eighteen years of renovation experience, purchased the three-story mansion and began extensive restoration. "I used to attend a girls' boarding school near here, in Chambersburg," she explained, "where my mother owned and operated a resort." The combination of business skills she learned from her mother, and her renovation and artistic skills learned as an adult, proved to be invaluable when she purchased The Mercersburg Inn.

The inn's grand entrance features polished chestnut paneling. Walking between two rose-colored scagliola columns, you can climb to the second floor by way of a graceful, curving double staircase, with unusual serpentine banisters. Sunlight filters through stained-glass windows.

The public rooms are all elegant but comfortable. The grand hall has four sets of French doors that are opened during balmy summer evenings, and a fireplace to warm the room in the chill winter. But it's the large, airy sunroom that seems to offer the most luxurious setting for relaxation. White wicker furnishings and floral cushions on the window seats create a perfect atmosphere for sipping mint-laced iced tea. In the winter the fireplace roars, and scenes of snowy delight can be seen through the large windows.

For indoor entertainment, the bowling alley that once took up the basement has been removed and made into a game room, where guests can play billiards and board games, or watch television or a VCR.

Fran's artistry is quite evident in the inn's spacious guest rooms, each uniquely decorated. Most of the rooms have handmade cherry canopy beds and down comforters. She has made excellent use of fabrics for swagging, around beds and windows, to create a sense of romance. Antiques and tastefully hung artwork complete the mood. All rooms have meticulously restored baths.

Swiss chef George Vetch prepares a six-course meal every evening. As you sit in the mahogany-paneled dining room amidst leaded glass chandeliers and antique cabinets and sideboards, you will be served an exquisite meal, both in flavor and beauty, on Limoges china.

I began my meal with a curried butternut squash and apple-almond soup that had a smooth texture and subtle flavoring. After an appetizer of grilled sea scallops with saffron poached potatoes, I was served a tender breast of duck, lightly coated with a port wine sauce, and accompanied by grilled quince and persimmons. A salad and dessert followed, and were of equal merit. The flavors of herbs from the inn's gardens and the freshness of the locally grown vegetables are evident in each dish.

Breakfast is also available, and can be enjoyed in the sunroom. By the way, the wallpaper in this room is a pattern that was used by Thomas Jefferson at Monticello.

Be sure to take advantage of the historical richness of the area and stroll through Mercersburg. The inn is also only an hour's drive to Harper's Ferry and the Gettysburg Battlefield. A stay at The Mercersburg Inn is country elegance at its best. We welcome the inn to *Country Inns and Back Roads.*

THE MERCERSBURG INN, 405 S. Main St., Mercersburg, PA 17236; 717-328-5231. A 15-guestroom (private baths) elegant country inn located in historical Mercersburg. All-size beds. Open year-round. Six-course gourmet meal with modified American plan; breakfast on B&B. Close to Harper's Ferry, Gettysburg Battlefield, hiking, skiing, boating. No smoking. Pets by special arrangement. Fran Wolfe Guy, Owner; John Mohr, Innkeeper.

Directions: Take Pa. Exit 3 from I-81 west on Pa. Rte. 16 to Mercersburg. The inn is on the left (Pa. Rtes. 16 and 75).

SMITHTON INN
Ephrata, Pennsylvania (1987)

"We want our guests to have a great Lancaster County experience. The Old Order people who live in this part of Pennsylvania live exactly as most of our forebears did. Customs have remained unchanged here. It's like being in touch with your own family's past."

I was to ponder that thought, expressed by Dorothy Graybill, many, many times during my visit to the Smithton Inn and the surrounding countryside at Ephrata, a predominantly Pennsylvania Dutch community.

"Unfortunately, the image of the Pennsylvania Dutch has been considerably distorted over the years, largely because of the efforts to commercialize some of the customs, language, and artifacts. We have developed a booklet with suggestions for touring and shopping that completely eliminates any of these places," Dorothy continued. "Both Allan and I make extensive and continuing trips throughout the countryside to make certain that our guests see the 'real' Pennsylvania Dutch life."

Dorothy was speaking of her associate at the Smithton Inn, Allan Smith, who is, among many other things, an excellent architect and woodcraftsman. We were having a chat in the truly handsome Great Room of the inn, and I couldn't help but feel that this room, with its fireplace, braided rug, comfortable furniture, and brightly polished hardwood floors, was an excellent place to start any adventure of this nature.

The inn is a pre-Revolutionary inn and stagecoach stop, built in 1763, and has been an inn for most of its many years. Each of the guest rooms has its own working fireplace or cast iron stove and can be candlelighted during the evening hours. Beds have canopies, soft goose-down pillows, and bright handmade Pennsylvania Dutch quilts. Red flannel nightshirts are an amusing touch for guests to wear if they wish. Something I particularly appreciate is the speaker on every bedside table with a volume control, so that guests can enjoy the tasteful selection of chamber music. And on cold winter evenings you may have your bed made with a featherbed. Allan is pleased to escort inn guests through the inn, pointing out many of the marvelously designed and constructed features, not only in the original building, but in the additions that are being made. He has a wonderful sense of history and an obvious affection for good craftsmanship.

In a recent note from Dorothy, she mentioned that they have finished redecorating a four-room suite and also the Gold Room, which sounds very elegant, with gold velvet draperies, a gold velvet and black leather chair and couch, and a queen-sized, canopied bed. This room is on the first floor and faces the garden and is most convenient for guests who cannot use steps.

"We serve a full country breakfast and a rather simple but nourishing evening meal at our guests' request," Dorothy told me. "It consists of an appetizer, soup, salad, and a meat pie. Dessert is a homemade ice cream with our exceptional chocolate sauce, which is a story in itself."

The well-known Ephrata Cloister, an 18th-century German Protestant monastic society, is situated just a few steps away. It is the scene of *Vorspiel*, a musical drama presented throughout the summer.

The entire area abounds in museums, crafts shops, antiques malls, summer and winter theater, concerts, winery tours, and art exhibits. There is also a summer-long Renaissance fair. Among several fine Pennsylvania Dutch restaurants are some located on picturesque Dutch farms.

I strongly suggest that our readers plan on staying at the Smithton Inn for a minimum of two nights and, if possible, three or more. The expert and caring guidance from the innkeepers provides every one with a "real Lancaster County experience."

SMITHTON INN, 900 W. Main St., Ephrata, PA 17522; 717-733-6094. A 7-guestroom (private baths) pre-Revolutionary inn in Pennsylvania Dutch country near Lancaster. King, queen, and double beds available. Breakfast included in room rate. Dinner served to houseguests by advance reservation. Those sensitive to traffic noise should ask for an inside room or the Gold Room. Open all year. Wheelchair access. Convenient to all of Lancaster County's cultural, historic, and recreational attractions. Ephrata Cloister nearby. Dorothy Graybill, Owner-hostess. (See Index for rates.)

Directions: Ṣmithton is located 11 mi. north of Lancaster, an 5 mi. south of Pa. Tpke. Exit 21. From north or south, take Hwy. 222 to Ephrata exit. Turn west on Rte. 322 for 2.5 mi. to inn.

STERLING INN
South Sterling, Pennsylvania (1974)

I could not resist it any longer—I had been listening to the gurgling waters of the Wallenpaupack Creek for about twenty minutes on a warm, lazy afternoon. I was sitting on a lawn chair about fifty paces from the back of the Sterling Inn, just two feet from the bank of the creek. The smell of the freshly cut lawn mingled with the scent of the forest on the other side of the water.

I kicked off my shoes, rolled up my pants, and waded out to stand on the flat, smooth shelf of rock in the middle of the creek. The water was clean and cool. There was a little pool about twenty-five feet away, deep enough for someone to sit in and have the water come up to his chest. A flash of red and another of blue signaled a cardinal and a bluejay darting into the woods, deep in the Pocono Mountains of Pennsylvania.

I climbed back on the bank and was drying my feet, when one of the other guests came and plunked down on a nearby chair. "I think this is one of the best-kept, neatest places that I have ever visited," she said. "It's as American as apple pie and fresh vegetables. The rooms are so comfortable, and I'm very glad I came. Don't you just love it here?"

Even if her enthusiasm hadn't been catching, I would have had to agree.

This was the friendly and unpretentious atmosphere that Alice Julian had in mind over a half-century ago when she acquired the Sterling Inn. That is the way her daughter and son-in-law, Carmen and Henry Arneberg, kept it, and the same way that the present owners, Ron and Mary Kay Logan, are keeping it today.

The Sterling Inn is on a back road in the Poconos. There are enticing hiking and walking trails on the inn property and nearby. One of them, Ron told me, leads to a waterfall on the ridge behind the inn. There is a very pleasant nine-hole putting green, a swimming area with a sandy beach, and a little pond with willow trees and a few ducks.

Guest rooms are in several very attractive buildings, all beautifully situated in the parklike surroundings. Some handsome new suites have been furnished with beautiful antiques, Franklin woodburning fireplaces, and decks overlooking the creek that I was wading in.

The menu includes such entrées as roast lamb, pot roast, and standing rib roast because, Mary Kay Logan says, "This is the kind of food that people serve only when they are having guests for dinner." All the baking is done in the warm, friendly kitchen.

In many ways this Pocono Mountain inn personifies the things that I find most delightful in country inns. For example, fresh flowers are on the dining room tables at all times, and there are books and magazines in all parlors and sitting rooms. When guests advise the inn of their arrival time, the inn automobile will meet buses and airplanes. Special diets can also be accommodated.

The inn is open year-round, and the setting is like a picture postcard. Winter activities include cross-country skiing and lessons, ice skating, sledding, winter hikes, and roasting chestnuts or marshmallows by the open fire. The horse-drawn sleigh rides are very popular.

In the blaze of autumn colors there are incredibly beautiful nature walks along Wallenpaupack Creek and hikes on woodland trails. Spring and summer at the Sterling Inn, of course, offer all sorts of outdoor enjoyment.

STERLING INN, Rte. 191, South Sterling, PA 18460; 717-676-3311. From Ct., N.Y., N.J., Md., Del., Wash., D.C.: 800-523-8200. A 56-guestroom (private baths) secluded country inn-resort in the Pocono Mountains, 8 mi. from I-84 and 12 mi. from I-380. All-size beds available. Modified American plan. Bed-and-breakfast rates available. Reservation and check-in offices close at 10 p.m. Breakfast, lunch, and dinner served to travelers daily. Jackets requested for dinner. Open year-round. Indoor swimming and spa, putting green, shuffleboard, all-weather tennis court, scenic hiking trails, xc skiing and lessons, ice skating, and sledding on grounds. Golf courses, horseback riding, major ski areas nearby. Gift shop and print gallery. No pets. Ron and Mary Kay Logan, Owners-hosts. (See Index for rates.)

Directions: From I-80, follow I-380 to Rte. 940 to Mount Pocono. At light, cross Rte. 611 and proceed on Rte. 196 north to Rte. 423. Drive north on Rte. 423 to Rte. 191 and travel ½ mi. north to inn. From I-84, follow Rte. 507 south through Greentown and Newfoundland. In Newfoundland, pick up Rte. 191 and travel 4 mi. south to inn.

TARA
Clark, Pennsylvania (1986)

Inspired by the world's most renowned movie, *Gone With the Wind,* Jim and Donna Winner restored a beautiful antebellum mansion located midway between Cleveland, Ohio, and Pittsburgh, Pennsylvania. They named it Tara.

When I first saw Tara from the rolling highways of western Pennsylvania I wondered if magically I'd been transported in time to the Old South of the early 1800s—the era before the Civil War, when grace and grandeur, honor, fine clothes, plantations, and Southern hospitality were the lifestyle.

The house, built in 1854, is one of western Pennsylvania's most famous historic landmarks. The mansion, with its two-story Grecian columns, overlooks 4,000-acre Lake Shenango, surrounded by rolling hills of maple and pine. The grounds are enhanced by a gazebo and many beautiful flowers.

Incurable romantics, Jim and Donna knew from the first time they saw what was to become Tara that it should definitely be a country inn. They have made it their home and have lavishly displayed their entire collection of antiques, art, rare china, and crystal throughout, including crystal chandeliers from Austria and a hand-painted Dresden chandelier from Germany. An antique brass chandelier featuring Steuben shades graces the circular stairwell.

There are thirteen guest rooms, all with working fireplaces. Each room has been carefully decorated to reflect the personality of a character from the book. For example, Miss Melanie's room is all feminine and

fluffy in yellow and pink, with bows and wicker furniture. Overlooking the lake, it boasts one of the best views in the house. Rhett's room is masculine and strong. Its focal point is a center-island bed with a canopy that rises to the nine-foot ceiling. The Katie O'Hara room has an 18th-century hand-carved bed and a hand-painted ivy floor. The "old maid's" stairwell descends to the lovely antique private bath below.

There are two main dining rooms, a tavern, and a patio café for outdoor dining in clement weather. Ashley's is for formal dining, with such offerings as medallions of beef, Norwegian salmon, and rack of lamb, an array of tantalizing desserts, and special gourmet coffees, all served on antique tables set with crystal and silver. The Old South Room is a true-to-life Southern-style dining room, serving fried chicken, smoked ham, grits, cornbread, and other Dixie favorites, all served family style. Stonewall's Tavern has walls of hand-hewn stone with beamed ceilings and offers a lighter, more informal menu.

Tara is just fun to browse through. There is an authentic, primitive slave kitchen, a primitive bedroom with a genuine rope bed, and a collection of antiques that date back to 1760. One of the pieces on display is a table that belonged to President James Buchanan and was used in the White House during his administration, just before the Civil War. The library itself is most impressive, with both old and new books, and one can read on the veranda or in Miss Pittypat's Parlor.

The day after Thanksgiving, 100,000 tiny white lights will be draped in the trees and bushes. The trees in the parlor are decorated in a Victorian mode, and those in the Old South Room will be done in an old-fashioned style. Bows and holly adorn the crystal chandeliers.

A letter I received from one of my Canadian readers said in part: "On our return from a trip to Washington, D.C., we were truly transported to the period when hospitality was a very special thing in the South and we experienced this at Tara. Every trip should include at least one outstanding and memorable experience and indeed our visit to Tara will be remembered for many years."

TARA, 3665 Valley View Rd., Box 475, Rte. 18, Clark, PA 16113; 412-962-3535. A 13-guestroom (private baths) mansion, 8 hrs. west of New York and 8 hrs. east of Chicago. Breakfast, lunch, and dinner served. Open year-round. Croquet, bocci, boating, fishing, swimming, carriage rides, bicycling, backroading, xc skiing, and golf. Not suitable for children. No pets. Jim and Donna Winner, Owners-hosts. (See Index for rates.)

Directions: Just inside the Pa. border on I-80 take Exit 1N and follow Rte. 18 north for 8 mi. Tara is located on the east side overlooking Lake Shenango. Art, plane

THE INN AT MILLRACE POND
Hope, New Jersey (1989)

The village of Hope, listed on the National Register of Historic Places, has been called the best-preserved historic community on the East Coast. Established in 1769 by a settlement of Moravians, the little township boasts over fifteen of the original stone houses still standing. The Moravians were a hardy and industrious people of German descent, who had emigrated from Moravia and Bohemia to escape religious persecution in 1735.

Their four-story stone gristmill now qualifies as the oldest building in Hope, since the log cabin that was built before the mill no longer exists. It is also on the National Register of Historic Places. When Gloria Carrigan and Dick Gooding discovered the mill, it was an imposing ruin. The shell was intact, but the inside was a disaster of rubble, boards, and litter.

However, the great Y-posts, hand-hewn celing beams, and interior stone walls and arches were still there, and as a builder and developer, Dick Gooding, along with an architect friend, had a vision of how to rescue this landmark structure.

When work was first started, Gloria told me, her mother came to see what was going on, and her only remark was, "You're dreaming." And of course, that's exactly what they were doing. Dick and Gloria's dream was to create an inn that was true to its Colonial origins, not only in architecture and furnishings but also in spirit. That was in 1986.

Today, the gristmill has been handsomely restored, with a below-stairs tavern, featuring an enormous walk-in fireplace, a spacious dining room, and generous guest rooms with modern baths on the second and third floors. Across a brick terrace, the miller's house has a charming little parlor and several guest rooms, and the wheelwright's stone cottage houses two spacious rooms, ideal for families.

All of the rooms reflect a classic simplicity, with Williamsburg colors, braided or oriental rugs, and a mixture of antiques and fine reproductions of Colonial-period furniture. With a nod in the direction of comfort and convenience, the lamps have dimmer switches, many of the tubs have whirlpools, and the beds have Sealy Posturepedic mattresses.

Right from the start, Gloria asked her three chefs, all graduates of culinary schools, to incorporate some basic Colonial foods, such as chicken, duckling, game, corn, and asparagus, into their innovative American cuisine. Their corn and mussel chowder is a great success, as are their cured salmon, rabbit in puff pastry, roast half duckling with apple and peppercorn sauce, and a mouth-watering list of desserts. The *New York Times* gave them a "Very Good" rating, which is high praise, indeed.

As I walked along the millrace with Dick, admiring the beautiful old maples and locusts and the green lawn that sloped up a little hill, he told me of how the Moravians had cut through twenty feet of rock and shale to make a channel for the water to flow by gravity from the pond to the mill.

I was fascinated by the ingenious way a series of short staircases had been arranged to create a landing or balcony just inside the entrance to the mill. Standing on this balcony and looking down into the millrace chamber, where the great skeleton of the sixteen-foot overshot wheel stands, seeing the narrow stream of water that still comes down the millrace from the millpond, just as it did in the 1700s, I got a real sense of the original use of this building.

THE INN AT MILLRACE POND, Box 359, Route 519, Hope, NJ 07844; 201-459-4884. A 16-guestroom (private baths) Colonial inn in a tiny historic Moravian village in western New Jersey, 70 min, from NYC across the Geo. Washington Bridge. Queen and twin beds available. Continental breakfast included in rate. Dinner served to travelers; reservations suggested. Open year-round. Wheelchair access to dining room. Delaware Water Gap Recreation Area, Waterloo Village with seasonal concerts, antiques and crafts shows, hiking, biking, fishing, canoeing, shopping, wineries, and winter sports in Poconos nearby. No pets. Dick Gooding and Gloria Carrigan, Owners-hosts. (See Index for rates.)

Directions: From Rte. 80 take Exit 12 to Rte. 521 and continue south approx. 1 mi. to blinker in Hope. Turn left on Rte. 519 down hill and drive past inn to parking area.

THE MAINSTAY INN & COTTAGE
Cape May, New Jersey (1976)

"Last year marked the opening of the Cape May Point Lighthouse, built in 1859. I've been working on it for the past seven years," Tom Carroll told me. He and Sue Carroll were bringing me up to date as we sat on the porch of the Mainstay Inn, enjoying a cup of tea. "We established a nonprofit organization, leased the lighthouse from the Coast Guard, and have opened it to the public. It's attracting hundreds of people daily."

"We're very proud of our involvement with the community," Sue said, "and of what we've contributed toward making Cape May one of the most beautiful and popular towns on the Eastern seaboard."

I've known Tom and Sue for thirteen of their eighteen years as innkeepers, and I've always admired their creativity and dedication. They have restored the Mainstay and the 1870 summer cottage next door with great fidelity to the period. In a town of hundreds of restored Victorian buildings, the Mainstay, built in 1872 as an elegant gentleman's club, is considered one of the finest examples of Victorian architecture and decoration.

To the original features that survived the years, such as the fourteen-foot ceilings with eight-foot chandeliers and many important furnishings, they added beautiful antiques and special touches. They used Bradbury & Bradbury silk-screened wallpapers; they had ceilings and walls decorated by an expert in stenciling; and they assiduously tracked down authentic fittings and fixtures.

The three parlors and huge guest rooms are almost all furnished in what is called Renaissance Revival. "It's flowing to the eye with graceful curves," Sue explained. "Walnut was used extensively during the 1870s, and there are very tall mirrors, tall headboards, and wardrobes. They're a shock compared to things today. Under some of the beds are chamber pots that roll out on wooden trays, and other beds have the original mosquito nets attached to small pulleys in the ceilings. I think the fun of staying here is that you are seeing furniture that would never go in your house, and it can be very exciting."

While we were chatting, I noticed an occasional horse and carriage clip-clopping by the inn. "Oh, yes," Sue said, "Cape May has regular horse-and-carriage and antique auto tours of the town."

Breakfast is served in the dining room or on warm days on the veranda, where even now I was enjoying the hydrangeas, tiger lilies, and roses blooming profusely in the yard. It's a wonderful place for afternoon tea and cookies, served after the house tour, conducted at 3:30 p.m. every day for visitors and houseguests.

In addition to myriad summer activities in Cape May, an annual Shakespeare Weekend is held at the Mainstay in March, and there's always a Dickens Christmas extravaganza in December.

The Mainstay and the Carrolls offer their guests a truly opulent Victorian experience on one of the most beautiful historical streets right in the center of a beautiful seaside Victorian town.

THE MAINSTAY INN & COTTAGE, 635 Columbia Ave., Cape May, NJ 08204; 609-884-8690. A 12-guestroom inn (private baths) in a well-preserved Victorian village just one block from the ocean. All-size beds available. Breakfast served to houseguests. Open every day from mid-March to mid-Dec. Fine restaurants, historic house tours, summer theater, sailboat trips, horse and carriage tours, concerts, military reviews, bird-watching, beach, boating, swimming, fishing, bicycles, riding, golf, tennis, and hiking nearby. Not suitable for small children. No pets. No credit cards; personal checks accepted. Tom and Sue Carroll, Owners-hosts. (See Index for rates.)

Directions: From Philadelphia take the Walt Whitman Bridge to the Atlantic City Expy. Follow the Atlantic City Expy. to exit for Garden State Pkwy., south. Go south on pkwy., which ends in Cape May, where pkwy. becomes Lafayette St. Turn left at first light onto Madison. Proceed 3 blocks and turn right onto Columbia. Proceed 3 blocks to inn on right side.

The date in parenthesis in the heading represents the first year the inn appeared in the pages of Country Inns and Back Roads.

THE STOCKTON INN, "COLLIGAN'S"
Stockton, New Jersey

When I checked in at the Stockton Inn, "Colligan's," I asked to meet manager-host Andrew McDermott and was ushered to the inn's tavern. I chuckled to myself as I walked in, thinking that was, of course, a most logical place to find a true Scotsman. But this Scotsman was busy at work, seeing to the full-service bar's supplies, and making additions to the inn's already extensive wine list. "Well, I see you found me," he said, smiling, as we shook hands. Andrew recently took over management of the inn and thoroughly seems to enjoy his work. As he finished up the orders, he gave me a brief history of the inn, starting with the tavern.

"This tavern has been here the entire life of the inn—since 1796. It really was called a 'public house' then, and we still like to run it that way. The local townspeople come at the end of the day to relax and enjoy themselves. We like the English-pub atmosphere."

The inn is built of lovely old stones, with white pillars, and a mansard roof on the third floor. The stone walls have a soft, weathered look that comes with Pennsylvania–New Jersey stone. "You know, this place has been said to have inspired the song 'There's a Small Hotel,' " Andrew told me as we entered one of the inn's dining rooms. Unusual murals depicting the countryside as it was during the early part of the 19th century decorate the plaster walls. Some of them have been carefully restored.

As he showed me to my room, I asked about any special activities that would be taking place during my stay. "You'll probably have to make a list in priority order since we always have more things to do than guests have time for. First, we have a great cabaret every Friday in the Garden Room, then there's jazz every Saturday in the inn's Silver Dollar Bar, and dinner at our French restaurant, The Fox, is a real special treat," he said enthusiastically. "We have a large menu, with at least a dozen entrees, ranging from rack of lamb to boneless lacquered duck, and our not-to-be-missed famous crab cakes. In the winter we serve ethnic meals on Friday evenings."

Andrew left me to settle in, suggesting I visit the antique show and sale at Prall's Mill later in the day. My Carriage House suite was handsomely furnished, comfortable, and ready with a laid fire for a cold evening. But, as it was August, I was truly grateful for the air-conditioner softly humming away. The other suites are located in the main inn, the Wagon House, and the Federal House.

The brochure on the desk in my room highlighted the inn's special offerings: two-night midweek getaways, romantic overnights, Veteran's Day weekend, Election Day, and the Fourth of July. I could see why the inn has so many return visitors.

As I left for the antique show, I flipped a nickel into the inn's

whimsical wishing well, wishing for . . . but then, that's my secret, and walked off humming "There's a Small Hotel."

STOCKTON INN, "COLLIGAN'S," Main St., Stockton, NJ 08559; 609-397-1250. An 11-guestroom (private baths) traditional inn in a Delaware River village. Lunch and dinner served every day. Continental breakfast included. Open all year. Weekends, two-night minimum. Queen beds. All of the scenic, historic, and cultural attractions of nearby Bucks County, Pa., and New Jersey. No pets. Andrew McDermott, Manager-host.

Directions: From N.Y., take N.J. Tnpk. south to Exit 10, then follow I-287 north of Somerville and exit on Rte. 22 west. Go 2½ mi., then take Rte. 202 south, past Flemington to the Delaware River. Use the last exit in New Jersey, marked Rte. 29, Lambertville and Stockton. Go 3 mi. north on Rte. 29 to Stockton. From Philadelphia, follow I-95 north to the Delaware River. Cross the Delaware to the first exit in New Jersey, marked Rte. 29 Trenton/Lambertville. Follow Rte. 29 north through Lambertville, approx. 17 mi. to Stockton.

"European plan" means that rates for rooms and meals are separate. "American plan" means that meals are included in the cost of the room. "Modified American plan" means that breakfast and dinner are included in the cost of the room. The rates at some inns include a continental breakfast with the lodging.

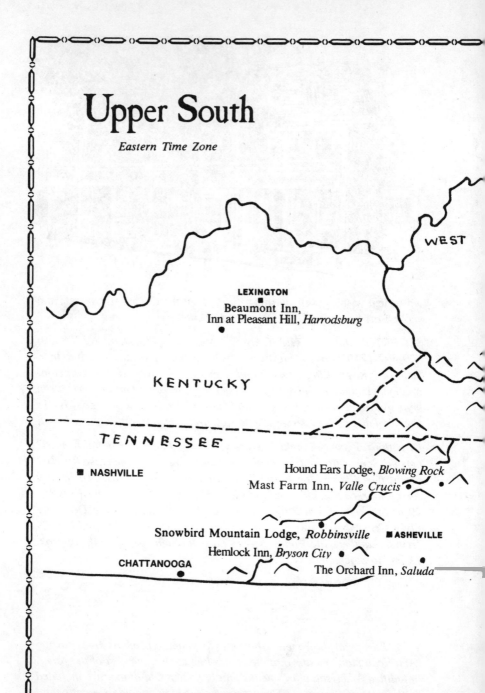

Upper South

Eastern Time Zone

WEST

LEXINGTON
Beaumont Inn,
Inn at Pleasant Hill, *Harrodsburg*

KENTUCKY

TENNESSEE

■ NASHVILLE

Hound Ears Lodge, *Blowing Rock*
Mast Farm Inn, *Valle Crucis*

Snowbird Mountain Lodge, *Robbinsville* ■ ASHEVILLE
Hemlock Inn, *Bryson City*
CHATTANOOGA
The Orchard Inn, *Saluda*

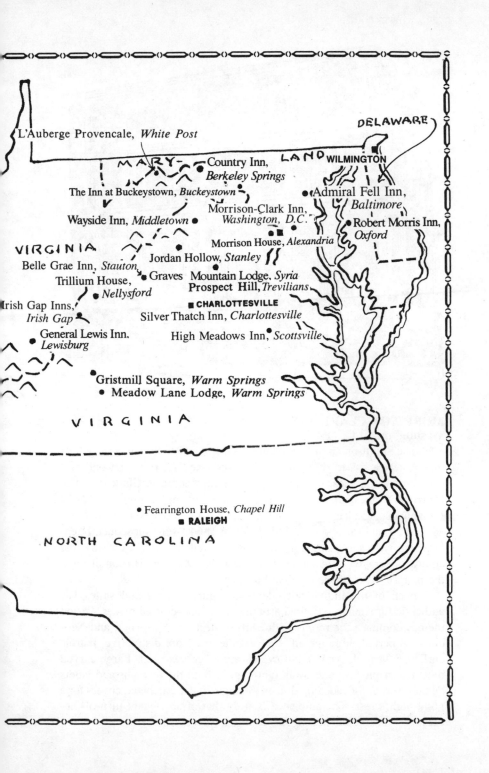

L'Auberge Provencale, *White Post*

DELAWARE

Country Inn, *Berkeley Springs* MARYLAND WILMINGTON

The Inn at Buckeystown, *Buckeystown* • Admiral Fell Inn, *Baltimore*

Morrison-Clark Inn, *Washington, D.C.*

Wayside Inn, *Middletown* • Robert Morris Inn, *Oxford*

VIRGINIA Morrison House, *Alexandria*

Jordan Hollow, *Stanley*

Belle Grae Inn, *Stauton*

Trillium House, • Graves Mountain Lodge, *Syria*
• *Nellysford* Prospect Hill, *Trevilians*

Irish Gap Inns, ■ CHARLOTTESVILLE
Irish Gap Silver Thatch Inn, *Charlottesville*

General Lewis Inn, High Meadows Inn, *Scottsville*
Lewisburg

• Gristmill Square, *Warm Springs*
• Meadow Lane Lodge, *Warm Springs*

VIRGINIA

• Fearrington House, *Chapel Hill*
■ RALEIGH

NORTH CAROLINA

MORRISON-CLARK INN
Washington, D.C. (1990)

The Smithsonian Institution in Washington, D.C. is one of the jewels that America has to offer the world. And one of the most wonderful accommodations near the Smithsonian is the Morrison-Clark Inn. The Morrison-Clark is the only historic inn in the nation's capital. The 1864 Italiante mansion has a lovely Shanghai porch and spacious bay windows. The two grand townhouses, completed in 1864, were subsequently enlarged in 1876 and a two-story veranda was added in 1917. In 1987, the additions were removed and a new addition was completed to complement the historic lines of the original building.

Each of the individually decorated guest rooms and suites has authentic furnishings, original artwork, and hand-crafted pieces. Period themes dominate the rooms with Early American, Victorian, and Neo-classical periods highlighted. Victorian textures are distinctive; marble curlicues, lace, damask, and raw silk are all represented. Large carved pine and maple armoires await clothing. Pull on the festoons and jabots and lower sound-deadening drapes. Snuggle under crocheted covers for a good night's rest. The ambience is truly that of an elegant turn-of-the-century Washington home. All rooms have private baths, television, telephones, individually controlled heating and air-conditioning, and computer access data ports.

The raw silk texturing is repeated in the inn's 120-seat restaurant, furbished with floor-to-ceiling mirrors. The main dining room displays Chinese art objects, a circular sofa topped by an imposing floral arrangement, and a unique collection of oxblood vases arranged on shelves.

Our dinner was quite spectacular, highlighted by chef David Fye's Southern dishes: she-crab soup, fried catfish, Louisiana pan-fried fish stew, and pan-roasted quail. The accompanying black bean and grilled onion cakes with orange and toasted chilies were wonderful. Other specialties include Louisiana crayfish bisque, roasted boneless chicken with old-fashioned mustard cream gravy, and a mouth-watering double chocolate espresso torte with anisette whipped cream. A quiet courtyard with a fountain is a perfect setting for informal outdoor dining.

There are three comfortable common rooms in which to relax after such a fabulous dinner: The club room, with high ceilings and cozy arm chairs, the parlor, with exotic Victorian furnishings, and the lovely marble-floored lobby. Traditional design themes such as red, white, and gray Spanish tile accent the lobby. Fabric of woven plum are layered on foyer walls. The club room is painted a lovely storm-cloud gray and is hung with splendid hunt-scene oils.

The Morrison-Clark Inn is centrally located three blocks from the Capitol Convention Center, and only eight blocks from the mall and the Smithsonian. It offers guests the comfort and uniqueness of a country inn in the city.

MORRISON-CLARK INN, 11th at Massachusetts Ave., N.W., Washington, DC, 20001; 202-898-1200 or 800-332-7898. A 54-guestroom Italiante mansion (private baths) near the Smithsonian Institution. Open all year. Queen, double, and twin beds. Continental breakfast included in room fee; lunch and dinner available. Close to subway, mall, Smithsonian, and Capitol Convention Center; 6 mi. to National Airport. Small pets and smoking accepted. DEC Development, Owners; Michael A. Such, Manager.

Directions: From Baltimore, take I-95 south to Balt-Washington Pkwy. Proceed to N.Y. Ave. At 5th St., N.W., go right on L St. and proceed 6 blocks. Hotel is on right.

The date in parenthesis in the heading represents the first year the inn appeared in the pages of Country Inns and Back Roads.

ADMIRAL FELL INN
Baltimore, Maryland

If you've always yearned for the free life of a sailor, spend some time at the Admiral Fell Inn and voyage back to Colonial Baltimore. Located in the rejuvenated, working waterfront community of Fells Point, the Admiral Fell Inn is the only historic inn on the waterfront.

Originally known as the Anchorage Hotel, the three connected buildings, constructed between 1850 and 1910, were used as a 28-room boarding house for sailors, then as a vinegar factory. Owner Jim Widman purchased the inn in 1984, and began what had to be a difficult renovation project. "Being an ex-navy officer, I never did quite shake the call of the sea," he told me as I registered. The friendly atmosphere of the inn is immediately noticeable; a partners desk adds a more personal flair than the standard hotel front desk.

Jim's attention to historical accuracy is apparent both in the interior and exterior. The oldest of the inn's buildings is a three-story columned structure of red brick with an early Victorian-style facade. The other two buildings are four-story, rough-cut tan brick, with facades of simplified Georgian detailing. Standing at the inn's bright red front doors, I thought I could almost hear the heavy hobnail boots of sailors as they passed on the cobblestones.

Each guest room is unique in design, and decorated with antique treasures and period pieces found along the Eastern Seaboard. Every room bears the name and displays a biographical sketch of a famous Baltimorian. My room was luxurious, with two pencil-point four-poster

beds, canopied in intricate lace work. All rooms have private baths (some with Jacuzzis), telephones, and television. Three rooms are designed to accommodate the handicapped.

Visiting the Admiral Fell Inn offers the same feeling as a stay at the home of a wealthy friend, so well are comfort and luxury married. The wood-burning fireplace in the large gracious sitting area of the drawing room highlights the room's emerald greens and warm reds, while the deep browns of Federal furniture are reflected in the polished brass fixtures.

In contrast, the skylit, four-story first-floor atrium, with its lush plants, is flooded with warmth and light all year. The library has an excellent selection of reading material and also serves as a cozy spot to share a continental breakfast with other guests. Or, you may choose to breakfast in your room, and spend time lingering over your complimentary morning newspaper.

The inn's English-style pub is a delightful place to sip a glass of beer and listen to local lore of the 18th-century waterfront. The pub offers lunch and light fare daily. Dinner can be enjoyed by candlelight in the elegant courtyard, or the inn's restaurant, famous for its fondues and fresh seafood. Baltimore has long been known for its ethnically diverse restaurants where you can satisfy a craving for anything from Mexican to traditional New England cuisine. Many excellent restaurants are within walking distance, or you can take advantage of the inn's complimentary van transportation. For a romantic evening excursion, take the water taxi.

Baltimore is a fascinating city to explore. Theaters, taverns, markets, jazz clubs, landmark homes, quaint shops, and boating facilities are close to the inn. For example, a short stroll through the Fells Point area will bring you to China Sea Trading, a curiosity shop worth at least an hour's investigation.

The Admiral Fell Inn has the kind of gracious hospitality and subtle elegance that inspired the comment of the couple who shared my table during breakfast: "We came for a weekend. We wish we'd come for a week." I echo their thoughts.

ADMIRAL FELL INN, 888 S. Broadway, Baltimore, MD 21231; 301-522-7377 or 800-292-4667. A 40-guestroom (private baths) charming inn on the historic Fells Point waterfront. Open all year. Double and king-size beds. Continental breakfast included. Light fare in the pub, and dinner in the restaurant, all week. Complimentary van service. Pet boarding service available. Jim Widman, Owner-host.

Directions: From I-95, go north on Russel St. to Pratt St. Turn right and continue east for 1 mi. around Inner Harbor on President St. (I-83) and Fleet St. to Broadway. Go right on Broadway and continue to end.

THE INN AT BUCKEYSTOWN
Buckeystown, Maryland (1987)

Buckeystown is a beautiful old (1731) village with a number of Federal homes and stone structures dating to the Revolutionary War. There are also many Victorian houses, but by far the most impressive is the Inn, as you can see from Jan Lindstrom's drawing. Spring is a wonderful time to be there, when the pink dogwoods, lilacs, and flowering fruit trees scent the air.

The capacious wraparound porch with its old-fashioned rockers is a perfect spot to sit and enjoy the fragrance and the sunset, while possibly sipping a sherry and chatting with other guests. On the evening of my visit, a Canadian couple joined me. They told me they always stop here on their trips to and from Florida.

A dinner bell at 7:30 p.m. sharp summoned us into the elegant main dining room, where two oak tables of eight were set with antique china, glassware, and silver. The room is grandly Victorian, with a bold butterfly, bird-and-flower-patterned wallpaper, oriental rugs, oak sideboards and cabinets, and a magnificent crystal chandelier.

Dan Pelz and his evening manager, Betty Farley, had cooked the family-style dinner of cream of yellow pepper soup with fresh dill, Bibb lettuce and cherry tomato salad with fresh basil vinaigrette, Cornish game hen glazed with lime and ginger, served with wild rice and fresh asparagus. Dessert was something wonderful with fresh strawberries called Strawberry Fool.

As Dan explained later, they have one seating for both breakfast and dinner, and there's always a set menu for dinner with complimentary wine and special breads.

Dan, who began the inn in 1981 with his close friend and partner, Marty Martinez, has been doing double duty since Marty's untimely death last year.

"Rebecca Shipman, my innkeeper, and our exceptional staff have been my mainstay," he said, "and we are all dedicated to maintaining the excellent reputation of the inn."

There are eight rooms and two cottages, all charmingly furnished with period pieces, as well as such modern comforts as good mattresses, electric blankets, and air conditioning.

There are interesting walks near the inn—the Monocacy River, where fisherman cast for bass, an ancient Indian dig in a rocky cliff, woods and farmlands—Dan calls the area a paradise for architecture buffs, historians, antiquers, and outdoors people. Buckeystown is within an hour of Washington, D.C., Baltimore, and Gettysburg, and within a half-hour of Harper's Ferry, Leesburg, and New Market (the antiques capital of Maryland). Nearby Frederick is a beautifully restored historic town with many sites of interest, nice shops, and all city conveniences.

I should also mention that innkeeping duties are shared by Joshua, a Maine coon cat, and an arrogant Persian named Priscilla.

THE INN AT BUCKEYSTOWN, Buckeystown, MD 21717; 301-874-5755. A 10-guestroom (5 private baths) inn in a historic village. Queen and double beds available. Rates include dinner and breakfast. Dinner served to travelers with 24-hr. advance reservation. Open year-round. Minimum stay of 2 days required on all holidays and on weekends from Oct. 1 to Jan. 1, and from Apr. 1 to July 1. Conveniently located to enjoy all of the historical and cultural attractions of the region. No facilities for children under 16. No pets. Two cats in residence. No smoking in dining room. Dan Pelz, Owner; Rebecca Shipman, Manager. (See Index for rates.)

Directions: Buckeystown lies 4 mi. to the south of the Buckeystown exit off I-270 in Frederick, and 5 mi. to the south of the Buckeystown exit off I-70 in Frederick. Inn is located on Maryland Rte. 85.

"European plan" means that rates for rooms and meals are separate. "American plan" means that meals are included in the cost of the room. "Modified American plan" means that breakfast and dinner are included in the cost of the room. The rates at some inns include a continental breakfast with the lodging.

ROBERT MORRIS INN
Oxford, Maryland (1970)

The Robert Morris is on the eastern shore of Maryland beside the Tred Avon River. One of the ways to reach it is via the famous Cape May–Lewes ferry, which I've been riding ever since my first visit. Oxford is, surprisingly enough, still one of the most unspoiled villages in North America. It has several pre-Revolutionary and Federalist houses that are remarkably well preserved. Incidentally, you can get a copy of "This and That About Olde Oxford, Maryland" by Howard B. Gerhardt at the front desk of the inn. It's an extremely well-written informal history of Oxford.

The decorations in the main house have always attracted attention, and the murals in the dining room made from 140-year-old wallpaper samples, depict scenes from other places in North America, including Natural Bridge, Virginia, and Boston Harbor. The guest rooms in the main house are decorated in a casual motif with country rugs and coverlets and a variety of interesting knickknacks on the walls, among which are the tops of china serving dishes of many different designs.

I think Wendy and Ken Gibson can be justly proud that in the eighteen years since they took over the inn they've gone from almost entirely shared baths to almost entirely private baths (out of thirty-three guest rooms, thirty now have their own bathrooms). And they have added the special touch of handmade pine mirrors and shelves.

Just down the block on the waterfront is Sandaway, with six guest rooms decorated in a country-romantic style. All have a view of the river. They are reserved for nonsmokers. As a matter of fact, in the main house, the entire third floor is restricted to nonsmokers.

The inn's location in the Chesapeake Bay area means that there is considerable emphasis on seafood at lunch and dinner—crabcakes, crab Imperial, oysters Gino, stuffed shrimp, and stuffed fish. There are, of course, other poultry and meat offerings as well.

One of their favorite stories about their legendary "light and lumpy" crabcakes is how Wendy and Ken sent some Robert Morris crabcakes to author James Michener in Sitka, Alaska, when he was working on a book there. "We heard that he was homesick for the Eastern Shore and our crabcakes. They made it via Federal Express in under forty-eight hours."

The Robert Morris is very much a family operation, with Ken's brother, Jay, handling the major innkeeping duties, while Wendy and Robert are very active and involved "behind the scenes," as Wendy puts it. Their two teenagers, Kent and Ben, are planning their move from being kitchen helpers and dishwashers to greater status as waiters, where they say "the money is." They have always had an entrepreneurial bent, as my Constant Readers will remember. Ben has designed T-shirts that depict all the things guests remember about the inn and Oxford. I hear they're selling like hotcakes.

The Gibsons have succeeded in keeping the Robert Morris simple and good. They have made it a policy not to accept groups or business conferences, keeping the atmosphere friendly and personal. A stay in this lovely inn beside the Tred Avon River is completely peaceful and quiet—a place to relax and enjoy the incredible sunsets.

The inn starts taking reservations on the tenth of January for the current year, and accommodations should be reserved as early as possible, even for midweek stays.

ROBERT MORRIS INN, Oxford, MD 21654; 301-226-5111. A 33-guestroom (30 private baths) waterside inn and lodge in a secluded Colonial community on the Tred Avon, 10 mi. from Easton, Md. Queen, double, and twin beds available. (Some rooms with private porches and some nonsmoking rooms.) European plan. Breakfast, lunch, and dinner served to travelers and guests daily. Open year-round except Christmas Day and Feb. 1 till mid-Mar. Wheelchair access to restaurant. Tennis, golf, seasonal river swimming, sailing, fishing, and bicycles nearby. Recommended for children over 10. No pets. Wendy and Ken Gibson, Owners-hosts; Jay Gibson, Manager. (See Index for rates.)

Directions: From Delaware Memorial Bridge, follow Rte. 13 south to Rte. 301 and proceed south to Rte. 50, then east on Rte. 50 to Easton. From Chesapeake Bay Bridge, follow Rte. 50-301 to Rte. 50 and proceed east to Easton. From Chesapeake Bay Bridge Tunnel, follow Rte. 13 north to Rte. 50 and proceed west to Easton. From Easton, follow Rte. 322 to Rte. 333 to Oxford and inn.

BELLE GRAE INN
Staunton, Virginia (1990)

Between the Allegheny Mountains on the west and the Blue Ridge Mountains on the east lies the fertile, green Shenandoah Valley. It's no wonder that this valley has been celebrated in song with the words, "Oh Shenandoah, I long to see you . . ." Known as America's First Frontier, the limestone-dotted hills, picturesque towns, stone farmhouses, and log cabins have seen early settlers pass from Pennsylvania on their way to historic towns like Lexington and Staunton.

Many of the inns in the valley have offered hospitality to travelers for over a hundred years. The Belle Grae Inn in Staunton is one of these. The Federal-style mansion was originally built in 1870. Innkeeper Michael Organ, a communications professor, saw the potential of the stately old home and restored it to its original splendor in 1983. While many of Virginia's inns are country inns, the Belle Grae revels in her classification as a city inn.

The inn takes its name from two of the seven hills on which the city of Staunton is built: Betsy Belle and Mary Grae. As you sit on the inn's spacious veranda, you get a splendid view of these two old Scottish ladies. The rambling Victorian is located in a quiet residential neighborhood in the center of the Newtown Historic District. Dogwoods, azaleas, and lilacs surround the house with lovely colors and scents during the spring.

Michael calls the inn's furnishings *collectics,* a most charming word for his collection of antiques, keepsakes, and reproductions that decorate the common rooms. The ten guest rooms are traditional Victorian colors of mauve, forest green, dusty rose, and steel blue, which accent the hardwood floors and antique furnishings. My room had a wonderful queen-size canopy bed, a desk with a comfortable chair, and a cozy fireplace. Some of the rooms have sitting areas, and one room, whimsically called the Pullman Car, has an antique Murphy bed. The private baths have pedestal sinks, along with full tub and shower units.

Suites are more luxurious, with four-poster beds, fireplaces, Oriental carpets, sitting areas, large dressing rooms, private baths, and telephones and televisions. The vintage brick townhouse suite is joined to the main inn by a footbridge, and from the suite's windows, the comings and goings of Staunton can be heard.

Afternoon tea is served with tasty tea cakes and cookies. I enjoyed my cup and shared my cakes with Bell Boy, the inn's well-behaved boxer, as I sat in a wicker rocker in the peaceful courtyard. Smells of garlic and onions occasionally wafted from the direction of the Belle-Grae Bistro as dinner preparations began. The Belle-Grae Bistro is Staunton's only indoor/outdoor cafe. Guests can enjoy à la carte dining on the terrace patio under umbrellas, and listen to live evening entertainment. Indoors, the Bistro's bright, sunny room overlooking the expansive lawn is a wonder-

ful place to begin your leisurely breakfast with coffee, juice, and pastries, followed by an omelet, fried tomatoes, and cheese grits.

Dinner is served in the more formal dining rooms of the original house or on the veranda. The inn's talented chef, Ken Hicks, focuses on distinctive and delicious recipes with a Southern flavor. A roast pork loin coated with orange glaze was served the evening I visited. The succulent pork was accompanied by tender new potatoes that had been browned in olive oil and sprinkled with chopped, fresh mint.

The Belle Grae Inn is on the walking tour of Staunton, a stroll that will take you through history. President Woodrow Wilson's birthplace is just seven blocks away, and the Statler Brothers' Museum, antique stores, and specialty shops are all nearby. I'm sure you'll find the Belle Grae Inn's hospitality more than worth your visit.

BELLE GRAE INN, 515 W. Frederick St., Staunton, VA 24401; 703-886-5151. A 10-guestroom (private baths) historic Victorian inn located in Virginia's Shenandoah Valley. Breakfast included; dinner Wed. through Sun., lunch Tues. through Sun. Open year-round. All-size beds. Monthly celebrations and seasonal activities. Near specialty shops and historical sites. Children over 10 welcome. No pets. Michael Organ, Owner-host.

Directions: From I-81 take Exit 57 west (Rte. 250W to center of Staunton). Rte. 250W intersects Rte. 254W (Frederick St.). Go left 6 blocks to inn.

GRAVES' MOUNTAIN LODGE
Syria, Virginia (1972)

For over 130 years, five generations of the Graves family have been innkeepers in the shadow of the Blue Ridge Mountains near Syria, Virginia. In the early 1850s, Paschal Graves opened an "ordinary," or inn, along the Blue Ridge Turnpike on land now part of the Shenandoah National Park. The ordinary was a natural stopping point for travelers making the seventy mile journey between Gordonsville and New Market. Here horses were changed to make the climb over the mountains, and farmers on foot herded their livestock to market along the turnpike or hauled wagonloads of bark and carts of apples, corn, and chestnuts.

Around 1857 the Graves family moved to their present location and for 100 years took in travelers and vacationers in their rambling farmhouse. Today's innkeeper is Jim Graves, and he can recall as a boy growing up the fun and work of having visitors arrive. Their cook fried chicken, baked hams and fresh fruit pies and cakes. Dinner was served family style and people came from all around to have chicken. As he said, "When we had a lot of guests in the summer, our family moved out of the bedrooms and slept on the porch. We didn't mind because vacationers usually brought children for us to play with. We became friends with many of them and later some came back to work on the farm."

A lot of very exciting things have happened since Jim was a young boy. He met and married Rachel Lynn Norman, who shared his enthusiasm. Even during their courting days they drew sketches and developed ideas for a rustic but modern mountain resort. They discovered that they had the same pedigree; they are both descendants of Captain Thomas Graves, who sailed to Jamestown in 1608. Rachel's family stems from Thomas Graves' oldest son, born in England, and Jim's family is descended from a younger son, born in Virginia. Twelve generations later their marriage united two branches of a 375-year family tree. By the way, this tree is pictured in the inn's booklet, "Mountain Hospitality."

One of the most colorful figures connected with Graves' Mountain Lodge was Jim's father, "Mr. Jack," who was still on the scene during my first visit many years ago. It was a common sight to see him come to dinner fresh from his farm chores, but in clean overalls, to be on hand to meet all of the guests and their children.

As I leafed through the pages of "Mountain Hospitality," which contains all this fascinating information, I realized that very little has changed since the original concept of Graves' Mountain Lodge four generations ago. The new lodge is a unique collection of old and new buildings, each with a history all its own. Over the years I have described the outbuildings that also serve as guest quarters. In recent years two additional buildings with tastefully furnished motel-type bedrooms enjoy a fantastic view of the great valley filled with cattle, sheep, farmland, and acres and acres of peach and apple trees.

What about the food at Graves' Mountain Lodge? Well, here is Rachel Graves telling me about Sunday night supper at Graves' Mountain Lodge. "Sunday night dinner will be country ham, cold fried chicken, country-fried potatoes and onions, green beans, baked tomatoes, corn pudding, coleslaw, maybe one or two other vegetables, and probably spiced peaches or apples. Usually on Sunday night we have hot fudge cake for dessert.

"Tonight, we will have between 250 and 300 people. Last Sunday, we had about 700 people.

"On Tuesday evenings we are now serving catfish with our country ham. Something our guests really enjoy is our 'fish and pay' trout pond. We'll either cook or freeze their catch."

The original Graves family, including Mr. Jack, I'm sure, would be glad to know that everybody is served family style inside the lodge and on the porch.

Although the lodge is operated on the American plan—three meals a day with lodging—those who want to stop by for a meal can call for a reservation and are always welcome.

GRAVES' MOUNTAIN LODGE, Syria, VA 22743; 703-923-4231. A 53-guestroom secluded, rustic resort-inn, including 8 cabins, 38 motel units, and 7 rooms in lodge on Rte. 670, off Rte. 321, 10 mi. north of Madison, Va., 38 mi. N.W. of Charlottesville, Va. American plan. Breakfast, lunch, dinner served to travelers by reservation only. Closed Dec. 1 to late Mar. Swimming, tennis, horseback riding, hunting, fishing, a special nature walk, rock hunting, and hiking on grounds. Golf nearby. Jim and Rachel Graves, Owners-hosts. (See Index for rates.)

Directions: Coming south from Washington, D.C., take I-66 to Gainsville. Follow Rte. 29 south to Madison, turn right onto Rte. 231 west, go 7 mi. to Banco, turn left onto Rte. 670 and follow 670 for 4½ mi. to lodge.

HIGH MEADOWS INN
Scottsville, Virginia (1990)

Occasionally I get a bit jaded as a travel writer. Difficult as it may be to believe, just as any job has its moments of boredom, so does mine. And then I stay at an inn like the High Meadows, and all of a sudden the world takes on a new glow, and I can't imagine having any other profession.

This gracious inn is located on the Constitution Route in the midst of the Virginia wine country. Located on 23 acres, the stately home is actually two separate houses joined by a great hall: one a Federal style and the other a Victorian. The home with its seventeen rooms, nine fireplaces, and original grained woodwork was recently placed on the National Register of Historic Homes.

When I arrived at High Meadows Inn I was greeted by innkeeper Mary Jae Sushka. Later during the weekend I was surprised to discover that Mary Jae has a chameleon career: During the week she is a securities and exchange commission senior analyst. After four years in Britain where Peter, her husband and fellow innkeeper, served as a liaison to the Royal Navy, the Sushkas returned to the United States to search for an inn. "We read a real estate ad for a 'restoration gem'," Mary Jae recalled. "What we saw was a hulk. No electricity. No plumbing." But the Sushkas saw the possibilities, and purchased the property the year Peter retired.

The surroundings are relaxed and pleasant. Guests can stroll through the rose gardens or spend time in the Pinot Noir vineyards. Numerous footpaths around two ponds and meandering creeks present tranquil, pastoral settings for contemplation.

Each of the seven guest rooms is quite unique and furnished with period antiques, some dating from the 1700s. Sitting areas with writing desks, reading materials and reading lamps, and at least one soft chair provide reason enough to stay in your room. A small crystal decanter of port wine and two small stemmed glasses invite a late-night toast. I was interested in each room's individualized leather-bound memorabilia book, containing before and after restoration pictures and a three- or four-page history describing the room's furnishings and method of restoration.

We stayed in the spacious Highview Room, one of two air-conditioned rooms on the upper level of the Victorian house, with its huge windows and original comb graining. All guest rooms include private baths, some with sitting showers and others with claw-foot tubs. As I sat reading in the room's Chippendale chair, I happened to glance up and notice an original steel engraving of "George Washington's First Interview with His Wife Martha." His hand was firmly planted on a similar splat-backed chair.

Rates include breakfast, afternoon tea, and Virginia wine with hors d'oeuvres before dining. Everything served at the inn is made on the

premises. Dinner is by candlelight and includes four courses. Coffee and peach wine are served afterward in either the main hall or on the west terrace. During the week, a European picnic supper basket is filled with such choice goodies as Roman beef loaf on fettuccine, lemon cole slaw with apples and currants, fresh fruits, brownies, fresh daisies, and the traditional red-and-white-checked tablecloth.

Tubing, canoeing, and fishing on the lazy James River can fill an afternoon, or you may prefer a more history-infused visit to nearby Monticello and the presidential homes of Monroe and Madison. I just stayed put, enjoying the pastoral surroundings. When I left, I was rejuvenated and happy to be the travel writer that I am.

HIGH MEADOWS INN, Rte. 20 South, Rte. 4, Box 6, Scottsville, VA 24590; 804-286-2218. A 7-guestroom (private baths) historic, renovated country inn located just minutes from Charlottesville. Open year-round. All-size beds. Full breakfast, tea, and wine and hors d'oeuvres included. Dinner on weekends; gourmet picnic baskets on weekdays. Close to outdoor activities and historic tours. Pets by prior arrangement. Peter and Mary Jae Sushka, Owners-hosts.

Directions: Take Exit 24 on I-64 in Charlottesville and proceed on Rte. 20 south for 17 mi. Cross Rte. 726 and the inn's private drive is ³/10 mi. further on your left.

THE INN AT GRISTMILL SQUARE
Warm Springs, Virginia (1977)

A wonderful old waterwheel, a square that was once the village center with the grain mill, a hardware store, a blacksmith's shop, and two private homes (one the former home of the miller)—this is what is known as Gristmill Square. There has been a mill on this site since 1771—the present mill was erected in 1900. Of course, the buildings have all been restored, and the grain mill has been designated a historical site.

This is one of my favorite places, with the wonderful scenery of the Allegheny Mountains, fields of wildflowers, birds, streams where trout dart and play, and most of all the pure mountain air. It's so exhilarating.

Gristmill Square is just down the road from the county courthouse in a village of two hundred souls, with a little brook running right through the town. There isn't a single traffic light in the whole county.

The former hardware store and the two private homes now house the inn's fourteen guest rooms, several of which have fireplaces and are decorated with antiques and old prints. They are all well outfitted with clocks, refrigerators, cable television, decorator linens, and fluffy towels. Magazines and wildflowers add an extra touch.

The Waterwheel Restaurant has been artfully fashioned from the grain mill, which was operated by the waterwheel. The heavenly aroma of the grain, the beige patina of the walls, and the geometric patterns created by the beams and posts make a most unusual setting for a candlelight dinner.

The menu features roast duckling with apricots, pan-fried trout with black walnuts, veal à l'orange, and broiled mountain trout.

The McWilliams family has also provided additional amenities for guests who enjoy longer stays. The Bath and Tennis Club has a swimming pool and tennis courts that are playable for most of the year, and there is a sauna in the Steel House. In one of the golfing capitals of the world, the famous Cascades and Lower Cascades golf courses are a short drive away. The Warm Springs Pools are within walking distance.

There is horseback and carriage riding nearby as well as exceptional trout fishing, downhill and cross-country skiing, and some of the most beautiful backroading and hill-walking to be found west of Scotland.

Adding to the cultural attractions of the area are the Garth Newel chamber music concerts, performed on summer weekends.

Bath County is located in the west-central portion of Virginia. The 540-square-mile area is within one day's drive of half the population of the northeastern United States. The elevations range from 4,477 feet above sea level to 1,140 feet, where the Cowpasture River flows into Allegheny County. Visitors began coming to the springs of Bath County as early as 1750 and it's been increasing in popularity every year since.

THE INN AT GRISTMILL SQUARE, P.O. Box 359, Warm Springs, VA 24484; 703-839-2231. A 14-guestroom (private baths) unusual restoration with a restaurant and many resort attractions in a small country town in the Allegheny Mtns., 19 mi. north of Covington. European plan. Restaurant open for dinner daily Tues.-Sun., and Sun. lunch. Lunch served May 1 to Nov. 1, Tues.-Sun. Restaurant closed Mon. Suggest calling for details. Tennis courts, swimming pool, and sauna on grounds. Golf at nearby Cascades or Lower Cascades. Skiing at Snowshoe, West Va., about an hr. away. Skating, riding, hiking, fishing, hunting, antiquing, and backroading nearby. Children welcome. The McWilliams Family, Owners-hosts. (See Index for rates.)

Directions: From Staunton, Va., follow Rte. 254 to Buffalo Gap; Rte. 42 to Millboro Spring; Rte. 39 to Warm Springs. From Lexington, take Rte. 39 to Warm Springs. From Roanoke, take Rte. 220 to Warm Springs. From Lewisburg, W Va., take I-64 to Covington; Rte. 220 north to Warm Springs. From northern W. Va. travel south to Rte. 39 east to Warm Springs. The inn is on Rte. 645. From Rte. 220 going north, turn left on Rte. 645 in Warm Springs. From Rte. 39W turn left on Rte. 692 and left again on Rte. 645 at Warm Springs.

IRISH GAP INNS
Irish Gap, Virginia (1990)

I was on my way to a tea party! And the most intriguing aspect of this tea party was its other guests: Holland Lops, English Lops, French Lops, and Netherland Dwarfs. I was particularly pleased that I would be enjoying my toast and marmalade with such international guests. Well, of course, I'm teasing. The other guests are really pedigreed rabbits belonging to the Irish Gap Inns' owner, Dillard Saunders. When she heard that I would be visiting, she invited me to join her, and the menagerie, at an Easter tea held for the children of Irish Gap, Virginia.

The Irish Gap Inns are tucked off the Blue Ridge Parkway on 285 acres of beautiful Virginia mountaintop woodlands and fields. Even though the parkway is close, the location is both remote and private. A gravel drive leads to the Bee Skep Inn and its partner, the Gatehouse B&B, that comprise the Inns. Dillard, a native Virginian, purchased the property in 1984, and lived in the old farmhouse while work was done on the inns.

With a background in interior design, Ms. Saunders successfully constructed the inns to look like turn-of-the-century hostelries: old in appearance yet modern on the interiors. "I wanted the inns to reflect an understated elegance," Dillard told me. Behind the inn, water cascades from a mountain-fed spring down a hand-built rock wall and into one of two ponds.

The Bee Skep Inn is built on the site of the property's original log cabin. Its large common rooms, built of oak beams with timber framing, overlook the ponds. The living room is spacious, with a dining area. English pine antiques, heart-pine floors, and colors of blue, white, and coral create an old-world ambience.

The four guest rooms have charming woodland names with decorative themes to fit. For example, the fox hunter room is done in red with navy plaid fabrics, has dark woods, oil paintings of fox hunts, and features four-poster beds and antique and reproduction furnishings. Each room has two beds, a private bath, television, and a small refrigerator and coffee maker. Window boxes, spilling over with flowers, and comfortable rockers await on each room's private sitting porch.

Dillard took me on a hike along the fern-covered banks of the creek, and we ended up at the back deck of the Gatehouse. This tidy white Victorian cottage has an airy wraparound front porch also. The great room is furnished with Early American primitive antiques and reproductions, and has a large fireplace for intimate winter evenings. A bedroom with a private bath is located on the main floor, and two other bedrooms share a bath upstairs. A small kitchen is available.

A complimentary breakfast is served at the Bee Skep and includes

fruit, French toast, eggs, sausage, tea and coffee, and an inn specialty, chocolate squash bread.

Dinner is by reservation, and can include such gourmet choices as veal scallops with lemon-garlic cream sauce, broccoli vinaigrette, and yellow squash parmigiana. Desserts are luscious. I sampled the fresh fruit cobbler and ended up having two servings. Most of the vegetables are garden fresh.

There are great outdoor activities available around the area that include bicycling on the Blue Ridge Parkway and fishing and swimming in the ponds. You might also like to give Dillard a hand when she feeds the rest of her farm family: seven dogs, five goats, turkeys, chickens, and three horses.

Oh, by the way, our tea party was quite elegant. The rabbits chose the watercress sandwiches and left the sweets for the children and me. It was an affair that would have satisfied even the Mad Hatter's expectations.

IRISH GAP INNS, Rte. 1, Box 40, Vesuvius, VA 24483; 804-922-7701. A 7-guestroom (4 in the Inn, all private baths; 3 in the Gatehouse, 1 private bath, 1 shared) inn on 285 acres of rural woodlands. All-size beds. Complimentary breakfast; dinner by reservation. Open all year. Bicycling, fishing, swimming. Near historic Lexington. Handicap accessibility. No pets. Dillard Saunders, Owner-host.

Directions: Located between milepost 37 and 38 on the Blue Ridge Parkway at Irish Gap. Take Parkway exit, then turn left at Private Road sign.

JORDAN HOLLOW FARM INN
Stanley, Virginia (1985)

I'm not sure of the protocol, but I think I'm godfather to a colt. It all happened on a visit to Jordan Hollow Farm, when a foal was born and Marley Beers named him Norman—I have his most recent photo, and he's a beauty.

"He'll have to earn his keep," she said, "because we are a working horse farm." Marley was very enthusiastic about their new Norwegian Fjord horses, which have a fascinating history that dates back to Genghis Khan. "We think they are more appropriate for a country inn. They are gentle and attractive, and we use them for riding and driving. We also have German Holsteiners, Quarter Horses, Appaloosas, and Arabians.

"It is not necessary to be a horse rider to enjoy yourself here. However, many of our guests, who have never ridden in their lives and have come for the wonderful Shenandoah Valley experience, begin to feel at home with these beautiful animals once they try one of our beginner rides. We carefully take only six or seven people at a time. Intermediate rides are available for more experienced riders who may choose to ride English or western saddles. We offer cart rides and driving lessons with our Fjords for another equestrian experience.

Marley and her Dutch husband, Jetze (pronounced yet-sah), purchased this former Colonial horse farm several years ago and began creating an inn for the enjoyment of their guests. Jetze speaks several different languages, and both of them have traveled widely and are sophisticated hosts. They met in Africa.

This African influence is mirrored in one of the three dining rooms with decorations from Africa. In many ways, they seemed quite in place with the rest of this wonderful atmosphere that is so removed from the hubbub of the city.

One of the engaging features of the inn is the pub, called the Watering Trough. Jetze has built an adjoining fountain and gardens with umbrella tables and chairs. On the night of my visit I sat up rather late with the innkeepers and another couple from Washington. I asked the gentleman what he enjoyed most about being here, and he said, "Just the peace and quiet and opportunity to read, take walks, and enjoy good food and good company."

This convivial atmosphere continues at dinner. Marley is the cook and describes the food as "country Continental" style, with plenty of fresh fruits and vegetables, and homemade breads and desserts. She particularly recommends their roasted quail and rib eye steaks.

The guest rooms in a modern lodge-style building are all furnished with comfortable, cozy country-inn furniture, with different types of beds and other pieces in each room, as well as dried-flower arrangements, calico comforters, and wonderful, thick, fluffy towels.

The latest news is that Norman now has a full brother named Simpson, who promises to be just as big a horse but even more handsome. Norman has shed his baby coat and is now a beautiful dark gray with flecks of white. He stands over sixteen hands and is still growing. I have a framed photograph of him in my study.

On a guest's birthday, along with a birthday cake, Marley and Jetze have revived the old Virginia custom of buttering that person's nose, thus "helping him to slide through the next year without difficulty." I guess I'll have to return to Jordan Hollow on Norman's and Simpson's birthdays and butter their noses!

JORDAN HOLLOW FARM INN, Rte. 2, Box 375, Stanley, VA 22851; 703-778-2209 or 2285. A 16-guestroom (private baths) restored Colonial horse farm 6 mi. south of Luray in the northern Shenandoah Valley of Virginia. Queen, double, and twin beds available. Open year-round. Breakfast, lunch, and dinner served daily to houseguests. Restaurant open to public for dinner by reservation. The horse center provides horses and lessons from beginner thru advanced. Scenic trail rides for various levels of skill. Volleyball, table tennis, board games, and walking on the premises. Swimming, hiking, canoeing, fishing, skiing, golf, tennis, auctions, museums, antiques, crafts shops nearby. Sorry, no pets; boarding kennel nearby. Marley and Jetze Beers, Owners-hosts. (See Index for rates.)

Directions: The inn is located 6 mi. south of Luray, Va.; 7 mi. from Rte. 211; 12 mi. from the Skyline Drive; and 19 mi. from I-81 at New Market. Go south from Luray 6 mi. on Rte. 340; turn left on Rte. 624; left on Rte. 689; and right on Rte. 626.

L'AUBERGE PROVENÇALE
White Post, Virginia (1988)

Swinging gently in the hanging wooden swing on the wide front porch, Celeste Borel and I had been talking about how she and Alain, her husband, had found this beautiful 1753 stone farmhouse and had opened a country inn. During a lull in the conversation, I heard a flock of geese honk their way across the sky and watched as they settled on a pond in the nearby field. Crickets chirped, and far off in a pasture cattle lowed.

As reluctant as I was to leave this tranquil and bucolic scene, the aromas wafting from the kitchen, where Alain was practicing his art, were too much for me, and I eagerly followed Celeste into one of the three cozy dining rooms, where other guests were just sitting down to tables set with snowy white linen, overlaid with blue cloths, sparkling crystal, and gleaming silver. It was a very pleasant dining room with a fireplace, polished wood floors, and walls lined with French paintings and prints, including a Picasso.

"How do you happen to have a picture of the Pope's palace and the bridge of Avignon on your menu?" I asked Celeste.

"Alain was born and raised in Avignon," she replied. "He started working in his grandfather's restaurant there when he was thirteen, and he has been in the restaurant business ever since." Later, when I saw all of the articles that have been written about L'Auberge Provençale and Alain's cuisine, I realized he has become quite famous as a French chef. They frequently have diners who have driven from Washington, D.C., ninety minutes away.

Alain showed me the huge herb and vegetable garden. "We also have two cherry trees, a purple plum, a peach, a pear, and an apple tree, as well as raspberry bushes."

Alain calls his menu "cuisine moderne—classic Provençale French combined with nouvelle, but in substantial portions." Some of his starters include sautéed sweetbreads with port, capers, and pine nuts; duck foie gras with pears and turmeric; and a Provençale rabbit soup. Entrées could be roast squab with fresh peaches, cloves, and cinnamon basil served with wild rice; Moroccan-style medallions of lamb; veal with pomegranate wine and green peppercorns; and several other choices. There are wonderful desserts, such as chocolate genoise with white chocolate mousse and mocha sauce and homemade ice cream in an almond tulip cup.

Guest rooms in the main house and in an adjacent cottage are attractively and comfortably furnished with antique and wicker pieces and pleasingly decorated in soft colors, flowered and white eyelet spreads, paintings, and fresh flowers. There are four-poster beds and white iron beds, and two of the rooms in the main house have fireplaces.

The next morning as I sat on the porch at breakfast, savoring one of

Alain's perfect omelets and watching as the landscape emerged from the lifting mists, I pondered on what an interesting set of circumstances we had here.

Deep in the farming country of the Shenandoah Valley, in the tiny early American village of White Post—so named because George Washington as a young surveyor had erected a white post there—Celeste and Alain Borel have created a French country inn and restaurant. This combination has drawn guests from far and wide; one guest even arrived by helicopter, setting down in their back yard.

"There's an airstrip across the road," Celeste told me, "and the man who owns it has been kind enough to let single-engine planes land there. Then, Billy Thompson, who restores antique autos in town, will pick up and deliver them in one of his classic cars, if they so desire." That's what I mean about an interesting set of circumstances.

L'AUBERGE PROVENÇALE, Rte. 340, P.O. Box 119, White Post, VA 22633; 703-837-1375. A 6-guestroom (private baths) French country inn and restaurant in Clarke County in the Shenandoah Valley, 90 min. west of Washington, D.C. Queen and double beds available. Breakfast included in room rate. Picnic lunches by arrangement. Dinner served Wed. to Sat., 6 to 10:30; Sun., 4 to 9. Open year-round. Antiques and country shops, Burwell-Morgan Mill, Blandy Farm, White Post antique car restoration, point-to-point horse races, Skyline Drive, and magnificent backroading nearby. Well-behaved children over 10 welcome. No pets. Celeste and Alain Borel, Owners-hosts. (See Index for rates.)

Directions: From Washington, D.C., take Rte. 50 to Rte. 340, where there is a 3-way traffic light. Turn left and continue 1 mi. to inn.

MEADOW LANE LODGE
Warm Springs, Virginia (1978)

I was wandering about in the great barn at Meadow Lane Lodge, located in Bath County, Virginia, a few minutes from the famous Cascades Golf Course in Warm Springs. Here, sheep and goats graze and gambol. Chickens, ducks, guinea fowl, geese, and turkeys inhabit the old horse stalls in the large stable and freely wander in the areas around them. Cats and kittens mingle, as do the farm dogs. No one hurts anyone and there is respect everywhere.

A few moments earlier I had reluctantly gotten up from a wonderful breakfast featuring a special recipe for scrambled eggs blended with some aromatic herbs, prepared by innkeeper Philip Hirsh. Although Phip, as he is called, is a retired executive, he still takes great pride in occasionally doing the Meadow Lane breakfast.

In the beautiful Allegheny Mountains, Meadow Lane Lodge is an integral part of the Hirsh estate, comprised of 1,600 acres of woods, fields, and streams. In such an atmosphere, tranquility and relaxation are almost guaranteed.

Two suites and three double bedrooms are available in the main house, while Craig's Cottage, named for a Hirsh grandson, will accommodate two to four people. The cottage boasts a big stone fireplace in a lovely high ceilinged bedroom with a large picture window looking over the meadows and mountains.

Cathy Hirsh led me off to one corner, saying, "Yesterday, Phip and I took a couple of hours off, and with two of the dogs went up into the woods to walk around the horse exercise track, which was hewn out of the forest by Phip's father. We saw lady-slippers in bloom and lots of trillium and dwarf iris. Then we drove along the Jackson River to the trout ponds and the spring where the wild azalea and dogwood are flowering, and the watercress is a great patch of vivid green. Our river is one of Virginia's designated scenic rivers and two miles of it flow right through the farm.

"On cool spring and fall mornings and evenings, the two fireplaces in the living rooms of the lodge are always in use. I'm sure you noticed that the upstairs rooms have screened-in porches with delightful views and breezes. Later on, our large front porch with its wicker furniture will be a scene for lots of relaxing and chatting with other inn guests."

Additional accommodations are offered in the center of the village of Warm Springs in the Francisco Cottage, which has been restored and furnished in the manner of the log house originally erected on the site, circa 1820. This cottage offers a very pleasantly furnished living room, porch, two bedrooms, kitchen, and bath, and an impressive view of the hillsides.

Cathy and Philip are excited about the newest addition to Meadow

Lane. "It has been designed like an old Pennsylvania barn with an overhang and beautiful stonework at one end," Cathy told me. "There are two guest rooms with baths, plus a vaulted-ceiling living room with a big picture window. The building looks old and fits in beautifully with the rest of the farm."

They report that their new six-wicket English croquet court is very popular with guests, and Meadow Lane Lodge is now a member of the U.S. Croquet Association.

MEADOW LANE LODGE, Star Route A, Box 110, Warm Springs, VA 24484; 703-839-5959. An 11-guestroom (private baths) lodge-inn on a portion of a large estate about 10 min. from the center of Warm Springs and near the famous Cascades Golf Course. Guestrooms are in the main house and a cottage on the grounds and also in Francisco Cottage in Warm Springs. A full breakfast is the only meal served. Open Apr. 1 thru Jan. 31. Minimum stay in the lodge is 2 nights; in Francisco Cottage, 3 nights. Dinners are available at nearby restaurants. Tennis court, swimming, horseback riding, and excellent fishing on grounds. Also, miles of hiking and walking trails. Golf, skeet and trap shooting nearby. Children over 6 welcome. Small dogs accepted with prior approval. Philip and Cathy Hirsh, Owners-hosts. (See Index for rates.)

Directions: From Staunton, Va., follow Rte. 254 west to Buffalo Gap; Rte. 42 south to Millboro Spring; Rte. 39 west to Warm Springs. From Lexington, take Rte. 39 west. From Roanoke, take Rte. 220 north to Warm Springs and Rte. 39 west to Meadow Lane Lodge.

MORRISON HOUSE
Alexandria, Virginia (1987)

Although this book is about country inns, I have received requests for my recommendations of places in cities. Morrison House in Old Town, Alexandria, about twenty minutes from downtown D.C., is not a country inn on a back road, but it is the answer to having quiet, elegant lodgings in an atmosphere that is quite reminiscent of Knightsbridge, London. Further, if you have business or pleasure in the nearby nation's capital it is a most rewarding experience to return to Old Town, with its rows of 18th- and 19th-century houses, diverting shops, and safe walking at night.

The four-story, Federal-style building is red brick with black shutters, with a porticoed entrance, supported by four Greek columns and reached by twin curved staircases encircling a fountain sculpture.

Seated in the small courtyard in front of the hotel, I was enjoying the freshness of the early morning air and thinking back over the events of my first visit on the previous evening. When I pulled up in front of the entrance, my automobile door was opened by a properly attired butler—not a bellboy, but a butler. I learned that this gentleman is a very important part of the service offered at Morrison House. He was relaxed, efficient, not pompous, extremely accommodating, and a veritable fountain of information about where to go in the D.C. area and how to get there. In the meantime, my car had been whisked away to the hotel's underground parking garage.

To the right of the foyer is the parlor, pleasantly elegant with Federal-style sofas and chairs upholstered in silk brocade. Gracefully draped floor-to-ceiling windows look out over a quiet street.

If all of this talk of butlers and European elegance seems a little stiff, let me assure you that it is quite relaxed, and designed to provide a very pleasant stay.

This is also true of the guest rooms, which have mahogany four-poster and canopied beds, made up in the European style with triple sheets. The bathrooms are done in Italian marble, and there are terrycloth robes and little reminders to the effect that should a traveler have forgotten such things as a toothbrush, comb, shaving cream, and so forth, the same can be obtained by calling the reception area.

All of the additional thoughtfulness and amenities reflected in this hotel are the result of the extremely broad travel experiences of owners Robert and Rosemary Morrison. I had a very enjoyable chat with them about various European and British hotels that we both have enjoyed, and, not surprisingly, one mutual favorite was La Résidence du Bois in Paris, included in the European edition of this book.

As might be expected, part of the Morrison adventure is its two restaurants, Le Chardon d'Or (the gold thistle), with contemporary French cuisine, and the Grill, which has an American grill-style menu. Both have an extensive wine list, with many wines available by the glass. Le Chardon d'Or, with its à la carte and prix-fixe menus, is open for Sunday brunch and dinner Monday through Saturday. The Grill is open for lunch and dinner every day. Breakfast is served at Morrison House every day, and room service is available twenty-four hours every day.

MORRISON HOUSE, 116 S. Alfred St., Alexandria, VA 22314; 800-367-0800; 703-533-1808 (VA); or 703-838-8000 (local). A 45-guestroom (private baths) elegant, luxury hotel in a historic section of Alexandria, 15 min. from D.C. Restaurants open for breakfast, lunch, and dinner; Sunday brunch. Open year-round. Metro a 10-min. walk; 3 mi. to National Airport.Conveniently located to visit all of the D.C. area historic, recreational, and cultural attractions. Attractive weekend rates. Robert Morrison, Owner-host. (See Index for rates.)

Directions: From National Airport, drive south on Geo. Washington Pkwy. to King St. Turn right and continue for 2 blocks and turn left on S. Alfred St. The hotel is on the left at midblock. From the Beltway/U.S. 495, take Exit U.S. 1 north to Prince St. Turn right and continue for 1 block to S. Alfred St. Hotel is on right side.

PROSPECT HILL
Trevilians, Virginia (1979)

As often as I have visited Prospect Hill, a restored plantation house outside Charlottesville, Virginia, I am always delighted by the wealth of information Bill Sheehan has compiled about the history of the inn.

Although the Roger Thompson family owned it in 1732, its real progress began when William Overton purchased the property and increased it to over 1,500 acres in 1840. He enlarged the original house by adding two wings and a spiral staircase.

As Bill says, "During the War Between the States the son of the owner returned to find everything in a completely rundown condition and of course the slaves were gone. I don't believe that he really ever recovered from this catastrophe."

Today, there are guest rooms in a late-18th-century style in the main house and in the outbuildings formerly occupied by slaves and servants of the plantation. Some include Uncle Guy's House, with rooms both upstairs and down, the Overseer's Cottage, with a suite, the Boys' Cabin, and slave quarters.

Further restoration and renovation have been going on industriously during the last few years. "We have renovated the old Carriage House, which was built sometime in the 1840s," Bill told me. "We have added four magnificent Palladian windows to the open archways on each end of the house to keep the original flavor of the building's use as a carriage house.

"Sancho Pansy's Cottage, named after a slave who followed his young master into war, was built in the 1800s and was last used as the hen house." Bill says since this was not quite as historic as the others, his wife, Mireille, decorated it to reflect her Provençal French heritage. With a working fireplace and a Jacuzzi, it is particularly popular with honeymooners.

"Perhaps equally exciting is Mammy Katie's Kitchen, which was built around 1720 and named after the slave, Mammy Katie, who was one of the few slaves who remained on the plantation after the Civil War. She probably helped raise young William Overton. The kitchen building has the original fireplace, exposed beams, and ceiling joists dating to the 1720s. We, however, in our tradition of having 18th-century bedrooms and 20th-century bathrooms, added a small deck behind the kitchen for breakfast in the morning, and a large bedroom with a picture window with a beautiful view across our pasture.

"Prospect Hill retains its original character of an 18th-century plantation while having all the modern amenities for our guests."

Dinner is served Wednesday through Saturday by reservation and the menu has some very French touches because Bill and Mireille travel

widely in France and the cuisine is patterned after their experiences. Their son, Michael, has been working with them since he graduated from college a few years ago, and all three of them do the cooking. Daughter Nancy, home on weekends, turns out marvelous desserts.

This part of Virginia really offers a most impressive historical experience, particularly with Monticello, Jefferson's home, and the reproduction of the Michie Tavern nearby. There are numerous historical markers in the area, and Charlottesville itself has the impressive campus of the University of Virginia and its wonderful Georgian buildings. All of this is set in the greening countryside with the Blue Ridge Mountains just a short drive away.

PROSPECT HILL, Route 613, Trevilians, VA 23093; 703-967-0844. An 11-guestroom (private baths) country inn on a historic plantation 15 mi. east of Charlottesville, Va., 90 mi. southwest of Washington, D.C. Bed and breakfast-in-bed Sun. thru Tues. Modified American plan with full breakfast-in-bed and full dinner. Dinner served daily by reservation. Breakfast always served to houseguests. Swimming pool. Near Monticello, Ashlawn (President Monroe's home), Univ. of Virginia, Montpelier, and Skyline Drive. Children welcome. No pets. Bill and Mireille Sheehan, Owners-hosts. (See Index for rates.)

Directions: From Washington, D.C.: Beltway to I-66 west to Warrenton. Follow Rte. 29 south to Culpeper, then Rte. 15 south thru Orange and Gordonsville to Zion Crossroads. Turn left on Rte. 250 east 1 mi. to Rte. 613. Turn left 3 mi. to inn on left. From Charlottesville or Richmond: take I-64 to Exit 27; Rte. 15 south ½ mi. to Zion Crossroads; turn left on Rte. 250 east 1 mi. to Rte. 613. Turn left 3 mi. to inn on left.

SILVER THATCH INN
Charlottesville, Virginia (1986)

I was intrigued by the historical rumor that the Silver Thatch Inn had originally been built by Hessian soldiers taken prisoner during the Revolutionary War. The small, two-story log cabin section of the 1780 Colonial building was used to house British soldiers, and now serves as a cozy sitting room where guests enjoy late-afternoon wine and cheese.

Joe and Mickey (Miriam) Geller purchased the lovely old clapboard inn in December 1988, and promptly began changes mirroring their own special visions. The inn has had several additions through the years. The newest, a guest wing, was constructed in the same Colonial architectural style as the original structure, so there isn't a tacked-on look that is often the outcome of modernization.

The total guest rooms now number seven, and there are plans to add more rooms in the near future. Decorated with Colonial antiques and folk art, the rooms all have antique beds dressed with charming country quilts, snowy white linens, and fluffy down comforters. All rooms have private baths, with wonderful, thick towels. Several of the rooms have fireplaces.

One of the first things Joe and Mickey did when they moved in was to hire well-known chef Moncef Meddeb, owner of Boston's renowned L'Espalier Restaurant, to direct the inn's already excellent restaurant staff. The three elegantly appointed dining rooms provide a lovely atmosphere in which to enjoy the creations of this experienced and creative team.

Dinner is served by candlelight. I ordered an appetizer of sautéed fresh shrimp with a confetti of fresh vegetables, served on a bed of tender angel-hair pasta. My dinner partner had a velvety sauté of shiitake and oyster mushrooms finished with a splash of Madeira. We then split an order of Santa Fe chicken, which was absolutely fantastic. Oven-roasted chicken had been coated with a tangy mixture of herbs and spices, then napped with crème frâiche and served with Southwestern accompaniments. All dinners are served with a simple Boston lettuce and radicchio salad dressed with balsamic vinaigrette. The wine list is excellent and features California and Virginia wines and French champagnes.

The Gellers have totally relandscaped the backyard, providing a picturesque spot where guests may enjoy outdoor dining. It's a wonderful place to have your continental "plus" breakfast that includes muffins, yogurt, granola, fruit, and beverages.

On my way to take a refreshing dip in the swimming pool, I was greeted near the tennis courts by Chuckles, the inn's friendly black and white "wanna-be" dog. "She has pretensions to be a Lhasa apso," Mickey laughed, "but in reality she's a stray we picked up in the parking lot of Bonwit Teller in Boston!" I found her to be most chic and certainly friendly.

The Silver Thatch Inn is located just eight miles from downtown Charlottesville and minutes from the University of Virginia, the Skyline Drive, and the Blue Ridge Parkway. Thomas Jefferson's Monticello and James Monroe's Ash Lawn provide an interesting experience, as does a visit to Michie Tavern. The area also has fox hunting and steeplechase events.

Whether you choose to wander the tranquil grounds in the summer, enjoying the dogwood in full bloom, or ski the afternoon away in the winter and snuggle by the fire in the inn's comfortable lounge, you'll enjoy your visit. And be sure to tell Chuckles how lovely she is. We all need a fantasy.

SILVER THATCH INN, 3001 Hollymead Dr., Charlottesville, VA 22901; 804-978-4686. A 7-guestroom (private baths) country inn on the outskirts of Charlottesville, 15 min. from the Blue Ridge Mtns. Queen, double, and twin beds. Continental breakfast to guests. Dinner is served Tues. through Sat. evenings. Closed Christmas and first two weeks in Jan. Swimming and tennis on premises. Golf, horseback riding, hiking, skiing, biking, jogging, and wonderful back roads available nearby. Convenient to visit Monticello, Ash Lawn, and the University of Virginia. No smoking. Children welcome. No pets. Mickey and Joe Geller, Owners-hosts; Debbie Taylor and Jennifer Wyer, Managers.

Directions: The inn is 2 hrs. south of Washington, just off VA Rte. 29. Turn east 1 mi. south of the airport road intersection onto Rte. 1520 and proceed ½ mi. to inn.

TRILLIUM HOUSE
Wintergreen, Nellysford, Virginia (1985)

First, I'd better explain Wintergreen. This is a ten-thousand-acre residential community-cum-four-season resort on the slopes of the Blue Ridge Mountains, three hours southwest of Washington, D.C., and an hour from Charlottesville. Tucked away in the mountains are two 18-hole golf courses, an extensive tennis compound, a sixteen-acre lake, landscaped swimming pools, an equestrian center, and ten ski slopes.

The Wintergreen gate is just one mile from the Reeds Gap exit of the Blue Ridge Parkway.

Now, Trillium House. A rambling cedar building with dormers and pitched roofs, this country inn at Wintergreen is named after one of the many species of wildflowers that grow in abundance in these mountains.

Rustic, but quite modern, the Trillium House makes an excellent first impression. After stopping at the gate, Trillium guests receive from the courteous gatekeepers directions upward through various clusters of condominiums to Trillium, on one of the highest points at Wintergreen. It happens to be directly across the road from the Wintergarden, a recreation complex with both indoor and outdoor swimming pools, exercise rooms, and a very attractive restaurant looking out on a splendid view of the Blue Ridge Mountains. It is just a short distance to one of the many ski lifts. Strange as it may seem to some northerners, this part of Virginia has first-rate downhill skiing.

I stepped through the double entrance doors at ground level into the "great room" with a 22-foot cathedral ceiling and Jefferson sunburst window. A massive chimney with a woodburning stove dominates the room. Across the back of this room and up a short flight of steps stretches a balcony with a most impressive library, and on the other side of the chimney is a big-screen TV-watching room and gathering place.

Hallways stretch out from both sides of this room, along which are guest rooms and suites, many of them containing heirlooms that Ed and Betty Dinwiddie have brought from their former homes.

The dining-room windows put the guest on almost intimate terms with the 17th fairway and green, and watching the chipmunks and squirrels and birds around the feeders provides entertainment at breakfast.

I would describe Trillium House as being basically informal. It is, after all, an area where one would come to enjoy all of the great outdoors, from walking and hiking to golf, tennis, and swimming. Gentlemen are comfortable with or without jackets at dinner, and Ed and Betty have a way of immediately making everyone feel at home.

Speaking of dinner, it is available on Friday and Saturday nights with advance reservations. Betty did all the cooking the first couple of years, but now they have Ellen English, whom they call their "super chef" and associate innkeeper. "Our dinner guests tend to come again and again to enjoy stuffed tenderloin of beef and Ellen's various chicken, veal, and seafood creations."

If you did not receive your confirmation in advance, it's necessary to have the gatekeeper phone ahead to Trillium House.

The Trillium House country-inn experience is much greater than I can describe in one edition. The entire area—the beauty of the mountains, the vistas, and the splendid facilities are almost beyond my descriptive powers.

TRILLIUM HOUSE, Wintergreen, P.O. Box 280, Nellysford, VA 22958; 804-325-9126; use 800-325-9126 between 9 a.m. and 8 p.m. A 12-guestroom country inn (private baths) within the resort complex of Wintergreen. Queen and twin beds available. Breakfast included in room rate. Dinner served Fri. and Sat. by advance reservation. Restaurant across the road open daily. Open year-round. Please call for reservations at times other than the dinner hour. Extensive four-season recreation available, including golf, tennis, swimming (indoor and outdoor pool), and downhill skiing, hiking, bird watching, and horseback riding. Ed and Betty Dinwiddie, Owners-hosts. (See Index for rates.)

Directions: From points north and east take the Crozet/Rte. 250 exit from I-64. Go west on Rte. 250 to Rte. 6 and turn left. Follow Rte. 151 south to Rte. 664; turn right on 664 to Wintergreen entrance. From Blue Ridge Pkwy., exit at Reeds Gap, going east on Rte. 664.

THE COUNTRY INN
Berkeley Springs, West Virginia (1975)

"Let me tell you about our West Virginia springhouse water, which is from right here in Berkeley Springs and is shipped as far away as Miami, Florida!"

Once again I was having lunch in the Garden Room at the Country Inn with Jack and Adele Barker, whom I have been visiting for more than half of the twenty-three years that I've been writing this book.

Although it was a very warm midsummer's day, the atmosphere in the Garden Room was really springtime. It has a translucent ceiling, and its many, many growing plants, red and white tablecloths, strings of tiny white lights, and flags from all countries create a very festive air.

Jack continued, "There is a TV station in Miami that did a test on bottled water, and our water came out number one. It's just plain good spring water, and we're happy that it satisfies the folks in Miami."

I had landed earlier that morning at the Washington airport and made the relatively short trip through the countryside to this eastern panhandle of West Virginia well in time for lunch.

The first thing we did was to tour Country Inn West. Each floor has a different decorative color scheme, and there is an elevator and rooms for the handicapped. Guest rooms in the new building are larger, with more sumptuous bathrooms, and provide an interesting contrast to the rooms in the older building, with their brass beds and individual furnishings.

The hallways throughout both of the buildings of the Country Inn are hung with prints, reflecting Jack's interest in paintings and art. In fact, one entire living room has been set aside to display these well-chosen works of art for sale to the guests. There are reproductions of Italian, Flemish, French, and English masters, as well as American primitives. In particular, there are excellent and reasonably priced reproductions of turn-of-the-century French theatrical posters.

Jack was particularly enthusiastic about the completed spa, where it is now possible "to take the mineral waters," for which this section of West Virginia is famous, right at the inn.

The talk at lunch turned to the kinds of entertainments that have been developed over the past few years. "We have live music each weekend for our guests' listening and dancing pleasure," Adele told me. "Special shows include Western Night and Hawaiian Night, when guests may dress in appropriate costume to fit the occasion. All of this takes place in the romantic Country Garden in a semitropical atmosphere.

The regular menu at the inn features varied and tempting homemade soups, with special attention to entrées of fowl, beef, seafood, and country fare to satisfy hearty as well as calorie-conscious palates. The bakery features hot Kentucky pie, fruit pies of apple, cherry, blueberry,

and strawberry, along with coconut cream, pecan and their special cheese cakes.

Almost since the very start there has always been something in the works. "The completion of our Renaissance Spa provides the use of relaxing Swedish techniques and deep muscle massage," Jack commented. "And we expect that our facial massage and make-up analysis will be equally attractive to our guests."

Another very nice custom that many guests will appreciate is the Sunday church service conducted by the staff in the meeting room.

This section of West Virginia, identified as the Potomac Highlands, offers boating and fishing as well as many, many antique shops and excellent backroading in every season. Guests come in the winter to enjoy the quiet peacefulness, and now, with the opening of Country Inn West and the new spa and massage facilities, more and more people will be able to enjoy this truly country-inn hospitality.

THE COUNTRY INN, Berkeley Springs, WV 25411; 304-258-2210. A 72-guestroom (60 private baths) resort inn on Rte. 522, 34 mi. from Winchester, Va., and 100 mi. from Washington, D.C., or Baltimore, Md. Queen, double, and twin beds available. European plan. Breakfast, lunch, and dinner served to travelers. Open every day of the year. Wheelchair access. Berkeley Springs Spa adjoins the inn. Hunting, fishing, hiking, canoeing, antiquing, championship golf nearby. Jack and Adele Barker, Owners-hosts. (See Index for rates.)

Directions: Take I-70 to Hancock, Md. Inn is 6 mi. south on Rte. 522.

The date in parenthesis in the heading represents the first year the inn appeared in the pages of Country Inns and Back Roads.

GENERAL LEWIS INN
Lewisburg, West Virginia (1973)

Does the General Lewis Inn have a ghost or not? There are those who say yes and those who say no. Owner Mary Hock Morgan is a disbeliever; however, her son Jim says he has heard the ghost. Innkeeper Rodney Fisher is skeptical, but mentions that some say the ghost could be a slave who was hanged. He points out that the huge hand-hewn beams in the dining room were taken from the slave quarters. I can't say; I've never heard a thing on my visits. I've always slept like a baby.

Mary's husband, Jim, doesn't let it disturb his sleep, either. He's up early to greet guests at breakfast, listening to their adventures on the road and plans for the day. Jim knows all the great back roads and scenic routes, and can suggest any number of possible trips to parks and historic sites.

The General Lewis, in the historic district of Lewisburg, is included in a walking tour of historic homes. The original part of the inn was built by John Withrow in 1834 as a private dwelling. When Mary's parents purchased the house in 1928, they made additions that retained the feel of the early period, and little has been changed since.

Over the years they filled the inn with antiques, and today there are wonderful collections to browse through. The walls of Memory Hall are hung with tools, guns, household utensils, and musical instruments— some of which were made by hand from the parts of covered wagons by early settlers of West Virginia. There are also collections of early glassware, pottery, china, and old prints.

The cozy parlor, with its low, beamed ceiling almost always has a cheery fire crackling in the fireplace, and there are lots of rocking chairs, a spinning wheel, antique wall hangings, portraits, and oriental rugs. The guest rooms all have four-poster, tester, or canopied beds.

The inn is surrounded by broad lawns, and in the rear there are fragrant flower gardens, tall swaying trees, and a charming little playhouse that has a completely furnished dollhouse inside. Lunch is served in the garden at umbrella-shaded tables when weather permits. Rodney told me it's very popular with the local ladies.

The menu features many items that I associate with country cooking—pork chops with fried apples, pan-fried chicken, apple butter, country ham, and home-baked cornsticks, to name a few. The entrée selection includes new specialties such as chicken Randolph, coquille St. Jacques, roast duckling, trout, veal, lamb, and a lean, smoky pork barbecue. The dessert menu offers homemade pies and other mouthwatering items.

Lewisburg's historic district is listed on the National Register of Historic Places, and it's a captivating little town. Established in 1782, and named after General Andrew Lewis who fought in the Revolutionary War, it is the third oldest town in West Virginia. Greenbrier County is one of the most scenic areas of the state, with many mineral springs, famous golf courses, rivers, and beautiful parks and forests.

In the center of it all is the General Lewis Inn, offering old-fashioned Southern hospitality, just as it has been doing for over half a century. And besides all that, there's the ghost—or not.

GENERAL LEWIS INN, Lewisburg, WV 24901; 304-645-2600. A 26-guestroom (private baths) antique-laden village inn on Rte. 60, 90 mi. from Roanoke, Va. European plan. Breakfast, lunch, and dinner served daily. Dinner reservations necessary. Dining room closed Christmas Day. Famous golf courses nearby. Mary Hock Morgan, Owner-hostess; Rodney Fisher, Manager. (See Index for rates.)

Directions: Take Lewisburg exit from I-64. Follow Rte. 219 south to first traffic light. Turn left on Rte. 60, two blocks to inn.

BEAUMONT INN
Harrodsburg, Kentucky (1979)

I love to visit Kentucky! There is a gentle quality to this landscape that matches the soft, unhurried accents of its people.

I paused for a moment in front of the Beaumont Inn, which dates well back into the days before the War Between the States, and tried to imagine what it was like when it began its career as a school for young ladies in 1845. Some years later it was Beaumont College, and in 1916 it was purchased by Mr. and Mrs. Glave Goddard and converted into the Beaumont Inn.

The ownership and management passed from Mrs. Goddard to her daughter, Mrs. Dedman, and then to Mrs. Dedman's two sons. Today, Bud Dedman is the owner, and his son, Chuck, following tradition, has become the fourth-generation innkeeper. To make it even more interesting, Chuck and his wife, Helen, have two children, one of whom, Dixon, although he is a very young lad, is already showing great promise as an innkeeper of the future.

Grasping the solid handle of the big front door, I stepped inside, and there was Chuck Dedman. "I can see that you're looking around for Dixon," Chuck said. "He had to go on a very important errand for me, but he'll be back soon. Come on, I'll show you to your room."

I trotted along behind him, once again impressed by the number of rare items that have been collected and put in proper cases here at the inn. A group of antique fishing lures caught my eye, along with other Beaumont memorabilia, such as the collection of saltcellars—handsome small dishes that were used before the saltshaker came into being. Chuck's mother, Mary Elizabeth, had gathered together at least one hundred or more in a glass case.

"Oh yes, mother just loves things like that, and her history of the inn is always appreciated by our guests," he remarked.

The decorations and furniture in all the parlors and guest rooms reflect American history. The hallways on the main floor have several cabinets with beautiful old china and silverware, and the sitting rooms have elegant fireplaces and rose-patterned wallpaper.

In previous editions I have shared with the reader some of my enthusiasm for the bill of fare at the Beaumont. Probably topping everything is fried chicken and real Kentucky ham. Let me assure you that these taste nothing like any other food that bears the same name. The chicken almost falls off the bone and it's just about perfect, only exceeded perhaps by the tangy taste of real Kentucky ham, which is darker than some others you might have seen. These can be ordered at dinner in combination, and in spite of the fact that the menu has many other things I almost always end up with that combination.

The Beaumont is a wonderful place for an early spring vacation.

There are three championship golf courses close by and some wonderful shopping. The food department of the gift shop at the inn features Beaumont Inn cornmeal batter mix, brown sugar syrup, green tomato relish, sweet pickle relish, chicken-cheese casserole, frozen fruit salad, and chopped country ham. These tempting foods are also served in the dining room. Let me recommend to one and all the cornmeal cakes that are served at breakfast. They have a taste like nothing else I have ever tried.

Chuck and I returned to the front hall and, sure enough, there was Dixon already greeting new guests and giving them some suggestions about things they might like to do.

It looked to me like it was going to be another splendid visit at the Beaumont Inn.

BEAUMONT INN, Harrodsburg, KY 40330; 606-734-3381. A 29-guestroom (private baths) country inn in the heart of Kentucky's historic bluegrass country. European plan. Lunch and dinner served to travelers; all three meals to houseguests. Lunch not available Mon. Open every day from mid-March to mid-Dec. Tennis, swimming pool, shuffleboard on grounds. Golf courses and a wide range of recreational and historic attractions nearby. No pets. The Dedman Family, Owners-hosts. (See Index for rates.)

Directions: From Louisville, take Exit 48 from east I-64 and go south on Ky. 151 to U.S. 127 and on south to Harrodsburg. From Lexington, take U.S. 60 west, then west on Bluegrass Parkway to U.S. 127. From Nashville, take Exit I-65 to Bluegrass Parkway near Elizabethton, Ky., then east to U.S. 127.

THE INN AT PLEASANT HILL
Shakertown, Kentucky (1971)

Betty Morris and I were driving down the twisty road that leads to the Shaker Landing on the Kentucky River, just a few moments from the Inn at Pleasant Hill. Soon, a handsome paddlewheel river boat, the "Dixie Belle," came into view, and already there were people waiting to board her for the morning cruise.

This cruise, very popular with the inn guests, follows the seventy-five mile course of the river, bordered by impressive 315-foot limestone cliffs. Betty, who is manager of the Inn at Pleasant Hill, told me that a running history of the Kentucky River, including its importance to the economy of 100 years ago and the contributions made by the Shakers, is part of this cruise.

By an interesting coincidence, just as she pointed out the great railroad trestle that traverses the river, a freight train went by, right on cue.

The Inn at Pleasant Hill is located in a restored Shaker community in one of the most beautiful sections of central Kentucky. The Shakers were members of a religious sect, the United Society of Believers in Christ's Second Appearing. They were actually an offshoot of the Quakers. The founder was Mother Ann Lee, who brought her ideas to America late in the 18th century.

The Shakers held some advanced social ideas. They were hospitable to visitors and took in orphans and unwanted children. Their fundamental beliefs were in hard work and austere discipline that sought perfection. This sense of perfection was extended into the design of their furniture, and many people learn about Shakers for the first time as a result of being attracted by the beauty and simplicity of the functional Shaker designs.

The Shakers lived in communal dedication to their religious beliefs of celibacy, renunciation of worldliness, common ownership of property, and public confession of sins, which culminated in the frenetic dances that gave them the name Shakers.

There were five "families" at Pleasant Hill, established in 1805. By 1820 it was a prosperous colony of five hundred persons. "Family" had a particular meaning, since the Shakers did not believe in marriage. Men and women, they maintained, could live more happily as brothers and sisters, helping one another, but living personally apart.

The Civil War, plus 19th-century industrialism and worldliness, seeped into Pleasant Hill, and the celibacy rules prevented the natural increase in their numbers. In 1910 they were dissolved.

The reception area of the inn is located in the Trustees' House, one of twenty-five or more restored buildings clustered along the single country road. To construct buildings of enduring strength, some with walls three or four feet thick, the Shakers quarried limestone from the river bluffs and hauled granite slabs a mile uphill from the river. Most of the buildings are a deep red brick or limestone.

The restaurant is on the first floor of the Trustees' House, and the guest rooms on the second and third floors are reached by two marvelous twin-spiraled staircases of matchless craftsmanship. There are many additional bedrooms on the second floor of restored Shaker buildings.

The experience of sleeping in a Shaker room is most refreshing. In my room were two single beds, each with its own trundle bed underneath. The Shaker rockers were classic, and the extra chairs were hung by pegs on the walls.

THE INN AT PLEASANT HILL, Shakertown, KY. P.O. address: Rte. 4, Harrodsburg, KY 40330; 606-734-5411. An 81-guestroom (private baths) country inn in 15 restored Shaker buildings on Rte. 68, 7 mi. northeast of Harrodsburg, 25 mi. southwest of Lexington. European plan. Breakfast, lunch, dinner served daily to travelers. No tipping. Open year-round. Suggest contacting inn about winter schedule. Closed Christmas Eve and Christmas Day. Ann Voris, Owner-hostess. (See Index for rates.)

Directions: From Lexington take Rte. 68 south toward Harrodsburg. From Louisville, take I-64 to Lawrenceburg and Graeffenburg exit (not numbered). Follow Rte. 127 south to Harrodsburg and Rte. 68 northeast to Shakertown.

THE FEARRINGTON HOUSE
Chapel Hill, North Carolina (1988)

In the 17th and 18th centuries, many English immigrants to America settled in North Carolina. That's why I was interested to learn that R. B. Fitch, a native North Carolinian, went back to England for inspiration in the design of the Fearrington House. When I saw the arrangement of attractive, low buildings with their roofs pitched at different levels, grouped around the courtyard, with the pump in the middle and all the little gardens, I immediately thought of the Bell Inn in Buckinghamshire.

And sure enough, R.B., as he prefers being called, told me that a visit to the Bell Inn provided him and his wife with their inspiration.

"Jenny and I have made several trips to England, collecting old furniture and antiques and original art. The old pine flooring, for instance, came from an 1850 London workhouse."

Included in the group of inn buildings is the sun room, where afternoon tea is available, and the garden house, which is a living room where guests can get together.

Jenny, R.B.'s wife, has created fourteen superb guest rooms, mostly suites, every one of which is completely different from the others. I thought I could hear the pristine strains of a Mozart quartet as R.B. was showing me the guest rooms, and I asked him where that heavenly sound was coming from. "We have a wonderful sound system in all the rooms, including speakers in the bathroom. It's a great way to brush your teeth," he laughed. He's got heated towel racks in the bathrooms too.

"Each room has been designed to take advantage of the wonderful vistas," R.B. told me. There are views of open fields, woods, gardens, nearby Bynum Ridge, and a country village.

The village is a story in itself. R.B. has turned a farmstead of over 600 acres into a tiny rural community where the homes of about 800 inhabitants nestle unobtrusively in the surrounding forest. The village center was once a cluster of old farm buildings.

Now, the old milking barn is a pottery with a resident potter, another farm building is now an excellent, well-stocked market and general store, and there is even a post office in the old blacksmith shop. Jennie's passion for gardening has resulted in the Dovecote, a wonderful country garden shop. The restaurant, a lovely white-columned farmhouse, is in the old Fearrington home, built in 1926.

Food, I discovered, was of paramount importance in their plans. They wanted to bring back Southern cooking at its finest, and the menu offers such interesting items as Carolina crab cakes with tomato and corn relish, Chatham County goat cheese salad, corn chowder with hickory-smoked duck sausage, crayfish fritters and creole butter, and grilled Carolina quail with savory cabbage and a ginger sherry sauce. Many of their dishes are featured in the handsome *Fearrington House Cookbook*.

There are many other more usual dishes, but everything is cooked and served with a special flair and accompanied by buttermilk biscuits and homemade breads. I couldn't make up my mind between the lemon meringue pie and a hazelnut meringue with chocolate ice cream and fresh raspberry sauce. They were both incredible.

I asked R.B. what his philosophy had been in creating this very interesting and outstanding settlement. "We've tried to blend it into the rolling countryside so that it looks like it's been around for a long time. The 650 acres that make up the village were in the Fearrington family for over 200 years, and when we bought it in 1974 our commitment was to preserve its heritage and beauty."

Fearrington House has recently joined a very select list of American inns that belong to the pretigious Relais et Châteaux.

About all I would add is that I can't think of another inn with the same level of luxury and elegance, in a more beautiful setting.

THE FEARRINGTON HOUSE, Fearrington Village Center, Pittsboro, NC 27312; 919-542-2121. A 14-guestroom (private baths) (mostly suites) luxury inn and village in rolling farm country 8 mi. south of Chapel Hill, the home of the Univ. of No. Carolina. Queen and double beds available. Breakfast included in room rate. Picnics available. Restaurant is open for dinner Tues. thru Sat. and Sun. brunch. Open year-round. Swimming pool, croquet lawn, crafts shops, country walks on premises. Cultural, social, and athletic events at Univ. of No. Carolina; also Duke Univ. and No. Carolina State Univ. nearby. Children over 12 welcome. Nearby kennels available for pets. No smoking in dining rooms. Jenny and R.B. Fitch, Owners-hosts. (See Index for rates.)

Directions: The Fearrington House is located halfway between Chapel Hill and Pittsboro on U.S. 15/501.

HEMLOCK INN
Bryson City, North Carolina (1973)

"What's it really like at the Hemlock Inn?" I've been joyously answering that question for a great many years as a result of some really inspiring visits with Ella Jo and John Shell. This time, however, I'm going to share with you a letter I received from Mr. and Mrs. J. Brooks Brown, which apparently was mostly written by Helen Brown. I think it puts us right into the picture at the Hemlock Inn.

"We have stayed fifteen times at the Hemlock Inn and would like to share with you some observations about it. My husband, Brooks, and I, who are in our mid-sixties, travel by car from our home in Jacksonville, Florida, in just one day's time for that delicious 6:00 p.m. casual, family-style dinner. . . .

"How great it is to sit around the large Lazy Susan tables with guests who seem to be in concert with our same needs — not all seeming to need the entertainment of radio, TV, golfing, swimming, guided hiking or walking tours, but, instead, much-needed rest and freedom from pressing responsibilities. There is the freedom to converse without competitive conversation, to spend one's day in quietness together in those beautiful surroundings — most particularly for us in long walks or hikes down at the historic Deep Creek region. This can be a short or long hike.

"At each Hemlock stay we find renewal in having had our day started by John's loving prayer of grace in the lodge; new expressions of love for each other in tranquil, quiet, beautiful wild-flowered surroundings; discussing and working out a few problems of our own or those of friends;

making plans for grandchildren, family, or friends, or in stopping by the wonderful melodious stream to picnic or just to enjoy.

"You might say that we have the freedom here to catch up on the 'loose ends of life' at our own pace and to celebrate life during this getaway week at a slower tempo. . . .

"Another uniqueness about Hemlock is the freedom of choice of accommodations. There are all kinds of guest rooms, including some in cottages with even room for our grandchildren. Of course, all of them have private baths.

"We have played the shuffleboard that you have described and noticed that many guests enjoy a good game of table tennis, the outdoor porch rockers, quiet reading or game playing in the cheerful book-filled mountain-view room or in front of the large stone fireplace. Many couples, singles, or families hop in their cars and manage to take untold trips to interesting 'nobs' or 'overlooks,' or hike on the scenic trails. Ella Jo says that there are over 700 miles of maintained trails in the Great Smokies.

"So, I might end by saying, if you have survived this long letter so far, Brooks and I leave Hemlock with renewed vigor, memories for our memory bank, healed spirits to continue to meet a busy life, and, as John Shell says, 'a grateful reverence for those God-given things we certainly have in abundance.' "

Thank you, Brooks and Helen Brown. I've taken a few editing liberties with your splendid letter, and I am delighted to share your feelings for the Hemlock Inn. Perhaps we'll meet there sometime in the near future.

HEMLOCK INN, Bryson City, NC 28713; 704-488-2885. A 25-guestroom (private baths) Smoky Mountain inn, 4 mi. from Bryson City and 60 mi. from Asheville. Modified American plan omits lunch. Breakfast and dinner served to travelers by reservation only. Sunday dinner served at noontime. Open late April to early Nov. Wheelchair access. Near Fontana Dam, Cherokee, and Pisgah National Forest. Shuffleboard, skittles, table tennis, hiking trails on grounds. Tubing, rafting, and tennis nearby. No pets. No credit cards. Ella Jo and John Shell, Owners-hosts. (See Index for rates.)

Directions: From Hwy. 74 take the Hyatt Creek Rd.—Ela exit. Bear right until you reach Rte. 19. Turn left on Rte. 19 for approx. 1 mi., and turn right at inn sign. Take county road to top of mountain.

HOUND EARS LODGE
Blowing Rock, North Carolina (1971)

There are very few sights more inspiring to the golfer in me than to look over the golf course on a pleasant June morning from the balcony of Hound Ears Lodge. In the foreground is a lake fed by a small mountain stream that winds its way through the valley. This lake also serves as a hazard for the final hole and a very good 9-iron shot to the green is necessary to stay out of trouble.

The fairways that stretch out in the distance toward Grandfather Mountain are being watered by great fountains sent forth by the automatic watering system. When this is completed and the mist burns off, there is revealed a ring of mountains around the entire area. However, in the meantime, the greenskeepers are busy sweeping off the moisture that has accumulated overnight and the head greenskeeper can be seen tootling about in his golf cart, making sure that everything is ready for another day's play.

I had arrived at Hound Ears early in June, just at the time when the special golf packages, in effect since April, were being replaced by the regular social season. It was a good opportunity for me to have a pleasant visit with David Blust, the innkeeper at Hound Ears, who actually started as a bellboy a number of years ago. It's hard to imagine a more enthusiastic devotee not only of Hound Ears, but of golf and of North Carolina. We enjoyed a few moments of listening to Gene Fleri, who plays piano in the pleasant lounge before dinner and in the dining room during dinner. It is said that he can play any song that anyone can name.

Hound Ears is a golf- and ski-oriented country inn, but is somewhat different in atmosphere than the other *CIBR* inns in North Carolina. It is a luxurious, modified American plan resort-inn, and the rates reflect the additional services and elegance. In the many, many years that I have been revisiting Hound Ears I've always found a very gratifying number of *CIBR* guests.

Among the many amenities offered are turn-down service each evening, the *Charlotte Observer* at the door every morning, fresh towels supplied to the rooms while guests enjoy dinner, and a careful monitoring of guests at the main gate by courteous custodians. Advance reservations are preferred; however, occasionally there are some guest rooms available.

The property surrounding Hound Ears has been purchased by home-owners who have built attractive, luxurious vacation homes, and who are very much involved in the future and welfare of the entire resort complex.

A great many of the guests are from Florida, and during the warm weather they escape to this very high mountain area to enjoy all of the relative coolness, as well as the golf.

During the winter, in addition to being near several downhill ski areas aided by snowmaking, Hound Ears also has its own beginners' and intermediate slopes, providing enjoyment for those of us who are looking for a less vigorous downhill experience.

The staff at Hound Ears is made up for the most part of students from nearby Appalachia College in Boone. These are very pleasant, alert young people who have grown up in the area, for whom Hound Ears is a source of pride.

The furnishings, appointments, interiors, and exteriors are carefully harmonized. For example, my room was done in complementary shades of brown and yellow. All of the buildings are set among the rhododendrons and evergreens, and in many places huge handsome boulders were allowed to remain where they rested. The road was built around them, curving and twisting and climbing.

Nearby Grandfather Mountain is a place where the Scottish clan gathering is held during the second week in July. Clan members gather from all over the globe to take part in athletic competitions, dances, and piping. There are also a number of other cultural and recreational events.

HOUND EARS LODGE AND CLUB, P.O. Box 188, Blowing Rock, NC 28605; 704-963-4321. A luxurious 25-guestroom (private baths) resort-inn on Rte. 105, 6 mi. from Boone. Each room has two double beds. Near natural attractions. Modified American plan. Meals served to houseguests only. Open year-round. Tennis, 18-hole golf course, swimming, and skiing on grounds. Robert Breitenstein, Owner-host. (See Index for rates.)

Directions: From Winston-Salem, follow Rte. 421 west to Boone, then travel south on Rte. 105 to inn. From Asheville, follow Rte. I-40 east to Marion then Rte. 221 north to Linville and Rte. 105 north to inn. From Bristol, Va., and I-81, follow Rte. 58 east to Damascus, Va., then Rte. 91 to Mountain City, Tenn., and Rte. 421 to Boone, and Rte. 104 south to inn (5 mi.)

MAST FARM INN
Valle Crucis, North Carolina (1988)

"People in this part of North Carolina are very fond of just sittin' and talkin'." Francis and Sibyl Pressly and I were engaged in one of the most popular activities at the Mast Farm Inn—porch-rocking. They were telling me about the outbuildings around the rambling old farmhouse, which is on the National Register of Historic Places as "one of the most complete and best-presented groups of 19th-century farm buildings in western North Carolina." The Mast Farm had grown from the tiny log cabin built in 1812 by David Mast.

"The building with the bell tower is the old smokehouse," Francis continued. "Then there's the spring house. Then if you move on around, you come to the old woodshed and the apple house, or ice house, which has foot-thick walls, and we still use it for storing our potatoes and apples."

"Are any of the other buildings used for anything now?" I wondered.

"Oh, sure, we do some woodworking and keep our tools in the old woodshed," Francis replied.

"There's a nest of wrens who are using the old wash house," Sibyl added. "It was considered to be a very innovative wash house because it was built right over a stream and it had lattice work above, so the cool breezes could blow through. There are still two big old iron pots in there."

"Actually," Francis said, "we've restored these buildings to show what an old mountain farmstead was like. We have really made every effort to remain faithful to the past in this entire restoration."

I would say that Francis and Sibyl have succeeded admirably in their objectives. The main house, its long porch stretching around the side with rocking chairs and swings, must look very much as it did in the early 1900s, when it was first turned into an inn. A stay at the inn feels very much like a step back in time, with no telephones or television to shatter the peaceful country atmosphere.

Both originally from North Carolina, Francis and Sibyl had been living in Washington, D.C., where Francis was an administrator with the National 4-H Council, and Sibyl a physical therapist in geriatrics.

In the few years since they began renovating the farmhouse, they have shored up foundations, buttressed walls and floors, painted, papered, brought in craftsmen for woodworking, and done all those things that are necessary to bring a neglected and derelict old house back to its former dignity and beauty.

Today, the rooms fairly sparkle with turn-of-the-century antique furnishings and mountain crafts. There are fresh flowers everywhere and as one of their guests told me, "The inn is squeaky clean from one end to the other, and the room appointments seem to have been chosen not for their country atmosphere, but to make the guests comfortable."

I can see that the Presslys are very good at putting their guests at ease. They are very welcoming and make a point of introducing everyone. When it comes to meals, Sibyl says, "We serve our guests the kind of food that we enjoy."

They describe it as "country cooking with a gourmet flair." That means vegetables and fruit from their garden down by the river. The menu is prix fixe and dinner might be an appetizer, sautéed mountain trout, vegetable strudel, corn pudding, garden vegetables, salad, fresh-baked rolls and cornbread. Dessert could be a fruit cobbler with ice cream, hot fudge cake, fudge nut cake, sour cream apple pie, or Shaker lemon pie.

But as I started to say, we were sitting out on the porch, rocking, and Sibyl and Francis were telling me about how they'd happened to come here. As I looked out over the beautiful mountain valley, I could see just what it was about these North Carolina hills that had attracted them so much.

MAST FARM INN, P.O. Box 704, Valle Crucis, NC 28691; 704-963-5857. An 11-guestroom (9 private baths) farmhouse inn set in a beautiful mountain valley between Boone and Banner Elk in western North Carolina. Queen and double beds available. Modified American plan includes breakfast and dinner. Dinner served to the public Tues. thru Sun. lunch. Reservations necessary. Open Jan. to mid-Mar.; May 1 to Nov. 1. Fishing, canoeing, golf, hiking, skiing, country walks, crafts, and country fairs nearby. Children over 12 welcome. No pets. No smoking. Sibyl and Francis Pressly, Owners-hosts. (See Index for rates.)

Directions: The Boone/Banner Elk area is accessible from any direction. Watch for Valle Crucis on NC 105. Mast Farm Inn is 3 mi. from Rte. 105 on Rte. SR 1112.

THE ORCHARD INN
Saluda, North Carolina (1985)

I had finished every last bit of the succulent chicken Madras and now I was trying to stretch out a scrumptious blackberry cobbler so it would last as long as possible. I peered through the window, where nature had just put on a marvelous sunset, high in the North Carolina mountains. A pinpoint of light in the valley far below caught my eye.

Ken Hough joined me for a moment, having completed the busiest part of his evening in the kitchen as chef. "Have you ever wondered who lives down there where we can see that light?" I asked. Ken, among a number of other careers, has been headmaster of a college preparatory school in Charleston and also an operatic tenor. He smiled broadly at my question and replied, "It's funny you should mention that because I've often wondered the same thing. Of course, we could never find it in the daytime and the chances are we could never find it by night either."

The inn is midway between Hendersonville and Tryon and, like some other North Carolina inns, has a truly spectacular view. I was very flattered a few years ago when Ken and his wife, Ann, who has a marvelous feeling for interior design, reprinted some things I had said about them in the 1985 edition of this book: "Because I spend so much time in an automobile, I have invented a little game of my own. I call it 'Inn Word Association.' I think of an inn, then think of words that I associate most readily with it.

"In the case of the Orchard Inn there are many words that come to my mind—flowers, original paintings, music, sculpture, a breathtaking view, cordiality, intellectual curiosity, good conversation, mountain tranquility, and the changing tones and colors as they are affected by the mists off the mountains at various times of the day.

"The Orchard Inn combines country farmhouse warmth with many touches of southern plantation elegance. It has oriental rugs, original artwork, baskets, quilts, and Flow Blue china. Ann has exercised splendid taste in decorating the ten guest rooms with antiques, including some with iron and brass beds and hand-woven rag rugs."

This inn has one of the most interesting second-floor hallways I have ever seen. Several bookshelves are loaded with books and magazines, including very old but readable ones. There are all kinds of unusual curios, dolls, children's toys, a dollhouse, and contemporary drawings, watercolors, and prints from the French Impressionists.

The dining room is in the wonderful, long, glassed-in porch overlooking the rolling peaks of the Warrior Mountain Range. It's really quite magical after dusk has fallen—every table is candlelit, and the strains of Schumann, Mozart, and Scarlatti float out into the gathering night.

Ann joined us at the table and mentioned that Ken's "Ladies Only"

cooking school was most successful this past winter. "We're going to continue it. We include walks, massages, and concerts, and the camaraderie is wonderful." If the reader is interested in learning more about not only the cooking school but other special weekends that are offered throughout the year, just drop the inn a line.

Ken and Ann excused themselves and once again I was left looking out into the darkness at that one single pinpoint of light. I wondered if perhaps they, too, might be looking up at the lights of the inn.

THE ORCHARD INN, Box 725, Saluda, NC 28773; 704-749-5471. A 12-guestroom (private baths) mountaintop (2,500 ft.) inn a short distance from Tryon in western North Carolina. Queen, double, and twin beds available. Breakfast included with room rate. Dinner available. Open year-round. Antiquing, hiking, wildflower collecting, birdwatching, and superb country roads abound. No pets. No credit cards. Ann and Ken Hough, Owners-hosts. (See Index for rates.)

Directions: From Atlanta, take I-85 north to I-26. Continue north to Exit 28 and Hwy. 176. Inn is on Hwy. 176, 2 mi. off I-26. From Asheville, take I-26 south.

"European plan" means that rates for rooms and meals are separate. "American plan" means that meals are included in the cost of the room. "Modified American plan" means that breakfast and dinner are included in the cost of the room. The rates at some inns include a continental breakfast with the lodging.

SNOWBIRD MOUNTAIN LODGE
Robbinsville, North Carolina (1973)

"That's quite a collection of hiking sticks," I said admiringly. Bob Rhudy handed me a particularly handsome one, "They're all made from native woods, wild cherry, butternut, maple, silver bell, wormy chestnut . . ."

Hiking is one of the favorite pastimes of the many nature lovers who are fortunate enough to find this lodge on the outskirts of the Joyce Kilmer Memorial Forest, where giant trees, twenty feet around at the base, tower 150 feet overhead. There is a regular schedule of guided wildflower hikes led by well-qualified and knowledgeable naturalists, as well as a June hiking week led by a veteran hiker, just when the mountain laurel is abloom.

Snowbird Mountain Lodge perches 2,880 feet high in the heart of the Nantahala National Forest. Standing on the spacious flagstone terrace, I felt as if I were literally hanging over crystal clear Lake Santeetlah, at least 1,000 feet below, and as if I could almost reach out and touch the majestic peaks of the Snowbird Range directly before me. It's nothing short of breathtaking. A few of the other less athletically inclined guests were sitting obviously mesmerized by the fantastic view, the sound of the breeze sighing through the pines, and the birds singing and flitting busily among the leaves. I heard one gentleman murmur, "I don't think I'll ever leave."

This is bird-watchers' heaven, especially at the Point, a ten-minute hike away, where the Rhudys have built a deck.

"It's our best view," Connie told me. "Some of our guests have identified over 100 species of birds. We have humming birds, cardinals, scarlet tanagers, whippoorwills, red-eyed vireos, all kind of warblers, and many more."

I think Snowbird is everything a mountain lodge should be. Built of chestnut logs and native stone, with a huge stone fireplace and a floor-to-ceiling window looking out to the mountains in the main lounge, the house is furnished in a homey, comfortable manner. Guest rooms are paneled in various native woods with matching furniture, and colorful bedspreads add a bright touch. The shelves in the lounge are packed with books, and there are board games and an upright piano for indoor amusement.

All three meals are included in the room rate, and the food is plentiful, wholesome, and tasty, with mountain trout, roast beef, fresh ham, steak, home-baked bread, fresh vegetables, and homemade desserts. A box lunch is provided for hikers and picnickers.

In addition to miles of beautiful hiking trails, there are trout streams and lakes for fishing, several rivers for canoeing, kayaking, rafting, or tubing, a stream-fed pool for swimming, motorboat trips, horseback riding, a Cherokee Indian reservation, and a number of lovely scenic drives. Bob and Connie are always ready to offer suggestions and advice on any of these pursuits. The atmosphere is altogether relaxed and friendly.

As one of their guests commented, "It's the kind of place you hope exists but never expect to find."

SNOWBIRD MOUNTAIN LODGE, Joyce Kilmer Forest Rd., Robbinsville. NC 28771; 704-479-3433. A 23-guestroom (21 private baths) inn on top of the Great Smokies, 12 mi. from Robbinsville. King, double, and twin beds available. American plan (room and 3 meals). Open from end of April to early Nov. Lunch and dinner served to travelers by reservation only. Shuffleboard, table tennis, archery, croquet, horseshoes, badminton on grounds. Swimming, fishing, hiking, backroading nearby. Guided walks for nature lovers by reservation. Not suitable for children under 12. No pets. The Rhudy Family, Owners-hosts. (See Index for rates.)

Directions: The inn is located at the western tip of No. Carolina, 10 mi. west of Robbinsville. Approaching from the northeast or south take U.S. 19 and 129; from the northwest take U.SD. 129, then follow signs to Joyce Kilmer Memorial Forest.

The date in parenthesis in the heading represents the first year the inn appeared in the pages of Country Inns and Back Roads.

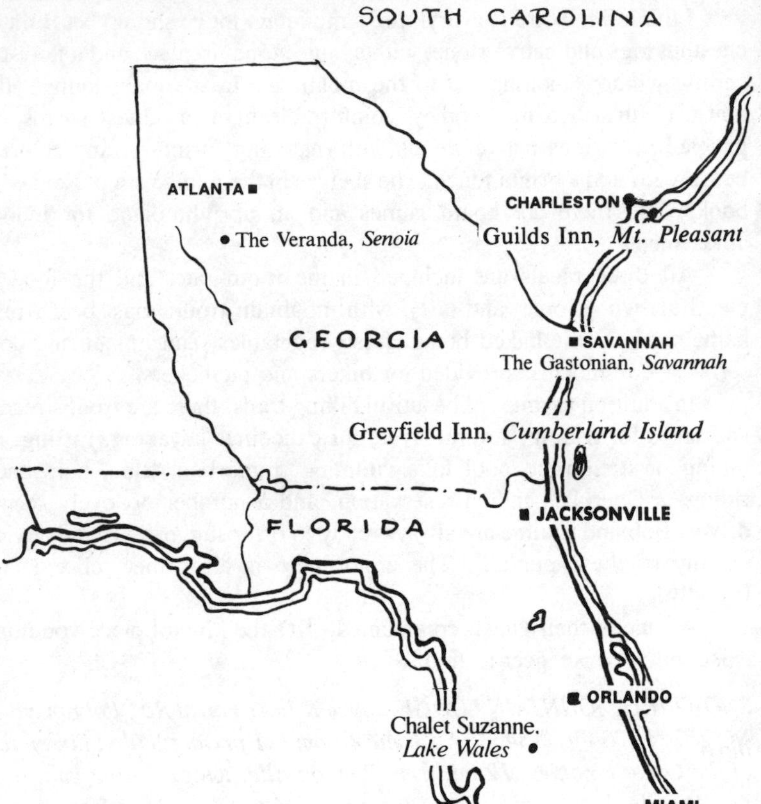

SOUTH CAROLINA

ATLANTA ■

CHARLESTON ●

● The Veranda, *Senoia*   Guilds Inn, *Mt. Pleasant*

GEORGIA   ■ SAVANNAH
The Gastonian, *Savannah*

Greyfield Inn, *Cumberland Island*

FLORIDA   ■ JACKSONVILLE

■ ORLANDO

Chalet Suzanne.
Lake Wales ●

MIAMI ●

Lower
South

Eastern Time Zone

CUMBERLAND ISLAND

Cumberland Island is the southernmost and largest of a chain of barrier islands that starts at Cape Hatteras and extends to the Florida-Georgia border. It is eighteen miles long and three miles wide at its widest point. There are 26 varieties of wild animals and 323 species of birds identified. The island has one road, Grand Avenue, a dirt and shell affair, which traverses the length of the island though the live oak.

In recent years the National Park Service acquired a great portion of the island and has taken the necessary action to forever maintain it as a nature preserve.

Marshland fringes much of Cumberland's shores, protecting them from the current and the tide. Its principal inhabitants are the ubiquitous fiddler crabs and long-legged wading birds. The live oak avenues create an atmosphere akin to a cathedral.

The eighteen-mile beach is the most striking feature of the island and one can walk for hours in delicious solitude except for the sanderling that scurry our of the clutching fingers of the waves, and the pelicans skimming the water. Shells abound and it's impossible to come back empty-handed.

The dunes, which are carefully protected, provide still another intriguing atmosphere. At the edge of the forest there is a group of lakes, which have their own particular wildlife. Egrets and herons fish these waters as well as ducks who stop off as they travel north and south.

Besides the wildlife there is a rich history of the island that covers pre-Columbian times as well as occupation by the Spaniards, the British, and later on some enterprising men from the new American republic. In the early 1800s there were a few plantations on the island, but after the War Between the States the island was dominated by the presence of the Carnegie family who raised an impressive mansion of brick and stone at Dungeness with formal gardens, swimming pool and stables. Unfortunately, it burned in 1959.

GREYFIELD INN
Cumberland Island, Georgia (1982)

I paid my first visit to this gorgeous, haunting part of the world in 1975. I had the pleasure then of spending part of a day with Lucy Ferguson, known to everyone as Grandma. She is the granddaughter of Thomas Carnegie (brother of Andrew). It was Grandma who first introduced me to Cumberland Island, with its eighteen-mile stretch of beach, fascinating dunes, and secret ponds. She also showed me the ruins of Dungeness, built by her grandparents, which unfortunately burned in 1959.

Once again, as on my first visit, I was on the ferry boat, *R.W. Ferguson,* and Captain Mitty Ferguson was updating me on Greyfield Inn. We left Fernandina Beach at 3:00 p.m. and were making the hour-and-a-quarter run up the passage between the island and mainland to the Greyfield dock.

"Of course, everything is much the same as it was when you were here the first time," he said, keeping a guiding hand on the wheel. "The Fergusons, including Grandmother, are still very much in the picture, so that we are a family team dividing the chores. We also have some excellent staff, including a wonderful naturalist/guide. Our guests rave about her tours, which explore many aspects of this magnificent island."

By this time the ferry was within sight of the Greyfield dock, and I could see once again the gleaming, three-story mansion through the mysterious grove of live oaks. Soon, with the other guests, I was bundled into the jeep and driven to the impressive front entrance of the inn with its majestic steps and broad veranda. As soon as I stepped inside, it all returned to me: the paintings, the oriental rugs, the mahogany furniture, the silver on the sideboard, the great fireplaces, and the great collection of books.

I joined the other guests at dinner in the candlelit dining room and the conversation dealt with the wonders of the unspoiled beach, where the magnificent loggerhead sea turtles lay their eggs, and where guests sometimes can see the young hatching. The shore birds and the marine life are there, as are deer, wild horses, wild turkeys, and the dense live oak forest.

The newest acquisition is a Jeep Scrambler for beach tours, which Mitty tells me the guests really love. The gazebo that stands in the meadow between the primary and secondary dunes is a great spot in which to get out of the sun at midday, to watch the sun rise and set, or just to lie about reading and watching the shore birds.

There were several guests who had been at Greyfield for many days who were saying, "It takes a day just to find out what is here, and at least two days more to explore it."

Several of the guests had seen a recent issue of *Audubon Magazine* with the article by John Mitchell on Cumberland Island and Greyfield Inn. This is one of the last remaining impressive nature preserves on the East Coast.

It was wonderful to be back at Greyfield once again.

Do not plan on visiting the Greyfield Inn if you have only one night, and be certain to check with the inn about the ferry schedules. The Greyfield Inn is the only public overnight accommodation on Cumberland Island.

GREYFIELD INN, Cumberland Island, GA (mailing address: Fernandina Beach, FL 32034); 904-261-6408. A 9-guestroom (1 private bath) mansion on an island off the coast of southern Georgia. King, double, and twin beds available. Accessible from Fernandina Beach, Fla., or on a National Park Service ferry from St. Mary's, Ga. Check with inn on ferry times. Rates include full breakfast and dinner, as well as either box lunch or informal noon meal. Open every day in the year by reservation only. Beachcombing, swimming, fishing, clam digging, photography, birdwatching, bicycles, walking and driving tours, natural history tour. No pets. The Ferguson Family, Innkeepers. (See Index for rates.)

Directions: The R.W. Ferguson leaves from the public dock at Fernandina Beach, Fla., at either 3 or 5 p.m., depending upon the day of the week (check with inn). Also check with inn on National Park Service ferry schedule from St. Mary's, Ga. Autos are left on the mainland. Island also accessible by small plane or helicopter.

THE GASTONIAN
Savannah, Georgia (1989)

Light splashes down the steps and across the sidewalk when the door opens to welcome frock-coated gentlemen with their bejewelled ladies in silks and satins alighting from their carriages. Sounds of gaiety and music spill out of the open windows. It is 1868 and another brilliant party is in progress at the opulent townhouse of the prosperous insurance broker, R. H. Footman. Next door, the equally opulent house is dim, as Aaron Champion and his wife join their neighbor's gathering. The Civil War has been over for three years, and Savannah society, spared General Sherman's wrath, is returning to sparkling life.

Well, I'm just daydreaming, but that's the sort of thing one does in this lavishly restored and decorated home. Hugh and Roberta Lineberger encourage such fantasies. After all, it was their own fantasy that brought them here in the first place.

"We were on vacation from our home in California, passing through Savannah on our way to a golfing holiday in South Carolina," Roberta told me, "when we started looking at some of these lovely old houses and dreaming about running a bed-and-breakfast inn." Within a matter of weeks they found themselves the owners of not one but two Italianate Regency homes, side by side, and were deep in the intricacies of renovation and restoration.

I must say, the Linebergers have done a magnificent job of creating a truly elegant inn out of these two historic homes. The houses are connected by an attractive curving walkway, elevated over the garden filled with fragrant myrtle and flowering dogwood.

I could go on at great lengths about the beautiful architectural

features and the equally beautiful American and European antique furnishings of the Gastonian. Roberta has decorated every room with great flair and taste, with lush fabrics and authentic Savannah colors. The rooms have working fireplaces, plants, and fresh flowers.

Some of the bathrooms are the most unusual I've ever seen. Many of the tubs are the kind, as Hugh puts it, "you can fill up to your earlobes and soak away in." One of them, fit for a Roman emperor, is in the Caracalla Suite, which has an eight-foot round whirlpool bathtub in front of a fireplace.

More important to me is the feeling of gracious hospitality. Having tea with Hugh and Roberta in the elegant Chippendale and Sheraton sitting room, facing a charming portrait of a lovely lady over the carved white-marble fireplace, I found them very warm and easy to talk with.

Roberta explained that although breakfast is sometimes served in the formal dining room, she usually cooks and serves it in the large, sunny kitchen. In addition to her legendary Southern-style breakfasts, "We welcome our guests with fresh fruit and wine," she said, "and have little extras, like turn-down service and Savannah sweets and cordials."

They have many amusing stories of their adventures in bringing the Gastonian into being, and their travels in Europe, collecting treasures for it. "I'm sure there's a story about that portrait of the lovely lady," I said. "Yes, indeed there is," Roberta replied. "The antiques dealer in southeastern England where we saw her had made a solemn vow to find the right home for her, and we had to promise him we would provide her with a most beautiful setting."

"Actually," Hugh commented with a smile, "we like to provide all our guests with a beautiful setting, as well as with real Southern hospitality."

It's my pleasure to welcome the Gastonian to our pages.

THE GASTONIAN, 220 E. Gaston St., Savannah, GA 31401; 912-232-2869. A 13-guestroom and suites (private baths) luxurious inn in twin townhouses in the Historic Landmark District of Savannah. King, queen, and double beds available. Complimentary full breakfast only meal served. Open year-round. Arrangements for horse-drawn carriage historical tours, dinner reservations, hot tub on premises. Golf and athletic club privileges, tennis, deep-sea fishing, Savannah River within walking distance, and all of the historic and cultural attractions in the largest Historic Landmark district in U.S. nearby. No children under 12. No pets. Smoking limited. Hugh and Roberta Lineberger, Owners-hosts. (See Index for rates.)

Directions: From I-95 take I-16 to Savannah. Take W. Broad St. exit, crossing Broad St. and continuing to Gaston St. and the inn at the corner of Lincoln St.

THE VERANDA
Senoia, Georgia (1989)

For a real taste of old-fashioned Georgia country hospitality, you can't beat the Veranda in the sleepy little town of Senoia (pronounced senoy). Ella Jo and John Shell at the Hemlock Inn in North Carolina had told me about it. The Veranda is listed on the National Register of Historic Places, and I understand the town itself may be added to the Register any day now. It's a toss-up as to whether the local hardware store, with one or more of "everything," or James H. Baggerly's Museum is the more fascinating place to visit.

Jan and Bobby Boal at the Veranda have a few museum-quality collections themselves. I loved Bobby's array of over 100 walking sticks, many of them made by her father and grandfather and others purchased all over the world, including one that belonged to Senator Robert A. Taft. Some other things that are a lot of fun are a huge old Wurlitzer player piano-organ with chimes, and a lot of music rolls, and the 1860s Estey pump organ with all kinds of turn-of-the-century sheet music and songbooks. They also have a vast and fascinating collection of kaleidoscopes and unusual puzzles and games.

When Jan and Bobby bought the house in 1985, it had been a private residence since the 1930s. Before that, it had been the Hollberg Hotel, built in 1906 when Senoia was a thriving cotton town with a new rail station. A rambling white clapboard building with a Doric-columned wraparound porch, it was built entirely with heart-pine lumber. Several rooms have the original pressed-tin ceilings, unusual prismed chandeliers, stained-glass window insets, and thin-planked wainscoting.

The Boals have completed the feeling of authenticity with their own heirlooms and antiques, including eclectic furnishings, oriental rugs, fine old books, prints, and etchings and a massive set of walnut book cases, once owned by President William McKinley.

All of the guest rooms are most attractively furnished with queen-sized beds, armoires, handmade quilts, rocking chairs, and fresh flowers. When I retired for the night, I found my bed had been turned down and a miniature kaleidoscope was on the pillow.

The Boals are two of the friendliest people you'd ever want to meet. While Bobby was busy in the kitchen, Jan entertained us with a tune on the pump organ. When he isn't playing the organ, serving meals, doing his thing making french toast for breakfast, and just generally innkeeping, Jan is a mathematics professor at Georgia State University.

Bobby says innkeeping is hard work but the rewards are many. She loves it when guests share her interest in the history of the area.

Be sure to make advance reservations for dinner, as you won't want to miss one of her "made from scratch" meals, including the crisp Georgia crackers that accompany the fresh fruit salad. Bobby has a large collection of regional and old family-secret recipes, along with many of her own original ones. Everyone tells her she should write a cookbook. One of her dinners might include cold peach soup, veal in puffed pastry, a ham and chicken casserole, homemade fruit sorbet, sourdough biscuits or sourdough bread, fresh vegetables, and some delectable dessert like lemon meringue sundae, Black Forest torte, or homemade angel food cake with fresh strawberries and whipped cream.

There's so much more to tell, but I'll leave it to you to discover the delights of a visit to this homey, comfortable inn where Southern hospitality reigns. I am delighted to welcome the Veranda to our pages.

THE VERANDA, 252 Seavy St., Senoia, GA 30276; 404-599-3905. A 9-guestroom (private baths) homey Victorian inn on the National Register of Historic Places in a quiet small town, 36 mi. south of Atlanta. Queen and twin beds available. Deluxe breakfast included; all meals available by reservation. Open year-round. Library, music, puzzles, games, gift shop, porch swings and rocking chairs, and special theme weekends on premises. Golf, tennis, fishing, historic walking tours, festivals, antiquing, Callaway Gardens, Warm Springs, private museum, and great hardware store nearby. No pets. Limited smoking. Bobby and Jan Boal, Owners-hosts. (See Index for rates.)

Directions: From Atlanta, take Rte. 85 through Riverdale and Fayetteville to Senoia city limit. Turn right at Seavy St. Inn is on corner of Barnes and Seavy Sts.

CHALET SUZANNE
Lake Wales, Florida (1973)

After my first visit to Chalet Suzanne a number of years ago, I wondered if it really did happen or was it like the musical *Brigadoon,* in which the fictional Scottish village returns for one day every 100 years. This is a reaction I frequently get from guests who visit this unusual country inn in central Florida. Sometimes they can hardly believe it.

However, there is no doubt that Chalet Suzanne really exists. The bridges, steeples, cupolas, minarets, peaked roofs, flat roofs, castle towers, domes, treasures, antiques, and pagodas are all there. It's a world of pastels in Bavarian, Swiss, Oriental, French, English, Turkish, Chinese, and every other style you can think of. The nice part of it is that the guest rooms are all comfortably furnished in this wonderful Arabian Nights atmosphere, with something special about each one, like a nice view, a private patio overlooking the swimming pool, or being close to the airstrip.

It was all started in the early 1930s by Bertha Hinshaw, and now her son, Carl, and his wife, Vita, are continuing with their own touches—the newest of which is a spectacular covered walkway to the dining area, graced by a beautifully carved window with Tiffany angel roundels from All Angels Episcopal Church in New York City.

To the people who live in Florida, Chalet Suzanne is best known for its exceptional food. In fact, it was recently awarded the Golden Spoon for the nineteenth consecutive year of being listed among the top ten restaurants in Florida. *Mobil Guide* has given it four stars and it has the *Travel-Holiday Magazine* award for fine dining. You've undoubtedly read about it in national magazines or seen it on TV—they get a lot of attention from the media.

Dinner is served in the wonderful around-the-world ambience of the dining rooms, with Persian tile tables, Venetian glass lamps, clocks, statuary, stained-glass windows, an old piano, and an eclectic collection of goblets and stemware—no two tables are set alike. By the way, there is a very intriguing little table for two set in the front window, which is reserved for honeymooners, if possible. Almost all the tables have a nice view.

Most of the guests visiting Chalet Suzanne for the first time order the well-known chicken Suzanne, beautifully browned and glazed. It is prepared by Carl, who, in addition to being the "chief pilot" of the inn's private airstrip, is also the "principal stirrer" in the soup factory, and in addition to everything else is the chef at the inn.

Dinner also can include the original baked grapefruit centered with a sautéed chicken liver, the famed Chalet Suzanne romaine soup, hearts of artichoke salad, petite peas in cream and butter, a grilled tomato slice, deliciously hot homemade rolls, a mint ice, and tiny crêpes Suzanne.

The remark "It's almost like a Disney movie" is frequently heard at Chalet Suzanne, and I guess it's more than a coincidence that Disney World and many other famous attractions, including the beautiful Cypress Gardens waterskiing shows, are just a short distance away.

Oh yes, there is a 2,450-foot airstrip at Chalet Suzanne owing to Carl Hinshaw's lifelong love of flying. The flying tradition continues because Carl and Tina's son, Eric, is also a pilot.

Never ones to rest on their laurels, Vita tells me they've been hard at work, tending the lush landscaping and gardens, restocking the lily pond with goldfish and waterlilies, adding a new fountain, and building a new flower conservatory and greenhouse.

They are busy bees, indeed, making sure their guests have a wonderful time at Chalet Suzanne.

CHALET SUZANNE, P.O. Drawer AC, Lake Wales, FL 33859; 813-676-6011. A 30-guestroom (private baths) phantasmagoric country inn and gourmet restaurant, 4 mi. north of Lake Wales, between Cypress Gardens and the Bok Singing Tower near Disney World. European plan. Dining room open from 8 a.m. to 9:30 p.m. Closed Mon. from June to Nov. Wheelchair access. Pool on grounds. Golf, tennis nearby. Lots of opportunity for good jogging. Not inexpensive. The Hinshaw Family, Owners-hosts. (See Index for rates.)

Directions: From Interstate 4 turn south on U.S. 27 toward Lake Wales. From Sunshine State Pkwy., exit at Yeehaw Junction and head west on Rte. 60 to U.S. 27 (60 mi.). Proceed north on U.S. 27 at Lake Wales. Inn is 4 mi. north of Lake Wales on 17A.

GUILDS INN
Mount Pleasant, South Carolina (1988)

I think there's something about a bow tie that indicates a wonderful lack of stuffiness on the part of the wearer. Guild (pronounced guile) Hollowell wears a bow tie and is warm, enthusiastic, and friendly an innkeeper as you'd ever want to meet.

Guild and Joyce and their five sons spent months restoring and remodeling their inn which began its life as a grocery store in 1888. They also created a restaurant called Supper at Seven. Now, John and Amy Malik manage the inn and see to the comfort of their guests.

Although Guilds Inn is not furnished with genuine antiques, you'd never know it. The furnishings are particularly fine reproductions of antique furniture; in fact, Guild showed me several pieces that have been meticulously copied from the DuPont collection at the Winterthur Museum, and they are most impressive. There are beautiful highboys, lowboys, secretaries, breakfronts, and many other handsome pieces that were made by the Kindel Furniture Company. I was interested to learn that the Hollowells own a furniture store down the street, where some of these pieces can be purchased.

The village of Mount Pleasant was originally settled by farmers and also served as a summer retreat for many Charlestonians in the late 19th century.

The entrance to the inn is through a picket fence at one side of the building and across a pretty lawn and garden. Joyce has done a handsome job of decoration, with rich colors in fabrics, carpets, and walls. There are many original paintings and engravings. Each of the six guest rooms has been carefully and attractively furnished with queen-sized or twin beds and some of the other pieces I mentioned. One room has a Connecticut tall-post bed of cherry with a handmade fishnet canopy. All rooms have whirlpool baths and telephones, along with turn-down service and the morning newspaper.

It's a make-your-own breakfast in the butler's pantry in the Morning Room, which is well stocked with juice, fresh fruit, muffins and pastries, cereal, sausage or ham biscuits, and, of course, coffee or tea. The sunny Morning Room is a pleasant gathering place for breakfast and conversation.

"We want to allow our guests to experience the more leisurely and gentle pace of village life," Guild told me, "and we've tried to carry that over into our restaurant. Our chef prepares many of the timeless recipes from Mount Pleasant's early days." Their Supper at Seven restaurant has a single seating with a fixed menu of four courses. Some of their regional specialties are fillet of beef on fried eggplant, seafood chowder, local channel bass in puff pastry, Caesar salad, tomato cups with fresh corn,

low country squash pie, fresh figs filled with white chocolate mousse, and bourbon chocolate pecan pie. I understand they have a wide reputation for their fine cuisine, and many guests make the short trip over the bridge from downtown Charleston to enjoy a leisurely dinner. There is also a small cafe in the front of the building that is a popular place for lunch.

Being so close to Charleston and yet away from "the madding crowd" makes the Guilds Inn an especially desirable stopping place. After a strenuous day spent taking in all the historic sights of Charleston or attending such famous events as the Spoleto Festival, it would be a blessing to be able to retreat to this peaceful and quiet inn.

GUILDS INN, 101 Pitt St., Mt. Pleasant, SC 29464; 803-881-0510. A 6-guestroom (private baths) small inn and restaurant in a quiet, residential neighborhood across the bridge from Charleston. Queen and double beds available. Breakfast included in room rate. Dinner served Tues. thru Sat., by reservation only. Open year-round. All of the cultural and historical attractions of Charleston nearby. Guilds Hollowell, Owner-host; John and Amy Malik, Managers. (See Index for rates.)

Directions: Take Rte. 17 or 701 in Charleston, and cross the bridge into Mt. Pleasant, taking Whilden St. south to Venning St. Turn right on Venning and go 1 block to Pitt St.

The date in parenthesis in the heading represents the first year the inn appeared in the pages of Country Inns and Back Roads.

White Gull Inn, *Fish Creek*

Stafford's Bay View Inn, *Petoskey*

White Lace Inn, *Sturgeon Bay*

LAKE HURON

LAKE MICHIGAN

MICHIGAN

SAGINAW ■ Montague Inn, *Saginaw*

The National House Inn, *Marshall*

DETROIT ■

Botsford Inn, *Farmington*

LAKE ERIE

Wooster Inn, *Wooster* ● CLEVELAND ■

OHIO

The Inn at Honey Run, *Millersburg* ●

INDIANA

White Oak Inn, *Danville* ●

COLUMBUS ■ ●

Buxton Inn, *Granville*

INDIANAPOLIS ■

Golden Lamb, *Lebanon* ●

CINCINNATI ■

THE BUXTON INN
Granville, Ohio (1976)

Ever since I learned about the connection between Granville, Massachusetts, and Granville, Ohio, on my first visit to the Buxton Inn in 1975, I've been fascinated by it. The fact is that Granville in western Massachusetts, just above the Connecticut border, is a very attractive town that happens to be well known in the area for having exceptionally fine cheese.

Granville, Ohio, the home of the Buxton Inn, has been called "Ohio's best kept secret." "It was founded in 1805 by a mass migration from Granby, Connecticut, and Granville, Massachusetts," Orville Orr told me. "The community is laid out like a typical New England village, as you can see, with broad tree-lined streets, a town square where pioneers built four churches, and the Denison University campus."

He continued, "We have over one hundred buildings on the National Register of Historic Places. Most of the businesses are located in the restored downtown area, where three blocks are dominated by the Avery Downer House, which houses the Robbins Hunter Museum, furnished with 18th- and 19th-century American and English furniture, paintings, and decorative accessories."

If I had only one word that might describe the Buxton Inn, it would be "flair." On each of my visits since that now memorable first one, when a very young Amy Orr conducted me on my first tour of the inn and the town, there has been something exciting either accomplished or in the developmental stage. It seems that all of the Orr family, including Audrey, Orville, Amy, and Melanie, have unusual talents that are expressed in the inn.

The Buxton was originally built in 1812, and the Orr family has re-created the atmosphere of an inn of that period, even to the point of having waitresses and hosts and hostesses dressed in carefully researched costumes of the time.

Actually, the inn is a reflection of 175 years of changing styles, with the tastes and fashions of owners and innkeepers of different eras represented in the fabrics and designs. "We tend to collect things from different periods anyway," Audrey told me, "and we've furnished our bedrooms and dining rooms with different themes. Originally, we used period chairs in one of the dining rooms and discovered that they were too small; people were sliding off. So we reluctantly took them out and put in new, larger chairs."

I've always been intrigued by the printed menu at the Buxton Inn, not only because it contains the very interesting history of the inn, but also because it has far more offerings than the average menu, including many varieties of seafood, and such hearty offerings as veal sweetbreads, baby beef liver à l'orange, and Louisiana chicken with artichoke hearts. Be sure to ask about the spareribs with a most marvelous barbecue sauce.

Perhaps it's the atmosphere of a college town that encourages the Orrs to reach out beyond the visible horizon. Many things have been done here over the years I've been visiting. There was the creation of the Wine Cellar and the Tavern downstairs, where the original drivers and settlers would be fed when this was a stagecoach inn after 1812. The gazebo and the fountain, the columns and colonnades in back of the inn, all create a feeling of Roman baths.

The most recent addition is a beautiful dining room, glassed in on three sides and with a glass roof, giving the room a greenhouse feeling. Still more of the nearby homes have been converted into further guest rooms, including the Warner House on the corner.

It is obvious to me that the Orrs are people with dreams and a capacity for inventiveness that has allowed them to continue to turn their dreams into realities—realities that fortunately become wonderful benefits for inn guests at the Buxton.

It's a bit of a distance from Granville, Massachusetts, to Granville, Ohio, but a trip to the Buxton is always a great pleasure for me.

THE BUXTON INN, 313 E. Broadway, Granville, OH 43023; 614-587-0001. A 19-guestroom (private baths) inn in a college town in central Ohio near Denison University, the Indian Mounds Museum, and the Heisey Glass Museum. European plan. Lunch and dinner served daily. Closed Christmas Day. Golf, tennis, horseback riding, cultural activities nearby. No pets. Orville and Audrey Orr, Owners-hosts. (See Index for rates.)

Directions: Take Granville exit from I-70. Travel north 8 mi. on Rte. 37 into Granville.

THE GOLDEN LAMB
Lebanon, Ohio (1970)

Sandra Reynolds and I were seated in the lobby of the Golden Lamb, waiting for Jack Reynolds to finish a telephone call, and then we were all going to walk up the street to the Warren County Museum.

Just to be in this lobby is to partake of a generous helping of the American past. Among other things, there was a lamp, the base of which was made out of a candle mold, and a curly maple table. An old coal stove that was used 100 years or more ago is still in use today. Always on hand is a big punch bowl, where guests and friends may enjoy a modicum of refreshment. There are quite a few examples of Shaker crafts in the lobby and elsewhere in the inn, including Shaker boxes, dowels, chests, and Shaker-style furniture in the dining room.

"The Shakers came to this section of Ohio during the 19th century and attracted buyers from all over the country with their fine farm stock, medicinal herbs, furniture, and other household essentials," explained Sandra. "Their community, Union Village, was sold by them over a half century ago, but we have a lot of local interest in their culture, and the Warren County Museum has a considerable area devoted to Shaker memorabilia."

If Ohio could be called the "mother of presidents," the Golden Lamb might be called the "mother of country inns," because it is a significant force in providing inspiration for many innkeepers to preserve the best of the old, and at the same time to back it up with good innkeeping. Throughout the inn are found artifacts, furniture, and furnishings that have been collected from America's past that in a sense give us a real feeling of appreciation for what our forebears thought was beautiful, useful, and promising.

The building dates back to 1815 and was built on the site of an original log cabin erected by Jonas Seaman, who was granted a license in 1803 to operate "a house of public entertainment." Even before roads were built many guests came on foot or horseback to the inn. Here, in the warmth of the tavern's public rooms, they exchanged news of the world and related their own experiences. Many famous people have stopped here, including ten United States presidents as well as Henry Clay, Mark Twain, and Charles Dickens. Overnight guests may stay in rooms that are named for some of the great and near-great, both national and international, who have enjoyed accommodations here in the past.

Since this lovely old inn is a part of the heartland of America, it stands to reason that the main dishes would be representative of American cooking. There is beef in many forms, rainbow trout, and fried Kentucky ham steak. Roast duckling with wild rice dressing, flounder, Warren County turkey, and pork tenderloin are some of the principal entrées.

When possible, vegetables from the nearby verdant Ohio countryside are used.

Each guest room is named for a famous guest and is filled with antiques. When the rooms are not occupied, visitors may stroll through the halls and peek at the collection of chests, wardrobes, tables, and beds.

One of the most rewarding times to visit this inn is during the Christmas holiday season, when it is decorated literally "to the nines." Planning starts in July, with decisions on the theme and the menu. It is also the scene for the Cincinnati Art Club annual show.

THE GOLDEN LAMB INN, 27 S. Broadway, Lebanon, OH 45036; 513-932-5065. A historic 18-guestroom (private baths) village inn in the heart of Ohio farming country on U.S. Hwys. 63, 42, and 48. Twin and double beds available. European plan. Complimentary continental breakfast. Lunch and dinner served daily except Christmas. Golf and tennis nearby. No pets. Jackson Reynolds, Manager. (See Index for rates.)

Directions: From I-71, exit Rte. 48N, 3 mi. north to Lebanon. From I 75, exit Rte. 63E, 7 mi. east to Lebanon.

"European plan" means that rates for rooms and meals are separate. "American plan" means that meals are included in the cost of the room. "Modified American plan" means that breakfast and dinner are included in the cost of the room. The rates at some inns include a continental breakfast with the lodging.

THE INN AT HONEY RUN
Millersburg, Ohio (1984)

Partially hidden in its woodsy setting, the Inn at Honey Run blends into the forest of maples, ash, oak, poplar, black walnut, butternut, and hickory. And many of those woods, as well as other native materials, can be found throughout the inn. The spectacular free-standing fireplace in the living room is of native matched-vein sandstone. The many colorful quilts on the beds and the walls are made by local craftspeople.

Marge Stock's dream was to create an inn that was nearly indiscernable from the forest and fields that surround it. Floor-to-ceiling windows, outside decks that literally thrust themselves into the forest, bird feeders everywhere, all enhance the enjoyment of nature.

Although the architecture may be very contemporary and dramatic, the hospitality is old-fashioned and personal. Marge and Margret Schlichting, her manager, have a great staff of cheerful, friendly people who really make their guests feel at home.

Marge sent me up the hill to see her latest pet project, an earth-sheltered building with twelve new guest rooms. At first I thought they looked like great rock-rimmed cups or pockets tilted into the hill. Then I could see why Marge called them "Honeycombs"—they did bear a resemblance to a honeycomb, albeit one of giant and rock-ribbed proportions. As I came up the curving drive and gazed across the wildflower-strewn field, I marveled at how imperceptibly these new structures were tucked into the hill, and this was before the azaleas, junipers, heather, cotoneaster, and other shrubbery had grown to further camouflage them.

I'd made the trip out to Ohio specifically to see Marge's new project. "An earth shelter has so many practical advantages," she told me. "In addition, it has a feeling of great serenity and peace." This is, to my knowledge, the first earth-sheltered building with public accommodations in the country.

As I walked toward the huge square concrete arch that burrowed into the hill, I wondered if it would feel like a cave inside, but when I stepped into the entry hall, I had an instant feeling of space and light. The ceiling soared thirty feet to a skylight, and a spacious, carpeted staircase wound around to the second floor.

As with the main inn, the feeling is very contemporary. In each guest room, a massive fireplace wall of native Ohio sandstone rock has a cut-out section for a built-in cabinet, which hides a remote-control TV. Every conceivable modern convenience is provided in these rooms.

Beyond the sliding glass doors of each room is a private patio where you can almost reach out and touch the vivid wildflowers. Off in the distance are rolling forested hills, interspersed with patches of green cultivated fields. I watched from my patio as a beautiful sunrise spread its rosy fingers through the trees, as my neighbors could have done since all the rooms face east. It's a perfect place for quiet contemplation and feeling close to nature.

Meals are made from scratch, with such things as pan-fried trout from Holmes County waters, steak, baked ham, and roast loin of pork, which as Marge says, "comes with fresh applesauce."

There is so much more to tell about this very special place and about Marge and her ability to make her dreams come true, but you will discover those delightful surprises for yourself.

THE INN AT HONEY RUN, 6920 Country Road 203, Millersburg, OH 44654; 216-674-0011. A 36-guestroom (private baths) country inn located in north-central Ohio's beautiful, wooded countryside. King, queen, and twin beds available. Continental breakfast included in room rate. Lunch and dinner served Mon. thru Sat. Advance reservations only. Sun. breakfast and eve. buffet served to houseguests only. Closed Jan. 1 to 15. Wheelchair access. Ample opportunities for recreation and backroading in Ohio's Amish country. No facilities for small children. No pets. Marjorie Stock, Owner-hostess. (See Index for rates.)

Directions: From Millersburg, proceed on E. Jackson St. (Rtes. 39 and 62) past courthouse and gas station on right. At next corner turn left onto Rte. 241. At 1 mi. the road goes downhill. At 1³/₄ mi. it crosses the bridge over Honey Run; turn right immediately around the small hill onto Rte. 203 (not well marked). After about 1¹/₂ mi. turn right at inn sign. (Watch out for the Amish horse-drawn buggies.)

The date in parenthesis in the heading represents the first year the inn appeared in the pages of Country Inns and Back Roads.

THE WHITE OAK INN
Danville, Ohio (1989)

I think wood is the big story here at the White Oak Inn. It begins when you drive up the two-lane scenic route and you first see the inn's sign on the great white oak from which the inn takes its name. This was originally a working farm of several hundred acres. In 1915, George Crise set up a temporary sawmill on the land and, taking trees from the surrounding woods, fashioned the timbers that went into the three-story, gambrel-roofed house. As Jim Acton says, "He was a real craftsman." All of the doors, moldings, and cabinetry throughout the house are testimony to his craftsmanship. The guest rooms are named for the woods with which they are furnished—oak, poplar, ash, maple, walnut and cherry.

When James and Joyce Acton were looking for an inn, they took a drive through the hills and down into the oil-drilling and farming community near Danville, across from the Kokosing River. "The moment we saw the house," Joyce exclaimed, "we knew this was it, it was so big and so nice."

A bearded Jim Acton greeted me as I drove up and pointed out some of the grand old trees on the property. Two friendly Labradors—Lady Chardonnay, or Charlie, and Captain—frolicked around us. Joyce and Jim are one of those couples who dropped out of corporate life to take up innkeeping, and they seem to have taken to it with great gusto. They are very friendly, hospitable people and make their guests at home, introducing them by name over the complimentary wine and cheese offered in the afternoon.

The strains of a Beethoven quartet greeted me as I walked through the beveled-glass front door, and Joyce mentioned that they are lucky to receive the Ohio State University FM station, with fine musical offerings. The living room is a very comfortable, pleasant room with sofas, rocking chairs, a nice brick fireplace, paintings, flowers, and a small game table.

Joyce told me she really likes to have a two-day notice on dinner reservations. Their menu is usually something like beef Wellington, chicken breasts with mushrooms and wine sauce, or veal scallopini.

Dinner is served family style in the dining room, where there are two seven-foot-long, handmade white oak tables, antique kitchen chairs, a china closet with crystal, a sideboard, a chandelier, candles, and blue tablecloths. Joyce serves a hearty breakfast of french toast, from her own homemade bread, with sausage, and there are fresh fruit and freshly baked pastries.

A candlelight dinner can be arranged in front of the fire in the White Oak guest room for an intimate tête-à-tête or a special occasion.

The guest room doors have grapevine wreaths with plaid bows, and the rooms are decorated with fresh flowers, starchy ruffled curtains, and high, firm beds with hand-sewn quilts, some made by the Amish and others bought from antiques dealers.

Jim mentioned that their special weekends, such as the Country Inn Cookery Weekend, the Naturalist Weekend, and the Photography Weekend, have become very popular.

This is a homey kind of place where you can pull up a chair in the kitchen and have a good old-fashioned chat with Joyce, or you can just sit on one of the oak swings on the spacious front porch and smell the fragrant viburnum.

We are happy to welcome the White Oak Inn to the pages of *Country Inns and Back Roads*.

THE WHITE OAK INN, 29683 Walhonding Rd., Danville, OH 43014; 614-599-6107. A 7-guestroom (private baths) 1915 farmhouse-inn on 14 acres of farmland and woods in the scenic Kokosing River valley, 15 mi. east of Mt. Vernon in north central Ohio. Queen and double beds available. Complimentary breakfast; dinner served to houseguests by 2-day advance reservation. Closed Thanksgiving and Christmas. Board games, 2 porch swings, nature walks, bird-watching on grounds. Inquire about the special weekends. Roscoe Village, restored canal town, 25 mi., largest Amish population in U.S., 30 mi. No smoking. Joyce and Jim Acton, Owners-hosts. (See Index for rates.)

Directions: From either I-71 or 77, take U.S. Rte. 36, 11 mi. east of Mt. Vernon, or 43 mi. west of Newcomerstown to Ohio Rte. 715. The inn is located on the left of Ohio Rte. 715, 3 mi. from U.S. Rte. 36.

WOOSTER INN
Wooster, Ohio (1988)

The soccer ball came toward me in an arc, and for just a moment I thought perhaps I was back at college again myself. There was a fair-sized crowd for this soccer game at Wooster College, where some co-eds stood on the edge of the field. In the near distance the Gothic buildings were somewhat reminiscent of my college in central Pennsylvania.

Meanwhile, the ball hit the ground right in front of me. I considered all the possibilities and then gave the ball a sort of half-hearted kick that returned it to the referee.

It was early fall and the rolling countryside between Akron and Millersburg had beautiful tints and hues of autumn. The cornfields were fallow in their own shades of beige, and the roads across the Ohio countryside followed the contours of the land, where cattle peacefully grazed and occasional small villages gave me the unmistakable feeling of being in America's heartland. The town of Wooster is actually the hub of many highways leading off in all directions.

I had arrived a bit earlier than anticipated, and Willy Bergmann, the manager of the Wooster Inn, suggested that since there was going to be a soccer game I might get a kick out of it, little knowing the accuracy of his prediction.

The Wooster Inn, which offers full services, reflects a great deal of the town-and-gown spirit with its furnishings and location right on the edge of the campus. During the college year the cultural events on the campus, such as lectures, concerts, plays, and art exhibits, are open to the public, and of course that includes the inn guests. During the summer the Ohio Light Opera performs several productions in the college theater. There are also various types of athletic events, providing an interesting diversion for the pleasure of business travelers who might find themselves in Wooster.

The architecture of the inn has generous amounts of what I guess is American Georgian, and it fits very well with the campus buildings. One of its attractive aspects is its view of the college golf course, which is open to guests throughout the year. All-weather tennis courts are also nearby.

The newly decorated lobby is most attractive, with comfortable chairs and tables arranged in conversational groupings, where guests who are waiting to be called to dinner or perhaps waiting for someone to join them can take in this collegiate atmosphere.

The dining room is straight off the lobby, and the big bay windows have a splendid view of the rolling golf course. The tables are set with crisp white tablecloths, fresh flowers, and candles. I asked Willy Bergman to tell me about some of the main dishes on the menu. "We are well known for serving fresh rainbow trout," he said. "Our guests also enjoy veal

scallopini Dijon. I guess our tastes out here represent the Midwest because our pork chops basted with honey are very popular. The students also like the fettucini with scallops and shrimp." Those are just a few of the over sixteen items on the dinner menu. That night I had a most enjoyable dinner with Willy and found the pork chops basted with honey much to my taste. I decided to try them at home at the next opportunity. Breakfast features such specialties as pecan waffles, and there is a wide selection on the luncheon menu.

Guest rooms at the inn have been very tastefully furnished. All or most of them have views of the golf course, the soccer field, or the nearby residences. There certainly was no disturbing noise during the evening.

As we were finishing off the dessert, Willy said, with a twinkle in his eye, "I happened to be looking out the window of my office when that soccer ball landed in front of you, and I wondered why you didn't give it a good healthy kick."

"Well, to tell you the truth, soccer never was my game."

THE WOOSTER INN, Wayne Ave. and Gasche St., Wooster, OH 44691; 216-264-2341. A 17-guestroom (private baths) pleasant inn on the campus of the College of Wooster, about 60 mi. southwest of Cleveland. Queen, double, and twin beds available. Air conditioning, telephone, and TV in room. Breakfast included in room rate. Breakfast, lunch, and dinner served every day. Open year-round. Wheelchair access. Convenient to all of the college cultural and athletic events. Golf and tennis nearby. Willy J. Bergmann, Manager. (See Index for rates.)

Directions: Wooster is the hub of U.S. Rtes. 30 and 250 and Ohio Rtes. 3, 585, and 83. Locate the college and then ask for directions to the inn.

BOTSFORD INN
Farmington Hills, Michigan (1969)

I go back a long time with the Botsford Inn, but not way back to 1836 when it was first built by Orrin Weston as a home, or to when the famous Botsford family took it over and converted it into an inn. But I have been visiting it for quite a few of the more recent years.

I can remember when I first heard of the Botsford Inn, my reaction was, "Who would expect to find a New England country inn in Detroit?" I soon learned that it wasn't really in Detroit, but Farmington Hills, and the people in Farmington Hills will tell you that there's quite a difference. It's a very pleasant residential town. The inn was a stagecoach stop on the road from Grand Rapids on Lake Michigan, and, in fact, at one time the Grand River plank road followed an Indian trail that went on to Lansing and Detroit.

I strolled around the surprisingly spacious grounds and the rose garden, which was originally created by Mrs. Henry Ford, admiring the towering pine, maple, and elm trees. I realized that some of the more elegant features of the 19th century have been preserved at the Botsford, many by Henry Ford, who restored it in the 1920s. I think it is remarkable that such a valuable piece of property has not gone the way of the wrecking ball and bulldozer long before now.

One of the principal reasons for this must be attributed to the devotion of the present innkeeper and owner, John Anhut, who has a weakness for country inns. Following Mr. Ford's example, John has succeeded in holding back time. For example, in two sitting rooms there are many furnishings from Henry Ford's house, including a beautiful little

inlaid spinet, a horsehair sofa, music boxes, inlaid mahogany tables, and spinning wheels.

The older sections of the inn have very low ceilings, huge beams, and handsome fireplaces with big andirons. One of the more celebrated features of the inn is the second-floor ballroom, where, at a country dance, long ago, Henry Ford first met the young lady who was to become his wife.

I'm certain that innkeeper Botsford and preserver Ford would approve of the contemporary changes that innkeeper Anhut has made, including guest rooms with reproductions of Colonial furniture, air conditioning against the Detroit summer heat, and tennis courts.

It's also certain that the farmers, drovers, and traveling men of the past century would nod their heads in approval at the hearty offerings from the Botsford kitchen today. These include braised short ribs of beef with jardinière sauce, frogs' legs sautéed in chablis, Botsford old-fashioned chicken pot pie topped with flaky buttered crust, and roast prime rib of Western beef au jus. Their cherry cobbler has become so famous it was featured in a cartoon in the *Detroit News.*

Many birds can be glimpsed through the floor-to-ceiling windows of the restaurant, which overlook a garden courtyard, and cards on the tables help guests to identify the feathered visitors.

What appeals greatly to me about this inn is John Anhut himself. As busy as he is, he makes a concerted effort to meet every one of his guests. "Some of them have really become old friends to me," he said. "I think it's the best part of having a country inn."

The Botsford tradition of hospitality, begun during the Indian trail days, is continuing now with the Anhut family. In 1836, it was a day's journey from the banks of the river, where Detroit was a burgeoning city; today, it is just a short drive from the hustle and bustle of the Motor City. Worthwhile reminders of the past have been preserved and, best of all, the spirit of country innkeeping and community service is very much alive.

BOTSFORD INN, 28000 Grand River Ave., Farmington Hills, MI 48024; 313-474-4800. A 65-guestroom (private baths) village inn on the city line of Detroit. European plan. Dinner served daily except Monday. Breakfast and lunch Tues. thru Sat. Sun. brunch. Closed Christmas and New Year's Day. TV, telephone, and air conditioning in rooms. Wheelchair access. Tennis on grounds. Greenfield Village, skiing, and state parks nearby. John Anhut, Owner-host. (See Index for rates.)

Directions: Located in Farmington Hills on I-96, easily accessible from major highways in Michigan.

MONTAGUE INN
Saginaw, Michigan (1989)

Secret panels and passageways behind the library walls? What does it all mean? I think it means that this grand Georgian mansion was built in the middle of Prohibition (1929) and the owners may have had some things they wanted to hide. Otherwise, the Montagues were pillars of the community—manufacturers of soaps and hand creams, subsequently bought by the Jergens Company.

Today, innkeeper Meg Brodie-Ideker stores their bottles of home-made herb vinegars in the secret closet, and guests sip their before-dinner aperitifs or wine in the book-lined library, without ever guessing what lies behind the white paneled walls.

This had been another mouldering mansion in the once-opulent Grove area of Saginaw, when Norman Kinney and his partners found it in 1985. Norman Kinney has become something of a celebrity in the field of inn restorations, and his expertise is in great demand. The National House in nearby Marshall and now the Montague Inn are prime examples of his talent.

As Norman points out, he and his wife, Kathryn, had a lot of help from the four other couples who pooled their resources and pitched in to bring this beautiful home back to vibrant and elegant life. It is now listed on the National Register of Historic Places.

Driving through busy, industrial Saginaw, I marveled at the green oasis, known as the Grove, on the east side of the city, where grand old mansions and the many huge trees reminded me that lumber barons had once prospered and lived here.

I turned off the wide boulevard and drove through the parklike grounds of the Montague Inn around to the back parking area. Meg, who was cutting flowers, greeted me with a welcoming wave and a bright, charming smile. "Do I see the glint of water over there?" I called, gesturing toward a line of trees at the edge of the lawn. "That's Lake Linton," she replied, coming over to me, her arms loaded with colorful tulips and daffodils, "and across the water is Ojibway Island—it's a wonderful spot for picnics, and the Saginaw River is just beyond that."

"Kathryn has a wonderful herb garden over on the side of the house. She has all of the usual herbs as well as lovage, bergamot, lemon balm, scented geraniums, baby's breath, and many edible flowers. We use them in our salad dressings, soups, and sauces, and our chef likes to dress his dishes with the edible flowers."

I knew the inn had established a reputation for gourmet dining, and my dinner that evening convinced me it was well deserved. My smoked salmon appetizer, served with fresh fruit puree and bleu cheese, was delightfully different and the medallions of tenderloin were perfectly grilled and seasoned. The black-and-white-uniformed waitresses served dinner with smooth, cheerful efficiency. The dining room was most inviting, the tables set with sparkling crystal and silver and fresh flowers, the large bay window looking out across the lawns to the lake.

This is a very gracious house, with several bay windows, fireplaces, white paneled walls, and a beautiful cantilevered, curved staircase rising above the circular foyer. Furnished in fine mahogany antiques, oriental rugs, and original paintings, the atmosphere is one of elegance and comfort. Most of the guest rooms are spacious, and all are attractively decorated. The original tile bathrooms have unique art deco fixtures.

The architecture, atmosphere, decor, and service remind me of the country house hotels of Great Britain. I'm delighted to welcome the Montague Inn to our pages.

MONTAGUE INN, 1581 So. Washington Ave., Saginaw, MI 48601; 517-752-3939. An 18-guestroom (2 with shared bath) Georgian manor inn on 8 acres in a parklike setting in the Grove area of the city. European plan. Complimentary continental breakfast. Open year-round. Wheelchair access. Picnic lunches, Lake Linton, special events on grounds. Ojibway Island, Japanese Garden and Teahouse, children's zoo, Hoyt Park with skating rink, boat races, and fishing in Saginaw River nearby. Meg Brodie-Ideker, Owner-hostess. (See Index for rates.)

Directions: From I-75, take Holland Ave. (Rte. 46), bearing right onto Remington Ave. Turn left at Washington Ave. and continue to inn.

THE NATIONAL HOUSE INN
Marshall, Michigan (1978)

Barbara Bradley, the innkeeper at the National House Inn, was helping me to assimilate the experience of the unusual town of Marshall. "Mr. Brooks was the most important factor," she said. "He was the man who had the vision for Marshall. But everybody in the town has joined in. We are proud of the homes and the museums, and we all work together. I'm sure the National House could not have been restored if it hadn't been a community effort. People helped out in so many ways.

"This is probably the oldest remaining hotel building in Michigan," she remarked. "We learned that it was open in 1835 and undoubtedly was the first brick building of any kind in our county. It is now listed on the National Register of Historic Places.

"At one time it was a windmill and wagon factory and more recently an apartment building," she continued. "Restoring it was hard work, but underneath the dirt and grime of dozens of years there was the solid, beautiful structure of the original brick as well as irreplaceable woodwork. The apartments from the old building were converted into sixteen guest rooms and baths.

"As you can see, Marshall is very much a Victorian restoration, and we have had a great deal of fun discovering new Victorian pieces for the inn, among which is an antique wooden cash register that was discovered in the cellar. There is also country stenciling in the Andrew Mann bedroom and some other rooms. Our gardens continue to attract more and more attention."

To me, one of the most striking features of the National House is the passionate attention to detail. For example, each guest room has its own ambience, and there are colorful comforters, old trunks, marble-top

tables, bureaus, dried-flower arrangements, electric lamps that are reproductions of gas lamps, candle sconces with reflectors, little corner sofas,
and special care with doorknobs. Special attention is also given to the
linens. The bedroom windows overlook either the residential part of town
or a beautiful fountain in the center of the town park.

Breakfast is the only meal served and is offered every morning in the
dining room, where there is an interesting collection of chairs and tables
from great-grandfather's day. The color tones are warm brown and beige.
The breakfast, included in the room tariff, offers home-baked goods,
selected teas, and the best coffee in Calhoun County.

The inn has a very interesting and well-designed newsletter containing much information about the town of Marshall and the inn itself. It also
has a generous sprinkling of the recipes that enhance the breakfast menu.
I'm sure they would be happy to send you one on request.

In the years since I began visiting Marshall, a great many of the
buildings and homes of the town have been added to the State of Michigan
Historic Sites and to the National Register. The town contains the finest
examples of 19th-century architecture in the Midwest.

Marshall is situated on Interstate 94, Michigan's historic highway,
which started as an Indian trail. There are six historic sites that can be
visited along this road on which the development of the territory can be
traced.

The National House has five weekend specials, which include visits
to private homes by candlelight. The inn will be happy to supply any
reader with further details, including the dates.

*THE NATIONAL HOUSE INN, 102 South Parkview, Marshall, MI 49068;
616-781-7374. A 14-guestroom (private baths; 2 share a shower) elegantly restored Victorian-period village inn. European plan includes
continental breakfast. No other meals served. Open year-round. Closed
Christmas Eve and Christmas Day. Marshall is the finest example of 19th-
century architecture in the Midwest, with 15 State Historic Sites and 6
National Register Sites. Tennis, golf, swimming, boating, xc skiing nearby.
Barbara Bradley, Manager. (See Index for rates.)*

*Directions: From I-69, exit at Michigan Ave. in Marshall and go straight
1½ mi. to inn. From I-94 use Exit 110 and follow old Rte. 127 south 1½
mi. to inn.*

*The date in parenthesis in the heading represents the first year the inn
appeared in the pages of* Country Inns and Back Roads.

STAFFORD'S BAY VIEW INN
Petoskey, Michigan (1972)

First, a little background: Stafford's (as it is known in the area) is on the edge of the Bay View section of Petoskey, which is a summer resort community that grew up around a program of drama, music, art, and religious lectures and services. The community began in the late 1800s, when people rode on the Grand Rapids/Indiana Railroad or on lake steamers to reach this part of Michigan. The early residents built Victorian homes that are scattered throughout Bay View today. Last July it was officially designated a National Historic Landmark. It has been on the National Register of Historic Places for some time.

Stafford met his future wife, Janice, at the inn, where both of them were on the staff. Since that time, their family has grown to include Reg, who attended the Cornell University Hotel School and now manages a nearby family restaurant; Mary Kathryn, who is also involved in the hospitality field and finishing her senior year at MSU; and the youngest, Dean, who was always a big hit as a small boy wearing a tuxedo helping his father at the famous Sunday brunches is now a freshman at Delta College.

Janice tells me that Mary Kathryn was Reg's assistant at their restaurant in Charlevoix. "They made a dynamite team. It's funny, guests tease them about being so young, and yet they are a little older than we were when we took over the inn. I felt sorry for them because of the number of hours they were working until I remembered how many hours Duff and I put in during the early years.

"They were finally able to restore and rebuild ten new rooms on the third floor and thanks to Judy Honor, because it was her project, they are lovely. New windows, new walls, and a new floor plan. The only 'old' that remains are the outside walls, and some nooks and crannies.

"No two rooms are alike. Each is wallpapered in exciting Clarence House prints with a Victorian flare and bright, bright flowers. All the antique furniture and rocking chairs that they have been saving all this time have been refinished and are in the rooms. They have even created a mini-lobby for guests to gather in up there. All is very cozy and comfortable.

"Janice's favorite room, which Judy calls Grandmother's room, because it is blue with pink rosebuds, is located in the tower and incorporates her old room when she was a hostess and first met Stafford. That part is a lovely sitting room that overlooks the bay; even the old dresser that she used has been refinished and fits right into the decor."

Constant hard work and dedication to people, service, and to quality have been their watchwords. The inn is no longer a quaint, homespun, charming hotel. It has become a first-class sophisticated delight—a

pleasure to own and to share with the discriminating guest. That nice young couple that took over this business in 1961 have matured, and so has their business.

STAFFORD'S BAY VIEW INN, Box 3, Petoskey, MI 49770; 616-347-2771. A 30-guestroom (private baths) resort-inn on Little Traverse Bay in the Bay View section of Petoskey. Bed-and-breakfast plan includes full breakfast. Breakfast, lunch, and dinner served daily to travelers. Open daily May 6 to Nov. 1; Thanksgiving weekend; Dec. 26 to Mar. 24. Wheelchair access. Lake swimming and xc skiing on grounds. Historical Festival events, 3rd weekend in June. Bay View cultural programs in July and Aug. Golfing, boating, tennis, fishing, hiking, alpine ski trails, scenic and historic drives, and excellent shopping nearby. Stafford and Janice Smith and Judy Honor, Owners-hosts. (See Index for rates.)

Directions: From Detroit, take Gaylord exit from I-75 and follow Mich. Rte. 32 to Rte. 131 north to Petoskey. From Chicago, use Rte. 131 north to Petoskey.

"European plan" means that rates for rooms and meals are separate. "American plan" means that meals are included in the cost of the room. "Modified American plan" means that breakfast and dinner are included in the cost of the room. The rates at some inns include a continental breakfast with the lodging.

OLD RITTENHOUSE INN
Bayfield, Wisconsin (1980)

"Jerry was still working on his music degree at the University of Wisconsin, and I had just gotten a teaching job. We came to Bayfield on our honeymoon in 1969, and as soon as we saw this lovely old house we fell in love with it."

At first I thought Mary Phillips was speaking of the present building that houses the Old Rittenhouse Inn, but I soon realized she was really speaking of what was known for many years in Bayfield as "The Mansion."

"In 1973, we came back on a visit and noticed *this* house and wondered how we could have missed it on previous visits. We bought it for a song, and it's been our expanding home ever since." The Old Rittenhouse Inn is a Queen Anne-style mansion with an unusually wide veranda, decorated with hanging flowers and wicker furniture.

The sequel to this interesting episode is that the Phillipses did eventually buy and restore the Mansion (now called Le Château Boutin) with the aid of their partner, Greg Carrier. A third house, called Grey Oak, is also now a part of the Old Rittenhouse Inn.

These two musician-innkeepers have refused from the very start to accept the idea that Bayfield was simply a summertime resort area. They began by staging Christmas and Valentine's Day dinner concerts at the inn, and these developed into many more activities. The success of their

programs made it necessary to expand, and so today the original five guest rooms have been augmented by another fifteen, and Mary finally has a full and proper kitchen.

Antiques being one of Jerry's sidelines, each of the guest rooms has been handsomely outfitted with antique furniture, and all but one of them have their own fireplace.

It may be that Jerry and Mary are best known for their dinners. Jerry, resplendent in a Victorian tailcoat, describes the menu to his dinner guests, and it is also given in detail by the waitress later on. The fixed-price dinners start with several soups and a variety of entrées, including Lake Superior trout cooked in champagne, lamb, seafood crêpes, scallops, or chicken Cordon Bleu. The breads and preserves are all home-made. Their gourmet foods are also on sale at the inn and through a mail-order business that includes jams, jellies, marmalades, candies, fruit cakes, and many other delicious gifts.

The Phillipses have prepared a splendid new brochure entitled "The Old Rittenhouse Inn: An Innside Outlook." My copy lists every special event, seminar, festival, workshop, concert, and island adventure that can be enjoyed in Bayfield or on nearby Madeline Island throughout the year. Just to give you a quick idea, there's the Blossom Festival in June, the Christmas Dinner Concerts in December, ski touring under the auspices of the Audubon Society, and summer-day sails galore. The brochure continues with two cooking workshops, Valentine Sweetheart specials, two Murder-at-the-Mansion Mystery Weekends, a Bed and Breakfast Workshop in February, and, of course, the famous Apple Festival in October. The Phillipses will be glad to send you your copy.

It has certainly been a pleasure for me to visit and revisit the Old Rittenhouse Inn and enjoy good fun, good eating, and wonderful hospitality.

OLD RITTENHOUSE INN, Box 584, 301 Rittenhouse Ave., Bayfield, WI 54818; 715-779-5765. A 10-guestroom (private baths) Victorian inn in an area of historic and natural beauty, 70 mi. east of Duluth, Minn., on the shore of Lake Superior. King, queen, and double beds available. European plan. Breakfast, lunch, and dinner served to travelers. Open May 1 to Nov. 1; weekends through the winter. Advance reservations most desirable. Extensive recreational activity of all kinds available throughout the year, including tours, hiking, and cycling on the nearby Apostle and Madeline Islands. Not comfortable for small children. No pets. Jerry and Mary Phillips, Owners-hosts. (See Index for rates.)

Directions: From the Duluth Airport, follow Rte. 53-S through the city of Duluth over the bridge to Superior, Wis. Turn east on Rte. 2 near Ashland (1½ hrs.), turn north on 13-N to Bayfield.

THE WHITE GULL INN
Fish Creek, Wisconsin (1979)

This is actually going to be a tale of not one inn, but two inns. One is the White Gull Inn, where I have been visiting Jan and Andy Coulson and their two daughters, Meredith and Emilie Lindsley, for quite a few years. The other inn is the Whistling Swan, which the Coulsons purchased and have remodeled and redecorated. Both inns are located in the heart of Fish Creek's historic section.

The White Gull is a full-service inn, built as part of a large resort area more than seventy-five years ago, when hundreds of tourists would arrive in Fish Creek from Chicago and Milwaukee aboard steamships. Nowadays, guests drive or fly to Fish Creek because the beautiful waterfront, the main street, and the sparkling atmosphere have remained unchanged.

The main inn is a white clapboard, three-story building with an air of informality. The rooms, which have been increasing in numbers over recent years, are tidy and neat, and have been undergoing a steady redecorating program. Behind the inn, Cliffhouse has four guest rooms, each with a fireplace, which makes it especially popular in the winter.

In the Midwest, the White Gull is justifiably famous for its traditional Fish Boils, featuring freshly caught lake fish, boiled potatoes, homemade coleslaw, fresh-baked bread, and cherry pie. Russ Ostrand has been the master boiler for over twenty years. He prepares a roaring fire, and the fish are boiled in two huge iron cauldrons. He also plays the accordion and leads everybody in lots of singing and clapping of hands.

Besides the Fish Boils, the White Gull also has a more familiar evening menu.

The Whistling Swan, a bed and breakfast inn, has four bedrooms and three suites with antique beds and dressers, comfortable reading chairs and reading lights, carpeting and wallpaper that matches the fabrics. Most of the bathrooms have the original meticulously reglazed tubs, pedestal sinks, and brass fixtures.

A continental breakfast featuring fresh-squeezed orange juice and freshly baked pastry is served in the summer on the huge veranda, and guests take their ease in wicker chairs and rockers. Wintertime guests have a full breakfast at the White Gull, and dinners are taken at the White Gull by Whistling Swan guests, if desired.

Jan and Andy have also opened two shops in the Whistling Swan, one of which sells unusual gift items plus a distinctive line of women's and children's clothing, elegantly displayed in antique armoires and dressers, and the other features more masculine items and gifts for men.

And so Jan and Andy and Joan Holliday and Nancy Vaughn and the remainder of the staff at the White Gull and the Whistling Swan continue to make progress in some respect with each passing year. I'm sure it won't be long before Meredith, eleven years old, and Emilie Lindsley, five and a half, will be taking over some of the innkeeping duties themselves.

Door County is a wonderful place to visit in any season of the year and, thanks to the presence of two fine inns, it's a great place for a holiday.

THE WHITE GULL INN, Fish Creek, WI 54212; 414-868-3517. A 14-guestroom inn with 4 cottages (13 private baths) and additional guestrooms in the Whistling Swan in a most scenic area in Door County, 23 mi. north of Sturgeon Bay. Queen, double, and twin beds available. (Bookings for the Whistling Swan: P.O. Box 193; 414-868-3442.) Open year-round. European plan. Breakfast, lunch, and dinner except Thanksgiving and Christmas. Fish Boils: Wed., Fri., Sat., Sun. nights May thru Oct.; Wed. and Sat. nights Nov. thru April. All meals open to travelers; reservations requested. Wheelchair access to restaurant. Considerable outdoor and cultural attractions; golf, tennis, swimming, fishing, biking, sailing, xc skiing, and other summer and winter sports nearby. Excellent for children of all ages. No pets. Andy and Jan Coulson, Joan Holliday, and Nancy Vaughn, Owners-hosts. (See Index for rates.)

Directions: From Chicago: take I-94 to Milwaukee. Follow Rte. I-43 from Milwaukee to Manitowoc; Rte. 42 from Manitowoc to Fish Creek. Turn left at stop sign at the bottom of the hill, go 2½ blocks to inn. From Green Bay; take Rte. 57 to Sturgeon Bay; Rte. 42 to Fish Creek.

WHITE LACE INN
Sturgeon Bay, Wisconsin (1988)

The first time I visited Dennis and Bonnie Statz at the White Lace Inn a number of years ago, I was doing some research for one of my other books, *Bed and Breakfast, American Style.*

At that time Dennis was working on the Garden House in the rear of the Main House, and we had a long talk about his plans for the garden area.

Since then not only is the Garden House a *fait accompli,* with fireplaces in the six guest rooms, but all the wonderful things associated with its name have actually come true, with myriad flowers everywhere.

So now, with the Garden House and another more recent addition, the luxurious Washburn House, the White Lace Inn offers fifteen guest rooms in three historic Victorian houses. Each room has period wallcoverings, floral print fabrics in roses, peaches, and earth tones, polished hardwood floors, and many antiques. There are thick towels, good linens, warm comforters, extra pillows, good lighting, and many other things I like to find in country inns. Both the main house and the Washburn House boast double whirlpool bathtubs, too.

I was curious about the name White Lace. I suggested that perhaps it was just a nice, pleasant, evocative term, but Bonnie assured me that indeed there was "something of white lace in every one of the guest rooms." It's kind of fun to find the white lace in each room. In one room it's the hand-knotted lace canopy on a bed; in another it's the Battenberg lace border on the cloth covering a table; in another, it's filmy lace curtains.

Bonnie and Dennis are both originally from Wisconsin. He had graduated from the Engineering School at the University of Wisconsin at Madison and she had studied interior design before they were married. They had moved to Connecticut, and when the "inn idea" got too strong to be ignored, they looked all over New England without success, until a friend suggested that they visit Door County in Wisconsin.

They found what they'd been looking for on a quiet street in the residential area of Sturgeon Bay, within five blocks of the bay and two blocks of the downtown National Historic District. Bonnie and Dennis put many hours of hard work into bringing three nearly ruined houses back to life, and they have succeeded in creating a very special inn with a warm and intimate atmosphere.

A word or two about Door County, which is sometimes called one of the the best-kept secrets in the country. Lots of Wisconsin natives have never been there. I know of people who always look heavenward when extolling Door County's virtues. It's a good four-season resort area. Winter days can be spent cross-country skiing on the trails in the state parks or snowshoeing in the woods. After returning to the inn, it's fun to stand in front of the crackling fire and exchange information and enthusiasms with other guests. Of course, being on the lake, Door County in the summertime offers ever-expanding vacation delights, including sailing, windsurfing, fishing, and swimming.

I thought that it might be a bit quiet during the winter, but Bonnie assured me they have many full weekends between January and March, when people bring their cross-country skis and make a wonderful time of it.

Guests at the Garden House and the Washburn House enjoy continental breakfast at the Main House. Different kinds of home-baked muffins and Scandinavian fruit soup are featured each day, as well as juice and plenty of aromatic hot coffee. The coffee pot is always on the stove at other times as well. "No one has ever left the table hungry at breakfast time here," Dennis said.

WHITE LACE INN, 16 N. Fifth Ave., Sturgeon Bay, WI 54235; 414-743-1105. A 15-guestroom (private baths) bed-and-breakfast inn in one of Wisconsin's attractive resort areas. Open year-round. Conveniently located near all of the cultural and recreational attractions in Door County. Special 3-, 4-, and 5-night packages available from Nov. to May. No pets. Dennis and Bonnie Statz, Owners-hosts. (See Index for rates.)

Directions: From the south take the Rte. 42-57 bypass across the new bridge, turn left on Michigan, and go right on Fifth Ave.

THE ST. JAMES HOTEL
Red Wing, Minnesota (1981)

Once the premier hotel and meeting place of Red Wing, back in the 1870s when this thriving river town was the largest primary wheat market in the world, the St. James was sinking fast by the 1970s, when the Red Wing Shoe Company stepped in, in 1977, to rescue it from the wrecker's ball. Civic and community pride combined to revitalize and restore the entire downtown area, with the hotel as its centerpiece. It was a huge project, and today there are many handsome, 19th-century buildings with decorative stone and brick cornices and turn-of-the-century window treatments.

The St. James Hotel, listed on the National Register of Historic Places, has been authentically restored and refurbished with faithful reproductions, not only of furniture, but of all the fixtures, including brass soap dishes, towel racks, doorknobs, and the like.

The hotel is a modern accommodation of today, but serves as a reminder of opulent days gone by. In addition to excellent reproductions, the photographs and prints from a bygone era are further reminders of the past. Many of the walls are hung with pictures of Red Wing, taken over a hundred years ago, both of the town and the river steamers that made the town a regular stop. *If Walls Could Talk* is an unusual and fascinating history of the old St. James Hotel.

What excites me most is that this small hotel in the heart of America could have been torn down and gone the way of so many others, but instead it is making a contribution that bids fair to endure for at least another hundred years.

Turn-down bed service and the morning newspaper at the door are a couple of the niceties that add to the pleasure of a visit to the St. James. Bed linens and towels are of prime quality, and the quilt for each bed was especially designed and made to harmonize with the furnishings and colors of the room. Many of the rooms look out upon the Mississippi River, where the unending flow of barges provides constant entertainment. The *City of Red Wing* excursion boat departs from the wharf just behind the hotel for those who would like a closer look at the river. A new park, just across from the hotel, adds a very pleasant vista down to the river.

The Port of Red Wing Restaurant on the lower level of the hotel is picturesque, with walls of rough limestone quarried from the nearby bluffs. The Veranda Cafe, in the rear of the shopping court, offers breakfast and light meals, and the Victorian Dining Room offers elegant dining next to the Historic Lobby.

The Sheldon Auditorium, which housed Garrison Keillor's "Prairie Home Companion" a few years ago, as well as theater productions and St.

Paul Chamber Orchestra concerts, has just been given a three-million-dollar remodeling job. The rededication celebrations will be going on for a long time, with multimedia sound and light shows, concerts, plays, film festivals, and many other events.

Red Wing is a lively little town with lots to see and do, and at the St. James you're right in the center of it all.

ST. JAMES HOTEL, 406 Main St., Red Wing, MN 55066; 612-388-2846. A 60-guestroom (private baths) restored country town hotel on the Mississippi River, 50 mi. from Minneapolis. Queen, double, and twin beds available. Open all year. Breakfast, lunch, and dinner served to travelers. Wheelchair access. This is an in-town hotel with no sports or recreation on the grounds, but swimming, tennis, hiking, golf, bicycling, backroading, community events, and river sightseeing trips are all very convenient. No pets. Gene Foster, General Manager. (See Index for rates.)

Directions: From Minneapolis/St. Paul Airport take Hwy. 5 east, exit on Hwy. 55 to cross Mendota Bridge. Follow Hwy. 55 to Hastings where it joins Hwy. 61. Follow Hwy. 61, 22 mi. south into Red Wing. Accessible by Amtrak.

The date in parenthesis in the heading represents the first year the inn appeared in the pages of Country Inns and Back Roads.

SCHUMACHER'S NEW PRAGUE HOTEL
New Prague, Minnesota (1979)

John Schumacher, who is one of the most energetic and cheerful people I've ever met, was telling me about some of the main courses at his inn. "Our game menu includes pheasant, quail, venison, and rabbit served in various ways. In addition, there is a full poultry menu, lots of fish and seafood, some Czech dishes, including sausages, and several veal dishes. As a matter of fact, I think there are about fifty-six main offerings on the menu.

"There's a special 'healthy heart cuisine' menu for people who are so inclined and also a menu for lighter appetites, including sauerbrauten sandwiches. Of course, desserts like apple strudel, torte, and cheesecake will cancel out all of your good intentions."

John is a very innovative chef, having graduated at the top of his class from the Culinary Institute of America. He and Kathleen are young innkeepers who gain great satisfaction and personal fulfillment in running a country town inn. As he says, "It's been a wonderful experience since I first came to New Prague, and right from the start there were many things that had to be done, but it's been a highly satisfactory arrangement. Fortunately, I'm a chef and I feel that a great deal of our reputation centers around the fact that the food is something that I can control."

The building for Schumacher's New Prague Hotel was built in 1898 and originally was called the Broz Hotel. It was designed by Cass Gilbert, the same architect who designed the George Washington Bridge, the Supreme Court building in Washington, and the State Capitol in Saint Paul.

If the menu and the food are impressive, then the inn's guest rooms are equally so. Each is named for a different month and has an atmosphere and personality all its own. For example, "January" has "three-bear beds"—two beds put together to make a king-sized bed. Many of the

guest rooms have a folk-art theme; however, "April" features an antique Victorian three-piece settee and a king-sized custom round bed with a mirrored headboard.

There's a high canopied bed in "May," and the mustard-colored walls are decorated with white Bavarian daisies. "October" is in a deep mulberry, accentuated by painted pink chrysanthemums. (Now that I've got all those names straight, John tells me they are thinking of changing them.)

"We've been to Europe several times," John pointed out, "and I believe the decorations and cuisine here reflect my identification with Germany and Czechoslovakia. We have imported cotton-covered goose-down comforters and pillows, and there are many central-European decorative touches, such as wood carvings, as well as stenciled paintings by the Bavarian artist, Pipka.

Three of their recently remodeled rooms now have fireplaces and whirlpool tubs for two.

John and Kathleen recently returned from a trip to Bavaria, loaded with treasures for their two new dining rooms, their new gift shop, and many of their guest rooms. You will find charming Bavarian chandeliers, Bavarian pine furniture, and 200-year-old Bavarian pine wainscoting. Their gift shop is literally a treasurehouse of Czechoslovakian glassware, porcelain, beer steins, German folk-art ceramics, Austrian crystal, Polish plates, and Bavarian lamps, dolls, and pictures.

New Prague is just thirty-five miles south of the Minneapolis/Saint Paul metropolitan area, and besides the fun of staying at Schumacher's, there is a surprising number of things to do nearby, including golf and tennis. Cross-country skiing is twenty minutes away, and there are a number of lakes within a thirty-minute drive. The Minnesota River is just nine miles away and is ideal for canoeing. The area is excellent for biking as well as running.

SCHUMACHER'S NEW PRAGUE HOTEL, 212 West Main St., New Prague, MN 56071; 612-758-2133. (Metro line: 612-445-7285.) An 11-guestroom (private baths) Czechoslovakian-German inn located in a small country town, approx. 35 mi. south of Minneapolis and St. Paul. King, queen, and double beds available. European plan. Breakfast, lunch, and dinner served to travelers all year except 2 days at Christmas. Wheelchair access to restaurant. Good bicycling and backroading nearby; also xc skiing, tennis, and golf, No entertainment available to amuse children. No pets. John Schumacher, Owner-host. (See Index for rates.)

Directions: From Minneapolis, take Rte. 494 west to Rte. 169 south to Jordan exit. Turn south on Rte. 21 for 9 mi. to New Prague. Turn left to Main St. at the stop sign, and the hotel is in the second block on the right.

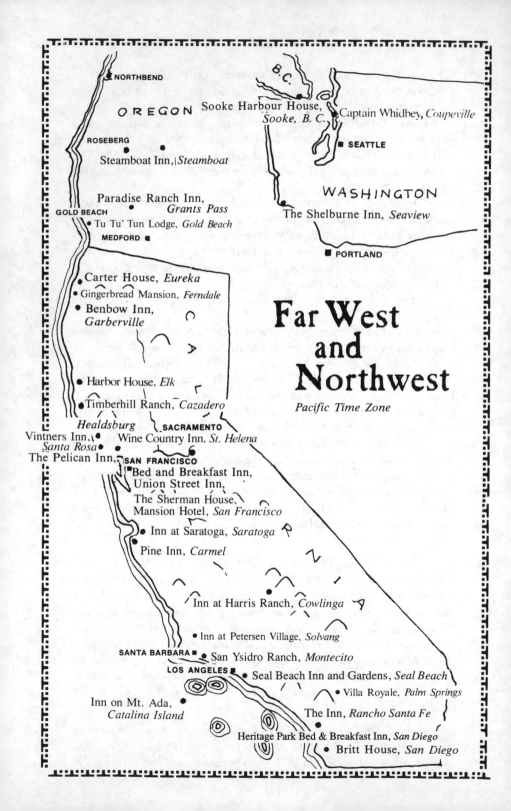

NORTHBEND

OREGON

ROSEBERG

Steamboat Inn, *Steamboat*

Paradise Ranch Inn,
Grants Pass

GOLD BEACH

Tu Tu' Tun Lodge, *Gold Beach*

MEDFORD

Carter House, *Eureka*

Gingerbread Mansion, *Ferndale*

Benbow Inn,
Garberville

Harbor House, *Elk*

Timberhill Ranch, *Cazadero*

Healdsburg

Vintners Inn,
Santa Rosa

The Pelican Inn,

Wine Country Inn, *St. Helena*

SACRAMENTO

SAN FRANCISCO

Bed and Breakfast Inn,
Union Street Inn,

The Sherman House,
Mansion Hotel, *San Francisco*

Inn at Saratoga, *Saratoga*

Pine Inn, *Carmel*

Inn at Harris Ranch, *Cowlinga*

Inn at Petersen Village, *Solvang*

SANTA BARBARA

San Ysidro Ranch, *Montecito*

LOS ANGELES

Seal Beach Inn and Gardens, *Seal Beach*

Villa Royale, *Palm Springs*

Inn on Mt. Ada,
Catalina Island

The Inn, *Rancho Santa Fe*

Heritage Park Bed & Breakfast Inn, *San Diego*

Britt House, *San Diego*

B.C.

Sooke Harbour House,
Sooke, B. C.

Captain Whidbey, *Coupeville*

SEATTLE

WASHINGTON

The Shelburne Inn, *Seaview*

PORTLAND

Far West
and
Northwest

Pacific Time Zone

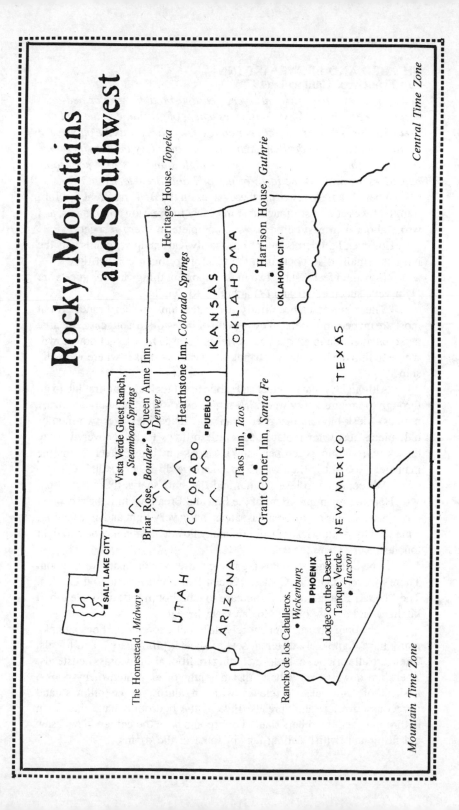

Rocky Mountains and Southwest

Central Time Zone

Mountain Time Zone

Heritage House, *Topeka*

KANSAS

OKLAHOMA

Harrison House, *Guthrie*

OKLAHOMA CITY

TEXAS

Vista Verde Guest Ranch, *Steamboat Springs*

Queen Anne Inn, *Denver*

Briar Rose, *Boulder*

Hearthstone Inn, *Colorado Springs*

COLORADO

PUEBLO

Taos Inn, *Taos*

Grant Corner Inn, *Santa Fe*

NEW MEXICO

SALT LAKE CITY

The Homestead, *Midway*

UTAH

ARIZONA

Rancho de los Caballeros, *Wickenburg*

PHOENIX

Lodge on the Desert, *Tanque Verde*, *Tucson*

THE BED AND BREAKFAST INN
San Francisco, California (1979)

Good, bad, or indifferent, every bed-and-breakfast inn or bed-and-breakfast home on the West Coast owes a debt of gratitude to the Bed and Breakfast Inn in San Francisco. For quite a few years it was the only one of its kind, and now I understand that there are over fifty in that city alone. It's a pity they did not all borrow the high standards and admirable objectives, as well as the idea, of the Bed and Breakfast Inn.

When it came to rewriting these pages on the Bed and Breakfast Inn, frankly, I was at a loss. I found that my early impressions of this inn, as I wrote about it in past editions, were complete in every respect.

However, I think this letter from Marily Kavanaugh explains why the inn has remained so popular in the face of so much competition.

"Bob and I feel that the two most important things for our guests are (1) a very special staff and (2) attention to details.

"There are other beautifully decorated inns in San Francisco but most are owned and operated by a group of investors. In our case, we give personal attention to all our guests. Telling guests how to get downtown, where to find the best pizza or handknit sweaters—this is where we really shine.

"Although we have a great staff, Bob and I feel it is our first job to go through the rooms every week. We notice everything that only an owner notices—desk blotters that need changing, magazines over two months old, plants ready for replacement, little pillows to be recovered, soap dishes with a chipped corner—the list goes on. I never feel this is the manager's job—it is the owner's job, and we do it very well.

"We continue to love the inn and the staff seems to love it, too."

Here are my impressions of the Bed and Breakfast Inn: the reception room, used as one of the breakfast areas, has a very light and airy feeling, enhanced by white wicker furniture, many flower arrangements, and light touches everywhere.

Some of the guest rooms are named after various parts of London. There's Covent Garden, Chelsea, Green Park, and Kensington Garden. The Mayfair Flat has a spiral staircase to a bedroom loft, a double tub, a kitchen, and a view of the Golden Gate Bridge.

Each room provides an entirely different experience. For example, many have completely different sets of sheets, pillowcases, and towels. There are all varieties of beds, including traditional shiny brass bedsteads. There are flowers everywhere, thermos jugs of ice water, many books, baskets of fruit, electric clocks with an alarm, down pillows, and gorgeous coverlets and spreads. Five of the bedrooms have their own bathrooms, and the others share. Four rooms have the garden view. I saw old-fashioned British ceiling fans in some of the rooms.

The location of the Bed and Breakfast is another virtue. Charlton Court is a little dead-end street off Union, between Buchanan and Laguna. San Francisco is such a "walking place" that it's convenient to many things. The nicest part of it is that when people get tired of walking, they can always take the cable cars!

THE BED AND BREAKFAST INN, Four Charlton Court, San Francisco, CA 94123; 415-921-9784. A 10-guestroom (6 private baths) European-style pension in the Union Street district of San Francisco. Queen, double, and single beds available. Convenient to all of the Bay Area recreational, cultural, and gustatory attractions. Continental breakfast is the only meal offered. Open daily year-round. Not comfortable for children. No pets. No credit cards. Robert and Marily Kavanaugh, Owners-hosts. (See Index for rates.)

Directions: Take the Van Ness Exit from Rte. 101 and proceed to Union Street. Charlton Court is a small courtyard street halfway between Laguna and Buchanan, off Union.

BENBOW INN
Garberville, California (1974)

The owners-innkeepers of the Benbow are Patsy and Chuck Watts, whom I have known for many years. The one outstanding quality that each of them has in such marvelous abundance is enthusiasm, and all of the improvements and additions to this truly unusual northern California inn have been undertaken by them with great joy and love.

"Ever since Day One," said Chuck, "we have been very happy and have had a really tremendous time. It's a continuing challenge and we've gotten a great deal accomplished, but I like the idea that the future is big with plans."

"We feel that we are a destination resort-inn, able to accommodate and provide amusement and diversion for all our guests of any age," chimed in Patsy. "We have acquired some fabulous antique pieces, most particularly a magnificent carved buffet for the dining room. We have added a beautiful carved mantel for the fireplace in the lobby and have installed an antique mantel and a fireplace in the lounge.

"We will be having our wine tasting in November, and this has now become a semiannual affair, with many of the California boutique wineries represented."

I first visited the Benbow Inn in 1973 and was immediately intrigued not only with its location in the glorious redwood country of northern California, but also with its design, which shows definite influences of the Art Deco style of the early 1920s. There are also some touches of an English Tudor manor house found in the half-timbers, carved dark wood paneling, solid oak furniture, bookcases, hardwood floors, handsome oriental rugs, and truly massive fireplace in the main living room.

Some guest rooms are on the terrace and garden levels with private patios. With four-poster beds, antiques, and country fabrics, their decor is most attractive. Three of them have fireplaces and VCRs. Other guest rooms in the main inn had also been handsomely redecorated, and my own room, Number 313, was on the top floor and looked out over the gardens and a wonderful changing panorama of clouds.

The Benbow is, indeed, a destination resort-inn—in addition to swimming, it offers tennis on two tennis courts nearby, a good golf course within walking distance, hiking, and magnificent backroading. By the way, it's very accessible by public transportation since the Route 101 buses stop almost at the front door.

At Christmastime there's a twelve-foot tree with teddy bears playing drums hanging from every branch. Under the tree there are Patsy's very special antique, oversized toys. An antique sleigh is on the front porch filled with presents and wreaths. Holly and masses of decorations are all over the inn.

On Christmas Day there is a special two-seatings Christmas dinner and everyone has a wonderful time.

Incidentally, in the fall and all through the holidays, English tea and scones are served in the lobby. Chuck's mother, Marie, is the tea lady.

The Benbow also has a film library with over 300 classic films. These are shown every evening. On one of my visits I cheered and wept a little at James Cagney's great portrayal of George M. Cohan in *Yankee Doodle Dandy*.

Patsy, Chuck, and Truffles (their new Afghan hound, the most photographed canine in northern California) are having a wonderful time greeting guests, sharing their enthusiasm, and providing their own bubbling brand of warmth and hospitality. In short, they're model innkeepers. I'm glad they and the Benbow Inn found each other.

BENBOW INN, 445 Lake Benbow Dr., Garberville, CA 95440; 707-923-2124. A 55-guestroom (private baths) English Tudor inn in the redwood country of northern California. King, queen, and twin beds available. On Rte. 101 near the Benbow State Park. European plan. Breakfast, lunch, and dinner served to travelers daily. Open mid-Apr. to Nov. 28; re-open Dec. 17 for holiday season. Swimming on grounds; golf, tennis adjacent. Hiking and magnificent backroading. Chuck, Patsy, and Truffles Watts, Owners-hosts. (See Index for rates.)

Directions: From San Francisco follow Rte. 101 north 200 mi. and exit at Benbow.

BRITT HOUSE
San Diego, California (1981)

Lying abed in the morning in this exquisitely and lovingly furnished bedroom of the Britt House, I couldn't help thinking that Daun Martin, with her attention to important details, has placed her truly valued guests in an atmosphere of at least ninety years ago, with authentic furniture, wallpaper designs, lighting fixtures, and other significant features.

True, to begin with, she has a most remarkable Victorian house, as you can see from the Jan Lindstrom drawing. A marvelous stained glass window flanking the stairwell is a truly magnificent work. The preservation of the handcarved doorways and moldings and the interior make it an almost living museum.

My mind drifted back to my arrival on the previous afternoon when Daun had shown me to the Camphor Tree Room, a quiet, intimate bedroom done in forest green, teal, and peach, with a carved oak dresser and a matching headboard for the queen-sized bed. True to its name, it has a thrilling view of the eighty-year-old camphor tree surrounded by ferns and flowers, and also has its own balcony where breakfast can be taken. This is typical of other rooms, all of which are done with an abundance of lace curtains, velvet swags, beautiful woods, oversized couches, and marble-top dressers.

The Britt House's answer to "down the hall" bathrooms is to provide their guests with terry cloth bathrobes. It's wonderful to slip into one of these after a shower or a bath.

Daun's affection for animals has created an additional special feature at the Britt House. Not only is there Barney, a sociable big, shaggy Bouvier de Flandre (mixed with sloth, as one guest remarked), but there is also a collection of stuffed animals of all kinds to be found in every bedroom. Usually they hold a welcoming note, personally addressed to each guest. Some of the animals are even taken out to dinner by guests. I know you won't believe this, but it's true. They sit them at the table, and everybody has lots of fun.

Britt House breakfasts are quite special. Freshly squeezed orange juice, eggs in a variety of styles, freshly baked yeast breads, sweet butter and honey, and European coffee, prepared filter-drip style, or tea are provided on the individual trays taken to each room. On Sunday morning, Daun's famous cinnamon twist bread is served with eggs over hash. There's a formal afternoon tea, too.

There are four bathrooms, two on each floor, and one has handsome twin antique bathtubs and bubble bath. The bathroom next to the billiard room offers a luxurious Finnish sauna that is available to all guests.

The Cottage, with its own private bath, just a few steps from the handsome camphor tree is decorated in cream, blue, and gray, and has a

romantically cozy bed-nook with a canopy, a full-sized bed, a kitchen, and a porch that faces the main house and the beautiful gardens.

These gardens have a remarkably tall hedge that protects the house, and provides excellent privacy. Regardless of what time of year I visit the Britt House, there always seems to be a profusion of flowers in bloom.

BRITT HOUSE, 406 Maple St., San Diego, CA 92103; 619-234-2926. A 10-guestroom bed-and-breakfast inn (one private bath) a short distance from Balboa Park with its world-famous zoo, Museum of Art, Man and Natural History. Reuben H. Fleet Space Theater, and the beaches, desert country, and Mexico (13 mi.). Queen, double, and twin beds available. Breakfast only meal served (special dinners can be arranged with advance notice). Open all year. Sauna on grounds; jogging, biking, skating, bicycles nearby. No pets. Smoking on front porch only. Daun Martin, Owner-host. (See Index for rates.)

Directions: Take Airport-Sassafrass turnoff coming south on Hwy. 5. Proceed on Kettner. Turn left on Laurel; left on Third; right on Nutmeg; right on Fourth St.; and go down one block to the corner of Fourth and Maple.

CARTER HOUSE
Eureka, California (1988)

When I first included the Carter House in my book *Bed and Break-fast, American Style,* I said it was "definitely a class act." I'm happy to say I haven't changed my mind.

Looking for all the world as if it had been standing on the hillside in Eureka for at least a hundred years, the house is actually an exact replica of a circa 1884 San Francisco house that was destroyed in the 1906 earthquake. Mark Carter discovered the plans for the house, which had been designed by the same architects who built the famous Carson Mansion, and he and a crew of three built the four-story structure in 1982. They followed the original plans, handcrafting the intricate wood wainscotings and moldings. Their work is really a marvel of craftsman-ship in every detail.

Mark and his wife, Christi, are a warm and enthusiastic couple, and they've left nothing to chance in creating a most inviting atmosphere in this handsome Victorian inn. While retaining a period tone throughout the house, they have captured a light and airy feeling with whitewashed walls and large, undraped windows. Antique furnishings are comple-mented with polished oak floors, oriental rugs, marble fireplaces, green plants, and fresh-cut flowers. Mark also likes to exhibit the works of local artists, and he displays original contemporary paintings, ceramics, and baskets in the three main floor parlors.

There are wonderful views of Humboldt Bay and the marina as well as the remarkable Carson Mansion from the third-story guest rooms, which have high pitched ceilings. There are also guest rooms at street level, below the parlor, and a suite with a fireplace and Jacuzzi on the second floor. They are all beautifully furnished with antiques, down comforters, fluffy pillows, and a flannel robe in the closet. Three rooms share a bath and the other four have their own private baths.

Breakfast at the Carter House is something quite special. The dining room table is laid with a crisp white tablecloth, beautiful Flow Blue china, crystal, and silver. The orange juice is freshly squeezed, the coffee is freshly roasted, and then there might be a honeydew and cantaloupe cup with a sauce of freshly diced mint leaves, Cointreau, and anise, or perhaps a poached pear in caramel sauce, or kiwi with puréed raspberries. There is almost always a just-baked fruit muffin and an egg Benedict or Florentine, and sometimes there is a smoked salmon platter. The *pièce de résistance* is Christi's melt-in-your-mouth apple-almond tart, constructed of paper-thin layers of phyllo pastry. This is just a sample, because Christi loves to cook, and she's always trying out new ideas.

They are now offering dinner for houseguests at Hotel Carter across the street. The menu changes every day, depending on what is available locally, and fish and seafood are frequently featured. Some of their entrées have been fillet of red snapper with a mustard and basil sauce, grilled yellow-fin tuna, and fillet of beef with a peppercorn sauce. Fresh vegetables and a green salad accompany dinner, and a choice of two appetizers and two desserts is also available. The desserts, which are Christi's department, sound scrumptious—fresh lemon tart with lemon cream sauce or chocolate mousse pâté with a Grand Marnier sauce.

The Carter House is on the fringe of Eureka's Old Town, where there are many beautifully restored turn-of-the-century buildings. This downtown restoration is one of the best I've seen and is not as commercial as many. It is right on the waterfront of Humboldt Bay.

Oh, one other thing. Mark has a 1958 Bentley, in which you may arrange to be transported to or from the airport. As I said, this is definitely a class act.

CARTER HOUSE, 1033 Third St., Eureka, CA 95501; 707-445-1390 or 444-8062. A 7-guestroom (4 private baths) Victorian mansion in a waterfront town in northern California, 200 mi. north of San Francisco. Queen and double beds available. Breakfast and afternoon tea are included in room charge. Dinner is served daily to houseguests during the summer. Open all year. Scenic cruises in Humboldt Bay, scenic drives, golf, Carson Mansion, Clarke Museum, antiques and crafts shops, art galleries, and restaurants nearby. No pets. Mark and Christi Carter, Owners-hosts. (See Index for rates.)

Directions: Take Hwy. 101 to Eureka. The inn is on the corner of L and Third Sts.

THE GINGERBREAD MANSION
Ferndale, California (1989)

"We use a cold-water process that eliminates the acidity in coffee," Wendy Hatfield was telling me the secret of the wonderful coffee they serve at the Gingerbread Mansion. "A drop of vanilla also gives it a special aroma and flavor," she added in a confidential murmur.

What a fun place this is! They've created some bathrooms you could write poems about. The Rose Suite's bath is the most spectacular, with a high, mirrored ceiling, a beautiful stained-glass window, hanging plants, and French garden wallpaper. The effect is really like being in a lovely light and airy garden. The great old ball-and-clawfooted tub stands on a raised platform with a white spindle-posted railing around it. And there's bubble bath for all.

Ken Torbert and Wendy have made a showplace of this Victorian marvel. It is probably the most photographed inn in northern California. In the small town of Ferndale, which is something of a Victorian marvel itself, the Gingerbread Mansion is a standout. With its peach and gold turrets, gables, widow's walk, intricately carved finials and spoolwork— and its remarkable topiary trees and bushes and formal English gardens— it is a sight to behold.

Rescued in 1981 by Wendy and Ken from a checkered past as a private residence, a hospital, an American Legion hall, and finally an apartment house, its Queen Anne and Eastlake architecture now provides an elegant setting for guests who enjoy its four parlors and nine guest rooms.

The furnishings are, of course, Victorian, but of the comfortable kind, and there are several fireplaces to cozy up to. Afternoon tea and cake are served in the parlors, where there are books and magazines, along with a 1,000-piece jigsaw puzzle of the inn.

As I started to say, Wendy and Ken take an acute interest in their breakfasts, served on a lace tablecloth in the formal dining room, which overlooks the marvelous garden with its fountain and thirty-foot-high fuchsias. In addition to their specially brewed coffee, they serve fresh fruit, freshly squeezed orange juice, local cheeses, hard-boiled eggs, and home-baked muffins, cakes, and breads. Wendy's "Very Lemony Lemon Bread," awarded first prize by Julia Child, might be on the menu.

Ferndale is called the Victorian Village, and with good reason. The Scandinavians, Swiss-Italians, and Portuguese who settled here in the late 1800s prospered as dairy farmers and built splendid houses in town in the prevailing Carpenter Gothic, Queen Anne, and Eastlake styles. Still intact 100 years later, the buildings were given a spectacular Victorian paint job by the entire community in the late 1960s, and the town has been designated a state historical landmark.

Strolling down the main street, I found all sorts of interesting shops, including businesses that have been in operation since the 1800s—the pharmacy, the local newspaper, a wonderful old mercantile store—as well as an old and rare bookshop, a candy factory, a blacksmith, and many crafts shops and galleries.

Ken tells me there are a number of excellent restaurants in the area. Wendy or Ken or one of their cheerful helpers can tell you more about all of the delights awaiting you at the Gingerbread Mansion and colorful Ferndale.

THE GINGERBREAD MANSION, 400 Berding St., Ferndale, CA 95536; 707-786-4000. A 9-guestroom (private baths) Victorian mansion in a historic landmark Victorian village in northern Calif., 5 mi. from the Pacific Coast. Queen beds and rooms with queen and twin beds available. Breakfast and afternoon tea included. Recommendations and reservations made for restaurants within walking distance. Open year-round. Garden, games, puzzles, and bicycles on premises. Unique village for sightseeing, shopping, antiquing, visiting crafts shops, art galleries, museum, repertory theater, coastal drives, Avenue of the Giants (redwoods), river activities, festivals, and many other events nearby. Children over 10. No pets. No smoking. Wendy Hatfield and Ken Torbert, Owners-hosts. (See Index for rates.)

Directions: From Hwy. 101, take Fernbridge exit and continue 5 mi. to Ferndale.

HARBOR HOUSE
Elk, California (1975)

This is another good place to greet spring, because spring comes lustily and vigorously in this part of the world, and the sea in its many moods washes ashore gently or raucously, but the rhythm never ceases. I awaken in the morning to look through the trees to the great rock formations that seem to have been thrown almost helter-skelter from the end of the headlands. Helen and Dean Turner, the innkeepers, had thoughtfully provided a very comfortable chair in the window, with a perfect view of the sea stacks and tunnels, which, along with the arches, caves, and small islands, provide an unusual view from the inn.

This particular group of rock formations was at one time a staging area for the loading and the unloading of lumber schooners. Fortunately, the story of this community has been graphically presented in the unusual brochure of the inn, with dramatic photographs showing just the scenes that I have described.

The subtitle for Harbor House on the rustic sign on Route 1 is "By the Sea." Fewer words are more apt than these. Although the main entrance is on the highway, the immediate focus of all the attention is in the rear of the inn, which looks out over the Pacific, and almost every guest room has this view.

The main building of the inn was built in 1916 as an executive residence. The construction is entirely of virgin redwood from the nearby Albion Forest. In fact, it is an enlarged version of the "Home of Redwood" exhibit building of the 1915 Panama–Pacific International Exposition in San Francisco.

Guest rooms in the main building and adjacent cottages are individually heated and have private baths. Fireplaces and parlor stoves are stocked with wood, and some of the accommodations have sun decks.

I reflected that were it not for the dominance of the sea, the view from the *other* side of the house across the meadows and into the low coastal hills could be thought of as very beautiful.

Because Helen and Dean Turner have always had a great deal of involvement and interest in the arts, from time to time Harbor House presents programs by soloists and chamber music players. The living room with its wood paneling provides an ideal atmosphere. As Helen says, "So many artists live on the coast and an intimate concert in the living room is a wonderful way to hear them." Also, Helen tells me, "Sometimes these concerts are spontaneous and informal, as a talented guest sits down at the Steinway or picks up the guitar."

Our dinner was the nice, slow, mellow kind I love and get so rarely. It was such pleasant, unhurried service. We were free to be alone together or speak to others if we wished, a wonderful blend of solitude and society.

We got wonderful pictures of all the colorful flowers and scenery. Beautiful as the pictures are, they do not capture what it was like to be there, or explain why I felt homesick when I had to leave.

Harbor House is an example of the very few "New England country inns" to be found in California.

HARBOR HOUSE, 5600 S. Hwy. #1, Box 369, Elk, CA 95432; 707-877-3203. A 6-guestroom, 4-cottage (private baths) seaside inn, 16 mi. south of Mendocino, overlooking the Pacific. King and queen beds available. Modified American plan omits lunch. Breakfast and dinner served daily to houseguests. Open year-round. Private beach, ocean wading, abalone and shell hunting, fishing, and hiking on grounds. Golf, biking, boating, ocean white-water tours, deep-sea fishing, and canoeing nearby. Unsuitable for children or pets. No credit cards. Dean and Helen Turner, Innkeepers. (See Index for rates.)

Directions: Elk is approx. 3 hrs. from Golden Gate Bridge. Take Hwy. 101 to Cloverdale, then Hwy. 128 west to Hwy. 1. Continue on Hwy. 1 south 6 mi. to Harbor House.

The date in parenthesis in the heading represents the first year the inn appeared in the pages of Country Inns and Back Roads.

HERITAGE PARK BED & BREAKFAST INN
San Diego, California (1987)

"Yes, we call ourselves a bed and breakfast inn, but since we offer dinner to our guests, that makes us a full-service inn." Lori Chandler and I were enjoying a candlelight dinner in the unusually commodious Queen Anne room, with a waitress costumed in late Victorian fashion. This remarkably restored mansion is located in the seven-acre Victorian preserve of Old Town, San Diego. "Yes, it has won us a 'People in Preservation' Award," Lori proudly told me.

"It stood vacant here in the Park for two-and-a-half years collecting mold, dry-rot, and severe floor and roof damage," she said. "Then my mother, my two sisters, their husbands, and I saw the possibilities and we spent hundreds of hours in research. Fortunately, we found the original floor plan, which enabled us to restore the house very authentically."

Heritage Park is set in a very quiet enclave of painstakingly restored Victorian homes, surrounded with flowers and shrubs. The pleasant cobblestone street is for pedestrians, and cars are parked in the back.

"The mansion was built in 1889," Lori pointed out, "and has the typical Queen Anne characteristics, including a variety of chimneys, shingles, a two-story corner tower, and an encircling veranda. Featured in the *Golden Era* magazine in 1890, it was called an 'outstanding, beautiful home of southern California.' "

There are nine distinctive guest rooms, each furnished and decorated in a popular style of the late 19th century. Incidentally, the antiques and collectibles are offered for sale, and as Lori says, "You can keep your special occasion with you forever."

Our catered dinner, at which we were joined by Lori's mother, Mary, consisted of five courses, and I could have chosen from baked chicken marinated in herbs, lemon, and butter or roast leg of lamb; however, I opted for large shrimp served with feta cheese. There is also a simpler Victorian country supper. We were eating at the table in the bay alcove window in the Queen Anne room, a guest room, where normally a couple would have breakfast or dinner brought in.

The full breakfast includes omelets, quiches, soufflés, a fruit cup with fresh fruit, and Lori's very special award-winning Strawberry Jam Loaf.

"I hope you will share with your readers the joy that we feel about Old Town, San Diego," she said, as we walked out to the front veranda to enjoy dessert and coffee. "It was a mission at first, established in 1769. Old Town, San Diego, was officially classified as a State Historic Park and incorporated in 1968; there are tours available to visit the original buildings.

"I've done a lot of other things up to this time in my life," she said, sighing contentedly. "However, I think that my background in antique collecting, interior designing, entertaining, public relations, and teaching has finally come to one focal point, and I'm content to be an innkeeper indefinitely."

Lori has proudly written to me that Heritage Park is the first B&B in Southern California to be selected as the Small Business of the Month by the San Diego Chamber of Commerce. Lori shows a lot of ingenuity in running her inn, and hardly a month goes by that she hasn't arranged some special events or activities that make the inn a very lively place indeed.

HERITAGE PARK BED & BREAKFAST INN, 2470 Heritage Park Row, San Diego, CA 92110; 619-295-7088. A 9-guestroom (5 private baths) restored Victorian mansion in the heart of Old Town, San Diego. Queen and double beds available. A choice of catered dinners is offered. Breakfast included in tariff, as well as evening refreshments, and nightly showing of vintage films. Open year-round. Special festivities at Christmas. Wheelchair facilities. Balboa Park, the famous San Diego Zoo, and other cultural activities and entertainment in the San Diego area. No accommodations for children under 14. No pets. No smoking. Lori Chandler, Manager. (See Index for rates.)

Directions: From Los Angeles follow I-5 south to Old Town Ave. off ramp; turn left on San Diego Ave. and right on Harney.

THE INN
Rancho Santa Fe, California (1974)

Aromatic eucalyptus trees, orange trees, bougainvillea, acacias, palm trees, and Brazilian pepper trees—fragrance and color. That was my first impression of this elegant but unassuming inn, spread out in hacienda-style cottages with red tile roofs amid terraced gardens, shaded by the towering eucalyptus trees. Six gardeners keep the twenty acres verdant and manicured, with broad lawns, clipped hedges and shrubs, and ornamental flowers of all kinds, including gorgeous roses.

This is a quiet haven, where the atmosphere though conservative is not at all stuffy. The mood is set by the Royce family, including owners Dan and his sister, Dorothy, who are third-generation hoteliers and are very much in evidence, along with their now grown-up offspring, also on the inn staff.

They see to it that everything runs like clockwork for their guests, who are usually found around the pleasantly sheltered heated swimming pool, on one of the three tennis courts or one of the two nearby 18-hole golf courses, or down at the Del Mar beach, where there are dressing rooms and showers, or in their whites playing a serious game of croquet on the regulation English croquet lawn.

There are several dining areas in the main building, and Dan assured me that gentlemen wear coats and ties at dinner. The Garden Room overlooks the pool and gardens and is decorated with lattice and painted murals; the Vintage Room is modeled after a traditional tap room, the charming Library Room is lined with over 4,000 books, and the Patio Room opens out onto a patio flanked with brilliant poinsettias and hanging plants. Dan tells me that on some summer weekend evenings there's dinner and dancing on the patio under the stars.

Before and after dinner, guests usually gather in the lounge area, a huge thirty-by-forty-foot room, with a high, beamed, cathedral ceiling, handsome fireplace, comfortable sofas and chairs, and filled with Royce family heirlooms. There are some exquisite oriental objets d'art, collected by Dan's grandmother during her travels in China—wall tapestries, dolls, vases and bowls, and a magnificent piece of needlework in gold thread. Dan pointed out that the antique boat collection mounted on the walls around the room are very intricately tooled ships' models.

Guest rooms in the main building and cottages are decorated with pleasant California-style furnishings. The cottages contain from two to ten guest rooms, some with kitchens, fireplaces, or private patios.

The town of Rancho Santa Fe is one of the most attractively designed that I have ever visited. It has been well described as a "civilized planned community." The homes, estates, shops, and buildings have been created in perfect harmony with nature's generous endowment of climate and

scenery. One of the dominating factors is the presence of the gigantic eucalyptus trees.

One of the most useful and gratifying amenities at the Inn is a map showing many short motor trips to points fifty miles away, including Lake Elsinore to the north and Tijuana, Mexico, to the south. I am personally acquainted with the rolling ranch and orchard country to the east as far away as Julian. All of these trips make a stay at the Inn worth several extra days.

The Inn is one of the few small American hotels that belong to the prestigious Relais et Châteaux, the world-famous French organization.

THE INN, P.O. Box 869, Rancho Santa Fe, CA 92067; 619-756-1131. A 75-guestroom (private baths) resort-inn, 27 mi. north of San Diego Freeway #5 and 5 mi. inland from Solana Beach, Del Mar. European plan. Breakfast, lunch, and dinner served to travelers daily. Open year-round. Wheelchair access. Pool, tennis, and 6-wicket croquet course on grounds. Golf, Delmar, and ocean nearby. Day trips to Balboa Park, San Diego Zoo, Wild Animal Park, Sea World, harbor cruises, La Jolla shops and galleries, Old Town San Diego, and backroading. Daniel Royce, Owner-host. (See Index for rates.)

Directions: From I-5, take Exit S8 and drive inland about 6 mi. The Inn is on Paseo Delicias at Linea del Cielo.

THE INN AT HARRIS RANCH
Coalinga, California (1990)

The Inn at Harris Ranch and the Harris Ranch Restaurants do not fit my criteria for inclusion in this book; however, an exception is being made because of its high quality and its location as an oasis on the seemingly endless, and often searingly hot, stretch of I-5 joining Northern and Southern California. Located in the fertile San Joaquin Valley, the soft pink stucco inn and restaurants are surrounded by lofty palms. Red tile roofs, stately archways and balconies, along with cool terra-cotta Mexican floor tiles, remind one of the early California haciendas.

The Inn is the newest part of the complex that makes up the legendary Harris Ranch. In the early 1900s, J. A. Harris migrated from Texas to establish one of California's first cotton gins. Two generations later, the ranch has grown to encompass 20,000 acres where cotton, melons, tomatoes, and lettuce, as well as an impressive variety of other crops, are grown.

Yet the name Harris Ranch most often connotes beef. The reputation for quality beef has been earned by word-of-mouth more than by advertising. Over 2,000 people a day enjoy breakfast, lunch, or dinner in one of the five dining rooms at the restaurant. Today, the beef plant processes more than 200 million pounds of high-quality beef a year. The Harris Ranch country store, which features fresh bakery products, can also pack Harris USDA choice beef to travel.

Entering the inn's double doors, a pink stone fireplace with huge matching columns meets your gaze. The lobby, with its polished granite reservation desk, is softened by antique-pine bookcases, lush plants, cowhide-covered sofas, and original oil paintings. Although the inn is large, with 89 rooms, the atmosphere remains intimate and casual. The luxurious guest rooms and suites are designed to create a refreshing country garden theme. Deep pile carpets, high ceilings, scrubbed pine furniture, hickory log chairs, and coordinated floral prints combine to make you feel very much at home. The bathrooms are cozy, with overhead heat lamps, double-basin sinks, and dressing areas. A state-of-the-art air-conditioning system, designed to be especially quiet, allows comfortable sleeping during the scorching summers. Many of the rooms have private patios or balconies that overlook the terraced courtyard, 25-meter Olympic-style lap pool, and large Jacuzzi spa.

A continental breakfast can be served in your room, or you can enjoy your meals at one of the ranch restaurants next door. A typical breakfast might include steak and eggs, buttermilk biscuits, hash browns, and fresh-squeezed orange juice. Omelets, corned beef hash, and other specialty items are also available. My particular favorite is the Harris Ranch *huevos rancheros*. Sunday brunch is offered in the grand ballroom between 10:30 a.m. and 3:00 p.m.

The Fountain Court Dining Room, the more casual Ranch Kitchen, or the intimate Jockey Club offer evening dining at its best. Fresh fruits and vegetables from the ranch farm, along with premium cuts of Harris Ranch beef, are prepared to order. Accompanied by the gentle splash of the courtyard fountain, I had a sumptuous meal of tender roast filet of beef that had been drizzled with a unique dried fruit and cabernet sauce.

Wines and champagne can be delivered to your room, and from May through September there is a poolside bar. A full-service bar/lounge, which offers entertainment on Friday and Saturday evenings, is located in the restaurant.

While you might feel as if you are in the middle of nowhere, a number of activities are available locally: jogging and walking trails located on the ranch grounds, and golf courses, tennis courts, and racquetball facilities are only a short drive from the inn.

The Harris Ranch Inn is comfortable, with an attentive staff and beautiful surroundings. Jack Harris would be proud to see that the empire he began in 1937 has not lost its focus: offering the highest in quality.

THE INN AT HARRIS RANCH, 24505 W. Dorris Ave., Rt. 1, Box 777, Interstate 5 and Hwy. 198, Coalinga, CA 93210; 800-942-2333 or 209-935-0717. An 89-guestroom (private baths) resort featuring a refreshing country atmosphere with elegant styling. Located just off I-5 approximately midway between San Francisco and Los Angeles. Open all year. Breakfast, lunch, and dinner available at the ranch restaurants. Nonsmoking rooms available. No pets. Private air strip. John and Carole Harris, Owners; Kirk Doyle, Manager.

Directions: North or south on I-5, take Harris Ranch exit at the junction of Rte. 198 east.

THE INN AT PETERSEN VILLAGE
Solvang, California (1989)

Hans Christian Andersen would feel quite at home in Solvang—it's a bit of Denmark in America. Settled by Danish farmers in the 19th century, it has grown into a thriving community with shops of all kinds, bakeries, restaurants, sidewalk cafes, windmills, and other tourist attractions. I understand there are good bargains to be had in imported Danish glass and other merchandise.

The village, with its half-timbered buildings, peaked roofs, and copper spires, is nestled among the sprawling ranches, farms and vineyards of the Santa Ynez mountains in central California, just north of Santa Barbara.

Playing a vital part in this lively community for the past thirty years, Earl Petersen was the architect for much of Solvang's Old World Village. He personally developed the Petersen Village and Inn, a European-style hotel overlooking an enclave of shops, arcades, and a courtyard that makes up the village.

Jim Colvin, manager of the inn and Earl's son-in-law, was on the scene the day of my visit, and he took me all around this picturesque establishment. "Earl and most of the family are in Denmark, attending their oldest son's wedding," he told me, "but almost any other time, you're likely to meet Earl, Delores, Stephanie, Aaron, Nancy, Adam, Jill, or Ari. They're all very much involved."

There's much to keep a big family busy in this bustling village within a village. The hotel lobby and guest rooms form a horseshoe around the courtyard and are all, in true European fashion, on the second and third floors above the shops. The inner rooms look down on the courtyard, where trees and flowers are growing and a fountain splashes.

The lobby is tastefully decorated with honey-colored mahogany paneling, groupings of comfortable, Queen Anne-style furniture, some Danish antiques, interesting prints, and carpeting imported from England. Because of the architectural design, guest rooms are in various sizes and shapes, with queen- or king-sized canopied beds, chintzes, pretty wallpapers, thick carpeting, and handsome tiled bathrooms. All of the rooms have views of either the courtyard or the mountains.

"Our inner courtyard rooms are the most popular, especially on the two weekends before Christmas when we have a pageant reenacting the birth of Christ," Jim explained. "We have choirs and musicians, llamas dressed as camels, Mary rides in on a donkey, and the shepherds have real sheep. Guests with rooms on the inner courtyard can open their windows and enjoy the whole pageant from their rooms."

The pleasing sound of a piano playing "It Had to be You" drifted out of the lounge as we approached it, and there were groups of people chatting and laughing, seated on checkered settees around nice coffee tables. "Our guests are treated to complimentary valley wines and cheese every day at six," Jim said, "and when Frank Engleman is here, he plays the piano. Frank is a delightful retired local gentleman who comes in most evenings. He plays anything anybody requests, and our guests really enjoy him."

Petersen Village has all kinds of interesting shops, a restaurant, and a tantalizing bakery, where the delectable pastries for the continental breakfast come from.

Solvang itself has no end of things to do, including horse-drawn trolley rides, tours at fourteen wineries, many horse farms in the surrounding hills, and a three-month summer season of Shakespeare, drama, and musicals performed under the stars in an outdoor theater one block from the inn.

Midway between northern and southern California, it's really a fun place for a stopover, and I can assure my readers they will find a warm welcome from Earl Petersen and his congenial family. We are happy to welcome the Inn at Petersen Village to our pages.

THE INN AT PETERSEN VILLAGE, 1576 Mission Drive, Solvang, CA 93463; 805-688-3121 (in Calif.: 800-321-8985). A 40-guestroom (private baths) European-style small hotel over a complex of shops in a Danish village in the Santa Ynez Mountains of central California. Complimentary continental breakfast only meal served; afternoon wine and cheese. Open year-round. All of the attractions of a lively small town, including summer theater, wineries, shopping, gliders, and balloon rides, and Santa Ines mission nearby. No children under six. No pets. The Petersen Family, Owners-hosts. (See Index for rates.)

Directions: From Hwy. 101, take Rte. 246 2 mi. to Solvang.

THE INN AT SARATOGA
Saratoga, California (1990)

A very good friend, who designs those amazingly wild computer games that perplex me beyond belief, recently wrote to me recommending the Inn at Saratoga. Apparently he had spent a think-tank weekend there and found it bucolic and charming.

Located in the foothills of the Santa Cruz mountains, the five-story modern hotel blends old-world hospitality with an English country setting. In the center of the quaint town of Saratoga, noted for its Mediterranean-like climate, the inn stands on a historical site that was once the location of a toll gate built in 1850 to transport great redwood logs out of the Santa Cruz mountains.

The English manor-style lobby is decorated in green, peach, and mauve, with prominent oak and brass accents. A platter of croissants and muffins is served here each morning, along with juices and huge thermoses filled with coffee and tea. Here, too, afternoon wine and hors d'oeuvres are set out around 4:00 p.m.

All forty-six guest rooms are designed for seclusion and privacy and have indoor and outdoor sitting areas that overlook bubbling Saratoga Creek and Wildwood Park. Towering eucalyptus, sycamore, and lush

elms, some over 200 years old, surround the inn and create a serene setting. Ruby red bougainvillea and heavily scented jasmine line the romantic pathways below.

The rooms have oversize beds, televisions, personal computer capabilities, telephones, built-in hair dryers, luxurious baths, and air-conditioning. White antiqued armoires and desks, along with comfortable love seats, furnish the sitting areas. Suites are larger and have the addition of whirlpool baths and European-style towel warmers. The executive and parlor suites may be combined for added comfort and convenience. Original California art decorates the walls, and floor-to-ceiling French windows make the rooms bright and airy.

The Inn at Saratoga is part of historical Saratoga Village. The area offers a wide variety of shopping possibilities including unique designer boutiques, quaint shops, and fine art and antique galleries. A number of award-winning restaurants featuring international cuisines are just three blocks away. Many cultural activities are available throughout the year. The famed Paul Masson Winery's Summer Festival, highlighting jazz greats like Ella Fitzgerald, and theater productions at the Flint Center are just a few. The inn is at the beginning of a self-guided historic walking tour, and in June the city celebrates its culture with the Blossom Festival.

Curving Highway 17 will take you to the Santa Cruz Beach and Boardwalk's looping roller coaster, and give you a chance to watch California's surfers in action. Stop on the way home for some wine tasting at the valley's best wineries, or have early afternoon tea at the Hakone Japanese Gardens.

I could see why my friend found the tranquility of The Inn at Saratoga conducive to the complex mental gymnastics he must do when designing computer games. Me? I just found my visit extremely refreshing and enjoyable. And that's what really matters.

THE INN AT SARATOGA, 20645 Fourth St., Saratoga, CA 95070; 408-867-5020. A 46-guestroom (private baths) modern hotel nestled at the foot of the Santa Cruz mountains in the town of Saratoga. Open all year. All-size beds. Continental breakfast included with tariff. Close to wineries, boutiques, fine restaurants, Paul Masson Winery summer concerts, and theaters. Tennis, swimming, windsurfing, horseback riding, and jogging and walking trails nearby. No pets. Jack Hickling, Manager-host.

Directions: From Rte. 280, take Rte. 85 (Saratoga/Sunnyvale Rd.) to the intersection with Rte. 9 (Big Basin Way). Turn right on Big Basin, and go approx. ¼ mi. to 4th St., then turn right. Go ½ block. From Hwy. 17, take Rte. 9 exit (Los Gatos/Saratoga) to Saratoga. Turn left on Big Basin Way (Rte. 9), then right onto 4th St. The inn is ½ block on the right.

THE INN ON MOUNT ADA
Avalon, California (1990)

In 1921, when chewing gum magnate/philanthropist William
Wrigley, Jr. stood back and, in his mind's eye, saw a vision of a summer
home, he pulled out all the stops. Located on 5.5 acres of the lovely island
of Santa Catalina, high atop hills overlooking Avalon Harbor, the compound covers nearly 7,000 square feet, which includes a main house
ornamented with elaborate columns, arches, panel work, and handmade
moldings. The den, sun room, living room, card lounge, dining rooms,
and butler's pantry complete the first level. Six bedrooms fill the second
floor.

Eventually the property was donated to the University of Southern
California for use as a marine institute. The university funded rehabilita-
tion to meet electrical and plumbing codes, as the building had been
vacant for more than twenty-five years prior to the university's possession.

In February 1985, a thirty-year lease was signed by USC and the Mt.
Ada Inn Corporation, composed of island residents Susie and Wayne
Griffin, Marlene McAdam, and ex-residents Suzie and Scott Wauben,
and the property was transformed into a B&B inn.

With backgrounds in home economics, restaurant management,
computer bookkeeping services, interior design, and civic affairs, the
partnership had the necessary combination of business experience to
operate such an undertaking. "Everyone in Avalon has chosen to live here
as an alternative life-style to the mainland," explained Susie Griffin, the
assistant innkeeper and conference center coordinator.

The Georgian home, listed on the National Register of Historic

Places, offers the stately architecture of detailed French doors, and paneled insets and dentil molding. Thought to commemorate the Bay of the Seven Moors, the L-shaped terrace is composed of seven configurations of local terra-cotta tile.

The common rooms are classical, restful, and deceptively custom designed by the best in the business. Views to the ocean are commonplace, and sumptuous couches and rattan furniture invite conversation. Crafts indigenous to the area are found in the form of rare Catalina pottery, an art practiced by island craftsmen in the 1920s.

The six guest rooms are detailed with old-world antiques. Chandeliers, carpeting, drapery fabrics, bedding are thoughtfully created and coordinated by specialty designers. The installation of acoustical insulation to provide adequate privacy was one aspect of upgrading that took place when the rooms were prepared for guests. Most rooms have queen-size beds and all have private baths.

A hearty breakfast is included with the room tariff, and may offer bran muffins, freshly squeezed orange juice, poached pears with strawberry glaze, a mushroom, onion, jack and cheddar cheese omelet, bacon, and bagels. Hot and cold appetizers, freshly baked cookies, a coffee and tea tray, soft drinks, fresh fruit, and mixed nuts are available at all times. Late-afternoon relaxation is accompanied by red and white wines, sherry, port, beer, and champagne.

"We call our style of food Cuisine of the American Pacific," Susie told me as she handed me my dinner menu. The freshest of ingredients are used, and are prepared with a combination of French and Oriental influences. I had the abalone platter with fresh Oriental noodles and tender vegetables. The egg-batter filets, with a lemon-butter, shallot, and garlic sauce, were so tender that they practically melted under my fork.

The Inn on Mount Ada is a five-minute drive from town, by golf cart only, if you please. The island only allows travel by such unintrusive means. In fact, I had one of the most serene mornings of my life as I stood on my balcony at 5 a.m. watching a spectacular sunrise, with the sounds of small birds and the sea to keep me company. Transportation from the mainland to Santa Catalina is by boat from Long Beach, San Pedro, and Newport Beach. Helicopters are available from Long Beach and San Pedro. I had a wonderful 15-minute ride on Island Express helicoptor service. I highly recommend it.

THE INN ON MT. ADA, 398 Wrigley Rd., P.O. Box 2560, Avalon, CA 90704; 213-510-2030. A 6-guestroom (private baths) elegant Georgian Colonial on the fabled island of Santa Catalina. Open all year, except Christmas. Breakfast included. Dinner available some evenings. No pets. Susie Griffin and Marlene McAdam, Owners-hosts.

Directions: Boat or helicopter from mainland.

MADRONA MANOR
Healdsburg, California (1988)

Many Easterners visiting northern California for the first time are struck with the unusual number of Victorian homes and buildings. I was reminded of this once again during a short drive around downtown Healdsburg on my way to Madrona Manor. I turned in at the impressive archway, flanked by a rainbow mass of flowers, and drove up the long winding drive to the three-story mansion. From the rambling front porch, I turned to look over the grounds and noticed that Madrona Manor sits on top of a knoll with flower gardens, sculptured hedges, numerous varieties of trees and bushes, and acres and acres of lawn.

I heard a step behind me and realized that the couple coming out the front door were the innkeepers of Madrona Manor, John and Carol Muir. "Oh, I see you are enjoying our view," John said.

Like the Old Rittenhouse, Madrona Manor is furnished with beautiful Victorian antiques. There is a 100-year-old square piano in the music room, and throughout the house are massive pieces of carved walnut and mahogany furniture and oriental carpets. "Five of our rooms have the antique furniture of the original owner, John Paxton, who was a San Francisco financier," Carol told me. "He built this house and also the Carriage House in 1881."

One of the guest rooms has a ten-foot-high canopied bed and a huge armoire. The others have carved headboards, chaise longues, dressing tables with beveled mirrors, original light fixtures, and period wallpapers. There are fourteen-foot-high ceilings and many fireplaces with brightly painted tiles.

"I love fireplaces," I told John. "How many of your guest rooms have them?" He thought for a moment. "We have nine rooms with fireplaces, including the four we added in the third-floor rooms, which were originally servants' quarters. These rooms have antique-reproduction furniture.

John, a former engineer, converted the Carriage House into more guest rooms, and has used vast amounts of carved rosewood for lamps and tables, as well as door trim and paneling. Guests gather in the huge lobby to shoot pool, work on an ongoing jigsaw puzzle, or sit by the cheery fire. There is a Garden Suite surrounded by lawn and flowers and another building with a very private country bedroom and suite. Madrona Manor is listed on the National Register of Historic Places as a historic district.

However, I think the big story at Madrona Manor is the food. Their big, efficient kitchen is a delight to behold, and includes a wood-burning oven, a mesquite grill, and a separate smokehouse. The Muir's son, Todd, is in command. The Muirs are obviously very proud of his talents as a chef. "Todd's cooking has attracted the attention of *Gourmet* magazine, and we have guests who drive all the way from San Francisco just for dinner," John told me. I'd certainly be happy to make the trip for the dinner I had, which included a wonderful crusty goat-cheese soufflé seasoned with rosemary and garlic, a perfect green salad, and mesquite-grilled monkfish that was absolutely delicious. I couldn't resist trying the Mexican flan with rose petals (delightful). There is a prix-fixe menu and an à la carte menu. Everything is given special and interesting treatment and served with great aplomb.

Later that night, as I stood on the balcony of my room, looking out over the beautiful view, with Mount Saint Helena to the east, I thought a stay here in the Sonoma wine country at this beautiful inn is a very special experience.

MADRONA MANOR (Romantik Hotels), 1001 Westside Rd., Box 818, Healdsburg, CA 95448; 707-433-4231. An 18-guestroom, 2-suite (private baths) Victorian mansion in the heart of Sonoma County wine country, 65 mi. north of San Francisco. All-size beds. Breakfast included in room rate. Dinner served daily; reservations recommended. Open year-round. Wheelchair access. Swimming pool on grounds. Golf, tennis, hiking, canoeing, fishing, winery tours nearby. Children and pets welcome by prearrangement. John and Carol Muir, Owners-hosts. (See Index for rates.)

Directions: From San Francisco, follow Rte. 101 north to the 2nd Healdsburg exit. Continue north and turn left at Mill St. (first stoplight), which becomes Westside Rd.

THE MANSION HOTEL
San Francisco, California (1990)

Unique, elegant, and certainly out of the ordinary, the Mansion Hotel offers guests a visit they will long remember. Settled in a prestigious neighborhood that includes some of San Francisco's most splendid homes, the hotel is only a short walk from the refurbished Fillmore district and Union Street, where some of the city's most unusual and fashionable boutiques, restaurants, and clubs are located.

From the moment you arrive and step into the grand foyer, welcomed by the soft tinkle of crystal chandeliers, there is an aura of excitement. To the strains of Bach's "Invention in C-Major," a large multicolored macaw screeches "hello" from his perch. Inventive murals tell the life story of The Mansion. Tapestries, artifacts, great paintings, and sculptures surround you—treasures of times past.

The parlor is an impressive example of Art Nouveau, and is dominated by a 9-foot turquoise jardiniere. "Sotheby's wanted it shipped to New York," said Mansion owner Bob Pritikin as he took me on a tour. Built in 1887 by Senator Chambers, the twin-turreted Queen Anne Victorian is one of San Francisco's original Grandes Dames, and a designated San Francisco landmark.

An author, advertising agency owner, and entertainer, Bob hosts a nightly Victorian Cabaret Theater that includes a fabulous magic show and a ghostly concert on the grand piano by The Mansion's resident ghost, Claudia. Claudia performs requests until the evening's end, when she completes her concert with a Scott Joplin rag, accompanied by guests who have been supplied with a multitude of rhythm instruments. Billed as

America's Foremost Concert Saw Player, Bob often treats guests to a performance of "Moonlight Saw-nata." "I just love to step up to my saw and warble," he laughed. "You know, I've played with Liberace and Johnny Cash!"

The common rooms display more than a million dollars' worth of art and antiques, including works by Turner, Reynolds, and the famed sculptor Benjamin Buffano. The Mansion's dining room features a breathtaking stained-glass mural, one of the world's largest. The turn-of-the-century masterpiece stretches 32 continuous feet. "I'm not sure if I'm staying in a hotel or an art museum," said fellow guest Mildred Salway.

Murals are a theme throughout the hotel, appearing in each guest room. The rooms are furnished with valued antiques and decorated with whimsy and drama. Most rooms have queen beds, and all have additional sofa beds and private baths. Special gifts of candy and silk roses await guests, as do fresh flowers.

Breakfast, which is included in the room rate, is opulent. Eggs any style, fresh-squeezed orange juice, jumbo "banger" sausages, hot cheese potatoes in mini-crocks, toasted crumpets, cereal, and fresh ground coffee are served in the breakfast kitchen, or on request, you may have breakfast in bed.

The Mansion offers elegant evening dining. Master chef David Coyle was formerly the personal chef to the Duke and Duchess of Bedford. Chef Coyle's artistry has regaled some of the crowned heads of Europe, including the Queen Mother of England. "But we give every Mansion guest the royal treatment," smiled Coyle. The Mansion's restaurant is restricted to the pleasure of its guests and may include a menu of fennel soup, filet of elk, or roast grouse. A list of fine California and French wines is available, along with a full beer selection, including San Francisco's rare steam beer.

Packing my bags just prior to checkout, I couldn't help but wonder how Claudia had met her demise. When asked, Bob just smiled and glanced toward the soft tinkle of the chandelier. I guess I really never do want to know. The magic and elegance of The Mansion Hotel should remain a mystery.

THE MANSION HOTEL, 2220 Sacramento St., San Francisco, CA 94115; 415-929-9444 or 800-826-9398. A 19-guestroom (private baths) Queen Anne Victorian located in one of San Francisco's most lovely neighborhoods. Open all year. Within walking distance to shops, restaurants, and clubs. City bus and taxi curbside; cable car 4 blocks away. Full breakfast included, lunch available, dinner by reservation. Telephones in rooms. Pets welcome. Bob Pritikin, Owner-host; Denise Mitidieri, Manager.

Directions: Ask directions to Pacific Heights in San Francisco.

THE PELICAN INN
Muir Beach, California (1988)

The Pelican is about as close to being an English West Country inn as one could find. I could well imagine that I was seated in the Lobster Pot in Mousehole in Cornwall. The Pelican has an Inglenook fireplace with the inscription, "Fear knocked at the door, Faith answered; No one was there." There's a resemblance to the Royal Oak Inn in Yattendon, the place where I like to stay on the nights before my departures from England.

The waitress came in with a platter of most tempting snacks, including bangers, ribs, cheese, and soup. When I remarked on how tempting they all looked, Susan replied, "We've added many new items to our menu. Our luncheon menu now includes a plowman's lunch of hot rolls, cheddar or Stilton cheese, chutney, tomatoes, and whole small onions, as well as cottage pie, bangers and mash, and fish and chips." Ed added, "Dinners include beef Wellington, rack of lamb, and prime rib with Yorkshire pudding, as well as fresh fish dishes."

Susan and Ed were good friends with the original owner of the inn, Charles Felix, an Englishman. Charles designed the inn, with its Tudor half-timbers and white exterior, and ran it most successfully for quite a few years. When he and his wife, Brenda, decided to go back to England, Susan and Ed were ecstatic at the prospect of becoming the new owners of the Pelican.

"Charles, of course, is a very hard act to follow," said Susan, "but I'm happy to say that one of our best moves was to make Barry Stock the manager of the inn. He's from Devonshire, England, where he ran some establishments. It was in Exeter that he met his wife, Pamela, an American girl from Newport Beach, California. She lured him out here, and in the course of time they visited the Pelican and were smitten immediately. He was Charlie's right-hand man and managed the inn while he was away."

Almost on cue, Barry walked in and I had the pleasure of being introduced. He proved to have a very attractive English accent and soon all of us were enthusiastically conversing. When I asked him about Pamela, he said, "Her passion is the inn garden. She cultivates many different species of flowering plants, all of which could be found in an English garden."

Susan and Ed excused themselves to go back to their other inn, and Barry suggested that I might like to have a look around the inn.

"Susan and Ed have really done a masterful job of freshening up the inn," he said. "We painted, we repaired, we exchanged furniture that wasn't authentic to the period. We have several new Asian rugs with a 16th-century design, and we uncovered some beautiful wood floors, as you can see. I'm happy to say that we've received many compliments from

guests who have been coming here for years, and this includes various members of Charles's family."

Our stroll took us abovestairs to the guest rooms, many of which have four-poster and half-tester beds. The Hogarth prints, which I admired on my first visit a number of years ago, were still in place.

"We now have a proper 'snug,' which is really an English term for a living room," Barry explained. "It's been furnished in 17th- and 18th-century English antiques and has a library and a fireplace. When we're not having a special party here, inn guests use it, and it is a popular place for them to curl up and read or to mingle with other guests."

Barry and I returned to the dining room, which was taking on a festive dinner air. The lights were reflected on the many carved chairs, beautiful old tables, and massive sideboards.

THE PELICAN INN, Muir Beach, CA 94965; 415-383-6000 (for reservations, call between 9:30 and 4:30). A 7-guestroom (private baths) English inn on the northern California coast, 8 mi. from the Golden Gate Bridge. Queen-size beds available. Breakfast included in tariff. Lunch and dinner open to the public. Open year-round. Wheelchair access to dining room. Swimming, beachcombing, backroading, walking, and all San Francisco attractions nearby. Ed and Susan Cunningham, Owners; Barry and Pamela Stock, Managers. (See Index for rates.)

Directions: From Golden Gate Bridge follow Hwy. 101 north to Hwy. 1/Stinson Beach exit. Turn left at traffic lights and follow Hwy. 1/Stinson Beach Rd. 5 mi. to Muir Beach. (Do not go to Muir Woods.)

THE PINE INN
Carmel, California (1990)

I found it hard to believe that I was sitting in the oldest commercial building in Carmel-by-the-Sea as the domed glass ceiling of the Pine Inn's gazebo rolled back to reveal a vibrant blue sky. I also found it difficult to imagine that the original hotel had been rolled on pine logs right down Ocean Avenue to its present location. Yet, it was true. This lovely, authentic Victorian inn, with its subtle updating, has lost none of the classic elegance that has charmed guests for over three generations.

Located in the center of Carmel, within walking distance to the beach, The Pine Inn was originally built in 1890 as the Hotel Carmelo. After the precarious log-rolling move, the hotel opened in 1904 to an overbooking of guests who were finally accommodated in tents pitched on adjoining lots.

Such a whirlwind opening made way for what has become quite a tradition. "See you at the Pine Inn," became an oft-used phrase as the town of Carmel expanded around the inn. From the very beginning, celebrities frequented the guest register. "We can't lay claim to George Washington," manager Hoby J. Hooker told me. "But at least the actor who played him on television slept here." While that actor's name pales against our first president's, the list of celebrated guests is noteworthy: Bing Crosby, Frank Sinatra, Howard Duff, Red Skelton, Ernie Ford, Mel Ferrer, and Tarzan himself, Johnny Weissmuller.

Those who are not quite as well known receive the same special treatment as celebrities. Each guest room is decorated with Chinese-style Victorian decor. Pierre Deuz fabrics, authentic period furnishings, and lovely artworks create a mood of old-fashioned comfort and charm. Of course, I always feel the height of pampering is excellent room service, an area where the Pine Inn excels. All rooms have private baths and all-size beds are available.

Since World War II, the inn's Red Parlor has been one of *the* places to imbibe. More than a local watering hole, the cozy decor and friendly atmosphere have established it as a traditional meeting place. Subtle lighting and rosy stained glass set an intimate mood. All sorts of rumors abound concerning the clientele. Apparently author John Steinbeck met his second wife here while dipping olives into extra-dry martinis. W. C. Fields is also said to have warmed a bar stool now and then. Sandwiches and evening pub fare are available.

The outdoor patio was converted to a gazebo in 1972 with the addition of the opening dome. Breakfast, lunch, and dinner are served here and in the Garden Room. Seafood from the Monterey Bay, fresh local vegetables, and the best in California wines make dining a pleasure. The Friday-night buffet and Sunday brunch are more than any epicure could hope for.

After brunch, step just outside the inn's main lobby to the patio complex of Pine Inn Shops. Known as Little Carmel, due to the diversity of unique boutiques, you will find original fashions, men's clothing, antiques, and jewelry.

The picturesque town of Carmel can be covered easily on foot. Some of the best art galleries on the West Coast are located in the area, and for those interested in a day "on the links," seventeen world-class golf courses are within driving distance. Other points of interest include Fisherman's Wharf, the Seventeen-Mile Drive, and the incomparable Monterey Bay Aquarium.

THE PINE INN, Ocean Ave. at Lincoln, Box 250, Carmel, CA 93921; 408-624-3851. A 49-guestroom (private baths) historic Victorian inn located in beautiful Carmel-by-the-Sea. All-size beds. Open all year. Breakfast, lunch, and dinner available. Restaurants, boutiques, galleries, and beaches within walking distance. Exceptional golf, Monterey Bay Aquarium, and Fisherman's Wharf nearby. No pets. Richard Gunner, Owner; Hoby J. Hooker, Manager.

Directions: From Coast Hwy. 1, take Ocean Ave. west to Lincoln St.

The date in parenthesis in the heading represents the first year the inn appeared in the pages of Country Inns and Back Roads.

SAN YSIDRO RANCH
Montecito, California (1990)

Waiting to check in at San Ysidro Ranch's reception desk, I was certain that I had seen famous chef Julia Child stroll through the cozy Hacienda Lounge. Michael Ullman, the Ranch's general manager, confirmed my suspicion. "Oh, yes, she's one of our guests. A large number of celebrities have considered the Ranch a second home since it opened in 1893," he said. I was impressed with the list, which included honeymooners John and Jacqueline Kennedy, Paul Newman and Joanne Woodward, Bruce Springsteen, and Barbra Streisand. Writer Somerset Maugham used the haven of the Geranium House to complete some of his finest works. Sinclair Lewis wrote in the closet of the Oak Cottage, away from the spectacular but distracting ocean views. Sir Laurence Olivier and Vivien Leigh plighted their troth in the old-fashioned wedding garden.

It's easy to see why San Ysidro Ranch attracts romantic couples and those who just want to retreat to the rustic residential atmosphere. Nestled at the foot of the Santa Ynez Mountains, forty-three cottages are tucked into the 540-acre grounds, of which the main grounds and garden remain virtually unchanged since the original land grant adobe was built in 1825. Hundred-year-old trees and wide terraces of pungent citrus, flowers, and herbs surround the lawns. Hedges heavy with flowering jasmine and honeysuckle perfume the air.

Each cottage has its own personality. California-country charm is enhanced by polished antiques, cozy upholstered pieces in soft yellows and blues, fluffy pillows and coverlets, and cushioned wall-to-wall carpeting. Ten bungalows have private outdoor Jacuzzis, and all have wood-burning fireplaces and wide sun decks for lounging. King and twin beds are available, and all cottages have full baths with tub/shower combos. A special touch: Your name is engraved on a wooden sign outside your cottage to make you feel at home.

Complimentary morning coffee, newspapers, and an Honor Bar, where guests mix their own drinks, are located in the Hacienda Lounge. Here also are the Ranch's only television, and videos, should you decide to come out of hiding.

I had difficulty choosing among the outdoor entertainment possibilities. Tennis at one of three courts, golf, hiking, swimming in the sunny Ranch pool, or horseback riding? I chose to mount up and explore the resort's 500 acres of canyon wilderness trails that wind through forests, bubbling creeks, and chaparral. I felt gloriously invigorated by the unspoiled beauty that surrounded me.

After a soak in my private Jacuzzi, I dressed for what I knew would be a special dining experience. Formerly the Plow and Angel, the Ranch restaurant took on a new name with the arrival of French chef Marc Ehrler. Now known as the Stonehouse, Ehrler characterizes the restaurant's cuisine as "fresh." The fixed menu is adapted every three months to make maximum use of fresh ingredients in the Ranch garden. "It makes it interesting and motivates me to try new things," Ehrler told me. Ehler has his own herb garden, and cures the restaurant's meat and fish in a smoker. Breakfast and lunch are also available, and all meals can be served in your cottage.

San Ysidro Ranch is just five minutes from downtown Montecito and Santa Barbara. Few inns can provide such privacy, comfort, calmness and personalized service so close to the hustle and bustle of civilization.

SAN YSIDRO RANCH, 900 San Ysidro Lane, Montecito, CA 93108; 805-969-5046. A 43-guest cottage (private baths) California-country retreat at the foot of the Santa Ynez Mountains. Open year-round; 2-night minimum. Very private. European plan. Breakfast, lunch, and dinner available. Tennis, swimming, golf, horseback riding, hiking. Five min. from Santa Barbara. Pets allowed with deposit. Claude Rouas and Bob Harmon, Owners; Michael Ullman, General manager; Jan Martin Winn, Manager.

Directions: Take the San Ysidro exit off Hwy. 101; head toward the hills. Follow San Ysidro Rd. to San Ysidro Lane, which ends at the Ranch.

THE SEAL BEACH INN AND GARDENS
Seal Beach, California (1981)

I became a Marjorie Bettenhausen fan when I first visited the Seal Beach Inn, which at that time was little more than a motel from the 1920s. It had one very important thing going for it, however, and that was Marjorie's vision, talent, and enthusiasm. In the intervening years, she has developed it into a showplace that welcomes guests from all over the world, as well as stars from nearby Hollywood.

Here are some observations from Marjorie herself about the inn: "It is a fairyland of brick courtyards, old ornate street lights, blue canopies, objets d'art, fountains, shuttered windows, window boxes, and vines. We are a family-run inn, a place of character, a thoughtfully designed place where guests are pampered and our service is friendly and caring.

"From the very start we saw the opportunity to create an inn that would have the ambience of inns that we have visited in southern France. We've been very fortunate since 1980, when you first visited, Norman, in having been discovered by many feature writers and also in having been on TV many times."

The French Mediterranean appearance is enhanced by the truly extraordinary gardens. All of the lodging rooms are named after flowers, including fuchsia, gardenia, and camellia. The full-time gardener keeps the flowers blooming even in winter with considerable aid from the mild year-round weather in this part of California. There are rare vines, climbing vines, flowering bushes, sweet-smelling bushes, deciduous trees, evergreen pear trees, and a wonderful variety of a cascading willowy tree that looks like a weeping willow, but really isn't. It stays green all year.

Lush plantings and antique newel posts are beside each guest room door, and in the rooms, lovely luxurious comforters and dust ruffles set off the wrought-iron headboards. The bridal chamber, with its very own veranda beside the pool, is much in demand.

In addition, there are the Royal Villas, six of the most romantic, lavish suites imaginable. Marjorie says, "In all of California there are none that are more exquisite!"

The entrance to the inn from the street is through a three-sided square, around which the guest rooms are situated, and this is indeed a flower-filled courtyard, lit by street lamps that were rescued from the scrap pile at nearby Long Beach. There is a red English telephone booth in one corner, and a kiosk (that would be quite at home in Nice) has notices of all the nearby attractions. The library is an elegant guest salon with an impressive fireplace, books, and games. Breakfast is served in a small, cozy French-style tea room, presided over by a cheerful hostess.

Breakfasts are lavish, with quiche or other intersting egg casseroles,

freshly squeezed juices, home-baked pastries, breads, cereals, their own granola, seasonal fruits, cheeses, freshly ground Viennese coffee and an assortment of imported teas. A special treat is the giant chocolate chip cookie presented to each arriving guest.

Marjorie maintains that it takes many years to establish an inn par excellence and declares that "we finally are reaching the end of inn adolescence and moving into golden maturity. We want to be the best inn in the state, not just in beauty but in the warmth and love in which we serve."

So now it can easily be seen why I am a Marjorie Bettenhausen fan.

THE SEAL BEACH INN AND GARDENS, 212 5th St., Seal Beach, CA 90740; 213-493-2416 or 213-430-3915. A 22-guestroom (private baths) village inn located in a quiet residential area of an attractive town, 300 yds. from beach. King, queen, and double beds available. Breakfast only meal served. Restaurants within walking distance. Open all year. Near Disneyland, Knott's Berry Farm, Lion Country Safari, Catalina Island (20 mi. offshore), and California mountains and lakes 2 hrs. away. Long Beach Playhouse, Long Beach Music Center nearby. Swimming pool on grounds. Tennis, beach, biking, skating, golf nearby. No pets. Marjorie and Jack Bettenhausen, Innkeepers. (See Index for rates.)

Directions: From Los Angeles Airport take Hwy. 405 Freeway south to Seal Beach Blvd. exit. Turn left toward the beach, right on the Pacific Coast Hwy., left on 5th St. in Seal Beach, which is the first stoplight after main street. Inn is on the left, 2 blocks toward the beach on 5th St.

THE SHERMAN HOUSE
San Francisco, California (1990)

"Luxury, elegance, and tasteful comfort" is the way The Sherman House is described in its brochure. I would add impeccable service and graciousness. I requested a ride from the airport and knew my stay would be a special one when I was promptly met by the hotel's chauffeur in a vintage car. As I settled into the comfort of the leather seats, I readied myself for a visit that would take me back to a time when travelers were treated as if they were guests in a private home.

The Sherman House is chiefly Italiante in style. The magnificent, asymmetrical white-frame three-story structure is located in the prestigious Pacific Heights area of San Francisco, near famed Union Street with its unique boutiques.

In January 1981, Manouchehr Mobedshahi, an Iranian-born San Franciscan entrepreneur, purchased the Sherman House and began major restoration work. Both the main house and the original Carriage House were lifted so new concrete basements and foundations could be poured. Additionally, new steel beam supports were added to bring the buildings up to seismic code.

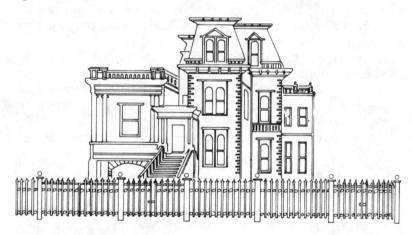

Since the home is a Designated Historical Landmark, no torch or chemicals could be used to remove the peeling exterior and interior paint, so it had to be painstakingly stripped by hand. Restoring the Sherman House to its original condition was quite a feat, but the results are spectacular, right down to the recreated plaster ornamentation and entrance posts and handrails. Besides the home's magnificently refinished hardwood floors, the solarium was refloored in black and white marble, and the bathrooms were done in black South American granite.

Both the public and individual rooms have been sumptuously decorated in French Second Empire, Austrian Biedermeier, and English Jacobean motifs and antiques. I was escorted to my room by the concierge as there is no traditional check-in. If requested, your luggage will be unpacked by the attentive staff, only one of the many services available, including tailoring, securing of opera and symphony tickets, and personalized shopping. If you must work while you travel, special arrangements can be made for stenographic, word-processing, translation, telegram, and telex services.

The elegant bedrooms have marble wood-burning fireplaces, draped canopy beds, and feather-down comforters. Modern features include wet bars, wall safes, televisions (even in the bathrooms!), and whirlpool baths. There are spectacular views of the Palace of Fine Arts, the Golden Gate, San Francisco Bay, and the hills of Marin.

I particularly enjoyed spending time in the hotel's large west wing, which consists of a three-story music and reception room, containing a platform for musicians, and a ceiling glowing with an ornate, leaded-glass skylight. The blue finch in the room's birdcage may cheerfully perform for you as you sit.

The furnished gallery is also the spot to meet before a lavish dinner. Guests are served appetizers as the maitre d' discusses the evening's menu, which may include such specialties as duck breast with cognac and truffles. Prices are not given unless requested, and can run from $35 to $80 per person. Swiss chef Neal Langermann shops daily for fresh ingredients and will prepare special menus for guests. Following appetizers, guests are seated in the dining room where their previously ordered first course is served.

Just before leaving, I spent a few quiet moments in the replicated Victorian greenhouse to steep in the wonderful service and luxury I had experienced.

THE SHERMAN HOUSE, 2160 Green St., San Francisco, CA 94123; 415-563-3600. A 15-guestroom (private baths) intimate, restored Victorian in San Francisco's elegant Pacific Heights district. Open all year. Queen and twin beds. European plan. Near shops, restaurants, theater, and most sightseeing areas. Full concierge services. Limited smoking. No pets. Manou and Vesta Mobedshahi, Owners; Michael Levy, Manager.

Directions: From San Francisco Airport, go north on Hwy. 101. Follow signs to Golden Gate Bridge and exit on Franklin St. Bear left up the hill and continue for 18 blocks to Green St. Turn left on Green St. Sherman House is 5½ blocks down on the right.

TIMBERHILL RANCH
Cazadero, California (1990)

Standing in a clearing beneath spicy-scented, majestic redwoods, a thousand feet above the Pacific Ocean's coastal fog and wind, I could see why, in the 1800s, the Pomo Indians had chosen this sheltered bit of Northern California coast for their winter home. The serenity is a balm. Apparently the owners of Timberhill Ranch, Barbara Farrell, Tarran McDaid, and Michael Riordan, felt the same way when they left hectic corporate positions in San Francisco and purchased Timberhill.

Formerly a working ranch, and then the location of an alternative school, the main ranch house and ten cottages sit on 10 secluded acres. The ranch's other 70 acres are covered by meadows peppered with wild iris, bluebells, and forget-me-nots. Groves of blood red madrone and oak and fir neighbor stately redwoods. The ranch is surrounded by the 317-acre Kruse Rhododendron Reserve and the 6,000-acre Salt Point State Park. Miles of hiking trails traverse the park and meander to the sea.

As I hefted my bags, the shadow of a red-tailed hawk crossed over me. Watching this graceful bird ride an updraft, I hoped my grandfather had been right when he told me that it was a good omen.

The shake cedar exterior of the main ranch house may look rustic, but the interior will immediately dispel any worries of "roughing it." A cozy, cushion-strewn sofa beckons guests to sink in front of the large stone fireplace. Smaller grouped seating areas encourage conversation. And books, magazines, puzzles, cards, and games offer entertainment after the last bit of daylight steals the spectacular views.

Fresh flowers appear in abundance in the cottages as well as the main lodge. The cottages are also rustic cedar, and are comfortable and romantic. Each has a wood-burning fireplace, with wood already cut and stacked, mini bar, coffee maker, reading lamps and arm chairs, and luxury amenities like fluffy robes and hairdryers. Colorful quilts, handmade by local artisans, adorn the beds. Private decks look onto views of the surrounding natural landscape, not on other cottages or the two world-class tennis courts or heated swimming pool and hot tub.

Should you choose to become somewhat of a hermit, you can easily stay at your cottage until dinner, since breakfast is delivered to your door. Lunch can be arranged and the staff will make up a picnic basket if you decide to do some hiking.

At dinnertime, a wonderful six-course meal is served in the intimate candlelight dining room. The meal begins with a selection of appetizers, and leisurely progresses through soup, salad, a palate-cleansing sorbet, and entree and dessert. The menu changes nightly as the chef uses only the freshest of ingredients, and can include such specialties as roast Petaluma duckling with sun dried figs, or grilled Pacific salmon with

tomatillo coulis. All breads, pastries, and desserts are homemade, and a good selection of California wines is available.

On Sunday afternoon I decided that my hedonistic behavior needed to be tempered, so I grabbed my tennis racket for a bit of lobbing at the courts. Just as I bounced my first ball, two of the ranch's ducks, Mutt and Jeff, hurriedly waddled down, hoping to beg a treat. After greeting them, I turned back to my bucket of balls and, again, was crossed by the shadow of the redtail. This time I knew my grandfather had been right. It was a good omen. My stay at Timberhill Ranch had been nothing less than exceptional.

TIMBERHILL RANCH, 35755 Hauser Bridge Rd., Cazadero, CA 95421; 707-847-3258. A 10-cottage (private baths) secluded ranch resort on the spectacular northern Sonoma County coast. Open all year. Queen-size beds; twins available. Modified American plan. Handicapped and non-smoking cottages provided. Tennis courts, heated pool, and hiking trails on property. Close to beaches, whale watching, golf, and art galleries. Barbara Farrell, Tarran McDaid, and Michael Riordan, Owners-hosts.

Directions: Take Hwy. 101 north from San Francisco to the Washington St. exit in Petaluma. Go west thru Bodega Bay and continue north on Hwy. 1; 5 mi. past Jenner, turn right on Meyers Grade Rd. Stay on paved road for 13.6 mi. The inn is on the right.

UNION STREET INN
San Francisco, California (1981)

"We are Edwardian, not Victorian."

Helen Stewart and I were having breakfast, seated in the sunny garden at the rear of the Union Street Inn. The fragrance of lilacs, camellias, and violets filled the air, and an occasional hummingbird darted from blossom to blossom. Some guests were enjoying breakfast on the spacious deck overlooking the garden, and there was the unmistakable aroma of fresh coffee and croissants. In this quiet retreat it was difficult to realize that we were in the heart of one of San Francisco's most attractive shopping and entertainment areas. "I say Edwardian," Helen continued, "because we're rather proud of the fact that in a city that has so much Victoriana, we are a bit different. The Edwardians, already into the 20th century, were less ostentatious than their elders. Their ornamentation was tempered by a new conservatism, and we like to feel that many of our decorations and furnishings are understatements."

Helen is a former San Francisco schoolteacher, who found herself involved in a mid-life career change. She restored and remodeled this handsome turn-of-the-century building, using tones and textures that are not only in the period, but also increase the feeling of hospitality.

The bedrooms have such intriguing names as Wildrose, Holly, Golden Gate, and English Garden.

Two of the bedrooms have queen-sized beds with canopies, two have

gleaming brass beds; all have really impressive, carefully chosen antiques. The brochure of the inn explains the different color schemes for each room. "If reservations are made sufficiently in advance, and the guests can anticipate a mood, these can all be coordinated." Helen made this comment with the faint suggestion of a twinkle.

My room had one of the queen-sized beds with very pleasant dark green wallpaper and matching draperies, which were most helpful in keeping the sun from intruding too early. The walls were adorned with two of the well-known Degas prints of ballet dancers. I thought they were quite appropriate, remembering King Edward's fondness for pretty women.

One end of the room had been turned into an alcove containing a rather elegantly decorated wash basin with mirrors and generous, fluffy towels. A very handsome antique mahogany dressing table had a three-way oval mirror. This is typical of the appointments of the other bedrooms, and I found many welcome living plants in all of the bedrooms.

Helen has converted the old carriage house at the bottom of the garden into a very fetching accommodation, with a large bay window overlooking the garden, and its own Jacuzzi. The garden has been remodeled, and a Victorian-looking curved fence with a lovely old-fashioned gate has been added. It truly does resemble an English garden.

A glance at the comments from the guest book told me the story: "Happiness is staying here!" "What a refreshing change from typical hotel stays." "Like returning to visit an old 'friend.'" "We'll be back for a second honeymoon."

Very fine restaurants are within walking distance.

UNION STREET HOTEL, 2229 Union St., San Francisco, CA 94123; 415-346-0424. A 6-guestroom (private baths) bed-and-breakfast inn. King and queen beds available. Convenient to all of the San Francisco attractions. Breakfast only meal served. Open every day except Christmas and New Year's. No pets. Helen Stewart, Owner-hostess. (See Index for rates.)

Directions: Take the Van Ness exit from Rte. 101 to Union St.; turn left. The inn is between Fillmore and Steiner on the left side of the street.

"European plan" means that rates for rooms and meals are separate. "American plan" means that meals are included in the cost of the room. "Modified American plan" means that breakfast and dinner are included in the cost of the room. The rates at some inns include a continental breakfast with the lodging.

VILLA ROYALE
Palm Springs, California (1989)

The sights, sounds, and scents of summer were all around me—the tinkling plash of a fountain, the deeper splash of a diver plunging into the swimming pool, the twitter of birds, the hum of an occasional bee, and everywhere the color and fragrance of flowers. I was leaning back in a chaise longue in a little hideaway garden corner with a tinkling fountain and a Schubert serenade floating on the air. This was early in March, when there was still snow at the top of Mount San Jacinto, towering 8,500 feet above the desert floor, where lively, toney Palm Springs forms a green and glamorous oasis.

Earlier that March day I had found Villa Royale at the east end of town, sheltered from the wind blowing off the desert, and within its cluster of low, hacienda-style adobe buildings, red-tile roofs, and lush garden courtyards, I found a European ambience.

"We have architecturally altered each guest room to represent a different country," Chuck Murawski was taking me on the grand tour, after our initial meeting in the lobby. It was clear from the outset that gardens and flowers are an important part of the decor here. The lobby, with its Spanish tile floor, fireplace, many windows, and french doors brings the outside in, and that means cascades of bougainvillea, frothy hibiscus, roses, petunias, and flowering shrubs and trees of all kinds.

Chuck and I threaded our way over winding, tree-shaded, flower-lined brick paths and around little private gardens and patios as we looked in on one fabulous room after another. He and his partner, Bob Lee, have roamed the world over, and the vast booty they have collected now adorns the rooms of this very special inn.

There's an elegant Monte Carlo suite reflecting colors and motifs from the south of France with tiled floors, stucco walls, a king-sized bed, canopied and curtained in a homespun fabric; the Greek Room is decorated with things Greek, even to the olive tree on the patio. Every room evokes the style and atmosphere of the country it represents, not only in its furniture but in the wall treatments, fixtures, pictures, and artifacts. Among those countries represented are Spain, Morocco, Germany, Italy, and England.

"This is our outdoor living room," Chuck said, as we strolled through a covered patio with a fireplace and tables and wicker chairs. "Sometimes there are three or four languages going on at the same time."

Over a delicious glass of iced tea, seated in the delightful little breakfast arcade with its series of arched french doors looking out on the courtyard and one of the two swimming pools, Chuck told me that they have carried their international theme into their dining room.

"We serve a different cuisine from a different country each night; it's called the Europa Dinner. We also offer other à la carte choices, such as chicken with lemon and capers, oriental chicken with hoisan sauce, steak au poivre, a pasta dish, and fish, along with appetizers, soup, salad, sourdough rolls, and some wonderful desserts."

The dining room is very romantic with little alcoves, an indoor-outdoor patio, a fireplace, and classical music.

If there were an ocean nearby, I'd think I was on the Riviera. I am happy to welcome the Villa Royale to *Country Inns and Back Roads.*

VILLA ROYALE, 1620 Indian Trail, Palm Springs, CA 92264; 619-327-2314. A 34-guestroom (private baths) luxurious but informal desert inn, 80 mi. from Los Angeles. King, queen, and twin beds available. Some suites with kitchens. Air conditioners; some fireplaces and private spas. Complimentary continental breakfast. Dinner by advance reservation. Open year-round; 2-day minimum stay on weekends; 3 days on holidays. Wheelchair access. Bicycles and 2 swimming pools on grounds. Tennis, golf, celebrity tours, fashionable shops and restaurants, horseback riding, museums, art galleries, national parks, Indian canyons and waterfalls, balloon rides nearby. No children. No pets. Charles Murawski and Bob Lee, Owners-hosts. (See Index for rates.)

Directions: Palm Springs has an international airport. By car from L.A., take the San Bernardino Freeway (Rte. 10) to Rte. 111, which becomes Palm Canyon in Palm Springs. Continue thru downtown (about 4 mi.) to Indian Trail.

VINTNERS INN
Santa Rosa, California (1990)

At the hub of the northern California wine country, Vintners Inn offers the ambience of a village in the south of France, right down to its house wine made from grapes grown on the property. Owners John and Francisca Duffy set out to recreate the French Mediterranean feeling when they began thinking about a design for their inn. The Duffys traveled to Europe and searched the regions surrounding Provence, photographing historical buildings and hamlets to garner information and inspiration.

John, an ex-nuclear physicist, and Francisca, a former Pan Am flight attendant, met during a tennis game. Neither will tell who won, but the match led to marriage and their shared vision for the Vintners Inn.

A native of Belgium, Francisca supervised the decoration of the inn's forty-four red-tile-roofed units. The units are joined by matching tiled walkways and surround a central plaza with a tranquil fountain. Arched windows, wrought-iron railings, and patios create a relaxed ambience. Antique European pine furnishings have been restored and refinished to complement the charming country-print fabrics and floral-patterned wallpapers. The rooms offer beamed ceilings, wood-burning fireplaces, wet bars, and views of the lush 45 acres of Pinot Blanc, French Colombard, and Sauvignon Blanc vineyards. All rooms have private baths with luxurious oversized oval bathtubs.

The lobby sports an enormous wine basket, and along with old antique farm equipment decorating the walls, creates an old-world atmosphere. Plan to enjoy a glass of 1985 gold medal Sauvignon Blanc as you relax in the outdoor sundeck Jacuzzi and watch the colorful hot-air balloons as they drift overhead. There is also a VCR with a good movie library available for guests.

Breakfast is served in the sunlit dining room overlooking the courtyard. You'll enjoy a sumptuous buffet of fresh fruit and juices, cereals, homemade breads, and croissants along with teas and rich fresh-ground coffee. A luscious Belgian waffle (and Francisca knows how to make a *real* Belgian waffle), slathered with whipped cream and seasonal berries, can be made to order. For a romantic morning, you may choose to take your breakfast to your room.

When the Duffys designed their inn, they also provided a building to house the acclaimed restaurant John Ash & Company. Owner-chef John Ash focuses on local foods. He carefully selects produce from nearby farms, oysters from the Tomales Bay, chicken and game birds grown on Sonoma ranches, and the county's famous cheeses. The freshest of seafood is purchased from northern California and Oregon.

I had a wonderful dinner that began with a salad of fresh Oregon

scallops sprinkled with coriander. A flaky California sea bass, grilled with fresh herbs and served on a bed of flavorful eggplant came next, followed by a palate-cleansing sorbet of mandarin oranges.

My entree of boned quail stuffed with a forcemeat of veal, walnuts, and leeks, served on top of fresh spinach, was done to perfection.

To finish, I sampled local goat cheeses, with baby greens and roasted walnuts. Elegant desserts will certainly tempt you, but I just couldn't eat another bite. The restaurant's wine list is excellent and has been given the Sweepstakes Award for 1985, 1986, and 1987 by the Sonoma County Harvest Fair.

John and Francisca are happy to help you plan tours of the area and will make recommendations on wineries, restaurants, points of interest, and picnic areas. Guest privileges can be arranged at nearby clubs for tennis, swimming, golf, and racquetball.

The Sonoma County wine country is in one of the most beautiful valleys in northern California. As I stood on my balcony overlooking the lovely manicured vineyards, I could see why John and Francisca chose this very special spot for their inn.

VINTNERS INN, 4350 Barnes Rd., Santa Rosa, CA 95403; 707-575-7350 or 800-421-2584. A 44-guestroom (private baths) inn complex nestled in the center of a vineyard in the heart of the Sonoma Valley in northern California. Open year-round. Queen-size beds. Breakfast included. Dinner at John Ash & Co. Accommodations for handicapped guests. Children welcome. Pets by arrangement. John and Francisca Duffy, Owners-hosts; Cindy Young, Manager.

Directions: From Hwy. 101 about 3 mi. north of Santa Rosa, take River Rd. turnoff west. First left turn is Barnes Rd.

THE WINE COUNTRY INN
St. Helena, California (1978)

It was a wonderful day in March. There were new leaves on the trees, the spring flowers were in profusion, wild geese were flying, and the small vineyards in the little valley just below the inn were starting to perk up. The natural wild mustard, lupines, poppies, and live oak trees blended with plantings of oleanders, petunias, and Chinese pistachios. This inn, which I saw almost the first day it was opened, has now taken on the patina that comes as buildings put on additional years.

Three or four of us who were attending a meeting of the CIBR innkeepers were seated around the pool at the Wine Country Inn, enjoying the warm, welcome sunshine.

One of the visiting innkeepers complimented Jim Smith, the innkeeper, on what was then a new pool and Jacuzzi. "Thank you very much," he responded. "I've never received as many compliments about the inn as I have this year and a lot of that has to do with the pool. It's become a popular area for socializing and swapping stories as to which winery tours to go on and which restaurants to enjoy."

The guest rooms are furnished almost entirely in antiques; some have intimate balconies and some have patios leading to the lawn. Many of the rooms have fireplaces, canopied beds, tufted bedspreads, and handmade quilts, along with a generous supply of magazines and books, and big, comfortable, fluffy pillows.

Visitors to the Napa Valley enjoy visits to the many wineries, as well as to mineral baths, geysers, a petrified forest, and several Robert Louis Stevenson memorial sites. There are also a number of antique shops in the

area. Dotted with century-old stone bridges, pump houses, barns, and stone buildings, all of which are a delight to both painter and photographer, the manicured agricultural beauty of the valley contrasts with the rugged, tree-covered hills surrounding it.

In the many years since the Wine Country Inn was the first bed and breakfast inn in the Napa Valley there have been other inns created. However, I am convinced that it is still for me the most enjoyable experience in the valley. Patience and constant attention to details and maintenance have allowed the building, the trees, shrubs, and flowers to take on a real character of their own. It's hard to realize that it was actually built in 1975 as an inn. The architecture is batten board with a center section of stone and a mansard roof that is quite in keeping with the other winery architecture of this part of California.

On a more personal note I have to say that becoming acquainted with people like Ned and Marge Smith and their sons, Jim and Jeff, and watching the progress of such families over the years has always been a great source of satisfaction for me. Jim's little four-year-old Michael and his baby sister, Kelly Elizabeth, who will be close to two years old by the time this book goes to press, are well on their way to becoming third-generation innkeepers.

I think other innkeepers in California are fortunate to have such a model inn after which to fashion themselves. The care and consideration that have gone into the designing, and the result, prove that a country inn doesn't have to be old to be legendary.

It's the spirit that matters.

THE WINE COUNTRY INN, 1152 Lodi Lane, St. Helena, CA 94574; 707-963-7077. A 25-room (private baths) country inn in the Napa wine valley of California, about 70 mi. from San Francisco. Queen, double, and twin beds available. Continental breakfast served to houseguests; no other meals served. Restaurants within walking distance. Open daily except the week before and including Christmas. This inn is within driving distance of a great many wineries and also the Robert Louis Stevenson Museum. Swimming pool and spa on grounds. Golf and tennis nearby. No children. No pets. Jim Smith, Innkeeper. (See Index for rates.)

Directions: From San Francisco take the Oakland Bay Bridge to Hwy. 80. Travel north to the Napa cutoff. Stay on Hwy. 29 through the town of St. Helena, for 1¾ mi. north to Lodi Lane, then turn east ¼ mi. to inn.

The date in parenthesis in the heading represents the first year the inn appeared in the pages of Country Inns and Back Roads.

PARADISE RANCH INN
Grants Pass, Oregon (1988)

The Paradise Ranch Inn's land was originally a working ranch, homesteaded in 1913, with the full complement of horses, cattle, and other livestock. Nestled in the beautiful Rogue River Valley of southern Oregon, it has become a resort-inn with something for everyone. There are a heated swimming pool and spa, jogging and bicycle trails, a 4-acre pond stocked with rainbow trout and other fish, a lake with swans and ducks, a chip-and-putt green, horses and trails, and white-water rafting on the Rogue River. As if that weren't enough, there is also a recreation barn where any number of activities and special events take place.

Mattie and Oliver Raymond have run the ranch for nineteen years with the help of other family members, extending their hospitality to their many guests. It is a particularly appealing place for families and children. Unfortunately, this year will be the last one that the Raymonds will be in residence; they have had to sell the property, since small, wonderful resorts like this one have an increasingly difficult time surviving.

The white rambling ranch house, white fences, and neat outbuildings set against the backdrop of rolling green meadows make a delightful picture. The guest rooms are comfortably and individually furnished with beamed ceilings and double and queen-size beds.

Mattie is justly proud of their new chef, Cheryl Anderson, a graduate of the Western Culinary Institute in Portland. Cheryl uses fresh fruit sauces rather than creamed sauces over meat and fish, giving the dishes very unique and exotic flavors. The dining room has windows on three sides and overlooks the lake, with breathtaking views of the Cascade Mountains.

Pet fish in the Garden Pond have been trained to avoid fish hooks, so prospective fishermen are cautioned not to drop a hook. However, all paraphernalia necessary for fishing can be obtained from the ranch for fishing in the lake. "We use barbless hooks," Ollie told me, "because the fish are so plentiful we feel it is not very sporting otherwise." I guess it depends on the fisherman, right? I certainly would have done better with a barbed hook.

The game room in the barn has three pool tables, a beautiful ping-pong table, and shuffleboard. There's also a piano, and on cool days a cheery fire burns in the fireplace.

So, take advantage of this last year before the inn will be closed for changes. The new owners are planning to add a championship golf course, thirty-two additional rooms, a lodge room, a fitness room, a covered tennis court, and a bubble pool. While these changes will be grand, there is something so wonderful about the intimate quality of small resorts—a dying breed. If you enjoy white-water rafting or helping with the cattle

roundup, or just simply relaxing under a tree, Paradise Ranch Inn
shouldn't be missed.

*PARADISE RANCH INN, 7000 Monument Dr., Grants Pass, OR 97526;
503-479-4333. An 18-guestroom (private baths) ranch-inn nestled in the
beautiful mountains of the Rogue River Valley. Open year-round. Restaurant open to public; closed Mon. and Tues. Heated swimming pool, hot
tub, lighted all-weather tennis courts, fishing, surrey rides, hayrides,
trail rides, cattle roundup, recreational center, and children-watching
available on grounds. Spectacular Rogue River raft trips and all-day
horseback riding, Shakespearean Festival, Crater Lake, and Oregon
caves nearby. Children welcome. Mattie and Oliver Raymond, Owners-
hosts.*

*Directions: From the Bay Area follow Rte. 101 north to Crescent City and
Rte. 199 to Grants Pass; turn north on Rte. 5 and exit at Merlin. Go under
Rte. 5, turn right on Monument Dr. for 2 ½ mi. Ranch is on the left.*

*"European plan" means that rates for rooms and meals are separate.
"American plan" means that meals are included in the cost of the room.
"Modified American plan" means that breakfast and dinner are included
in the cost of the room. The rates at some inns include a continental
breakfast with the lodging.*

STEAMBOAT INN
Steamboat, Oregon (1984)

I was on the Umpqua Highway (Route 138) on my way for a visit with Jim and Sharon Van Loan at the Steamboat Inn, a country inn that is a steelhead fisherman's dream.

This is the heartland of Oregon, and after a pleasant trip from Crescent City and Eureka, California, up Routes 101 and 199, I thrilled to the scenery on I-5 from Grants Pass to Roseburg.

Now, having left the Interstate and turning east, I was getting the feeling of what inland Oregon is really like. There were many cattle farms and fruit orchards gradually giving way to the beautiful upland country, and soon the road was running parallel to the North Umpqua River.

This idyllic trip along the river ended as I arrived at the Steamboat Inn and was immediately taken in tow by both Jim and Sharon, who are two very friendly people, quite suited to innkeeping.

I was shown to one of the eight rustic cabins, all of which are joined by a deck that extends out over the river, and soon I was enveloped in the euphoria created by the melodious, ever-present sounds of the water rushing by on its way to the Pacific Ocean.

I joined the other guests on the new back porch of the lodge in time to be well introduced by Jim and Sharon and to admire the art that lines the walls. After hors d'oeuvres we were all invited to sit down around the great table (actually, a huge pine slab) in the dining area and enjoy the main course. Sharon explained that a typical dinner includes several vegetables, homemade bread or pasta, and a selected entrée of the evening. Our main dish that evening, appropriately enough, was game hens with a fruited wild rice stuffing, which won the $5,000 grand prize in a Best-of-Country-Inns recipe contest in a recent national competition.

Guests for longer stays at Steamboat will not have the same main course at dinner twice. By the way, dinner is generally served a half hour after dark each night during the summer months and around seven during the winter.

Following dinner, I had a chance to talk with Jim and Sharon about how they came to be located here. "Originally, we came because of Jim's enthusiasm for fly-fishing. Also, Jim started attending a hotel management school as a result of his experiences with visiting inns in Japan," Sharon responded. "Then it occurred almost simultaneously to all of us that this would be a wonderful place to raise a family, and it seemed like a viable way of involving everyone and still being able to make financial progress."

Jim continued, "Although fly-fishing for steelhead is a big activity here about three months of the year, the rest of the time there are many nonfishing guests who arrive with the intention of remaining for one night and who extend their stay for two or three. It's an excellent place for families.

"Our new hideaway cottages on Steamboat Creek Road feature a master bedroom with a king-sized bed, a bathroom with a soaking tub, a living room, kitchen facilities, a loft that can sleep two people, and a deck."

"Our guests enjoy the wonderful presence of the river," Sharon commented. "They can explore the waterfalls, swim in the creek, and return at night to put their feet up on the porch railing and read a good book. We also have frequent cooking classes that many of our guests enjoy. Information about classes is included in our brochure."

Incidentally, Sharon and Pat Lee have collaborated on a spectacular cookbook, *Thyme and the River,* which features gorgeous color photographs of the North Umpqua River and some of the menus served at the inn, as well as a history of the area and the inn. I think this just might become a collector's item.

STEAMBOAT INN, Steamboat, OR 97447; 503-496-3495 or 503-498-2411. An 8-cabin and 4-cottage (private baths) rustic riverside inn in one of Oregon's most spectacular river canyon areas, 40 mi. west of Diamond Lake and 70 mi. east of Crater Lake. King, queen, and double beds available. Open all year. Breakfast, lunch, and dinner served daily; breakfast is not included in the room rate. Dinner ½ hr. after sundown in summer, 7 p.m. in winter. Fishing, backpacking, and hiking in abundance. Sharon and Jim Van Loan, Owners-hosts; Patricia Lee, Manager. (See Index for rates.)

Directions: From Roseburg drive 38 mi. east on Rte. 138.

TU TU' TUN LODGE
Gold Beach, Oregon (1989)

My friend Jerry Arndt and I had just arrived after a glorious drive up the Pacific Coast Highway and through the redwoods. I must warn all shutterbugs to allow time for plenty of picture-taking stops driving through this spectacular country.

Tu Tu' Tun (pronounced to-TOOT'n) is right on the Rogue River, just seven miles from the ocean. The name comes from an Indian tribe that once occupied this river bluff; a rough translation is "people close to the river."

My first impression as we drove into the grounds was of two rambling, weathered wood buildings with lots of glass, surrounded by beautiful plantings of native shrubs, bright blooms, and a manicured apple orchard.

True to their reputation as gracious hosts, Laurie and Dirk Van Zante greeted us and invited us into the main lodge, where a fire crackled in the massive stone fireplace.

Since it had been necessary for me to visit Tu Tu' Tun in April, during its off season, I asked Dirk about some of their customs. "Well," this handsome young man replied, "as the sun sets on the western hills, guests listen for the ringing of the big brass bell, summoning them to join us for hors d'oeuvres, one of which on occasion has a mysterious ingredient. The guests have a lot of fun guessing, and Laurie enjoys mixing a concoction to reward the winner!"

As I understand it, during this gathering time Dirk and Laurie have a chance to mingle with the guests and tell tall tales of the Rogue. Guests love to share their stories of their day fishing or wild river boating. Birds, bear, beaver, and otter vie for the first place with the biggest catch of the day, although children may vote for how many deer they have fed in the orchard that afternoon.

As dinner begins, Dirk welcomes people into the dining room, where Lazy Susan tables are decorated with fresh flowers. Dirk seats the guests by name, another of the many ways people are made to feel special at Tu Tu' Tun. "We have a four-course set daily menu," Laurie told me, "including such items as fresh chinook salmon baked with lemon butter and served with caper sauce, or marinated rolled chicken breast in a light shallot Parmesan sauce. Creamy zucchini soup, salad made from locally grown greens, freshly baked rolls, and raspberry sorbet are among the many family recipes."

The madrona wood fires lit on the terrace during dinner provide a dramatic view for diners, as well as a gathering place after dinner where conversations continue. "I tend the fires," Dirk explained, "and I'll tell everyone when I see the salmon jumping or a bald eagle soaring overhead."

Furnishings are attractive, comfortable, and contemporary, and everything is immaculate. There are two suites in the main building and sixteen rooms in a motel-style building, where each room is decorated with logging, fishing, or mining artifacts. "Rooms are named after riffles in the river, and many returning guests request 'their' room, which might be 'Lobster Riffle,' 'Bear Riffle,' or 'Hog Eddy.' They have their favorite view and can enjoy reminiscing over what they wrote in the log book last season." Every room has a private balcony or porch overlooking the river, and there are always fresh flowers and plants.

This is experiencing the wilderness in a most civilized manner with two charming innkeepers. We are happy to welcome them to our pages.

TU TU' TUN LODGE, 96550 North Bank Rogue, Gold Beach, OR 97444; 503-247-6664. A 16-guestroom, 2-suite (private baths) contemporary lodge on the Rogue River, in a wilderness setting, 7 mi. from the Pacific Ocean in southern Oregon. European plan. Lunch served daily to registered guests only. Breakfast and dinner served to travelers by reservation. Breakfast and lunch baskets available. Open April 29 to Nov. 1. Heated pool, pitch-and-putt course, antique pool table, antique player piano, horseshoes, private dock and hiking trails on premises. Guides for steelhead and salmon fishing, whitewater excursions, hiking, scenic drives and flights, beachcombing, golf, horseback riding nearby. Pets welcome. Dirk and Laurie Van Zante, Owners-hosts. (See Index for rates.) Directions: From Rte. 101 follow signs for 7 mi. up north side of river to the lodge.

THE CAPTAIN WHIDBEY INN
Coupeville, Washington (1973)

There isn't a Captain Whidbey any more, but there is a Captain John Colby Stone, who is also the innkeeper. With his Master's License from the Coast Guard, he is able to take passengers for a special cruise in his classic sloop, *Aeolus,* on the peaceful waters of Penn Cove. Gliding past the lush pastures and forests of Whidbey, guests who take this excursion might catch a glimpse of a majestic bald eagle, a great blue heron, porpoises, dolphins, or even an Orca whale.

The Captain Whidbey Inn, built in 1907 of distinctly regional peeled madrona logs, has been included in the Ebey's Landing National Historic Reserve, established by Congress. It is a romantic and rustic hideaway by the sea, on the shore of Penn Cove, with the feeling of an old-fashioned New England inn.

The natural center of the inn is the living room, with a very big fireplace made of round stones. Here, everybody—houseguests and dinner guests alike—sits around talking and leafing through the dozens of magazines.

Some of the guest rooms are upstairs in the main house and an additional number of rustic lodges, called Lagoon Rooms, overlooking their own private lake, were built in the woods across the road from the main house a few years ago, and they have recently been remodeled and soundproofed. The guest rooms are tastefully furnished with antiques, and those in the main house have down comforters and featherbeds. A nice area for general relaxing has been set aside for houseguests on the second floor with floor-to-ceiling bookshelves jampacked with books.

The gazebo by the lagoon has a two-level dining deck with a grill overlooking the Cove. It's a great place to dine on the famous Penn Cove mussels, clam chowder, grilled Northwest salmon and halibut, along with other seafoods and local fruits and vegetables. All this and warm sun, gentle breezes, and spectacular vistas, with boats and seaplanes and the fluttering burgees of West Coast yacht clubs. The Cascade Range in the east is dominated by Mount Baker, over 10,000 feet high, and Mount Olympus in the west, at almost 8,000 feet.

Penn Cove mussels are a big story here, and an annual mussel festival is held by the inn during January. There's a mussel-eating contest, a seven-course mussel dinner cooked by the fine kitchen staff, a "Mussel Beach" party, and a mussel recipe contest.

Captain Stone was named hotelier of the year in 1988 by the Washington State Lodging Association, of which he is also president. He says the most fun for him was being grand marshal of last year's Fourth of July parade.

I'm very proud of John's progress over the years. I've known him ever since he graduated from college and joined Steve and Shirlie Stone in tending the inn. I know Steve must have felt great pride in John's accomplishments.

We have lost Steve Stone, "Innkeeper Emeritus"—that wonderful Nantucketer with the unmistakable accent and the corncob pipe. John wrote to me, "For many, Steve *was* the inn, and in his memory and following his tradition we plan to keep the inn a warm, hospitable 'bit of New England' in the Northwest."

I can't think of a better tribute to his memory.

THE CAPTAIN WHIDBEY INN, 2072 W. Captain Whidbey Inn Rd., Coupeville, WA 98239; 206-678-4097. A 33-guestroom (4 cottages) (20 private baths) country inn, on protected Penn Cove off Puget Sound, 50 mi. north of Seattle, 3 mi. north of Coupeville. European plan. Breakfast, lunch, and dinner served daily to travelers. Open year-round. Boating and fishing on grounds. Golf nearby. Pets allowed in cottages only. Capt. John Colby Stone, Owner-host. (See Index for rates.)

Directions: Whidbey Island is reached year-round from the south by the Columbia Beach-Mukilteo Ferry, and during the summer and on weekends by the Port Townsend-Keystone Ferry. From the north (Vancouver, B.C., and Bellingham), take the Deception Pass Bridge to Whidbey Island.

THE SHELBURNE INN
Seaview, Washington (1988)

"This little peninsula has the cleanest estuary in the country. We're kind of hidden away here, surrounded by waters and bays." David Campiche gestured out toward the wide expanse of sandy beach as he spoke. "There's an abundance of shellfish and oysters, salmon, sturgeon, and eight to ten varieties of whitefish. There are bird sanctuaries, state parks, big rock jetties with sea lions, and whale-watching, too." We had strolled out behind the inn and past some houses to the sand dunes bordering the beach. "This is one of the longest stretches of beach you'll find in the Pacific Northwest," he said. "It goes on for thirty miles."

I had driven down the coast with John Stone of the Captain Whidbey Inn in time for dinner in the Shoalwater Restaurant, which is actually part of the Shelburne Inn. I should explain that David Campiche and Laurie Anderson tend the inn, and their partners, Tony and Ann Kischner, run the restaurant. We had a dinner there that I can only describe as exquisite, starting with a smoked fish mousse served with a variety of assorted smoked seafoods. Then there were local escargots served with Oregon hazelnuts and butter. After that came a fillet of freshly caught sturgeon with a raspberry beurre blanc, followed by a green salad, which was followed by roast quail served with a marvelous sauce made from port wine, walnuts, and cream cheese. Among the dessert offerings was Ann's Cranberry-Swirl Cheesecake with Chocolate Cranberry Glaze, which placed first in a national contest. Tony Kischner is a most innovative restaurateur, and I'm not surprised that the restaurant has acquired national recognition, which, I guess, was started by the late James Beard when he wrote about the inn and the restaurant in his syndicated column.

Since the turn of the century there has been a Shelburne Inn in the tiny coastal town of Seaview. In those days wealthy Oregonians came by steamer and a narrow-gauge railway to spend their summers in the sleepy villages on Long Beach Peninsula, lazing on the pristine beach, fishing the bounteous waters, picking mushrooms, digging for clams, and clambering over the rocks around North Head Lighthouse, where the Columbia River empties into the Pacific Ocean.

In 1977, when David and Laurie found the Shelburne Inn, it was in a sad state. "There were cans in the rooms to collect the rainfall," David told me. He is a young, handsome fellow with a very relaxed, engaging manner. His bearded face is frequently wreathed in smiles. He speaks laughingly of the hard work of restoring and renovating an old building, but the etched and stained-glass windows, the tongue-and-groove wood paneling and open-beamed ceilings, brass chandeliers, and handsome antique-furnished rooms reveal how much thought and energy he and Laurie have lavished on the inn—and still lavish.

The inn is listed on the National Register of Historic Places. Many of their antiques were collected during their travels in Europe and England; in fact, several of their stained-glass windows were rescued from an old church in Morcambe, England.

Despite their ten years of work, David says, "We're still working on it, and with our schedule we're about three years from having it right." I can't imagine how it could be any more "right" than it is, but they say they'll know when they have the rooms "just right."

Laurie, blond and blue-eyed, picked wallpapers and paint and lighting fixtures as well as the antique oak dressers and braided rugs and homespun quilts for the brass beds, and now she keeps the rooms bright with fresh flowers from their garden.

Some of their edible flowers adorned my breakfast plate the next morning, when I sat down at the big oval oak table in the pleasant lobby, where guests gather for breakfast and sociability. David and Laurie do great breakfasts. David makes his own sausage, while Laurie does all the baking.

A lovely old-fashioned inn, superb food, and friendly, hospitable hosts—I suggest you make your reservations now.

THE SHELBURNE INN, Pacific Hwy. 103 and 45th Pl., P.O. Box 250, Seaview, WA 98644; 206-642-2442. A 16-guestroom (13 private baths) Victorian village hotel on Highway 103 on the Long Beach peninsula, 120 mi. northwest of Portland, Ore. Breakfast included in room rate. Shoalwater Restaurant open for lunch and dinner daily in the summer; check winter service. Reservations recommended. Gift shop and pub on premises. State parks, sandy beach, museums, fishing, and birdwatching nearby. No pets. David Campiche and Laurie Anderson, Owners-hosts; Tony and Ann Kischner, Restaurateurs. (See Index for rates.)

Directions: Take U.S. 101 to the Long Beach Peninsula. In Seaview, take Rte. 103 a short distance. Inn is on the left.

SOOKE HARBOUR HOUSE
Sooke, British Columbia (1988)

Standing on the bluff at the top of the steps leading down to the shore, I looked out across the Strait of Juan de Fuca to the Olympic Mountain Peninsula and off to the east to East Sooke Park. Across the way was a very beautiful farm, toward which Sinclair Philip waved an arm. "Do you realize that farm is inhabited by a family of cougars? Seventy percent of the world's cougar population lives on Vancouver Island." I was amazed to hear that. Sinclair, a handsome, dark-haired young man with a neatly clipped beard, continued, "You can see deer on that farm and on our property, too. Harbor seals, sea lions, and otters are out there, and we frequently see gray and killer whales, too."

I had to admit this was a remarkable location for an inn, and Sinclair was certainly a walking encyclopedia on the infinite variety of animal and plant life that flourishes here on sea and land. I was looking down at a beautiful rock garden that terraced the slope, and there were many other gardens laced with little gravel paths surrounding the white clapboard inn buildings. They boasted masses of vegetables, herbs, fruits, and edible flowers. Some garden chairs were grouped on the terrace facing the water.

This is a very informal, contemporary place with an emphasis on the natural surroundings. There are lots of plants and flowers, magazines and books, and modern paintings and wall hangings. One of the two dining rooms is arranged as a sort of living/dining room with a comfortable sofa and rocking chairs grouped around a fireplace, and on the other side of the room the dining area is lined with windows overlooking the water.

Sinclair and his wife, Fredrica, with the help of friends and others, who are variously architects, artisans, and craftspeople, have created an environment that is aesthetically pleasing in every way. Many of the guest rooms have their own private gardens and porches, with double whirlpool baths placed to afford spectacular views of the ocean.

Every room has a special theme that is carried out in the decor; for instance, the Herb Garden Room is surrounded by herbs, and the hand-painted ceramic tiles in the bathroom depict various herbs. This is a split-level room with a fireplace and a private porch with a hot tub for two. (All of the rooms have fireplaces.) Stained-glass windows made with real underwater objects decorate the Underwater Garden Room.

Sinclair was telling me about the Indian Room. "This is the largest and most spectacular room we have, with a balcony extending the entire length of the room. There is a bathtub for two in front of the two-sided fireplace with a view of the ocean. It has multiple skylights, a vaulted ceiling, and is full of Indian artifacts and masks. Victor Newman, a very well-known Kwakiutl carver, helped decorate it."

Fredrica was born and raised in France, and she and Sinclair met in Nice on the Riviera. This unusual and talented couple found Sooke

Harbour House in 1979, and in the intervening years they have established an international reputation for their imaginative and creative cuisine. With the abundance of the sea just outside their kitchen door, the daily changing menu features such unusual items as sea urchin, octopus, sea cucumbers, abalone, and limpets. Their chefs concoct the delicacies that have aroused the admiration of food writers from around the world. The restaurant has been rated as one of the top ten in Canada for several years, and one year as *the* best restaurant in Canada. Besides their incredibly fresh fish and seafood specialties, they draw from their vast gardens and obtain local organically raised meats, like lamb, duck, suckling kid, squab, and young rabbit to round out their menu.

Watching the sun set over the ocean, I tried to think of someone who wouldn't love to stay here. I couldn't think of a soul.

SOOKE HARBOUR HOUSE, 1528 Whiffen Spit Rd., R.R. #4, Sooke, B.C., Canada VOS INO; 604-642-3421. A 13-guestroom (private baths) disarmingly informal country inn with a sophisticated cuisine on the west coast of Vancouver Island, 23 mi. west of Victoria. King and queen beds available. Full breakfast and light lunch included in room rate. Open year-round. Wheelchair access. Bicycles available on premises. Beachcombing, birdwatching, nature walks, Botanical Beach, kayaking, windsurfing, scuba diving, hiking in Pacific Rim park, and excellent fishing for winter Chinook and Tyee salmon nearby. Children welcome. Well-behaved pets welcome. Smoking restricted in several rooms. Fredrica and Sinclair Philip, Owners-hosts. (See Index for rates.)

Directions: From Victoria, take Hwy. 1 west to Hwy. 14. Continue on Hwy. 14 to Sooke. Turn left at Whiffen Spit Rd. (approx. 1 mi. past traffic light) and continue to inn.

THE HOMESTEAD
Midway, Utah (1989)

I felt exhilarated as I gazed far out across the plains and lush meadows to the magnificent snowcapped Mt. Timpanagos and Uinta ranges. I had no idea that Utah looked so much like Switzerland.

I was headed for the Homestead in the Heber Valley of north-central Utah; I'd been hearing good things about it. When I turned into the wide drive bordered by white fences and saw a cluster of buildings, dominated by the white manor house, amid the spacious grounds, I thought it looked very good, indeed.

Carole and Jerry Sanders are a young, enterprising, and enthusiastic couple who brought the Homestead back from the brink of disaster in the space of two years. Although they are dedicated to historic preservation, the remodeling and restoration of the buildings were only part of their plans, Jerry told me over an excellent dinner. "When Carole and I first saw this valley we were taken by its naturalness and beauty. Then I saw my two boys, ages seven and ten, chasing butterflies across the lawn, and I suddenly knew that's what I wanted the Homestead to be—a place where people could take the time to smell the roses and chase butterflies."

"Wasn't this originally a mineral hot springs resort?" I inquired. "Yes," Carole replied. "Simon Schneitter started the Schneitter House Hotel in 1886—it was later renamed the Virginia House. He was one of the many Swiss who settled in this valley, and who still retain their ethnic traditions, with special festivities on Labor Day weekend."

Other diners who were busily engaged with their dinners and their companions all seemed relaxed and happy. We were sitting in the large dining room (there are several others), with a piano and fireplace, many windows, a cart with flowers, and a number of antique pieces. The tables were nicely set with tablecloths and china. The whole aspect was most pleasant and inviting.

"We have a wonderful chef," Carole said. "He can really do anything, but we prefer to offer good country-type food, such as prime ribs and steaks. Our country-fried chicken has become quite famous." I was enjoying that country-fried chicken even as she spoke.

"Besides chasing butterflies," I asked, "what other sorts of things do your guests do?" Jerry hastened to assure me that there is literally no end of activities available. "Our indoor pool has the mineral hot springs, and there are the outdoor pool and hot tub, along with all the usual resort activities, including children's activities. We have some special programs in the planning stages, one of which is a dude-ranch week, with riding lessons, breakfast rides, and overnight pack trips. We are also planning a health and fitness retreat."

The next morning, after a continental breakfast in my very attractive

room in the Virginia House, which is run as a B&B and has a lovely little solarium and a hot tub, I was given a tour around the inn and the grounds. The guest rooms in each of the several buildings are decorated in a different motif. They are all most inviting and absolutely spotless.

There are little walks threading through the lawns and gardens, and there are sixty acres of fields, streams, and meadows. And there are butterflies.

THE HOMESTEAD, 700 No. Homestead Dr., Midway, UT 84049; 801-654-1102. (Outside Utah: 800-327-7220.) A 92-guestroom (private baths) historic country resort-inn nestled in Heber Valley, one of America's most beautiful alpine valleys, 50 mi. southeast of Salt Lake City. Breakfast, lunch, and dinner served daily. European plan. (Virginia House and Milk House include continental breakfast.) Open year-round. Indoor mineral and outdoor pools, hot tub, tennis, bicycles, horseback riding, snowmobiling, xc skiing, buggy and sleigh rides, fishing, nature walks, shuffleboard, and volleyball on grounds. Golf, 4 major ski areas, Heber Valley railroad, hunting, and fishing nearby. No pets. Gerald and Carole Sanders, Owners; Britt Mathwich, Manager. (See Index for rates.)

Directions: From Salt Lake City, take I-80 east to Silver Creek Junction. Turn south on Hwy. 40/189 and in Heber City, turn west at Midway Lane (Rte. 113). Continue 5 mi. to Homestead Dr.

"European plan" means that rates for rooms and meals are separate. "American plan" means that meals are included in the cost of the room. "Modified American plan" means that breakfast and dinner are included in the cost of the room. The rates at some inns include a continental breakfast with the lodging.

BRIAR ROSE BED & BREAKFAST
Boulder, Colorado (1983)

I'm going to share a part of a sparkling letter I received from Emily Hunter, the innkeeper at the Briar Rose:

"The Briar Rose is filled with vacationers and business travelers. One couple is in the yard reading in the shade of the tulip tree and sharing tea as they unwind from the day. The sparrows, finches, and chicadees are sharing birdseed noisily in the quiet of the afternoon. The neighbor's calico cat sits patiently watching the lily pond for any goldfish he might have missed.

"Even though it's a warm summer day we are starting to prepare for winter. The split firewood is neatly stacked, the down puffs are sun-aired and ready for use, and the fireplaces are swept. It won't be long before we curl up in front of the crackling fire and wonder where these summer days have gone."

The ground-floor exterior of the inn is a beautiful rose-colored brick, with Queen Anne shingles on the second story. I noticed several other small houses in Boulder that featured some of the same basic design.

"Our new redecorating touch is the beautiful hand stenciling in our common areas. A late art nouveau design of a rambling briar rose was just painted by Larry Boyce, who has painted the vice president's office in Washington, D.C., as well as Bette Midler's house."

More as an accommodation to the guests than anything else, the Briar Rose offers a modest dinner consisting of fresh pasta topped with your choice of sauces, and a cooked vegetable. This is augmented by a simple dessert that goes along with dinner.

As Emily says, "Boulder is a great restaurant town, and there are good restaurants within walking distance, but we want to be able to offer dinner to those guests who are arriving really tired from a long trip and who don't want to take the trouble to go out for dinner. This is particularly true of business people, and if they want to have dinner in front of the fire or at the table—or even on the back porch in the summertime—they can take their tray and enjoy it wherever they like."

During the past few years Emily has gained a considerable reputation for conducting conferences and seminars on the basic subject of how to open a bed-and-breakfast inn. These are held several times a year, and I'd suggest contacting her to find out all of the details.

Emily's letter went on: "We have an ideal climate here in Boulder with four distinct and wonderful seasons. There are over 300 sunny days a year and many things for visitors to enjoy, both recreational and artistic. Of course, the mountains offer everything, including climbing, hiking, cross-country skiing. Some people say that the powder snow offers the best downhill skiing in the world. Biking is also very popular here in this part of Colorado and there are bicyclists everywhere, as well as joggers and runners."

BRIAR ROSE BED & BREAKFAST, 2151 Arapahoe Ave., Boulder, CO 80302; 303-442-3007. An 11-guestroom (6 private baths) inn located in a quiet section of a pleasant university town, approx. 1 hr. from Denver. Queen, double, and twin beds available. Open all year. Breakfast included in lodging rate. Evening meal available upon request. Tea and homemade shortbread served any time. Convenient to all of the many recreational, cultural, and historic attractions nearby. Limousine service available to and from Denver airport. Emily Hunter, Owner-hostess. (See Index for rates.)

Directions: From Denver, follow I-25 north and Rte. 36 to Boulder. Turn left on Arapahoe Ave. Briar Rose is on the right on the corner of 22nd St.

"European plan" means that rates for rooms and meals are separate. "American plan" means that meals are included in the cost of the room. "Modified American plan" means that breakfast and dinner are included in the cost of the room. The rates at some inns include a continental breakfast with the lodging.

THE HEARTHSTONE INN
Colorado Springs, Colorado (1979)

It was a most agreeable early August morning at the Hearthstone Inn. This time I was paying a visit in midsummer, when I could see the inn's beautiful lawn and flowers at their very best, and also sit on the front porch in one of the new handsome Tennessee country rockers.

I watched with amusement while a father, mother, and their four-year-old boy romped on the lawn, and then one of the staff came out and set up the croquet set. I had arrived just a few moments earlier, driving down from Denver and Boulder, and was immediately offered my choice of coffee or iced tea. "The coffee is on from early in the morning," explained Dot Williams, who with Ruth Williams (no relation), is the innkeeper at the Hearthstone.

Now I watched the few cars go by on Cascade Avenue, one of the most impressive streets in Colorado Springs, and reflected on the many changes I have seen in the considerable number of years since the first night I landed in Denver. I had been picked up by Dot and Ruth and driven out to the Springs. These two women had opened up the first inn in Colorado Springs, overcoming many difficulties. At that time there was only one house; now there are two houses, cheek-by-jowl.

The most recent development is the completion of Sheltering Pines, a totally different type of accommodation in nearby Green Mountain Falls. I had visited it when it was just a bit more than a gleam in the innkeepers' eyes.

"It is slowly developing its own following," Dot said. "The cool of the mountain evenings and the clear air of our mountain days make this part of Colorado a real boon for those who suffer from heat or allergies. Family reunions or groups are enjoying the patio, barbecue grill, and the many trees. It's quite a bit higher than Colorado Springs."

Sheltering Pines is actually a duplex with two completely separate living areas. Each has a completely equipped kitchen with everything provided, including all of the bedding and towels. In the summer it is rented only by the week, but the rest of the year it's available for shorter stays with a two-night minimum.

The Hearthstone itself is well known from coast to coast as being one of the truly impressive Victorian restorations, and it is on the National Register of Historic Places. Every room has been furnished entirely with Victorian furniture and decorations, and the outside of this wonderful combination of two rambling houses has been finished in carefully researched Victorian colors. Visitors will be surprised, as was I, to see how gracefully they reflect the Mauve Decades.

I always look forward to breakfast at the Hearthstone, and there is a wide variety of hearty breakfast offerings, not just the usual. "We never serve the same guest the same breakfast twice," Ruth declared.

Dot and Ruth joined me on the front porch, and we watched the squirrels, Minnie the Moocher and Pearl the Squirrel, and their friend, Jaws, eat themselves silly on sunflower seeds.

"I've always hoped that you would come out during Christmas some year," Ruth said. "Our guests all gather around for eggnog and the tradition of decorating the tree. Many guests bring a homemade ornament, and we tag each one with their name and the year, and it becomes a permanent part of each tree's decorations. Why don't you plan to come next year?"

I certainly would enjoy that experience very much!

THE HEARTHSTONE INN, 506 N. Cascade Ave., Colorado Springs, CO 80903; 719-473-4413. A 25-guestroom (23 private baths) bed-and-breakfast inn within sight of Pike's Peak, in the residential section of Colorado Springs. All-size beds. Complimentary full breakfast is the only meal served. Open every day all year. (Housekeeping units also available in Green Mountain Falls.) Convenient to spectacular Colorado mountain scenery as well as Air Force Academy, Garden of the Gods, Cave of the Winds, the McAllister House Museum, Fine Arts Center, and Broadmoor Resort. Golf, tennis, swimming, hiking, backroading, and Pikes Peak ski area nearby. Check innkeepers for pet policy. Dorothy Williams and Ruth Williams, Innkeepers. (See Index for rates.)

Directions: From I-25 (the major north/south hwy.) use Exit 143 (Uintah St.); travel east (opposite direction from mountains) to third stoplight (Cascade Ave.). Turn right for 7 blocks. The inn will be on the right at the corner of St. Vrain and Cascade—a big Victorian house, tan with lilac trim.

The date in parenthesis in the heading represents the first year the inn appeared in the pages of Country Inns and Back Roads.

QUEEN ANNE INN
Denver, Colorado (1990)

Charles and Anne Hillestad are a couple whose warmth and graciousness have made the Queen Anne Inn a restful haven in an active, cosmopolitan city. Charles, a transplanted Oregonian, moved to Denver to practice real estate law. He claims a particular interest in science fiction. Ann was raised on an Iowa farm where she developed her love for sewing, travel, music, and wildlife. The Hillestads' interests are apparent in the urbane ambience of their inn. Fine woods, stained-glass windows, original art, soft chamber music, fresh flowers, sherry, and a grand oak staircase attest to their appreciation for Victorian styling.

In the mid-1970s, Charles and Ann stepped in to help halt the demolition of homes on Denver's historic Tremont block. The Queen Anne Inn was one of these homes. The area is part of the oldest surviving residential neighborhood in Denver, which now borders on a fountain park and a buffer of open space.

Just four short blocks from the heart of Denver's central business district, the Queen Anne Inn offers a respite from the rigors of travel or the stress of everyday life. Listed as "one of the top ten places to spend a wedding night" by *Bridal Guide Magazine*, the inn appeals to the ro-

mance in everyone. "If you can't win the heart of your significant other at the Queen Anne Inn, give up!" Charles told me.

Each guest room has its own character and style. For example, the Rooftop Room has French doors that open onto a private deck with a panoramic view of the city and mountains. While all the rooms boast original art, the Aspen Room *is* a work of art. Located in the turreted peak of the inn, the room has a wraparound and overhead mural of an alpine aspen grove in fall color. What a splendid scene to gaze upon the first thing in the morning! Some of the rooms highlight pillared canopy beds. Others have gleaming brass beds or carved wooden headboards. Although the beds are antiques, the mattresses are new and firm. Both queen and twin beds are available. All rooms have private modern baths.

The common rooms are light and airy, with high ceilings and tall windows. A peach-toned background and crisp white trim create warmth. The living room, dining room, kitchen, and private garden are all available for guest use. I enjoyed a complimentary glass of afternoon wine with Charles as we relaxed on the garden deck. Both the Hillestads can recommend an impressive repertoire of attractions that are within walking distance from the inn: the Denver Chamber Orchestra and Symphony, the Center for the Performing Arts, the large Tivoli complex with movies, shops, restaurants, the Museum of Natural History, and the Denver Zoo. Galleries, clubs, and nearly fifty fine restaurants, many of which are five-star caliber, are close by. The Hallestads are pleased to help you design a day's itinerary.

Although lunch and dinner are not included in the room rate, Ann assured me that "anything from a picnic lunch to a three-course gourmet dinner" can be arranged with advance notice. A breakfast of fruits, breads, fresh-squeezed juice, homemade granola, yogurt, hard-boiled eggs, and special-blend coffee and teas is included in the tariff.

For a romantic evening, take a lovely tour in one of the Amish horse-drawn carriages that pulls up directly in front of the inn. Somehow the city atmosphere becomes distant and time stops, if only for one night.

QUEEN ANNE INN, 2147 Tremont Pl., Denver, CO 80205; 303-296-6666. A 10-guestroom (private baths) elegant Victorian within walking distance of downtown Denver, and only 1 hour from the Rocky Mountains. Open all year. Breakfast and afternoon refreshments included. Picnic lunch and gourmet dinner on advance request. Museums, shops, restaurants, and entertainment nearby. Smoking restricted. No pets. Children over 15. Charles and Ann Hillestad, Owners-hosts.

Directions: Take Exit 213 on I-25 to 23rd St., continuing to Tremont. Turn right for one block.

VISTA VERDE GUEST AND SKI TOURING RANCH
Steamboat Springs, Colorado (1987)

There seemed to be a ruckus in the side yard next to the main lodge at Vista Verde, where some children were practicing with the lariat. There was a great deal of shouting and laughing because they had lassoed one of the wranglers, and he was now on the ground. They were all standing around him as the Lilliputians stood around Gulliver. The other adult guests in the dining room and I crowded to the window to see what was going on. One of the mothers seated at my table noted somewhat wryly that this was the first night her young daughter hadn't worn blue jeans, and it was obvious that her little flowered frock was going to be grass-stained.

Afterward we all drifted back to the tables and most of the talk was about the day's rafting trip down the Colorado, and the guests who had been here previously said that it was always a different adventure.

Vista Verde is an activity-oriented guest ranch, with the major focus centered on horseback riding. However, as Frank Brophy pointed out, "We have lots of things like gold panning and guided hiking expeditions for people who may not care for riding."

It was my first real Colorado guest ranch experience, and I must say that I was tremendously impressed. It is situated at an elevation of 7,800 feet, surrounded by a national forest and a wilderness area. Guests share the environment with elk, deer, bears, foxes, coyotes, beavers, porcupines, and golden and bald eagles.

Lodgings are in individual hand-hewn cabins with hooked rugs, calico curtains, and Early American furnishings. All of them are carpeted, with spacious living rooms, cozy fireplaces, kitchens and baths, and from one to three cheerful bedrooms.

Guests are on the American plan rates, which include three meals a day, and what meals they are! Everybody is summoned by a ranch dinner bell, and, as you might imagine, home cooking is the rule. There are homemade breads, pies, and pastries, and fresh eggs from the henhouse. Meals are served family style in the main lodge or on picnic tables near the outdoor fireplace. Breakfast cookouts, steak barbecues, and fish fries all add to the fun. There's evening entertainment almost every night, with such diversions as a rodeo, square dancing, sing-alongs, story-telling, and even some guest talent as well.

There is an extensive children's program with a children's counselor. As Frank says, "In short order, we can have a five-year-old riding better than an eighteen-year-old."

For both the summer and winter guests, there is a spa and exercise center with a whirlpool, sauna, and exercise facilities to help them relax after a day out of doors, either in the saddle, on hiking trails or on skis.

In winter, there is cross-country skiing, horse-drawn sleigh rides, snowshoeing, and ice fishing right on the ranch, or just relaxing in front of the fire.

This account of Vista Verde's virtues must of necessity be somewhat limited, and I hope that it will pique your interest enough to write for a brochure, which contains far more extensive suggestions. I can assure you that it is right on the mark.

VISTA VERDE GUEST AND SKI TOURING RANCH, Box 465, Steamboat Springs, CO 80477; 303-879-3858. An 8 individual cottage (private baths) ranch, high in the Colorado Rockies. Full American plan includes breakfast, lunch, and dinner, as well as many activities. Open year-round. Inquire about minimum stays. Horseback riding and instruction, swimming, spa, sauna, exercise center, sleigh and hay rides; xc skiing on grounds and nearby in winter. Colorado River float trips, hunting, fishing, hot-air ballooning, tennis, swimming, golfing, and other summer sports nearby. No pets. Special cancellation policy. Mr. and Mrs. Frank Brophy, Owners-hosts. (See Index for rates.)

Directions: American Airlines, Northwest, and Airwest have nonstop jet service to Steamboat Springs during the winter with access from 150 major U.S. cities. In summer, the best plan is to fly to Denver and transfer to Continental Express Airways or take an easy and beautiful 4-hr. drive to Steamboat Springs. Once there, telephone the ranch for further instructions.

HERITAGE HOUSE
Topeka, Kansas (1990)

It isn't often that I have had the opportunity to stay in such a previously prestigious location as the Heritage House, the former residence of the historic Menninger Clinic. The midwestern, turn-of-the-century white wood-frame house was originally purchased in 1925 by C. F. Menninger and two of his sons, Will and Karl. After modifications, the home opened its doors as the Menninger Clinic on May 5, 1925.

Almost sixty years later, in 1982, the clinic moved to its present location. Unfortunately, the farmhouse was left vacant until 1988 and suffered damage due to vandalism. In 1988, it was chosen as the sight of the Topeka Designers' Showhouse Home and underwent major renovation. In June of that year, Don and Betty Rich opened the Heritage House as a country inn.

The Riches have been in the hospitality industry for quite some time and appreciated the historical significance of the building. Their daughter, Sarah, had spent more than three years working in hotels and was a natural for their choice as the Heritage House's manager. She met me as I checked in and warmly discussed the history of the home and her dedication to her job: "Since I'm the daughter of the owners, I run Heritage House as they would, with total professionalism and the finest of quality."

Sarah took me on a tour of the inn's unusual living room and parlor. Both are hand-painted, using a marbleizing technique. Hardwood floors, Oriental rugs, and traditional-styled furnishings create a comfortable,

inviting atmosphere. Multicolored floral patterns, and shades of peach and jade green give a refreshing feeling. Once the setting of the Menninger Clinic's afternoon staff conferences, the rooms' real focal point is a fabulous green Italian fireplace located in the parlor.

One of the benefits of the inn's renovation is that the fifteen guest rooms have been individually decorated by Topeka designers. The most historical are Dr. Will and Dr. Karl Menninger's studies. Dr. Will's has the original knotty pine paneling and has been finished with a southwestern theme emphasizing earth tones. An original painting by Dr. Will's widow hangs on the wall.

In contrast, Dr. Karl's paneled room is cool, decorated in shades of blue. An elegant mahogany four-poster bed and large picture window dominate the room.

Other rooms have a Kansas country decor, complete with pine furniture and ruffled curtains. The Magnolia Room features an exotic Oriental theme complete with a black-lacquered four-poster and an elevated Jacuzzi tub. The majority of rooms have private baths with shower/ tub combinations. All rooms have telephones and color televisions.

The ambience of the inn is decidedly not stuffy, including the friendly house bar off the entry's living room where guests are encouraged to mix their own drinks on the honor system. Breakfast, lunch, and dinner are available, with a full breakfast included in your room tariff.

The dinner menu is à la carte and can be enjoyed on the inn's new wood deck during good weather. I ordered a rich crab cannelloni appetizer, then had a crisp house salad followed by a fresh piece of Pacific salmon with dill sauce. For dessert, I decided to splurge on calories and savored the white and dark chocolate buttercream gateau.

Topeka has a variety of special events to provide entertainment while you're visiting. Summer brings the Sunflower Music Festival and Fiesta Mexicana. In the fall you can have fun at Railroad Days, the Huff 'n' Puff Balloon Rally, or Cider Days. The Heritage House is close to Gage Park, the State Capital, and, of course, the Menninger Foundation. I know you'll enjoy the town, and the hospitality of the Heritage House.

HERITAGE HOUSE, 3535 S. W. 6th St., Topeka, KS 66606; 913-233-3800. A 15-guestroom (11 private baths) country inn located near downtown Topeka. Open all year. All-size beds. Full breakfast included; lunch and dinner available by reservation. Smoking in common areas only. Seasonal events. No pets. Don and Betty Rich, Owners; Sarah Rich, Manager.

Directions: From Kansas City, take I-70 west to Topeka. Take the East Turnpike exit to Gage Blvd. Go south on Gage to Sixth St. (first stop light) and turn left. Heritage House is on the right.

HARRISON HOUSE
Guthrie, Oklahoma (1988)

In the rousing finale of that grand musical *Oklahoma!* is the line "You're doing fine, Oklahoma—Oklahoma, okay!" And after a visit to the lively town of Guthrie, smack in the middle of state, I'll have to echo those sentiments.

I was greatly inspired by the pioneering spirit of community in Guthrie, originally the capital of the Oklahoma Territory and later the state. The whole town is on the National Register of Historic Places.

The Harrison House is a perfect example of that spirit. Phyllis Murray was a volunteer in the restoration of one of the buildings in the downtown historic district. Her husband, Ron, was one of the local investors in the project to develop an inn in what had been a handsome bank and office building. They needed someone to furnish and decorate the rooms, and Phyllis took on the job.

Little did she realize how involved she would become. Today she is the innkeeper, and she loves it. "I wanted this inn to be special," she told me, "and I have always been partial to the Victorian period, so the idea of decorating it really appealed to me." And this is where the feeling of community comes in. Phyllis found everything she has used in the inn within the immediate area. This includes every piece of antique furniture, all of the fabrics and wallpapers, even the mattresses, made by a local company to fit the various-sized old beds.

"I felt that it was really important to have furnishings and the feeling of what Guthrie was like at the turn of the century, and also I wanted this restoration to benefit the local economy," Phyllis declared. "It has been wonderful to see the interest that people in town have taken in this project."

By the time she had finished her splendid job of decorating, she decided to stay on as its innkeeper. Phyllis is a very warm and hospitable lady, who seems to make her guests feel very much at home.

The Harrison House is a handsome red brick and sandstone building with an impressive arched entrance at the corner. The lobby is elegantly decorated with marble-topped tables, velvet upholstered chairs, deep green carpeting, and plum-colored draperies.

Upstairs is a parlor and dining area where a continental breakfast is served at tables set with old china and silver plate. "None of our china or silver matches," Phyllis laughed, "which makes it more fun—like being at Aunt Susie's or Grandma Murray's."

The guest rooms are all decorated differently with original antique beds and other interesting pieces, and they all have their own bathrooms. I noticed one room was named for Tom Mix, who had once lived here and worked just down the street.

I had a brief chat with Ron Murray, a slow-talking, soft-spoken gentleman, and he told me how the town had accomplished the restoration of the Pollard Theatre, right next door to the inn. In fact, some of the guest rooms extend over the theater. "It's the only full-time professional repertory theater in Oklahoma," he said. "It opened with *Guys and Dolls,* and there will be ten musicals and plays presented throughout the year.

"We have a lot of history right here in Guthrie," he added. "You know, this town was established during the famous 'Run of '89,' when the Oklahoma Territory was opened to settlers, and this is our 100th year."

Phyllis took up the thread, "Nearly everything of interest is within walking distance, including some excellent restaurants. Oh, there are all sorts of things to do and see here."

Looking over all the brochures and folders listing various events and sightseeing possibilities, I had to agree with her.

HARRISON HOUSE, 124 W. Harrison St., P.O. Box 1555, Guthrie, OK 73044; 405-282-1000. A 23-guestroom (private baths) in-town bed-and-breakfast inn in the historic district of a bustling southwestern town, about 20 mi. north of Oklahoma City. King and double beds available. Continental breakfast included in room rate. Open year-round. Golf, fishing, bicycles, paddle boating, horseback riding, museums, theater, concerts, rodeos, territorial home tours, special events nearby. Well-behaved children welcome. No pets. Phyllis Murray, Manager. (See Index for rates.)

Directions: Guthrie is located on I-35, about 20 mi. north of Oklahoma City. The inn is at the corner of West Harrison and First Sts.

GRANT CORNER INN
Santa Fe, New Mexico (1988)

While the overhead fan in the dining room whirled lazily and morning conversations rose and fell, I took in my surroundings with pleasure. Sun streamed in the large windows, the rose-colored woven mats with blue napkins in white rabbit napkin rings and the little vases of fresh daisies made a pretty pattern on the polished oak tables. The aroma of fresh-brewed coffee scented the air, and my fruit-filled pancakes were delicious. "What a way to start the day," I thought.

I leafed through Louise Stewart's cookbook, with over 300 of the recipes that she and her husband, Pat Walter, have used for their breakfasts, which have become so famous that local people make reservations just for breakfast. The Southwestern and Mexican influence makes for some exciting combinations—poached pears with raspberry sauce, spicy *huevos rancheros,* scrambled eggs with jack cheese and coriander, peach or pumpkin-raisin pancakes, wholewheat burritos brushed with butter and served with jalapeño jelly and sour cream, stuffed french toast, blue corn waffles, asparagus frittatas, strawberry frappe, and always the delicate sopapillas. Sopapillas, in case you've never tried them, are delicious fried pastries dusted with powdered sugar and served with butter and honey. I understand Pat is the creator of many of the breakfast specialties. There are also all kinds of homemade breads, fresh fruit, juices, various cereals, and still other choices.

Later, talking to Pat and Louise, I realized that they made a perfect combination and had both come to this challenge with especially tailored backgrounds. Pat was a builder and had taught space planning and design, and Louise had a degree in hotel management and was an interior designer. Between the two of them, they have whipped what was a dilapidated 1905 "ugly duckling" of a house into an elegant and delightful bed-and-breakfast inn.

Throughout the inn they have placed many of their personal belongings—family antiques and heirlooms, Indian and Mexican folk art, and other treasures they have collected over the years. "Our guests enjoy the special things and always take good care of them," Louise told me. "I think it's the extra touches that people remember—I know I do."

Every guest room has a personality all of its own, and each one is quite different from the others. One sunny room has a very southwestern feeling with Indian rugs, a natural pine bed with a handmade antique country quilt, and natural muslin bed curtains. Another room, with french doors opening onto a private porch, is more formal, with a white iron and brass bed, a handsome antique quilt and matching ruffled pillow shams and curtains, a European-style white telephone, and a beautiful bentwood upholstered settee. I noticed baskets of fruit on bedside tables. Thick

robes in rooms where the bathroom is "down the hall," and telephones, TV, and ceiling fans in all the guest rooms.

Conversation is easy in the cozy parlor, where afternoon refreshments are served. Although no other meals are served, Louise assures me that arrangements can be made for an elegant picnic lunch, and both she and Pat are always happy to help map out day trips to nearby pueblos and other diversions for their guests.

Santa Fe is a fascinating blend of Indian, Spanish, and Anglo influences, with a vibrant cultural life that includes art, drama, dance, and a lot of music. The Santa Fe Opera has become very well known, and its festival, along with a chamber music festival, is held during July and August. Grant Corner Inn is just two blocks from the city plaza and within walking distance of art galleries, shops, and the Repertory Theatre.

GRANT CORNER INN, 122 Grant Ave., Santa Fe, NM 87501; 505-983-6678. A 13-guestroom (7 private baths) bed-and-breakfast inn in downtown Santa Fe. All-size beds. Breakfast and afternoon refreshments included in room rate. Picnic lunches can be arranged. Closed last 3 wks. in Jan. Wheelchair access. Within walking distance of shops, galleries, restaurants, and theater. Indian pueblos, music and art festivals, hiking, rafting, and skiing nearby. Children over 5 welcome. No pets. Louise Stewart and Pat Walter, Owners-hosts. (See Index for rates.)

Directions: From Albuquerque on U.S. 25, go north on St. Francis, east on Alameda, north on Guadalupe, and east on Johnson.

THE TAOS INN
Taos, New Mexico (1990)

As I stepped into The Taos Inn's two-story lobby, I thought I'd made a mistake and arrived during the wrong weekend. The lobby was buzzing with groups here and there in rapt conversation, and I didn't think there could possibly be enough room for all of us. Folks were standing on the interior balconies overlooking the decorative tiled fountain that I later learned had been the original town well. Others were viewing the exceptional artwork and brightly colored handwoven rugs that hung on the adobe walls. And quite a rousing discussion was taking place around the large sunken pueblo-style fireplace that dominates one corner of the room.

When I asked manager Kathleen Crislip if, in fact, I had arrived on the right date, she laughed and said, "Oh yes, certainly. It's always like this around here. Many of these people are local residents, most of them artists. We sometimes call our lobby 'the community living room.'" She went on to tell me that the inn had been a center of social activity in Taos for more than 300 years.

Just a short distance from the Taos Plaza, the inn has a remarkable history and is the only hotel in Taos on the National Register of Historic Places. Portions of the building date back to the late 1600s. With its rounded corners, slanted walls, curved archways, and soft light, the structure is a beautiful example of Spanish and Indian architecture that utilized local wood and adobe materials.

In 1895, Dr. T. Paul Martin, Taos's first physician, bought one of five 19th-century houses that surrounded a small plaza. Later, Dr. Martin and his wife, Helen, purchased the other four homes and rented them to local artists, creating a center for the Taos art community. After the doctor's death in 1935, Helen enclosed the patio, connecting the residences, and opened the Martin Hotel. In 1982, the inn was sold to present owner Scott Sanger and fellow investors, who proceeded to do extensive renovation and additions, including a Jacuzzi room and swimming pool.

The inn's forty guest rooms feature pueblo-style fireplaces, antiques and handcrafted Southwestern furniture, hand-loomed Zapotec Indian bedspreads, and original art. The private baths are decorated with hand-painted Mexican tile and each has a shower/tub combination.

Meals are available at the now-famous Doc Martin's Restaurant, established in the doctor's original clinic. Apparently many early Taos residents were born right in one of the intimate alcoves of the restaurant! The restaurant is popular with locals and visitors alike, so much so that reservations are recommended. The menu features made-from-scratch New American cuisine and original and traditional New Mexican specialties. Tender blue-corn pancakes, *carne adovada,* fresh fruit, and fantastic stuffed *sopaipillas* are just some of the breakfast choices available. The restaurant wine list has been granted an Award of Excellence by the prestigious *Wine Spectator* and also serves a fine selection of aperitifs and beers. For a more casual meal you might like to stroll across the street to the colorful Adobe Bar for more inexpensive Mexican food, shrimp, oysters, and terrific margaritas.

Taos offers a wide variety of entertainment and activities. People-watching alone can provide a full day of fun. Art galleries, boutiques, fascinating architecture, and the 900-year-old Taos Pueblo are within walking distance. The inn hosts a twice-yearly Meet the Artist series where guests can discuss the creative process with well-known Taos artists, and you might just come away having discovered your artist within.

THE TAOS INN, 125 Paseo del Pueblo Norte, Taos, NM 87571; 505-758-2233 or 800-TAOS-INN. A 49-guestroom (private baths) authentic historic adobe just steps from the Taos Plaza. Open year-round. All-size beds. Breakfast, lunch, dinner, and Sunday brunch available, but not included. Close to galleries, the Taos Pueblo, shopping, skiing, musical performances, theater, and art festivals. No pets. Handicap facilities. Betty and Scott Sanger, Owners-hosts; Kathleen Crislip, Manager.

Directions: From Albuquerque, take I-25 north to Santa Fe. Take Exit 282 and follow signs to Taos and Espanola, picking up US 84-285 north. From Espanola take Rte. 68N to Taos. The inn is just north of the Taos Plaza on the right.

The date in parenthesis in the heading represents the first year the inn appeared in the pages of Country Inns and Back Roads.

THE LODGE ON THE DESERT
Tucson, Arizona (1976)

The slanting rays of the western sun, providing spectacular back-lighting for the great banks of clouds that seemed to skim the jagged peaks of the Santa Catalina Mountains, streamed through the casement window and lit up the interior of my spacious studio bedroom at the Lodge on the Desert.

Even though the afternoon temperature in September reached 85 degrees, I knew that later that evening I would want a fire in my fireplace to ease the chill of the cool desert night.

My bedroom was really most impressive, with three windows on two sides and a patio facing north. The two double beds had rich bedspreads that complemented the orange curtains, and an armful of freshly picked flowers lent an air of gaiety to the dark tones of the carved wooden tables and chests. The full-sized closet reminded me that many people come here to spend weeks at a time, enjoying the benefits of a friendly climate in both summer and winter, plus the many opportunities for outdoor recreation, as well as the pursuit of the arts.

Tucson is one of the most sophisticated cities in the Southwest, with many fine homes and attractive shops in the downtown area. The University of Arizona is an active cultural center with a continuing program of music, drama, and arts and crafts exhibitions.

"We are now into our second fifty years of family ownership. My father built the Lodge on the Desert outside Tucson in 1936," commented Schuyler Lininger, the *patrón grande* of this resort-inn. "Now the city has grown up around us; fortunately, we have no tall buildings to disrupt our guests' view of the mountains, and yet we are set apart by the hedges around the property. However, many of our guests find nearness to the center of things in the city most desirable."

Here in the Southwest desert, during the outdoor weather, everybody gathers around the swimming pool, and here is where many conversations and lasting friendships start.

For cooler days, the Lodge has a very spacious and inviting living room with lots of books, which guests are free to take to their rooms, a chess game, a jigsaw puzzle, and many opportunities just to sit and relax.

The guest rooms of the inn have been designed after the manner of Pueblo Indian farmhouses, the beige adobe color frequently relieved by very colorful Mexican tiles.

Although the dining room features many dishes of the Southwest, I found there were also such favorites as Chateaubriand for two, roast rack of lamb, and several veal dishes. Schuyler explained that he and Helen have gone to great lengths to bring milk-fed Wisconsin veal to the table in different versions. Incidentally, one of the most popular features of the inn

is breakfast served on the patios of the guest rooms in the beautiful early-morning sunshine.

I believe another guest succinctly summed up my feelings about the Lodge on the Desert while we were at the pool, taking advantage of that bright September sun to get a few more degrees of tan.

"What I like about it here," she said, "is the really endless variety of things that are going on in Tucson—the Art Center, the many different theaters, the new museum, the exhibition of Indian arts, the opera company, the ballet, the Tucson Symphony, the golf courses, the racetrack, and all kinds of sports events—it's so *civilized!*"

THE LODGE ON THE DESERT, 306 N. Alvernon Way, Tucson, AZ 85733; 602-325-3366. A 40-guestroom (private baths) luxury inn within the city limits. King, queen, and twin beds available. American and European plans available in winter; European plan in summer. Continental breakfast included in European plan. Breakfast, lunch, and dinner served to travelers every day of the year. Wheelchair access. Near several historic, cultural, and recreational attractions. Swimming pool and lawn games on grounds. Tennis and golf 1 mi. Attended, leashed pets allowed. Schuyler and Helen Lininger, Owners-hosts. (See Index for rates.)

Directions: Take Speedway exit from I-10. Travel about 5 mi. east to Alvernon Way, turn right (south) onto Alvernon (¾ mi.). Lodge is on left side between 5th St. and Broadway.

RANCHO DE LOS CABALLEROS
Wickenburg, Arizona (1971)

Rancho de los Caballeros is a rather elegant ranch-inn. A continuous program of watering and irrigation makes it a green jewel in the desert. This is especially true of the 18-hole championship golf course. Many of the guest rooms and suites are built around a carefully planned cactus garden and oversized putting green and are decorated in Arizona desert colors with harmonizing hues of tan, yellow, and brown. Each accommodation, or *casita* as they are called in this part of the world, has a private patio and many of them have fireplaces.

A program of planned activities for younger people is one of the reasons this ranch experience is so popular with families. "We feel that it is a good balance," says innkeeper Rusty Gant, "because children of all ages have several activities every morning, and in the afternoon they can join their parents for more trail riding or tennis or a swim in the pool. At dinner the childrens' counselor gathers them all together, and they even have their own dining room. They are kept occupied until bedtime. This has proven to be an excellent idea for both children and their parents alike.

"The idea of a winter vacation on a guest ranch in Arizona never occurred to us," said a letter I received from a Michigan reader. "Wickenburg seemed like such a long way and we weren't quite sure what kind of people would be there. We certainly weren't horseback riders and we thought we might feel out of place. However, we were reading your book about how much you enjoyed the noon buffet around the pool at Rancho de los Caballeros and getting some horseback riding tips from one of the wranglers, and we began to think that maybe we would enjoy it too.

"The trip from Detroit to Phoenix was quite short and the ranch car met us at the airport. When I talked with Ann Giles on the telephone she

assured me that we'd feel right at home and that we should bring our tennis rackets. She mentioned that golf clubs could be rented if we didn't want to carry them. We literally dragged our two early-teenage sons with us, and did their faces light up when almost as soon as we arrived they noticed other young people. I don't believe we saw them for the rest of the two weeks."

Rancho de los Caballeros . . . "the ranch of the gentlemen on horseback." The name alone has an unusually romantic, melodic sound, and its location in the high country is equally romantic. As my correspondent from Michigan said later on in her letter, "The mountains and the desert literally grow on you."

I love to sit on the terrace at sunset and watch the changing colors and dimensions of the Bradshaw Mountains far across the valley.

I've visited Rancho de los Caballeros many times since my initial visit in 1971 and have always had a marvelous time, so I am not at all surprised at the experience of my friends from Michigan.

On two different occasions during the last five years the annual meeting of the Country Inns and Back Roads Innkeepers' Association has been held at this ranch. These are men and women from all over North America as well as visitors from Britain and Europe who represent the highest ideals of innkeeping. We went back the second time because of all the services and provisions for entertainment and amusement.

As we were leaving, several innkeepers urged me to arrange for another meeting here again as soon as possible.

RANCHO DE LOS CABALLEROS, Wickenburg, AZ 85358; 602-684-5484. A 74-guestroom (private baths) luxury ranch-resort, 60 mi. from Phoenix in the sunny, dry desert. American plan. Breakfast, lunch, dinner served to travelers daily. Open from mid-Oct. to early May. Wheelchair access. Swimming pool, horseback riding, hiking, skeet shooting, putting green, tennis, and 18-hole championship golf course on grounds. Special children's program. No pets. No credit cards. Dallas C. Gant, Jr., Mrs. Francis L. Hayman and son, Owners. (See Index for rates.)

Directions: Rtes. 60, 89, and 93 lead to Wickenburg. Ranch is 2 mi. west of town on Rte. 60 and 2 mi. south on Vulture Mine Road.

The date in parenthesis in the heading represents the first year the inn appeared in the pages of Country Inns and Back Roads.

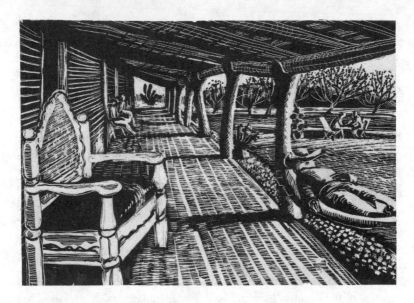

TANQUE VERDE
Tucson, Arizona (1970)

The postmark on the letter was "Caldwell, New Jersey." It said in part: "We've been reading about your last visit to Tanque Verde Ranch, just outside of Tucson. It sounds very intriguing. My wife and I are enthusiastic about the prospect of a new vacation experience in the desert country. The idea of staying at a ranch that may have even survived Indian raids, and your description of steak over mesquite fires and bird watching, are most inviting. However, it is a long way for us to go, and neither of us has ever been astride a horse. We're both about fifty years old and we'd like a little more advice as to whether we should venture forth on this trip."

Until my first visit to Tanque Verde in 1969, horseback riding for me consisted of a couple of short hauls on a Tennessee walking horse and one or two rides on the gentlest nag in my local livery stable. When I went out to Tanque Verde, I talked this over with the head wrangler, and he picked out a horse that he thought was the right size for my weight and had enough experience to guide me.

On that ride (the first of many during subsequent visits), I met a husband and wife from the Boston area, who were at a Western ranch for the first time and out on their first morning trail ride. We left the corral in single file and rode out into the desert. The entire experience was so exhilarating that by the time we got back to the ranch my Massachusetts neighbors were inquiring as to whether they could have more active horses and go for a longer ride the next day.

By the end of the week, these people had purchased some blue jeans, western shirts, cowboy hats, and boots, and knew all the horses by their first names.

Tanque Verde is a completely different type of country inn. There are many diversions, including both indoor and outdoor pools and an active tennis program. I spent one New Year's Eve there and had a great time with all the parents and children who had been there since Christmas.

In Tanque Verde's 100-year-old history as one of Arizona's pioneer guest cattle ranches, there are even stories of Indian raids. The ranch is set back in a semicircle of mountains, about a thirty-minute drive from downtown Tucson and the airport. The accommodations are in almost luxurious individual *casitas,* all of which have their own Spanish-style corner fireplaces. Everyone eats at long tables in the vaulted dining room, and there's nothing like the desert air to encourage big appetites.

One further point: Tanque Verde is open throughout the entire year, and during the summer there are many guests from Europe and Asia enjoying the full holiday in the desert. As innkeeper Bob Cote says, "We have so many guests speaking different languages, we could almost advertise that it's a good place for children to get some language tutoring."

This guest ranch was the first such accommodation to be included in *CIBR.* In subsequent years I have added a few others, both east and west. Tanque Verde, with genuine cordiality extended to all guests and its infectious informality, has served as a model for me.

TANQUE VERDE, 14301 E. Speedway, Tucson, AZ 85748; 602-296-6275. A 60-guestroom (private baths) ranch-inn, 10 mi. from Tucson. American plan. All-size beds. Breakfast, lunch, and dinner served to travelers by reservation. Open year-round. Riding, indoor and outdoor pool, tennis, sauna, exercise room, and whirlpool bath on grounds. Robert Cote, Owner-host. (See Index for rates.)

Directions: From U. S. 10, exit at Speedway Blvd. and travel east to dead end.

The date in parenthesis in the heading represents the first year the inn appeared in the pages of Country Inns and Back Roads.

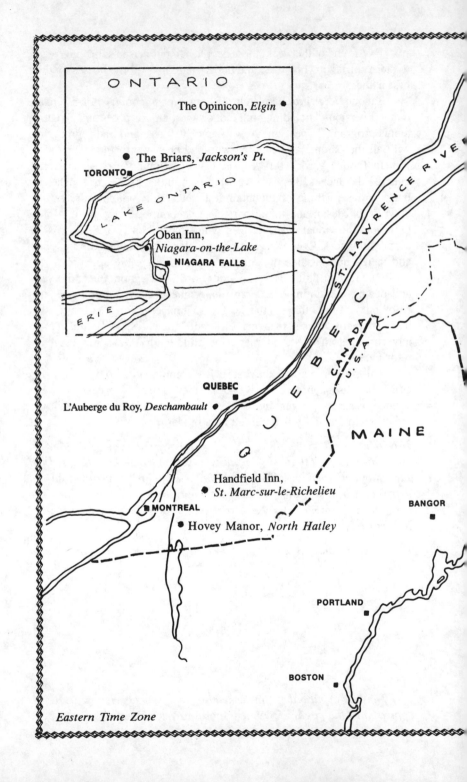

ONTARIO

The Opinicon, *Elgin*

The Briars, *Jackson's Pt.*

TORONTO

LAKE ONTARIO

Oban Inn,
Niagara-on-the-Lake

NIAGARA FALLS

ERIE

ST. LAWRENCE RIVER

CANADA

U.S.A

QUEBEC

QUÉBEC

L'Auberge du Roy, *Deschambault*

MAINE

Handfield Inn,
St. Marc-sur-le-Richelieu

BANGOR

MONTREAL

Hovey Manor, *North Hatley*

PORTLAND

BOSTON

Eastern Time Zone

GULF OF
ST. LAWRENCE

NEW

BRUNSWICK

Shaw's Hotel, *Brackley Beach*

P. E. I.

MONCTON

Marshlands, *Sackville*

CAPE
BRETON

SYDNEY

NOVA SCOTIA

Halliburton House, *Halifax*

HALIFAX

ALAIS

ATLANTIC

ANNAPOLIS ROYAL

Milford House, *South Milford*

YARMOUTH

OCEAN

Eastern and Maritime Canada

Atlantic Time Zone

MARSHLANDS INN
Sackville, New Brunswick (1975)

Every year I hear from a great many readers who have driven across Maine into New Brunswick to reach Nova Scotia and Prince Edward Island by the land route.

Almost all of these letters make some reference to the Marshlands Inn, just a few miles from the Nova Scotia border and the Prince Edward Island ferry. I'd like to reach back into the past to 1975 and share a portion of a letter from a honeymooning couple.

"Our itinerary from Calais, Maine, took us to the Marathon Inn off the coast of New Brunswick and then to the Marshlands Inn for a late lunch. The setting, decor, and food exceeded our expectations. We never expected to find such a sophisticated inn so far north.

"While paying our bill we found a copy of *Country Inns and Back Roads,* perused the table of contents, and noted your entry regarding the Marshlands. We found that we were in complete agreement with your comments and enjoyed your personal observations."

What was true in 1975 is for the most part still true these many years later. There has been one change recently at the Marshlands Inn. My dear friends Herb and Alice Read have sold the inn to Mary and John Blakely. Mary worked for four years at Marshlands as a hostess. She and John both come from England, where Mary's family had an English-style country inn in the Derbyshire hills. The Blakelys have been busy creating some very pleasant guest rooms in the carriage house, which they named Stonehaven. They tell me the rooms have oak floors and are furnished in antiques, "no reproductions, but the baths are modern."

In a conversation that I had with Mary, she filled me in on some of the new offerings being prepared by their French chef.

"Our chef calls the appetizer the entrée and the main dish, dinner," Mary told me. "He does traditional French cuisine as well as a little bit of nouvelle. One of his specialties is sauces.

"We have many new things on the menu, including cultivated mussels from Prince Edward Island or Nova Scotia. We serve them in wine or in stock, depending on the preference of the guest. We also have an excellent Caesar salad. We have specials three or four days a week, with appetizers and entrées. Incidentally, our chef does a halibut mousse with a pink peppercorn sauce and also a smoked cod mousse made with red peppers. We also have a Middle Eastern dish called cous-cous. This is a lamb dish with semolina.

"Of course, we still have the same dishes for which the Marshlands has gained such a fine reputation, including Atlantic and Miramichi salmon. Many of our guests ask for fiddlehead greens almost as soon as they check in."

The first thing that a newly arrived guest sees when entering Marshlands is the graceful, curving staircase, a carved settee, and many ancestral portraits. There are two high-ceilinged parlors for houseguests and diners waiting to be shown to their tables.

The guest rooms are almost all furnished in antiques and Persian rugs, and runners muffle footsteps in all the halls. Each guest room has a four poster bed and is decorated in a different color scheme and period wallpaper. My favorite room is on the third floor under the eaves, where there is a bow-shaped window with a sitting alcove, a leather-topped writing desk, a marble reading lamp, and a high dresser with a pedestal mirror.

One of the enduring traditions at Marshlands is the delicious hot chocolate, served every evening around ten o'clock. It's a time when guests who may have been otherwise occupied find themselves congregating and talking over the day's experiences.

Let me reassure my honeymooning couple from 1975 that the Marshlands Inn is all that it was during their visit and perhaps a great deal more.

MARSHLANDS INN, Box 1440, Sackville, N.B., Canada· E0A 3C0; 506-536-0170. A 25-guestroom (15 private baths) village inn near Tantramar Marshes and Fundy Tides. European plan. Breakfast, lunch, and dinner served to travelers daily. Open from Feb. thru late Nov. Golf, xc skiing, curling, hiking, and swimming nearby. John and Mary Blakely, Owners-hosts. (See Index for rates.)

Directions: Follow Trans-Canada Highway to Sackville, then Rte. 6 for 1 mi. to center of town.

THE HALLIBURTON HOUSE INN
Halifax, Nova Scotia (1989)

Sitting with William McKeever on the sunny deck of the courtyard, surrounded by flowers and trees, it was hard for me to realize that this small hotel is actually in the heart of historic downtown Halifax. William, who is a Yale graduate, moved his family to Halifax from Colorado to open the first European-style inn on Canada's Atlantic coast.

"Even though Halifax is undergoing a full boom," he said, "the pace is slower here and the people are less pressured. You can have gridlock at a four-way stop because everybody is waiting for the driver on the right to go first."

Halifax has certainly changed since my first visit years ago. I understand it is considered the leading North American city in historic building restoration, and they've done a remarkable job in recapturing the waterfront. Several shiny-glassed, tall office buildings exist cheek-by-jowl with 19th-century, once-decrepit warehouses and other historic buildings that have been spruced up and put to use as interesting shops, boutiques, and restaurants, with skywalks and pedestrian walkways.

The Halliburton House, only a few blocks from the waterfront, is actually three registered heritage townhouses side by side, built between 1809 and 1860. The main stone and brick building was the residence of Sir Brenton Halliburton, first Chief Justice of the Supreme Court of Nova Scotia. William and his wife, Berkley, and their partner, Charles Lief, set about renovating and restoring these houses to their former elegance and have succeeded admirably.

Stepping past the marble-floored entry, I found a library on the left, comfortably furnished in period antiques, with a fire glowing in the fireplace, over which presides an impressive portrait of Sir Brenton Halliburton. Around the walls are prints of Halifax harbor as it looked in the 1800s.

On the other side of the entrance hall is a cozy dining room, where there was much laughing and chatting among the guests who were enjoying the buffet breakfast. There were cereals, yogurt, fresh fruit and berries, fresh baked goods, teas and coffee, and gourmet preserves from Prince Edward Island. I noticed one guest was deeply engrossed in reading one of the local newspapers available on a side table. William commented that there were also regional and local magazines, guide books, and histories in the library.

"We offer a complimentary afternoon tea," he told me, "which includes many local delicacies, such as smoked mackerel and salmagundi (a local pickled herring), as well as tea cakes and scones." "And what about dinner?" I asked. "We serve dinner to our houseguests only, with advance reservations. The menu might include such dishes as steamed

Nova Scotia mussels, traditional seafood chowder, coq au vin, fresh fish fillets, as well as some delectable desserts."

The guest rooms, which come in various sizes, are all individually and pleasantly furnished and include cable TV and telephones. Some rooms have working fireplaces, others have private balconies, and a few have a refrigerator and a wet bar.

I took a short, bracing walk up Citadel Hill, whose history goes back to the 17th century and which served as a fort, protecting the most strategic harbor on Canada's Atlantic coast. The view of the harbor was spectacular, with the docks and wharves and all the little tugboats, naval vessels, and fishing boats plying the waters.

I am happy to welcome the Halliburton House Inn to our pages.

THE HALLIBURTON HOUSE INN, 5184 Morris St., Halifax, Nova Scotia, Canada B3J 1B3; 902-420-0658. A 35-guestroom (29 private baths) in-town inn on a quiet street in downtown Halifax. Double and twin beds available. Complimentary buffet breakfast and afternoon tea. Dinner served to houseguests only by reservation. Open year-round. Arrangements for sightseeing, walking tours, dinner reservations by staff. Maritime Museum, the waterfront with shops and restaurants, Citadel National Park, and Halifax Public Gardens nearby. No pets. William McKeever, Innkeeper. (See Index for rates.)

Directions: Nova Scotia, 90 mi, off the coast of Me., can be reached by auto via New Brunswick and by ferry from Portland, Bar Harbor, or St. John, N.B., arriving in Yarmouth, N.S. From Yarmouth, take Rte. 103 to Halifax. Halifax International Airport is a 30-min. drive from the inn.

MILFORD HOUSE
South Milford, Nova Scotia (1974)

Isn't there a saying that goes "the more things change the more they stay the same"? There's a wonderful old brochure from the turn of the century, describing the Milford House when A. D. Thomas was running it. He had established the hotel back in the 1880s as a way station between the Atlantic Coast and Annapolis Royal, but it soon became a haven for fishermen, sportsmen, and vacationers who loved rustic living.

The brochure declares, "It is a delightful and unspoiled spot on the outskirts of the real wilderness. . . . A really hot day is a very great rarity, and the nights are invariably cool . . ." There's a picture of two canoeists on a placid lake bounded by boulders and pines, and the brochure continues, ". . . cabins cluster cosily around the lakeshore . . . solid comfort is aimed at rather than elegance, and the beds, the food, and the attendants are excellent." The brochure closes with "Please engage rooms well in advance" and includes an impressive list of guests who recommend Milford House.

Well, things are much the same today under the expert management of Margaret and Bud Miller, who have been the innkeepers for over twenty years. Their daughter, Wendy, who gave me a guided tour on my first visit when she was only twelve, has become an officer in the Canadian Armed Forces and is presently stationed in North Dakota with NORAD. Their other daughter, Linda, often visits with her three young children, and they liven things up on the playground.

"We have many young families who come for the outdoor activities, and we are buying more high chairs and cribs every summer," Margaret tells me. "We keep the dining room serene and quiet by serving an early dinner for families with young children," she adds, "and we can usually provide a 'kid sitter,' when desired."

This is a great place for kids—what kid doesn't like to fish, paddle canoes, and explore the woods. As Bud says, "It's a place where dads and grandfathers can forever impress their kids."

On my last visit, my accommodations, like all the others, were in a tidy, rustic cabin where there were two bedrooms and a large combination sitting and dining room with windows overlooking still another view of the lake. There are over two dozen of these cottages situated well apart along the wooded shores of two lakes, within walking distance of the main lodge. Each cottage has its own lakeside dock, two to five bedrooms, a living room with a fireplace, electricity, and a bathroom with a tub or a shower. Some of them are insulated and contain housekeeping facilities ideal for a cross-country skiing holiday or just a secluded winter vacation. There were fresh flowers in my cabin, and although the furnishings were plain, everything was absolutely spick-and-span. All the cottages are provided with maid service, ice, wood, and kindling, delivered daily.

The main lodge has a comfortable living room, library, and games room. Breakfast and dinner are served in the huge old-fashioned dining room. It's hearty country home cooking, with vegetables from the garden, roasts, fresh fish, native blueberries, raspberries, and home-baked breads and pastries. Breakfasts are the kind that go on and on, with Red River cereal, oatmeal porridge, stewed prunes, bacon, ham, sausage, eggs, french toast, juices, berries, pancakes, homemade conserves, and other things.

Bud and Margaret are friendly people, and so are their waitresses. It's not only a place for lots of activities, but a place where you can sit and watch the sun go down and listen to the strange call of a loon floating across the lake—just as so many guests have done for a hundred years.

MILFORD HOUSE, South Milford, R.R. 4, Annapolis Royal, N.S., Canada B0S 1A0; 902-532-2617. A rustic resort-inn (private baths) with 27 cabins on 600 acres of woodlands and lakes, 90 mi. from Yarmouth, N.S., near Kejimkujik National Park. Modified American plan. Breakfast and dinner served daily with picnic lunches available. Open from June 15 to Sept. 15; fall and winter by special reservation. Tennis, fishing, croquet, canoeing, bird-watching, and swimming on grounds. Deep-sea fishing and golf nearby. Warren and Margaret Miller, Owners-hosts. (See Index for rates.)

Directions: From Yarmouth follow Rte. 1 to traffic lights in Annapolis Royal. Turn right and continue on Rte. 8, 15 mi. to inn. The Blue Nose Ferry from Bar Harbor to Yarmouth N.S., arrives in time for guests to make dinner at the Milford House.

THE BRIARS
Jackson's Point, Ontario (1980)

A recent note from John Sibbald mentions plans to re-create the Swallow Tower, the original 19th-century observation tower that was torn down when he was twelve. The view over the lake will be magnificent. He also adds, "We are now officially flying the barn swallow as our insignia. The swallow is not only an heraldic symbol of hospitality and good cheer but is very numerous around here and a great mosquito eater!" I'd say these are all important attributes for an inn.

There's an unusually large full-color map of the Briars and Lake Simcoe, prepared by John, in addition to some very informative literature, which you can obtain by writing the Briars.

I'll go into details about this map in just a moment, but first let me tell you about the Briars, a lush 200-acre estate on the south shore of Lake Simcoe, about forty-five miles north of Toronto. Guests are accommodated in cottages clustered by the lake or in handsome guest rooms in the Manor and its new wings. The inn is set in expanses of deep green lawns surrounded by sculpted hedges and giant pines. A peaceful river meanders through the golf course, and little streams wander under wooden bridges in the scenic woods and fields. I would term the Briars a distinctive Canadian resort that blends its rich past with modern facilities to offer an attractive holiday for guests with family or friends.

In the more than twenty years that I've been traveling in North America, I've come to the conclusion that while Canadians and Americans have lived side by side for many years and both speak the same language, there are still some subtle differences. For one thing, Canadians are basically more conservative than Americans. In this respect they are more like the English. I found that they prefer some of the more quiet things of life, such as good walking, quiet fireside reading, and a little less flamboyant approach to life in general.

And now to the map. In one corner it details a most interesting history since 1819, and traces ownership through more than 170 years to the present Sibbald family.

Actually, the Briars takes in so much territory and so many activities that it really requires this map to give a good overview. It shows the relationship of the Briars to the Red Barn and Peacock House, the gardens, the tennis courts, the wilderness, and of course the 18-hole golf course, the lake, and the village of Jackson's Point.

It shows the location of all of the many lakeside cottages and the golf clubhouse, as well as Saint George's Church, which I visited for the first time with John Sibbald a number of years ago, and the route of a great circle tour around Lake Simcoe with many points of interest.

With this map in hand it's easy for the guest to locate the many

recreational possibilities at the Briars. In winter the property becomes a snowy paradise for walking and cross-country skiing, skating, tobogganing, and snowshoeing. When the temperature falls there is a beautiful indoor pool, sauna, whirlpool, and exercise room.

In summer, there are two outdoor pools, all of the lake's recreational advantages, the golf course, lighted tennis courts, lawn sports, and wooded walking trails. There's fishing, sailing, and windsurfing every day of the year on Lake Simcoe.

Early on, one of the things that intrigued me greatly about the Briars was the fact that the Canadian novelist Mazo de la Roche lived in this area, which undoubtedly supplied her with the atmosphere later portrayed in her famous *Whiteoaks of Jalna* books. She was a guest in one of the cottages at the Briars during the last five summers of her life.

I pored over this map for at least an hour, discovering things that I had never known before about the Briars and Lake Simcoe.

THE BRIARS, Jackson's Point, Ontario, LOE 1LO Canada; 416-722-3271. A 91-guestroom resort-inn (private bath) on the shores of Lake Simcoe, approx. 45 mi. north of Toronto. Queen, double, and twin beds. Open every day. Breakfast, lunch, and dinner served to nonresidents. Summer activities include 18-hole golf course, two outdoor swimming pools, indoor swimming pool, whirlpool, sauna, lakeshore swimming, 5 all-weather tennis courts, and many lawn sports. Winter sports include xc skiing, skating, tobogganing, snowmobiling, ice-fishing, and curling. There is a children's program during the summer and Christmas holidays. Excellent for families in all seasons. John and Barbara Sibbald, Owners-hosts. (See Index for rates.)

Directions: Jackson's Point is located near Sutton, Ontario. From Hwy. 401, via Hwy. 404/Woodbine. Continue to Sutton and then Jackson's Point, 1/2 mi. east on Hedge Rd.

THE OPINICON
Chaffey's Locks, Elgin, Ontario (1981)

Ever since I was a boy I've been hearing about those wonderful, almost inaccessible, fishing and hunting resorts in Canada that are always situated on sylvan lakes and surrounded by primeval forests. Friends of my father would disappear a couple of times each year and return with tales of fish that practically leapt into the boat and game in Paul Bunyan dimensions. There were stories about highly voluble guides and idyllic days spent in the forest and on the water, followed by trenchermen's meals, very often including the day's catch.

In the summer of 1980 I found such a Canadian retreat with all of the virtues listed above, plus many more that make it a wonderful place for a rustic vacation.

The Opinicon resort-inn is situated on a lovely wooded hill overlooking Opinicon Lake, and surrounded by seventeen acres of well-groomed lawns, giant oaks, a large flower garden, and quiet spots in the woods or on the lake from which to observe nature. Accommodations are in the main building, an old-fashioned, two-storied, yellow clapboard residence with completely modernized rooms, many opening onto a porch or balcony. In the woods, set back from the lakeshore, are a series of cottages accommodating from two to eight persons each.

The cheerful dining room offers three sumptuous meals a day under the American plan, and I understand they've had the same chef for many years. Guests' freshly caught fish can be cooked and served at any meal, and the dining room is conducted like many old resort-inns that have now disappeared. I sat at the same table and had the same waitress for all my meals. She and the other waitresses were friendly young ladies from the area.

Innkeeper Al Cross, whose Bay State accent I recognized immediately, is from Newton, Massachusetts. His wife Janice's family has been running this resort-inn for many generations. Al is a somewhat rumpled type of man who is always on the go, greeting guests, taking care of their needs, and keeping the staff members on their toes.

With over 200 lakes in the area, the Opinicon is known for its great fishing. It appeared to me that about fifty percent of the guests in residence during my visit were interested in this sport, for which boats and experienced local guides can be arranged. The inn provides basket lunches, if desired.

On the other hand, many people enjoy the great variety of recreational activities available, including boating, lake and pool swimming, tennis, croquet, shuffleboard, horseshoes, table tennis, volleyball, and for the occasional inclement days, a good lending library. There's also an honest-to-gosh country store.

One of the most interesting things to do is to take the short walk to Chaffey's Locks, which are a part of the Rideau Canal System. This system was opened in 1832 to connect Kingston with Ottawa, thus avoiding the rapids of the St. Lawrence. It is still a navigable waterway, and the locks, models of stone engineering construction, are operated by hand by two gatekeepers.

The Opinicon is a great place to take the entire family for a real Canadian woods holiday. Rates have been structured in such a way that it is within the financial means of the average North American family, especially when you think of hungry kids eating three meals a day.

THE OPINICON, Chaffey's Locks, RR 1, Elgin, Ontario, Canada K0G 1C0; 613-359-5233. An 18-guestroom resort-inn on Opinicon Lake, part of the Rideau Canal System of eastern Ontario; 43 rooms also available in rustic cottages (private and shared baths). Full American and modified American plan. Open early April to late November. Fishing, boating, tennis, heated swimming pool, shuffleboard, bicycles on grounds, golf course nearby. Excellent for children of all ages. No credit cards. Personal checks accepted. Albert and Janice Cross, Owners-hosts. (See Index for rates.)

Directions: From south: Interstate 81 to 1000 Island Bridge to Ontario Rte. 401 west. Turn off Exit No. 645 at Rte. 32 (right), go north to Rte. 15, turning right (north). Follow to 2 miles beyond Elgin (bypassed). Turn left on Chaffey's Locks Rd. From east: Rte. 401 west to Exit No. 696 (Brockville), turn north (right) on Rte. 42, follow Rte. 42 to Crosby, turn south (left) on Rte. 15 for 2 miles and turn right on Chaffey's Locks Rd.

SHAW'S HOTEL
Brackley Beach, Prince Edward Island (1975)

I'm certain a great many of our readers enjoyed the Public Television presentation of *Anne of Green Gables,* an adaptation of Lucy Montgomery's splendid novel about a girl growing into young womanhood on Prince Edward Island. If you missed it, be sure to catch the reruns. Anne may never have actually existed, but her spirit is there, as well as an attractive, typical gabled house that she *might* have lived in.

Prince Edward Island is one of the great surprises of North America. For one thing, ocean water temperatures along the wide P.E.I. beaches average sixty-eight to seventy degrees in summer and the sun is excellent for tanning. It has one of Canada's finest national parks, stretching twenty-five miles along the Gulf of St. Lawrence. There are wild seascapes, breathtaking views, and an atmosphere of hospitality, because this has been a resort area for more than a century.

During the summer months there is an excellent theatre at the Confederation Centre of the Arts of Charlottetown, offering a choice of musicals that play to capacity houses almost every night.

Prince Edward Island is very popular in July and August, so reserve well in advance and be sure to obtain ferry information.

I first visited P.E.I. and Shaw's Hotel in 1974 and never thought that I could be this far north and find ocean water so wonderfully warm and enjoyable.

I had taken the ferry from Caribou, Nova Scotia, that morning. There is another ferry from Cape Tormentine, New Brunswick. It is possible to stay at the Marshlands Inn in Sackville and take the ferry over the next morning. I had driven down from the Inverary Inn on Cape Breton in northern Nova Scotia, so the Caribou crossing was more convenient.

I found that Shaw's was part of an original pioneer farm started in

1793, had become a hotel in 1860, and today, still has many of the characteristics of an operating farm.

Some of the accommodations are single and double rooms in the main building, a Victorian house with a brilliant red mansard third story. There are also individual cottages, accommodating from two to eight people. This is most convenient for families who return every summer. The cottages are spaced far enough apart to insure privacy. Five of them have their own fireplaces.

Shaw's Hotel is surrounded by many trees and broad meadows. The view from the dining room might include a sailboat bobbing along on the bay. There is a good mix of both Canadian and American guests, and Robbie Shaw says that there are always a few people from California, Washington, New York, and Alberta.

One of the most attractive features about Shaw's Hotel is the fact that it is only a short distance through the woods to the beach. All of this summertime outdoor activity, including swimming, sailing on the bay, deep-sea tuna fishing, golf, tennis, bicycling, walking, and horseback riding, contribute to very big appetites, so the main dishes include fresh salmon, lobster, mackerel, cod, and halibut. Dinners are fun because everyone is eager for a hearty meal, and enthusiasm is high after a day of recreation.

Children are particularly happy in this atmosphere. Robbie Shaw said he has had as many as twenty to thirty children at one time at the height of the season. "There is always plenty of elbow room," he said. "We don't have any trouble keeping the parents of the children amused either. Besides the beach, there are riding horses nearby, and it is fun to ride along the beach and on the bridle paths. I have been doing it all my life. My father, who passed away in 1985, always loved the children."

SHAW'S HOTEL, Brackley Beach, Prince Edward Island, Canada C0A 2H0; 902-672-2022. A 24-guestroom and 17-guest-cottage (some shared baths) country hotel within walking distance of Brackley Beach, 15 mi. from Charlottetown. American plan. Breakfast and dinner served to travelers daily. Open from June to Sept. Tennis, golf, bicycles, riding, sailing, beach and summer theater nearby. Pets allowed in cottages only. Robbie Shaw, Owner-host. (See Index for rates.)

Directions: Prince Edward Island is reached by ferry from either Cape Tormentine, New Brunswick (near Moncton), or Caribou, Nova Scotia. In both cases, after arriving on P.E.I., follow Rte. 1 to Charlottetown, then Rte. 15 to Brackley Beach. P.E.I. is also reached by Eastern Provincial Airway, VIA Rail Canada, and Air Canada.

HANDFIELD INN (Auberge Handfield)
St. Marc-sur-le-Richelieu, Quebec (1983)

The Richelieu River, part of the waterway that carries boats to the Saint Lawrence and down to the tip of Florida, was blue and sparkling in the summer sun. I was relaxing on the grassy banks directly in front of the newest group of traditional Quebec houses that had been redecorated and furnished by Conrad and Huguette Handfield and named Maison LaFlamme. The marina in front of Auberge Handfield (*auberge* is the French word for inn) had several visiting boats, and there were people sitting around the swimming pool enjoying animated conversations in both French and English.

In thinking about the new accommodations, I realized that the inn would become a resort-inn, since there were a great many things to do on the grounds or nearby.

Guest rooms in the main inn are furnished in the old Quebec style but with touches of modern comfort, including tile bathrooms and controlled heating. Many of them have rough wooden walls and casement windows overlooking broad fields. Huguette told me that most of these guest rooms are decorated either with antiques or furniture made by local craftsmen. Maison LaFlamme's guest rooms have a water view.

A summer visit here is really not complete without attendance at the summer theater presentation in a very cleverly converted ferry boat. The plays are all French comedies and have been commissioned by Huguette especially for performances at Auberge Handfield.

However, let's get back to the country inn aspects of Auberge Handfield. Certainly one of them would be the cuisine. As Conrad said, "There are two menus—one is traditional French cuisine and the other is nouvelle cuisine. So you see our guests can really have a choice for whatever may be their preference." I won't take the time here to list the main dishes except to say that I like French cuisine in any form, particularly the wonderful pastries on display for dessert.

The main dining room is very cozy and warm, and tables are on the sunny, converted, glassed-in porch. The natural wood contributes to a feeling of comfort and warmth. An interesting point is that the dining room is open all afternoon, so that guests can always get something to eat. It's open from breakfast until ten o'clock each night.

Auberge Handfield is essentially French, and it is not necessary to travel very far from any place in the United States or Canada to enjoy as French an experience as you would have in any village in France. The language is French, the villagers greet you in French, and the stores are French. They will help you out if you are in any difficulty. Essentially, it's a wonderful French experience.

I should also mention that sugaring-off parties are held from March until the end of April and are very popular with inn guests. They are held in a rustic sugar shack in a maple grove just a few miles from the inn. I have enjoyed them very much myself.

The Handfield Inn is a great many things: it is a venerable mansion that has seen a century and a half of history; an enjoyable French restaurant; a four-season resort; and perhaps best of all, it is an opportunity to visit a French-Canadian village that has remained relatively free from the invasion of developers. Its ancient stone houses and nearby shops remain untouched, and its farms still raise good vegetables and poultry.

HANDFIELD INN (Auberge Handfield), St. Marc-sur-le-Richelieu, Quebec, J0L 2E0, Canada; 514-584-2226. A 53-guestroom (private baths) French-Canadian country inn about 25 mi. from Montreal. Telephones and air conditioning in rooms. Different plans available. Please consult with inn in advance. Open year-round. Breakfast, lunch, and dinner served daily to travelers. Ladies are expected to wear a skirt or dress and gentlemen a coat at dinner. Summer French theater. All summer and winter active sports easily available. Many handcrafts, antique, and historical tours in the area. No pets. M. and Mme. Conrad Handfield, Owners-hosts. (See Index for rates.)

Directions: From Champlain, Victoria, or the Jacques Cartier bridges, take Hwy. 3 to Sorel, turn right at Hwy. 20. From the east end of Montreal, go through the Hyppolite LaFontaine Tunnel. Rte. 20 passes through St. Julie, St. Bruno, and Beloeil. Leave Hwy. 20 at Exit 112, turning left on Rte. 223 north. Handfield is 7 mi. distant.

THE HOVEY MANOR
North Hatley, Quebec (1973)

Steve Stafford slowed down the motor launch as we approached the inn's docks, and I had a wonderful view of Hovey Manor's secluded twenty-five acres sprawled across the hillside with its lovely English gardens and two beaches. In 1899, Henry Atkinson, a wealthy industrialist from Atlanta, purchased this prime site on Lake Massawippi. The antebellum-style home he built was inspired by George Washington's Mount Vernon.

In 1950, Robert F. Brown, the first innkeeper, ingeniously transformed the estate into a country inn which became renowned for its quality and charm. The present innkeepers, Steve and Kathy Stafford, purchased Hovey Manor ten years ago and have continued the tradition. Kathy's flair for decorating is evident throughout the property. Along with nine new deluxe rooms, all the bedrooms have been thoroughly upgraded and individually decorated. All have a private bath, most face the lake and many feature combinations of wood-burning fireplaces, canopy beds, whirlpool baths, and private balconies.

A few years ago, the cuisine at Hovey Manor underwent a dramatic transformation. Steve and Kathy succeeded in importing a talented Belgian chef, Marc de Canck, who has since been featured in Quebec's leading food magazine, *Sel et Poivre*. Marc serves a contemporary French cuisine and guests enjoy choosing from the varied, imaginative dishes. Steve says, "We've been delighted with the results of our improvements. Quebec's Ministry of Tourism has given us the highest rating for both cuisine (four forks) and accommodations (five fleurs de lys), which is rare for a country inn. The response from our guests has allowed us to remain open all year so that we've been able to develop a really good team. Turnover is low, and it makes Kathy and me happy to receive so many compliments regarding the friendliness and professionalism of our staff."

Although a traditional inn, Hovey Manor has all the resort facilities for a complete vacation experience. In summer there's an activities program, and canoes, paddleboats, windsurfers and tennis are free. Steve is an avid tennis player and happy to accept challenges from like-minded guests. Sailboats, water-skiing, and cruises are available at reasonable rates right on site. Guests are also treated to chamber music a few evenings a week and full English tea is served every day. This is also golf country with ten courses within a half-hour's drive from the Manor. There's summer stock at the Piggery Theatre, two minutes away.

Remember, this is the land of the maple leaf; fall foliage is wonderful and very accessible, being so close to Vermont. In winter, Hovey has fifty kilometers of groomed cross-country trails from its door. There's even a ski package offering inn-to-inn skiing, with the inn transferring the cars

and the baggage. For downhill skiers, there's a convenient interchangeable ticket, valid at four big mountains in the area, all with extensive snow-making equipment. In Hovey's historic Coach House bar you'll enjoy the unique après-ski atmosphere, and on selected evenings the chefs broil steaks and fresh salmon over the live charcoal hearth.

Whatever the season, I think that Hovey Manor provides a happy vacation experience. It's worthwhile as a destination in itself or as a convenient stopover point on your way to or from Montreal or Quebec City.

HOVEY MANOR, North Hatley, Quebec, Canada JOB 2CO; 819-842-2421. A 35-guestroom (private baths) resort inn (12 with wood-burning fireplaces) on Lake Massawippi, ½ hr. from U.S./Canada border. Queen, double, and twin beds available. Modified American and Euro-pean plans. Breakfast, lunch, dinner served every day. Open all year. Wheelchair access. Lighted tennis court, two beaches, sailing, canoeing, paddleboats, water skiing, windsurfing, fishing, xc skiing, and sleigh rides on grounds. Downhill skiing, horseback riding, racquet sports, and golf (10 courses) nearby; also many scenic and cultural attractions nearby. Sorry, no pets. Stephen and Kathryn Stafford, Owners-hosts. (See Index for rates.)

Directions: Take Vermont I-91 to Vermont/Quebec border and follow Rte. 55 to No. Hatley Exit 29. Follow Rte. 108E for 5 mi. to T junction at Lake Massawippi in North Hatley. Turn right for ¾ mi. to Hovey Manor sign and private drive on left.

Index

The rates listed here represent a general range of rates for two people for one night at each inn and should not be considered firm quotations. Breakfast may or may not be included, and tax and gratuities are usually not included. The rates cover both high and low seasons. It is well to inquire as to the availability or various plans and packages.

CB means continental breakfast included in price, no hot dish.
B means full breakfast included in price, hot meal.
MAP means breakfast and dinner included.
AP means 3 meals included.
Rates are approximate for 2 people for 1 night.

CB means continental breakfast included in price, no hot dish.
B means full breakfast included in price, hot meal.
MAP means breakfast and dinner included.
Rates are approximate for 2 people for 1 night.

B means full breakfast included in price, hot meal.
CB means continental breakfast included in price, no hot dish.
MAP means breakfast and dinner included.
*B&B or other rates available.
AP means 3 meals included.
Rates are approximate for 2 people for 1 night.

MAP means breakfast and dinner included.
CB means continental breakfast included in price, no hot dish.
B means full breakfast included in price, hot meal.
Rates are approximate for 2 people for 1 night.

MAP means breakfast and dinner included.
B means full breakfast included in price, hot meal.
CB means continental breakfast included in price, no hot dish.
Rates are approximate for 2 people for 1 night.

CB means continental breakfast included in price, no hot dish.
MAP means breakfast and dinner included.
B means full breakfast included in price, hot meal.
AP means 3 meals included.
Rates are approximate for 2 people for 1 night.

CB means continental breakfast included in price, no hot dish.
MAP means breakfast and dinner included.
B means full breakfast included in price, hot meal.
AP means 3 meals included.
Rates are approximate for 2 people for 1 night.

MAP means breakfast and dinner included.
B means full breakfast included in price, hot meal.
AP means 3 meals included.
CB means continental breakfast included in price, no hot dish.
Rates are approximate for 2 people for 1 night.

MAP means breakfast and dinner included.
CB means continental breakfast included in price, no hot dish.
B means full breakfast included in price, hot meal.
Rates are approximate for 2 people for 1 night.